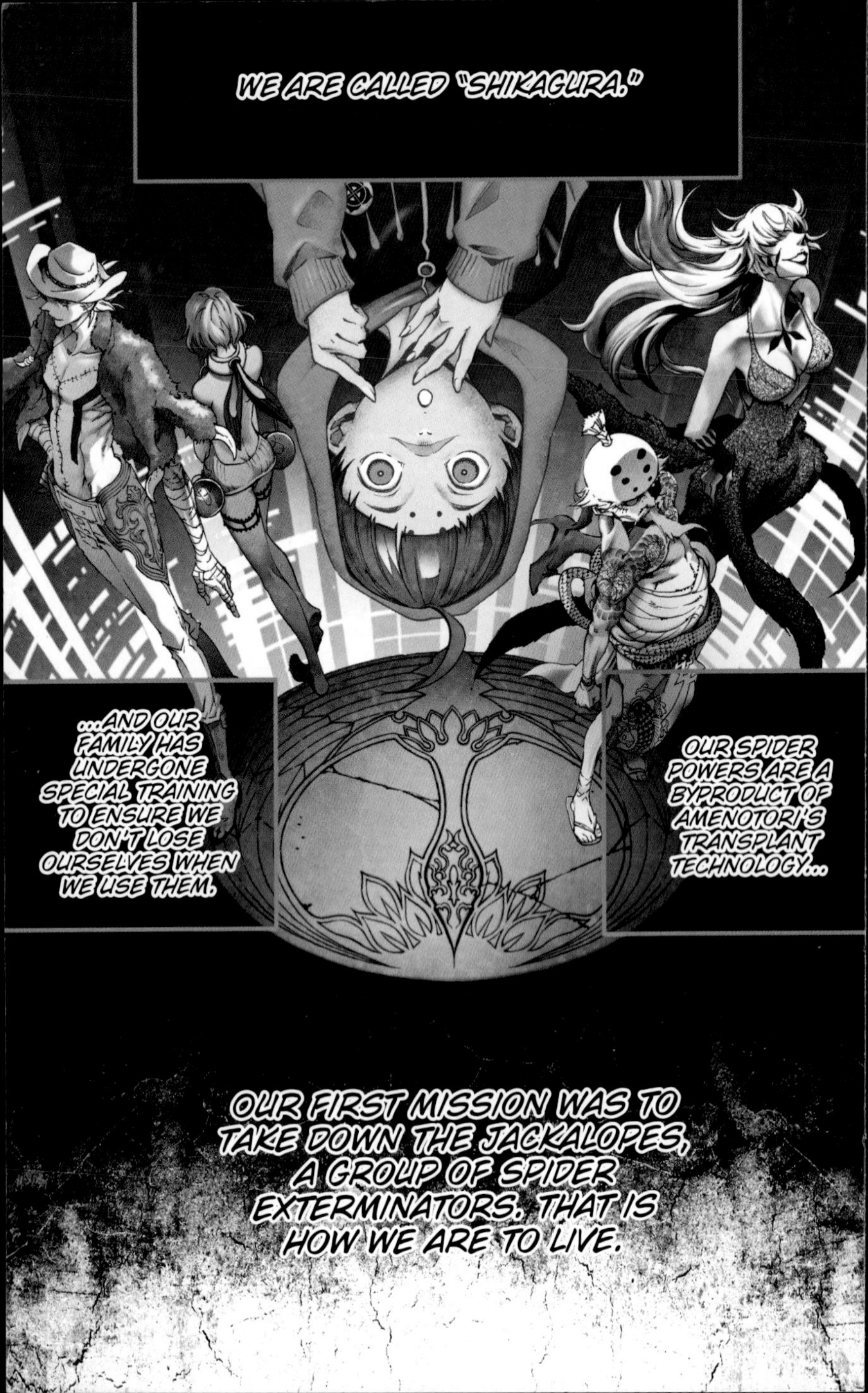

WE ARE CALLED "SHIKAGURA."
OUR SPIDER POWERS ARE A BYPRODUCT OF AMENOTORI'S TRANSPLANT TECHNOLOGY...
...AND OUR FAMILY HAS UNDERGONE SPECIAL TRAINING TO ENSURE WE DON'T LOSE OURSELVES WHEN WE USE THEM.
OUR FIRST MISSION WAS TO TAKE DOWN THE JACKALOPES, A GROUP OF SPIDER EXTERMINATORS. THAT IS HOW WE ARE TO LIVE.

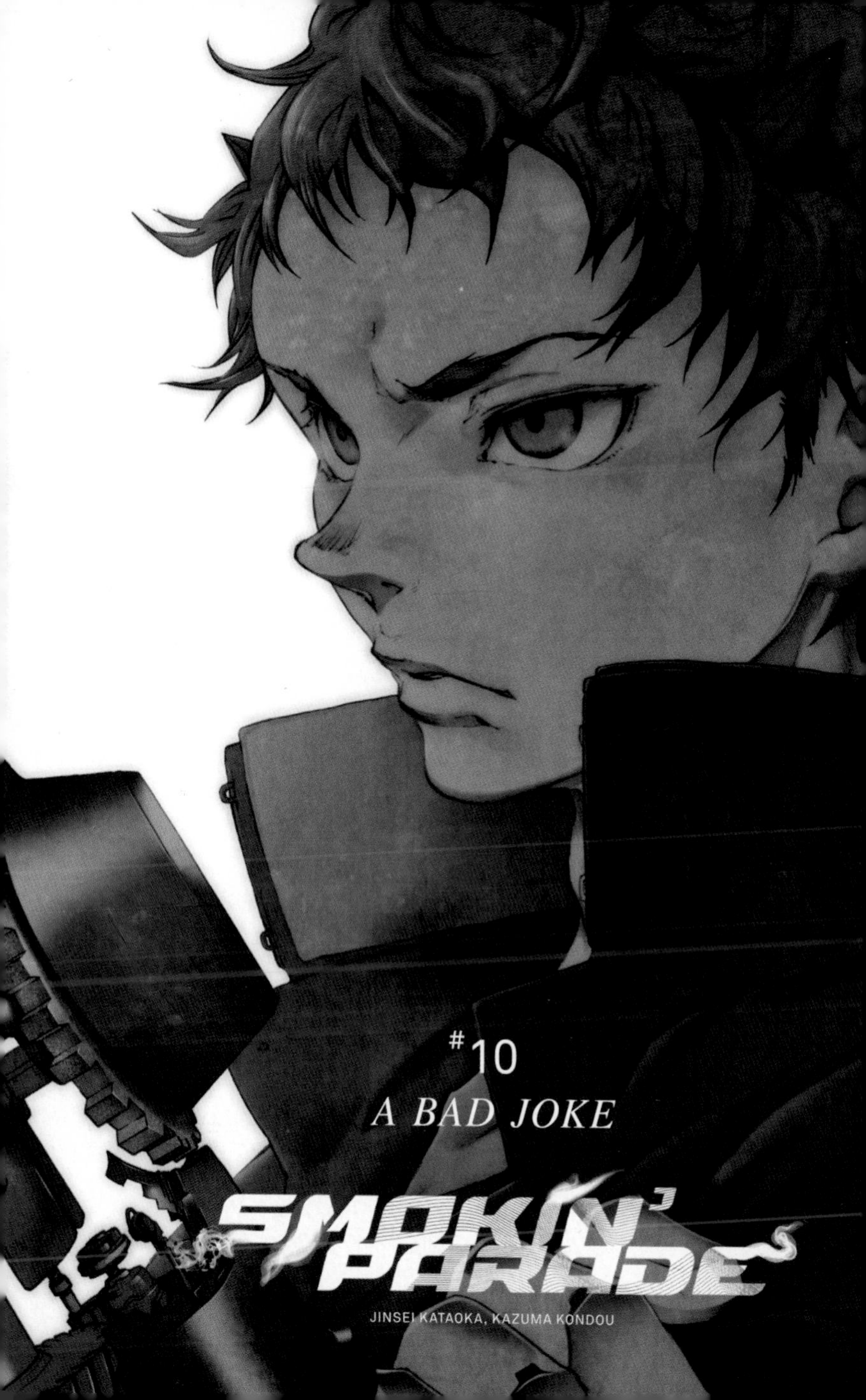
#10
A BAD JOKE
SMOKIN' PARADE
JINSEI KATAOKA, KAZUMA KONDOU

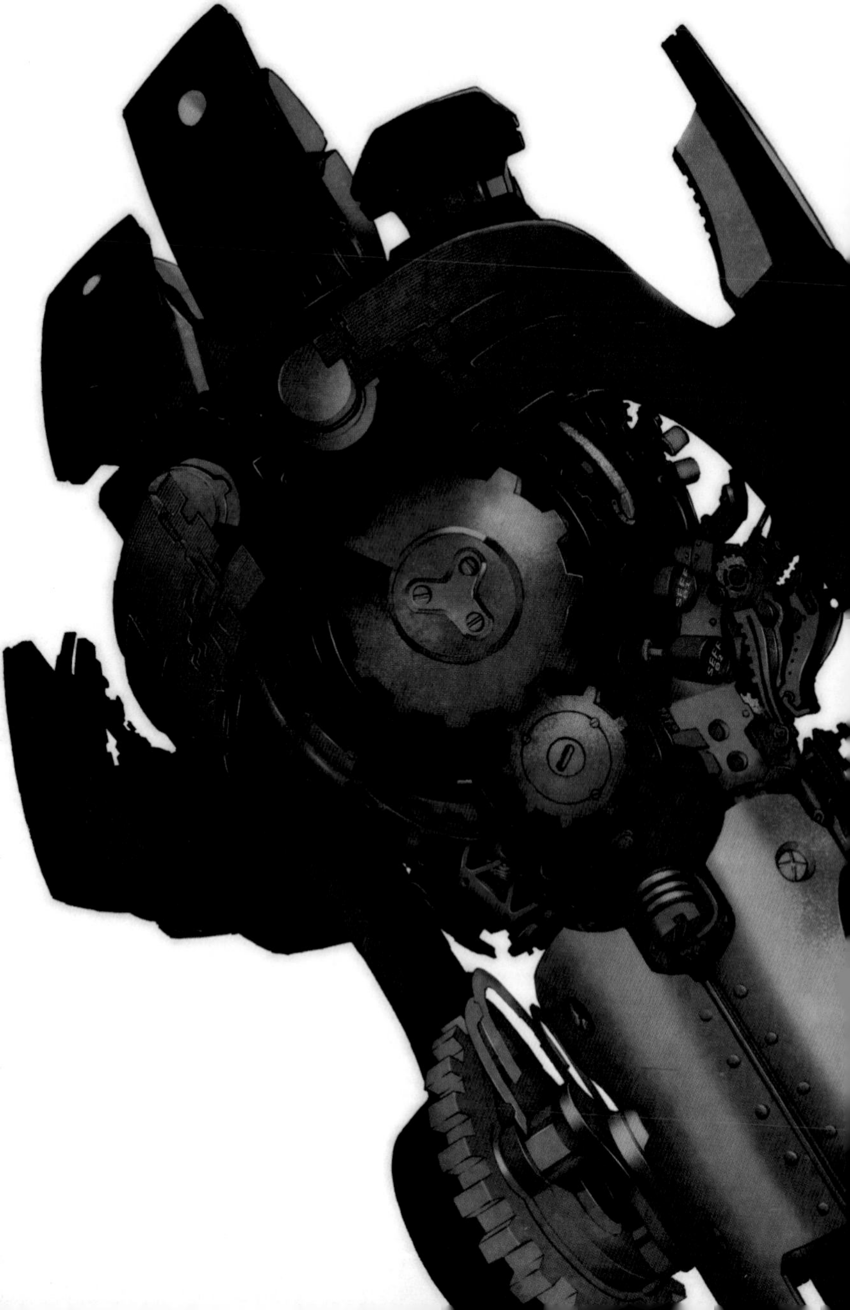
SEFF
SEFF

SMOKIN' PARADE

JINSEI KATAOKA, KAZUMA KONDOU

CONTENTS

001 #10
A Bad Joke

067 #11
Memories of Home

093 #12
Dying with Dignity

123 #13
Opposing Worlds

159 #14
Exposing Secrets

SMOKIN' PARADE

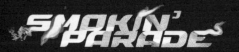

C H A R A C T E R S

AKUTA

A Jackalope who has taken a liking to Youkou because he sees himself in the kid. A heavy smoker with a sweet tooth.

YOUKOU KAKUJOU

A boy who lost both arms and his right leg when his younger sister turned into a Spider. He has replaced one missing arm with a Gear and joined the Jackalopes.

KOTOHARU

A member of the Jackalopes. He has an incredible amount of respect for Akuta and keeps a collection of items related to him.

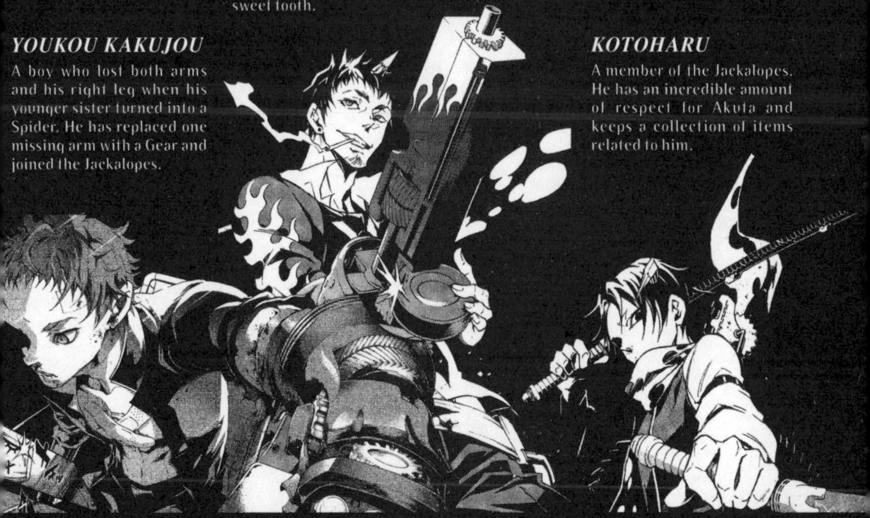

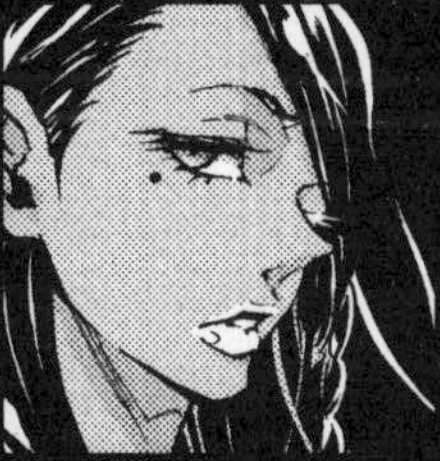

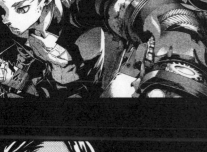

AMENOTORI

Amenotori, the revolutionary medical company that has made it possible to transplant any human part. This individual appears to have some connection to the company...?

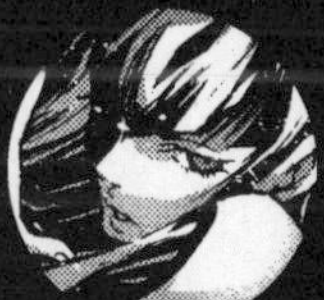

MIDARI

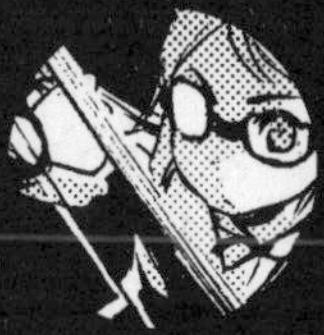

MATSUGO

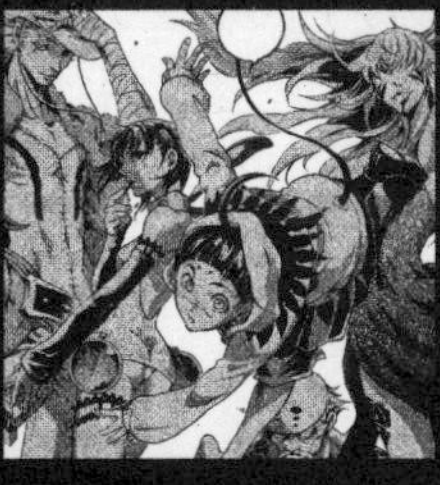

SHIKAGURA

A gang of Spiders that Kurama has sent after the Jackalopes.

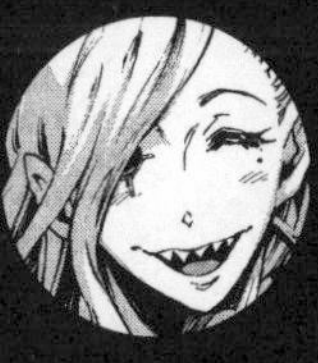

DOC

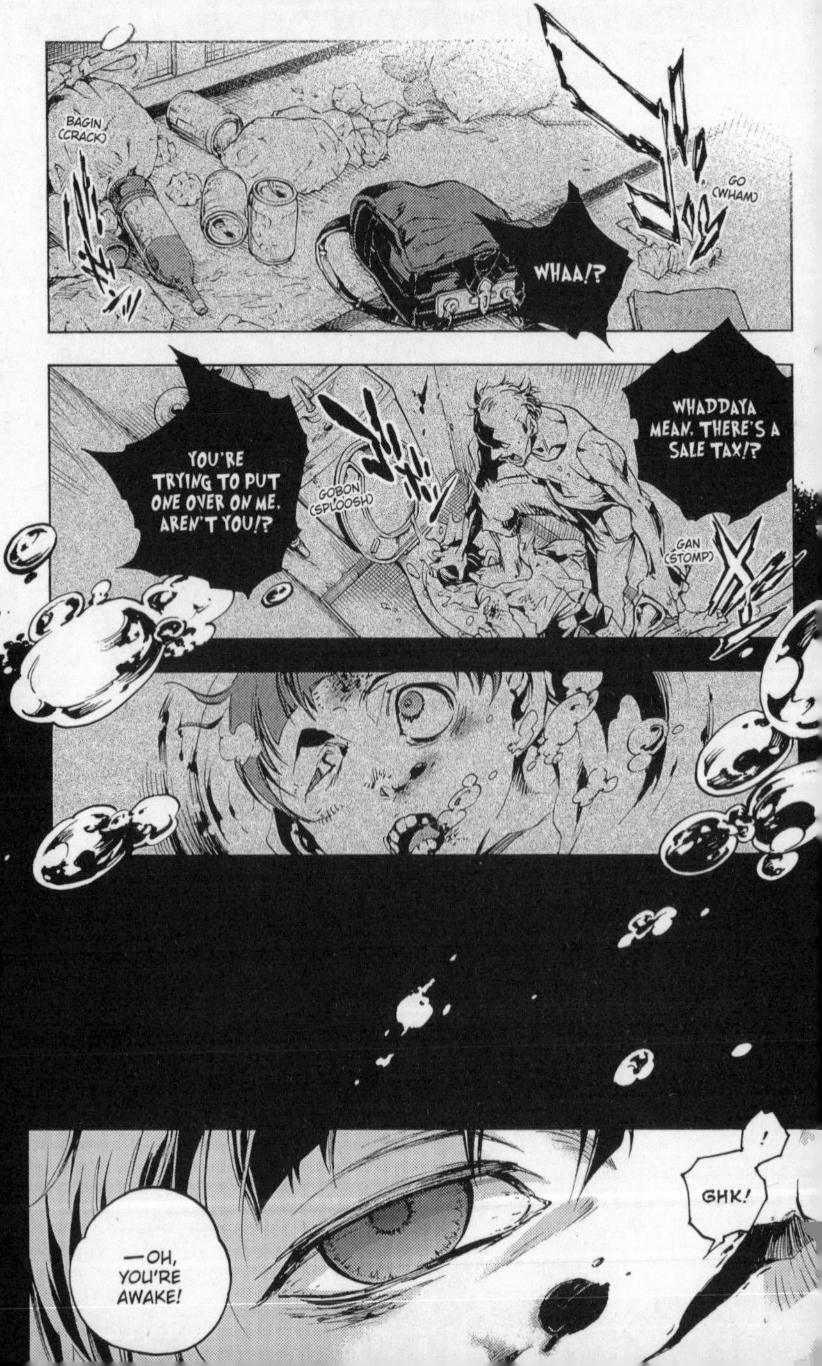
GO (WHAM)
WHAA!?
BAGIN (CRACK)
WHADDAYA MEAN, THERE'S A SALE TAX!?
GAN (STOMP)
GOBON (SPLOOSH)
YOU'RE TRYING TO PUT ONE OVER ON ME, AREN'T YOU!?
!
GHK!
—OH, YOU'RE AWAKE!

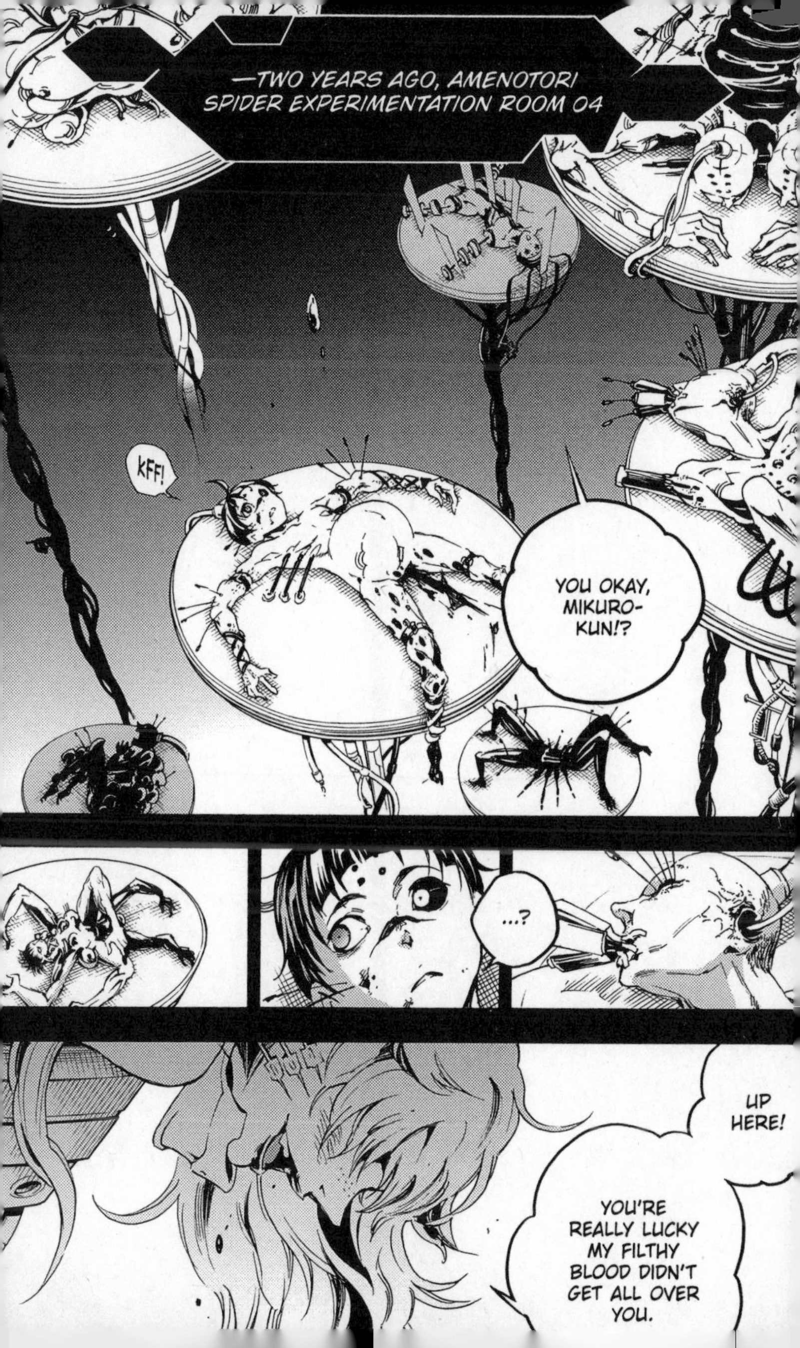
—TWO YEARS AGO, AMENOTORI SPIDER EXPERIMENTATION ROOM 04
KFF!
YOU OKAY, MIKURO-KUN!?
...?
UP HERE!
YOU'RE REALLY LUCKY MY FILTHY BLOOD DIDN'T GET ALL OVER YOU.

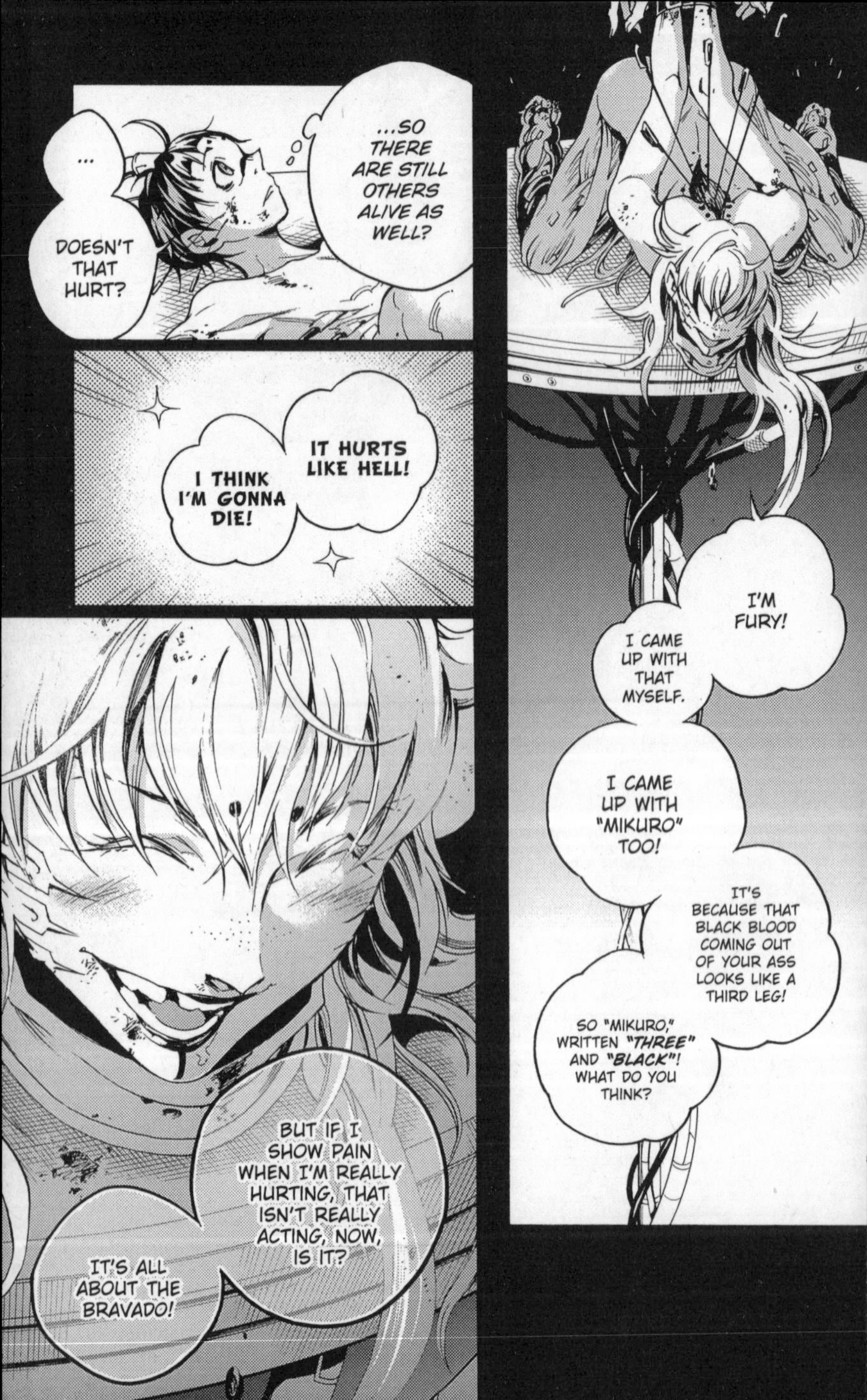
I'M FURY!
I CAME UP WITH THAT MYSELF.
I CAME UP WITH "MIKURO" TOO!
IT'S BECAUSE THAT BLACK BLOOD COMING OUT OF YOUR ASS LOOKS LIKE A THIRD LEG!
SO "MIKURO," WRITTEN *"THREE"* AND *"BLACK"*! WHAT DO YOU THINK?
...SO THERE ARE STILL OTHERS ALIVE AS WELL?
...
DOESN'T THAT HURT?
IT HURTS LIKE HELL!
I THINK I'M GONNA DIE!
BUT IF I SHOW PAIN WHEN I'M REALLY HURTING, THAT ISN'T REALLY ACTING, NOW, IS IT?
IT'S ALL ABOUT THE BRAVADO!

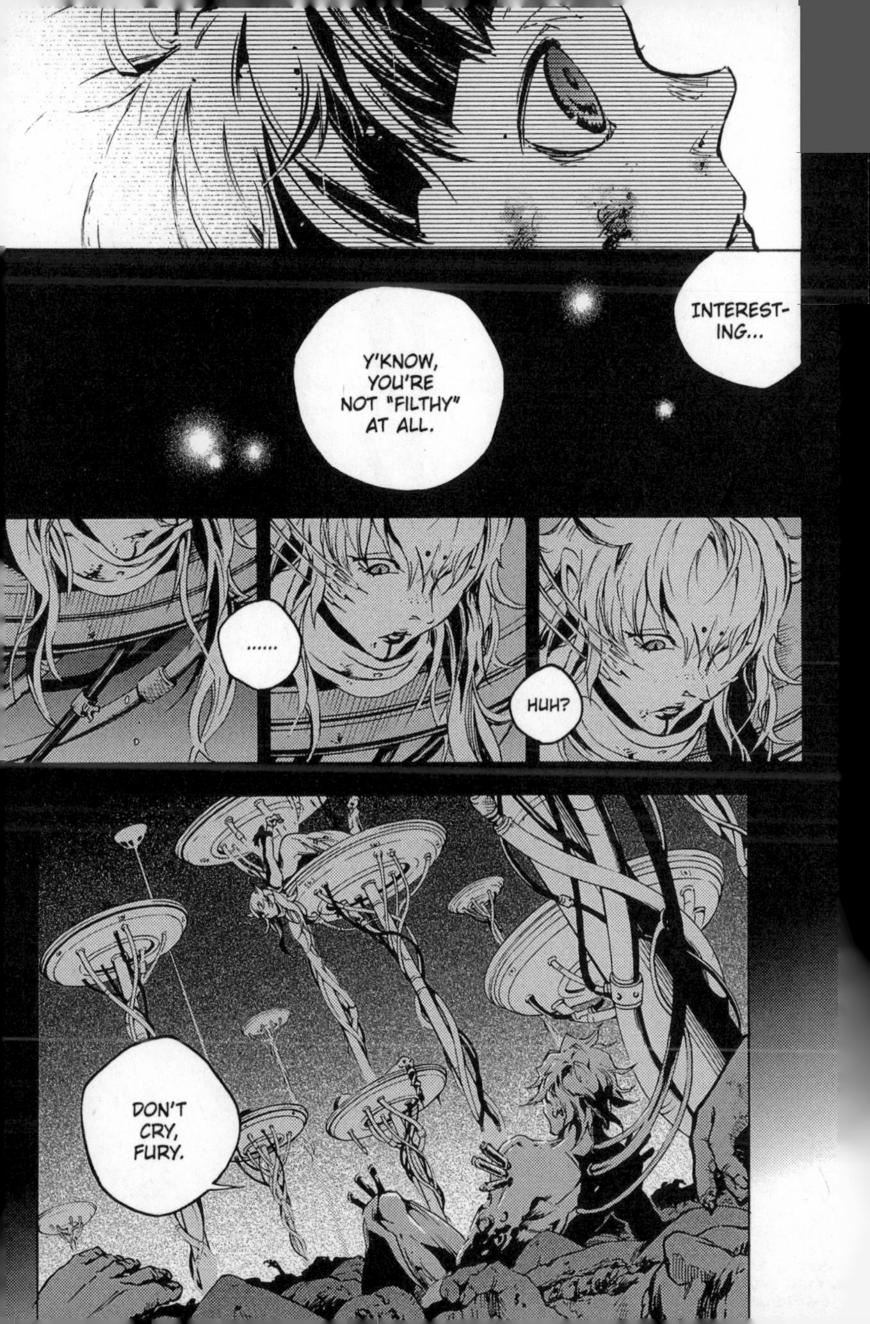
INTEREST-ING...
Y'KNOW, YOU'RE NOT "FILTHY" AT ALL.
HUH?
......
DON'T CRY, FURY.

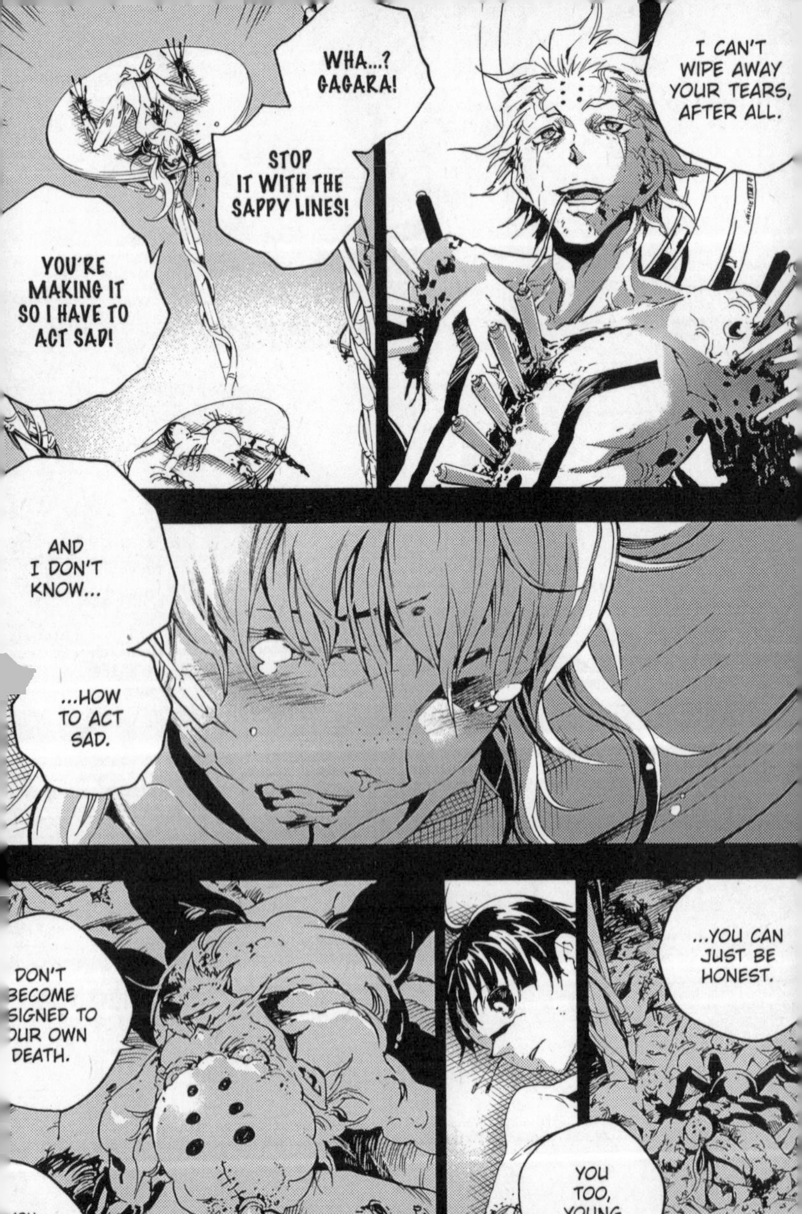
I CAN'T WIPE AWAY YOUR TEARS, AFTER ALL.
WHA...? GAGARA!
STOP IT WITH THE SAPPY LINES!
YOU'RE MAKING IT SO I HAVE TO ACT SAD!
AND I DON'T KNOW...
...HOW TO ACT SAD.
...YOU CAN JUST BE HONEST.
YOU TOO, YOUNG MAN.
DON'T BECOME SIGNED TO OUR OWN DEATH.
YOU BECAME DER AND

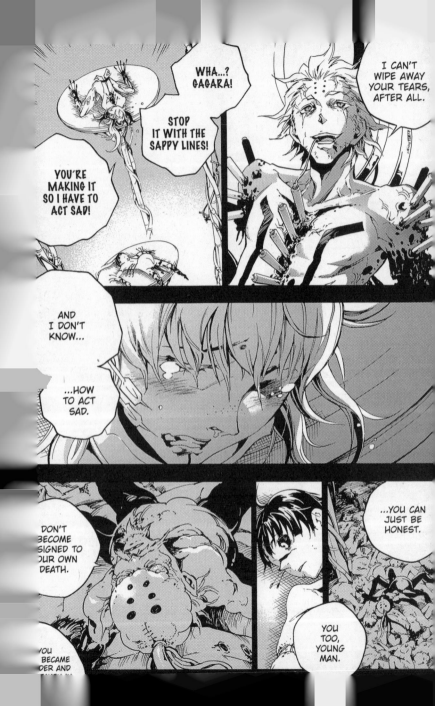

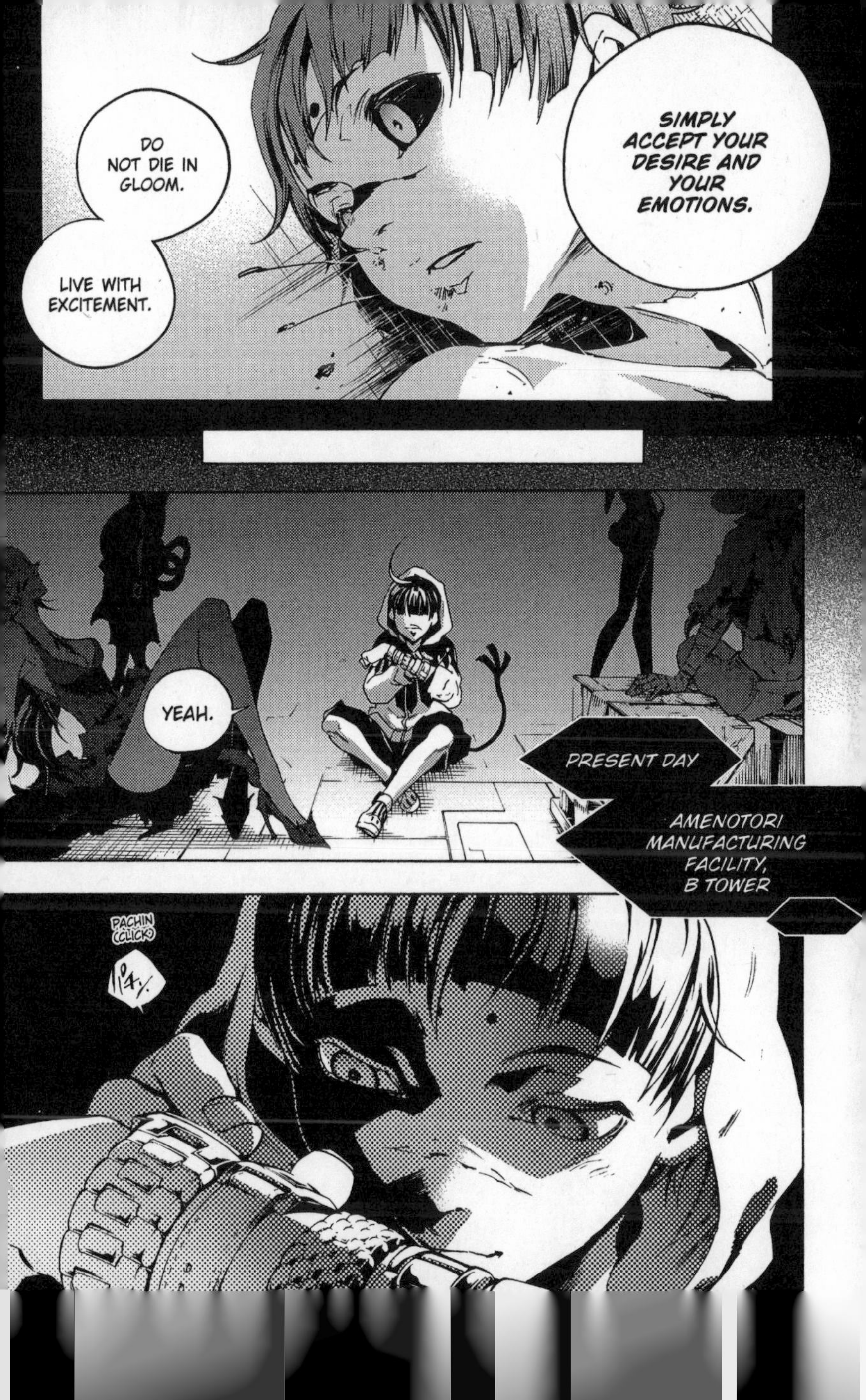
SIMPLY ACCEPT YOUR DESIRE AND YOUR EMOTIONS.
DO NOT DIE IN GLOOM.
LIVE WITH EXCITEMENT.
PRESENT DAY
AMENOTORI MANUFACTURING FACILITY, B TOWER
YEAH.
PACHIN (CLICK)

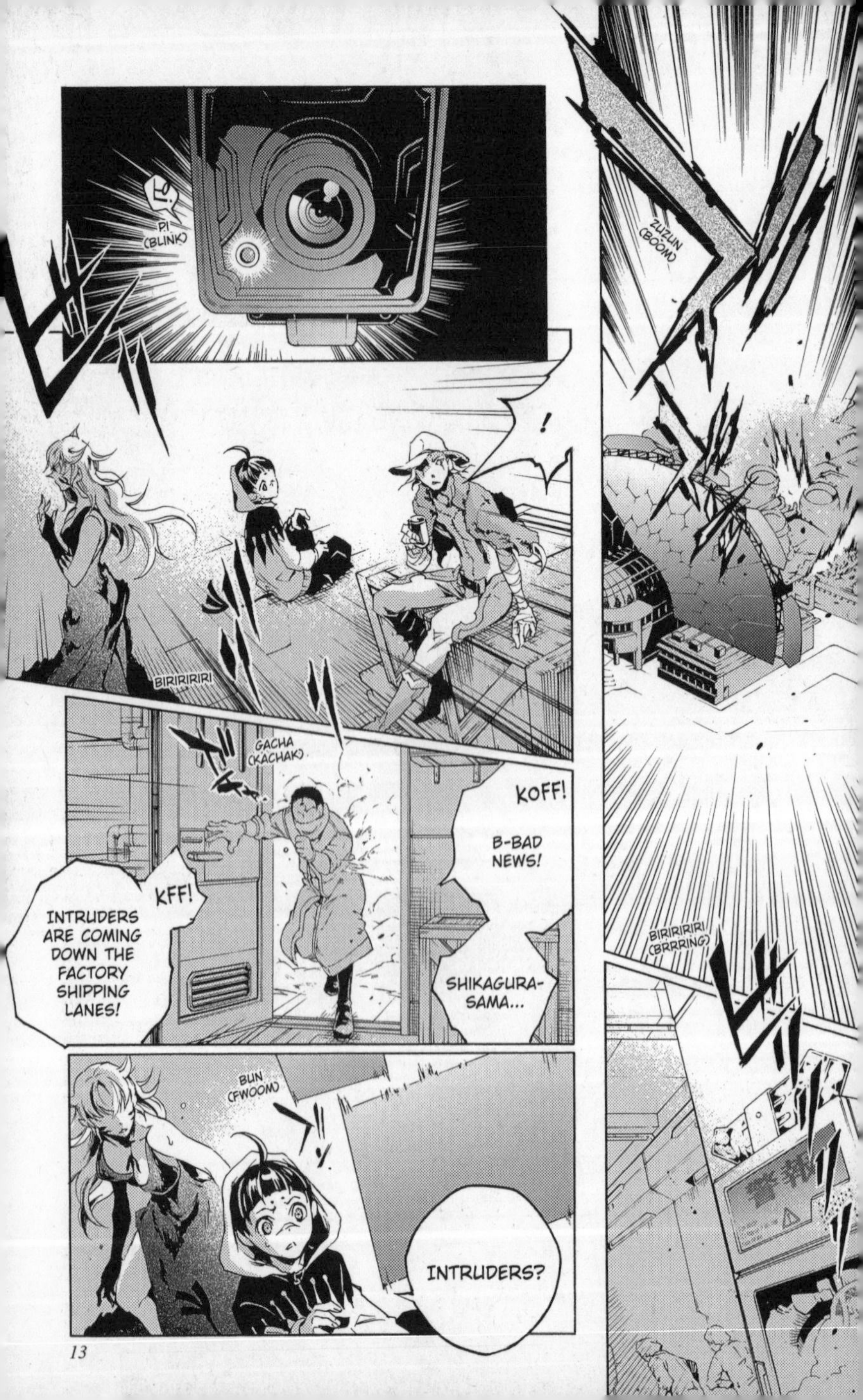
ZUZUN (BOOM)
BIRIRIRIRI (BRRRING)
P.I (BLINK)
!
BIRIRIRIRI
GACHA (KACHAK)
KOFF!
B-BAD NEWS!
SHIKAGURA-SAMA...
KFF!
INTRUDERS ARE COMING DOWN THE FACTORY SHIPPING LANES!
BUN (FWOOM)
INTRUDERS?

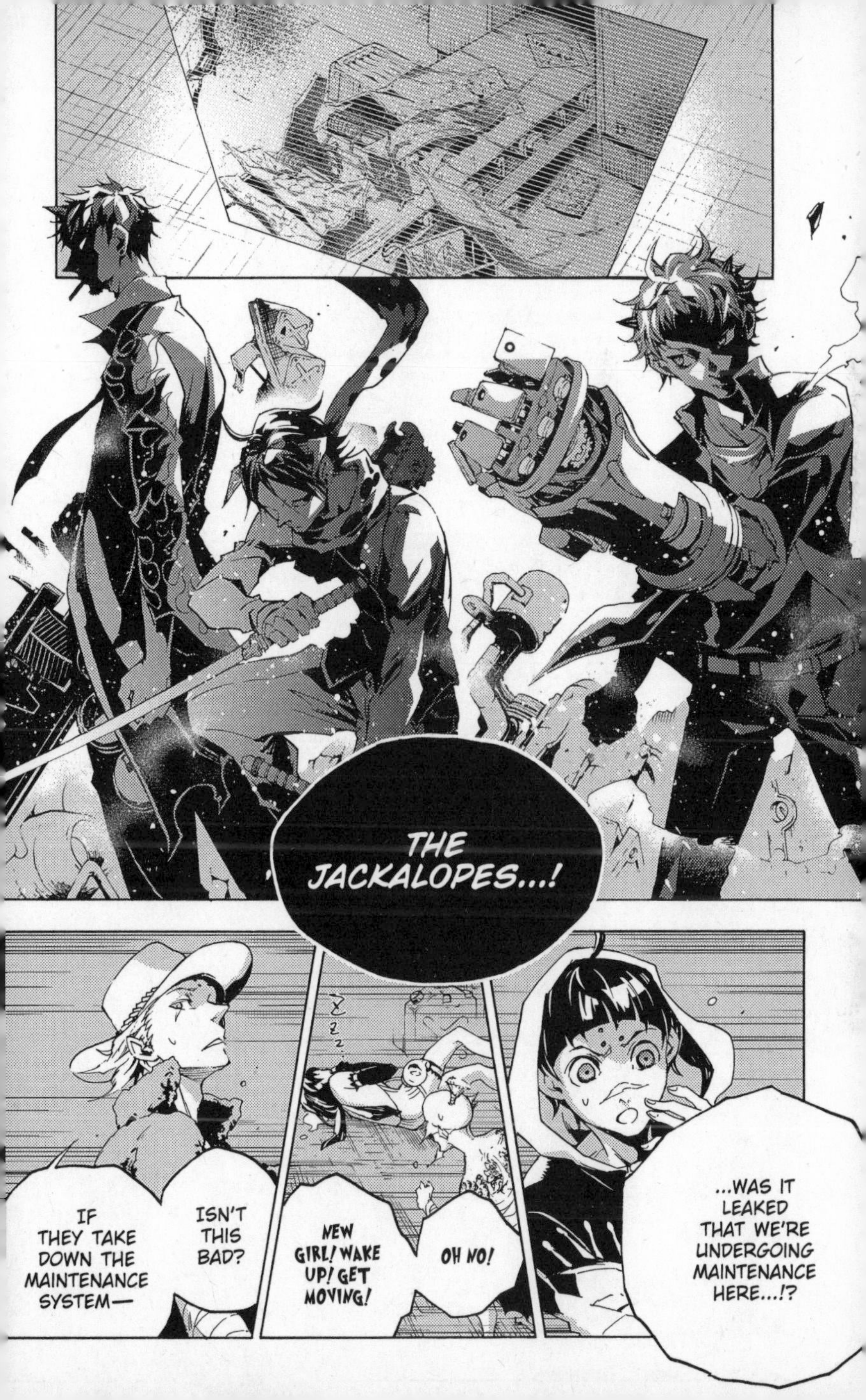
THE JACKALOPES...!
...WAS IT LEAKED THAT WE'RE UNDERGOING MAINTENANCE HERE...!?
OH NO!
NEW GIRL! WAKE UP! GET MOVING!
ISN'T THIS BAD?
IF THEY TAKE DOWN THE MAINTENANCE SYSTEM—

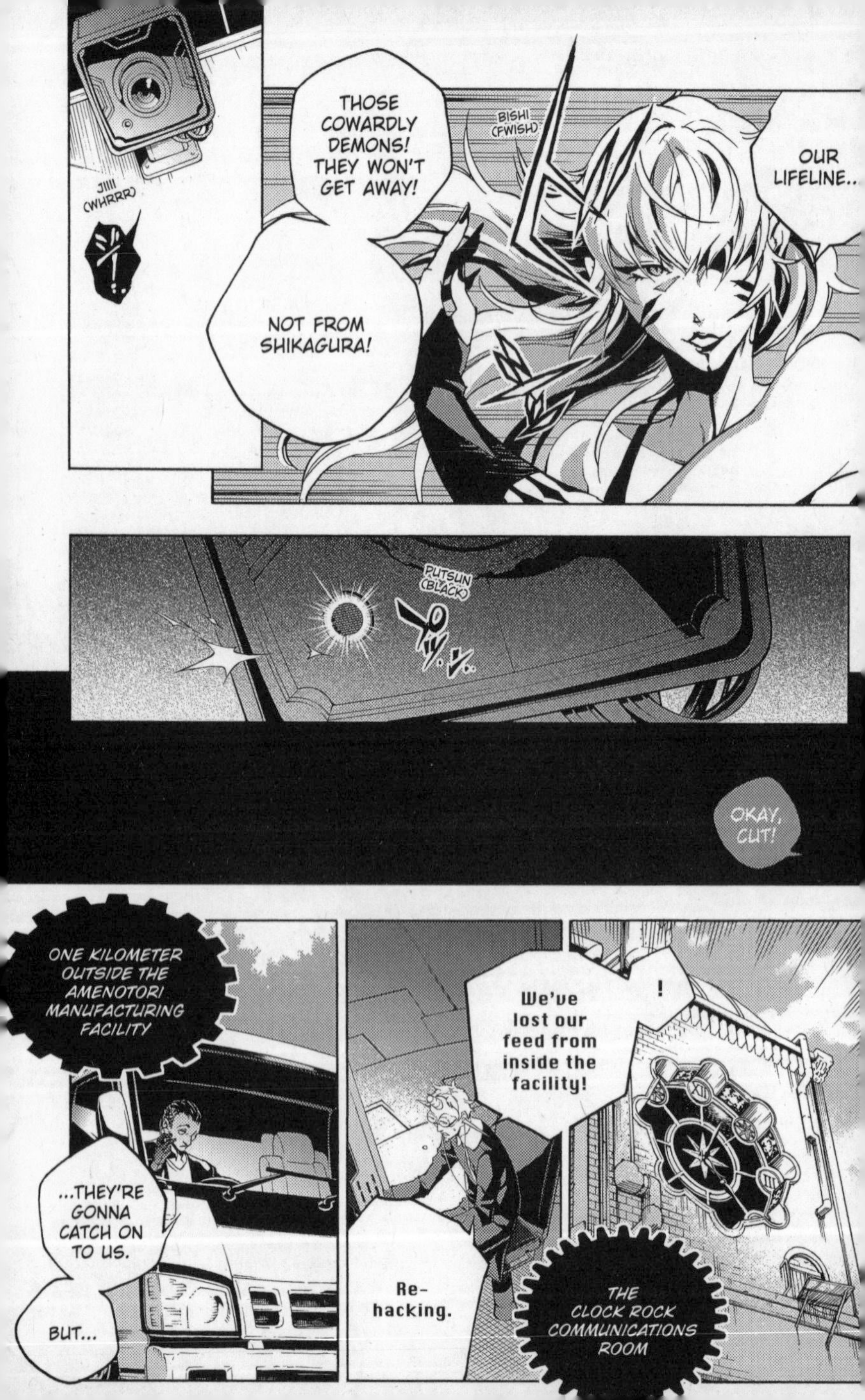
OUR LIFELINE...
BISHI (FWISH)
THOSE COWARDLY DEMONS! THEY WON'T GET AWAY!
NOT FROM SHIKAGURA!
JIIII (WHRRR)
PUTSUN (BLACK)
OKAY, CUT!
!
THE CLOCK ROCK COMMUNICATIONS ROOM
We've lost our feed from inside the facility!
Re-hacking.
ONE KILOMETER OUTSIDE THE AMENOTORI MANUFACTURING FACILITY
...THEY'RE GONNA CATCH ON TO US.
BUT...

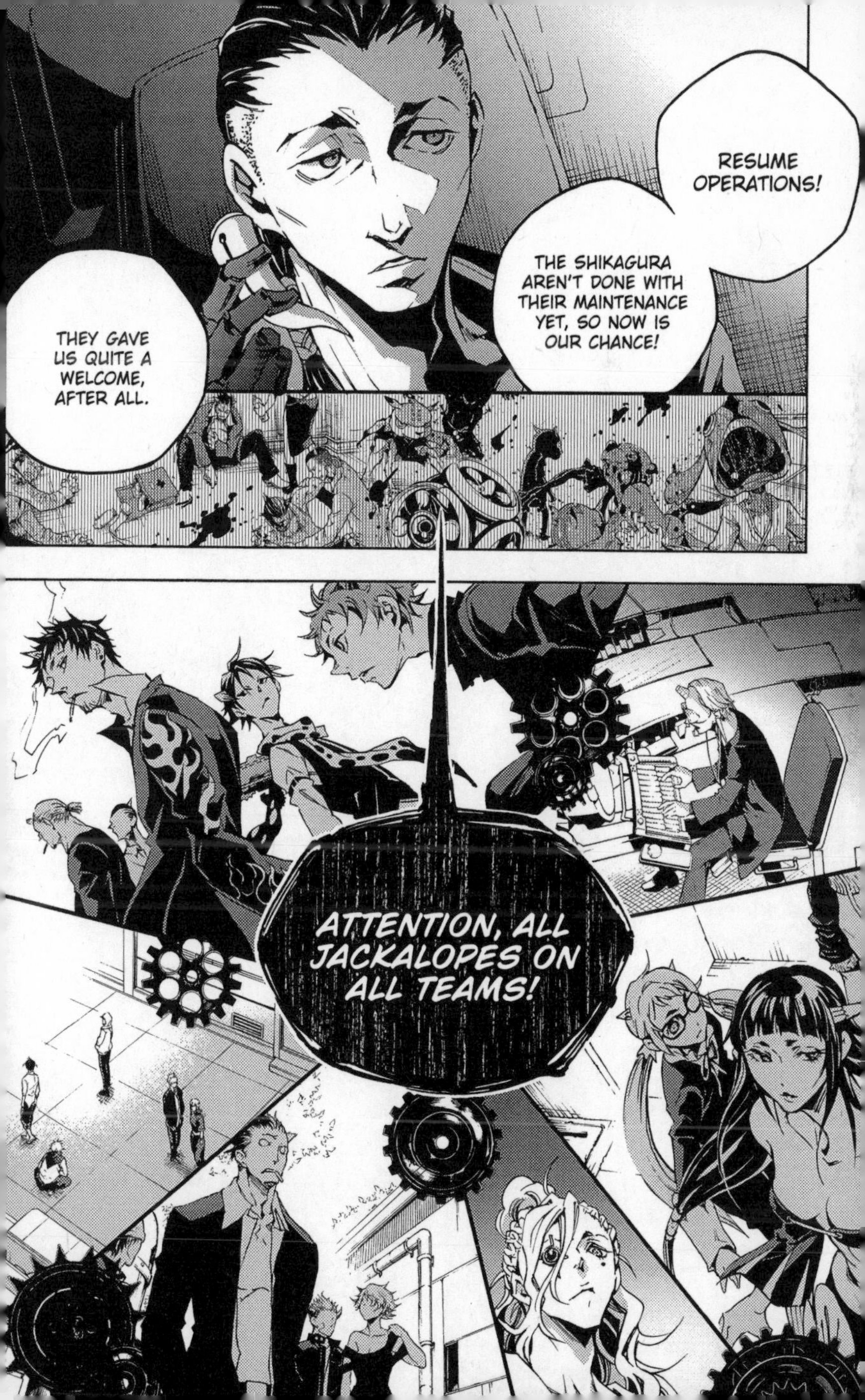
RESUME OPERATIONS!
THE SHIKAGURA AREN'T DONE WITH THEIR MAINTENANCE YET, SO NOW IS OUR CHANCE!
THEY GAVE US QUITE A WELCOME, AFTER ALL.
ATTENTION, ALL JACKALOPES ON ALL TEAMS!

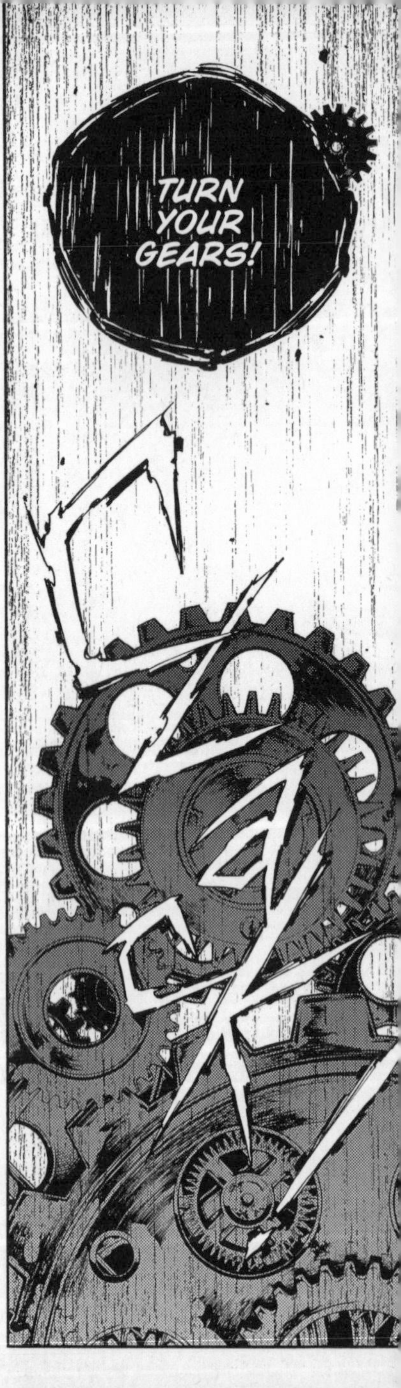
TURN YOUR GEARS!

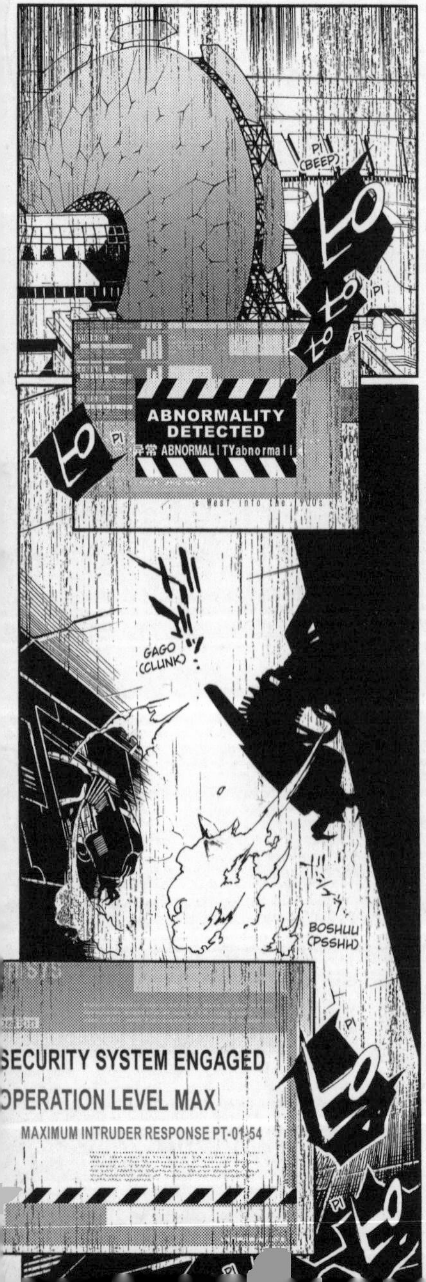
PI (BEEP)
PI
PI
PI
ABNORMALITY DETECTED
異常 ABNORMALITYabnormali
GAGO (CLUNK)
BOSHUU (PSSHH)
SECURITY SYSTEM ENGAGED
OPERATION LEVEL MAX
MAXIMUM INTRUDER RESPONSE PT-01-54
PI
PI

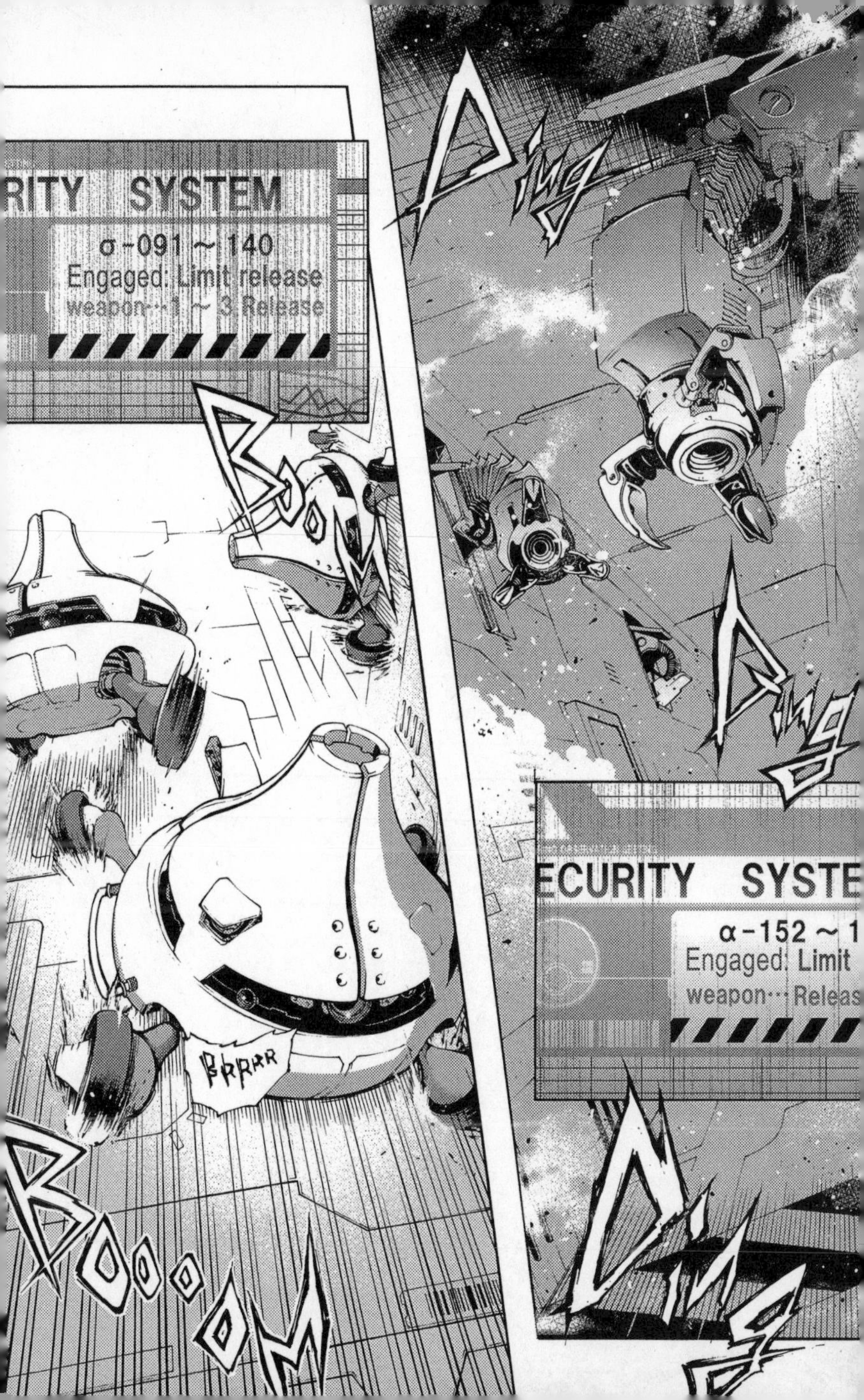
Ding
Ding
ECURITY SYSTE
α-152 ~ 1
Engaged: Limit
weapon··· Releas
Ding
RITY SYSTEM
σ-091 ~ 140
Engaged: Limit release
weapon··· 1 ~ 3 Release
BOOM
BRRRR
BOOOOM

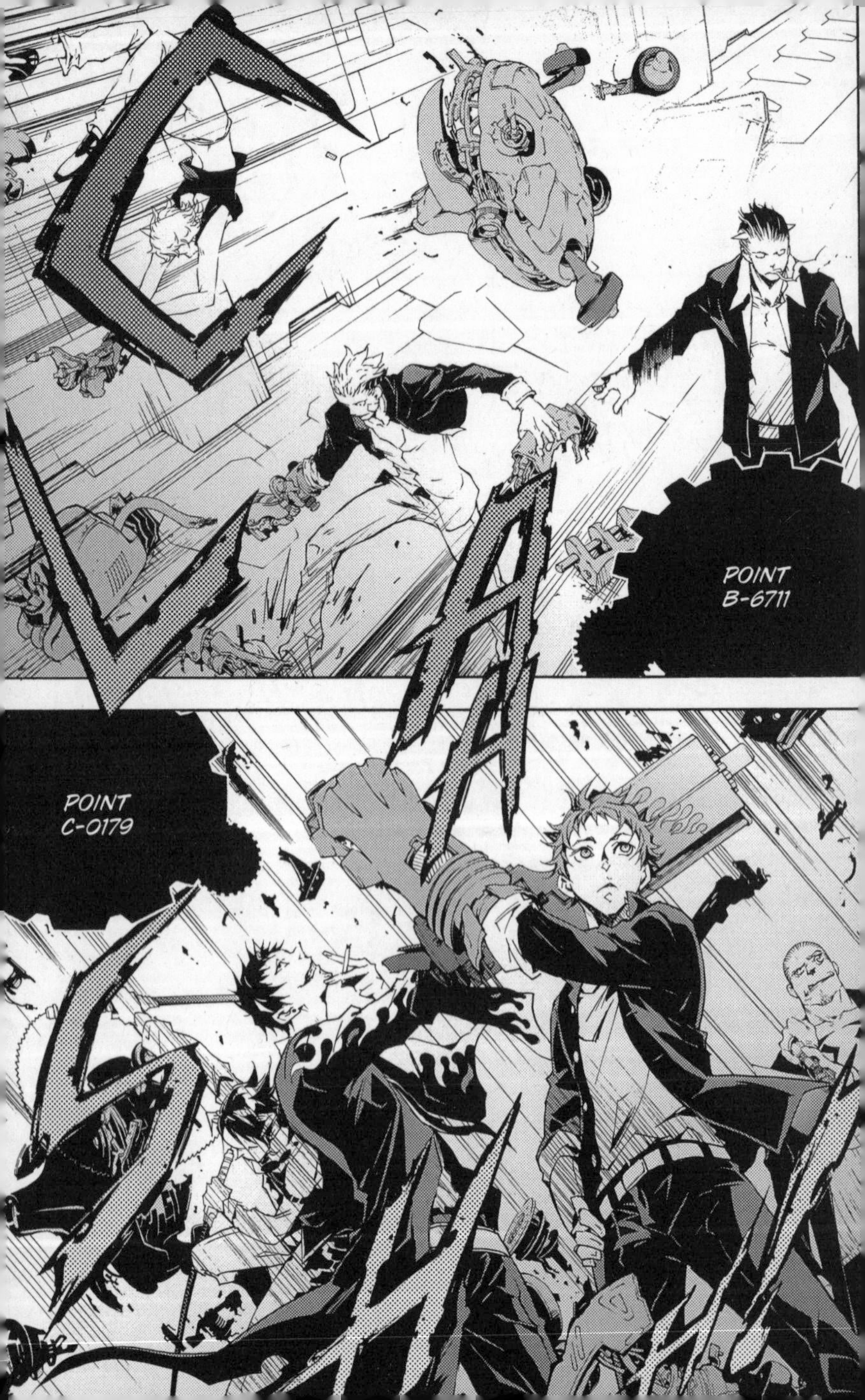
POINT
B-6711
POINT
C-0179

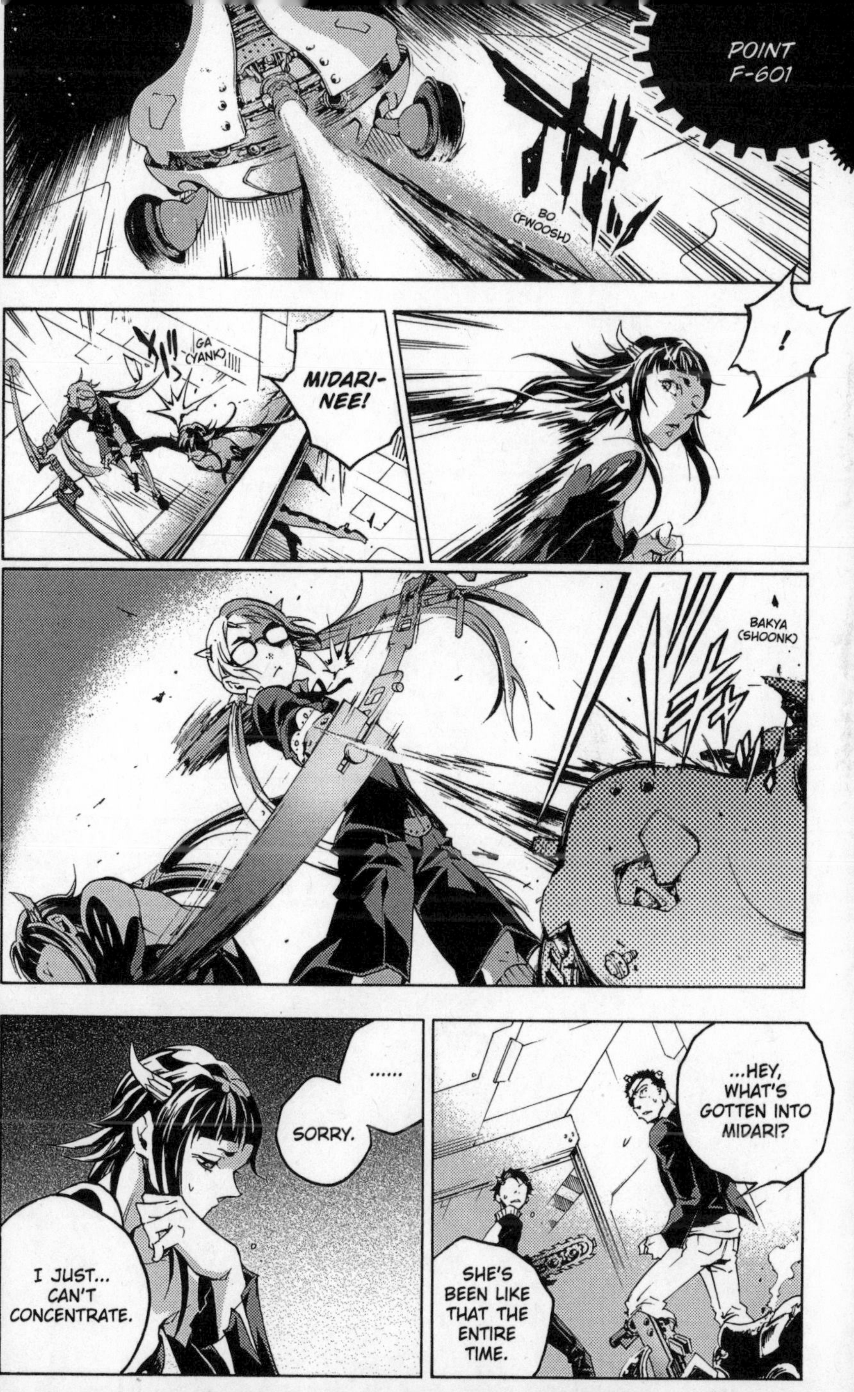
POINT F-601
BO (FWOOSH)
!
MIDARI-NEE!
GA (YANK)
BAKYA (SHOONK)
...HEY, WHAT'S GOTTEN INTO MIDARI?
SHE'S BEEN LIKE THAT THE ENTIRE TIME.
......
SORRY.
I JUST... CAN'T CONCENTRATE.

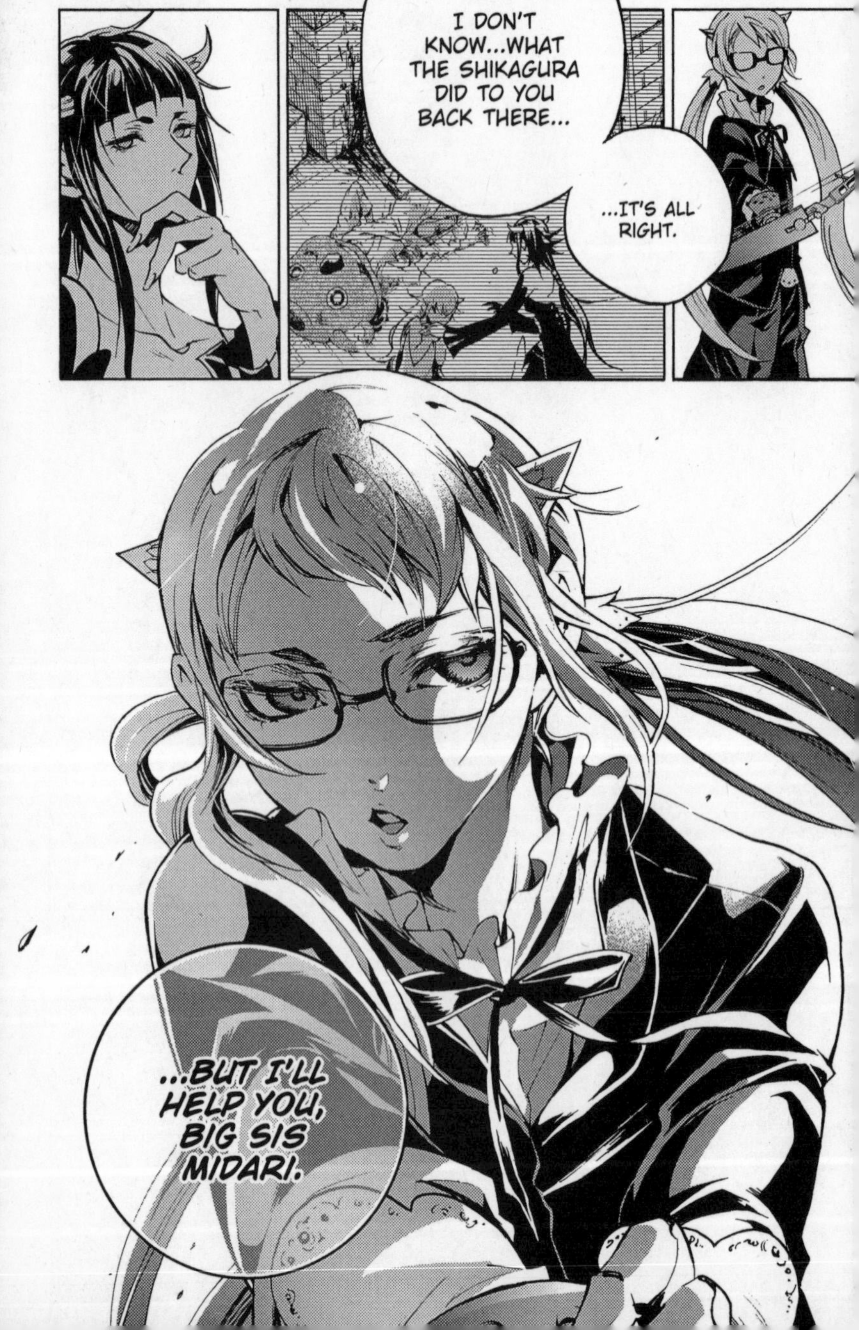
I DON'T KNOW...WHAT THE SHIKAGURA DID TO YOU BACK THERE...
...IT'S ALL RIGHT.
...BUT I'LL HELP YOU, BIG SIS MIDARI.

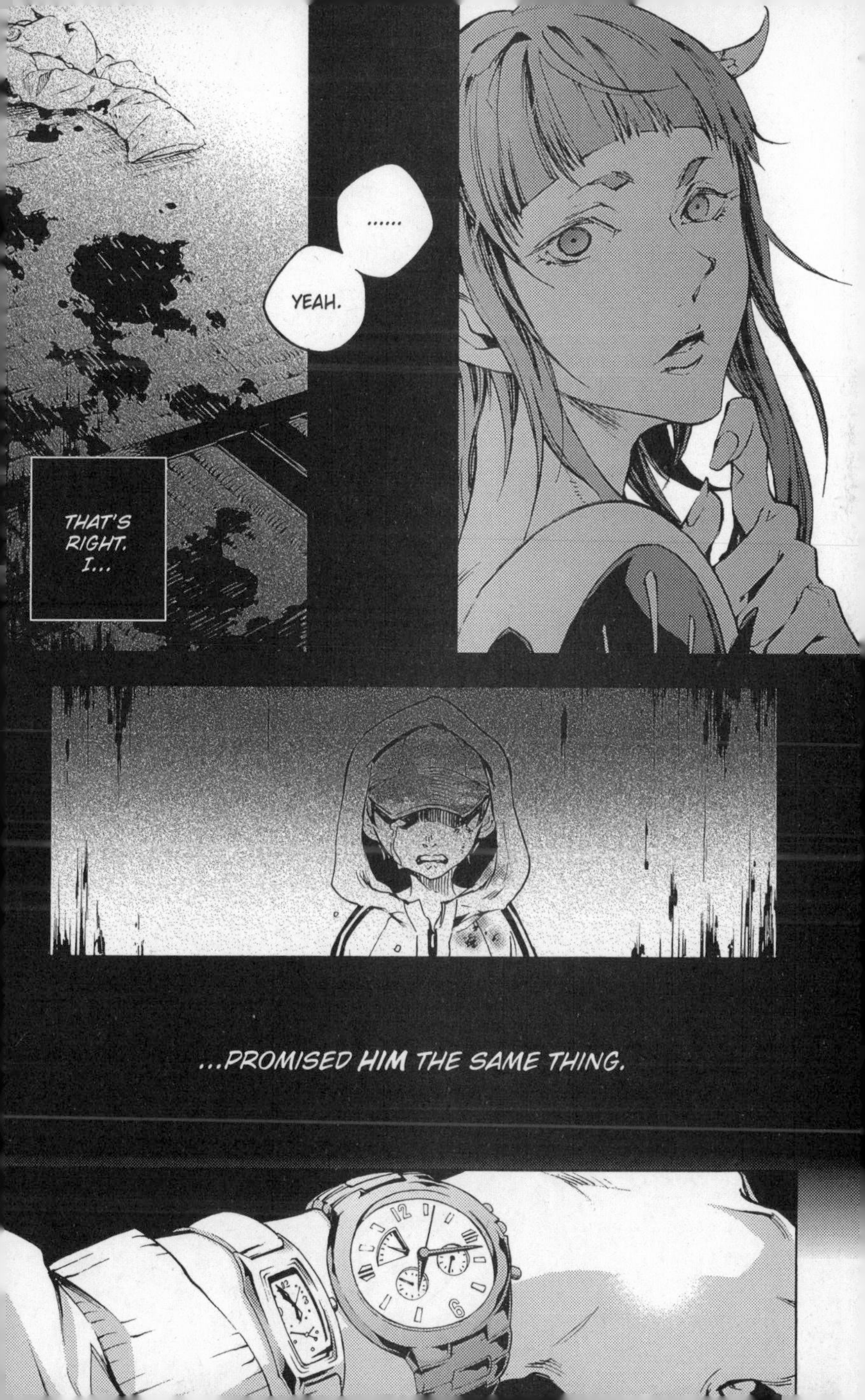
......
YEAH.
THAT'S RIGHT. I...
...PROMISED HIM THE SAME THING.

Defense system α-110—Offline.
θ-2219—Offline.
β-096—Offline.
—Offline.
—Offline.
PI (BEEP)
GAGAGA (KRZZT)
Route B 6711 secure!
Route C 0179 secure!
—Secure!
—Secure!

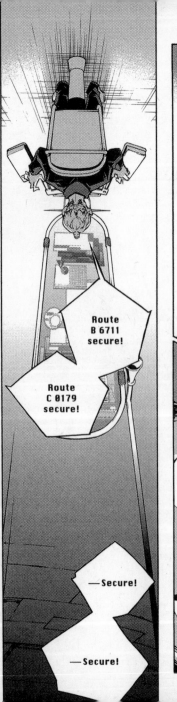

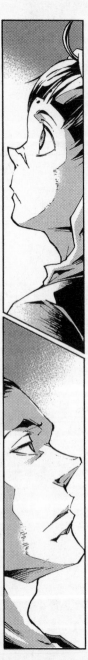

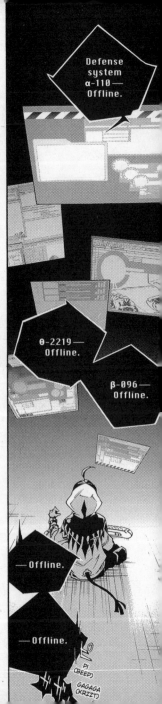

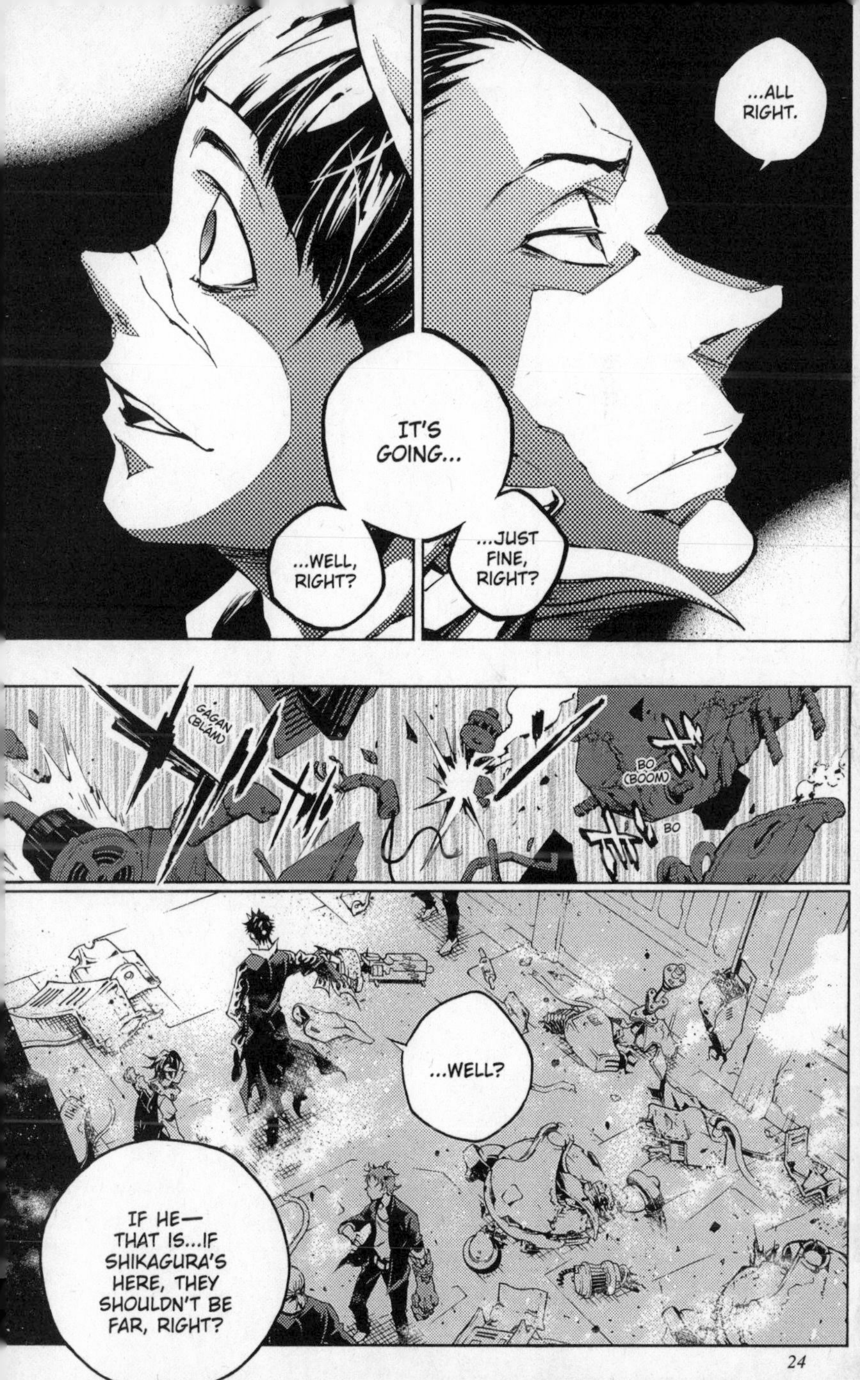
...ALL RIGHT.
IT'S GOING...
...JUST FINE, RIGHT?
...WELL, RIGHT?
BO (BOOM)
BO
GAGAN (BLAM)
...WELL?
IF HE— THAT IS...IF SHIKAGURA'S HERE, THEY SHOULDN'T BE FAR, RIGHT?

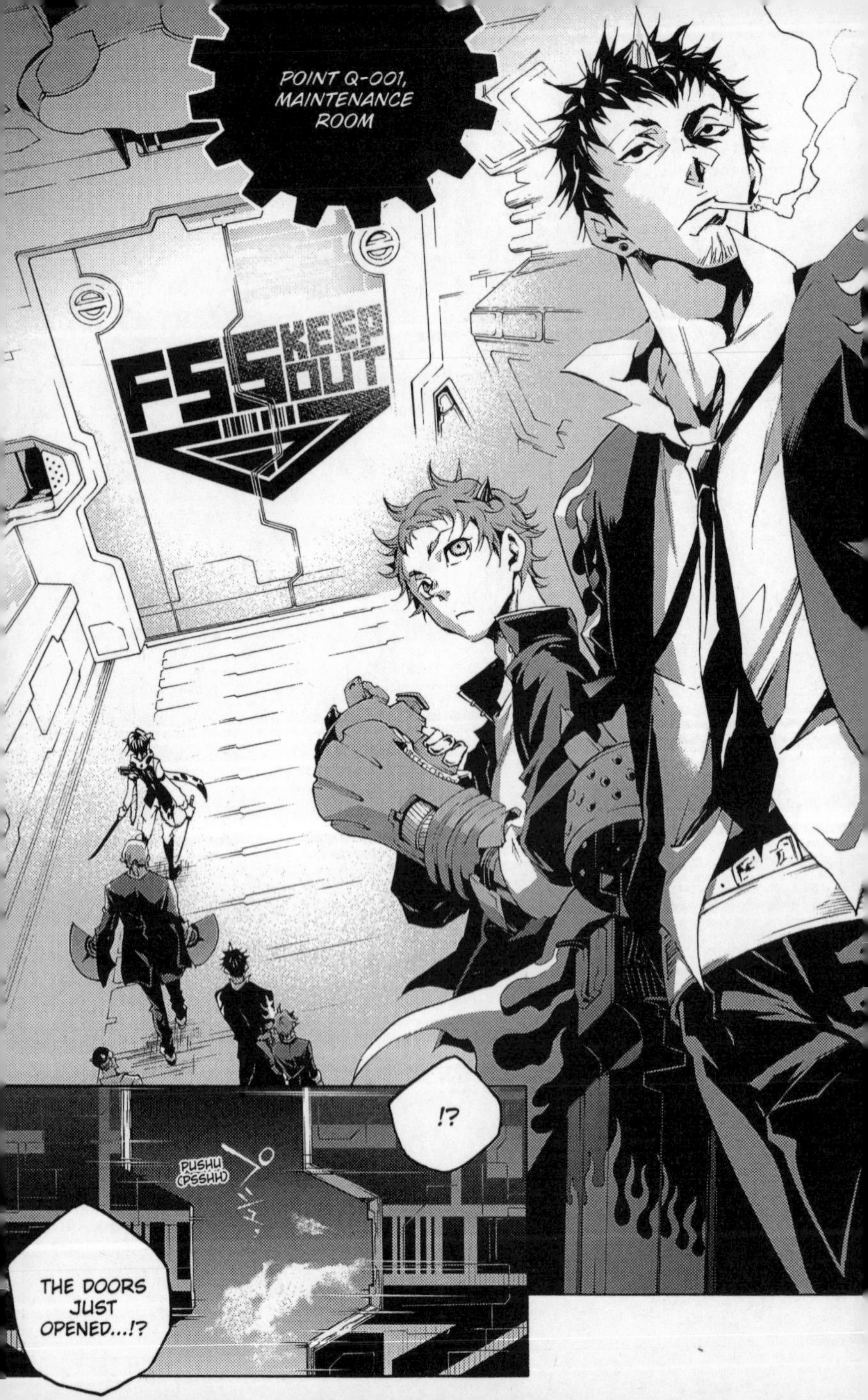
POINT Q-001, MAINTENANCE ROOM
FS KEEP OUT
!?
PUSHU (PSSHH)
THE DOORS JUST OPENED...!?

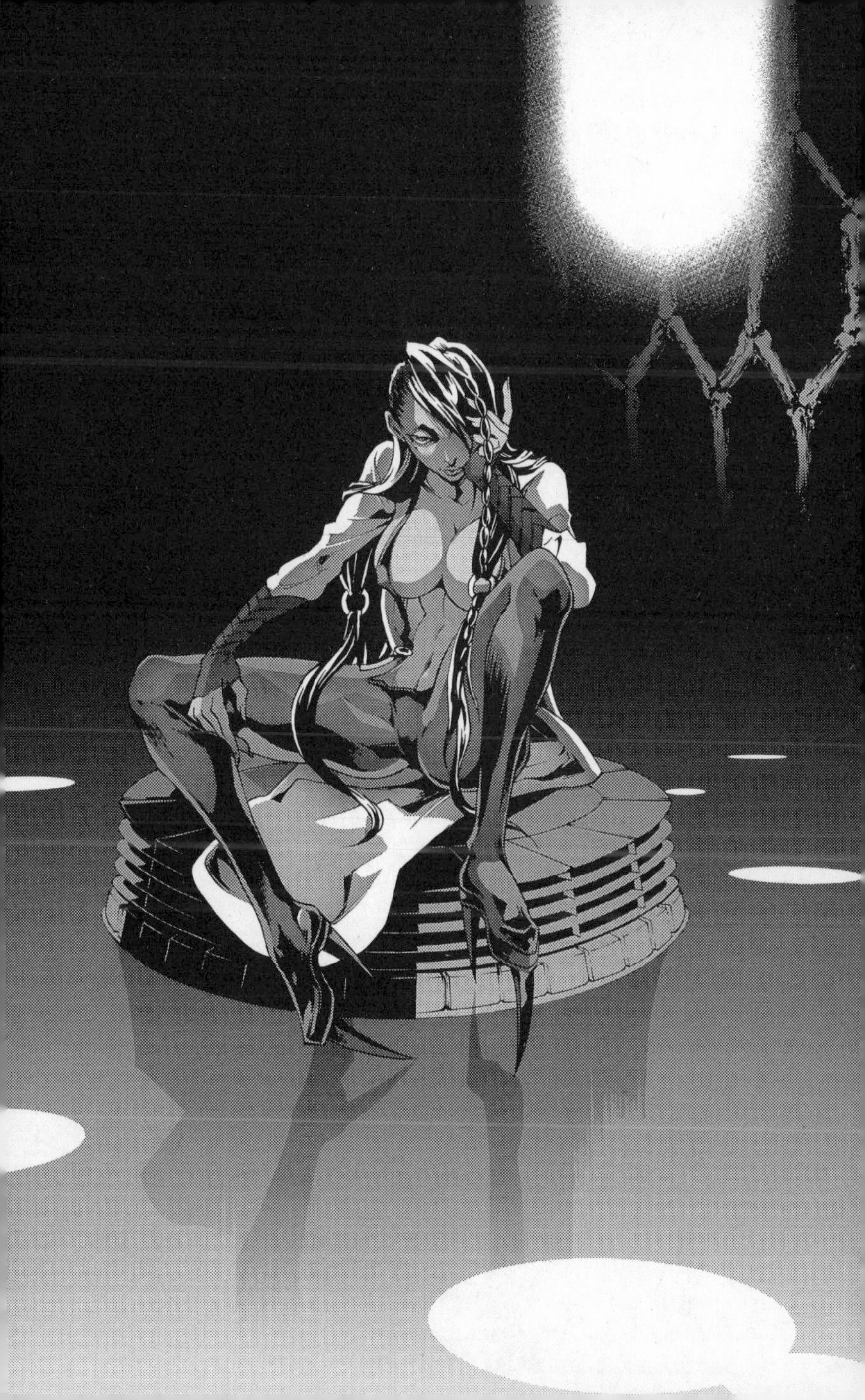

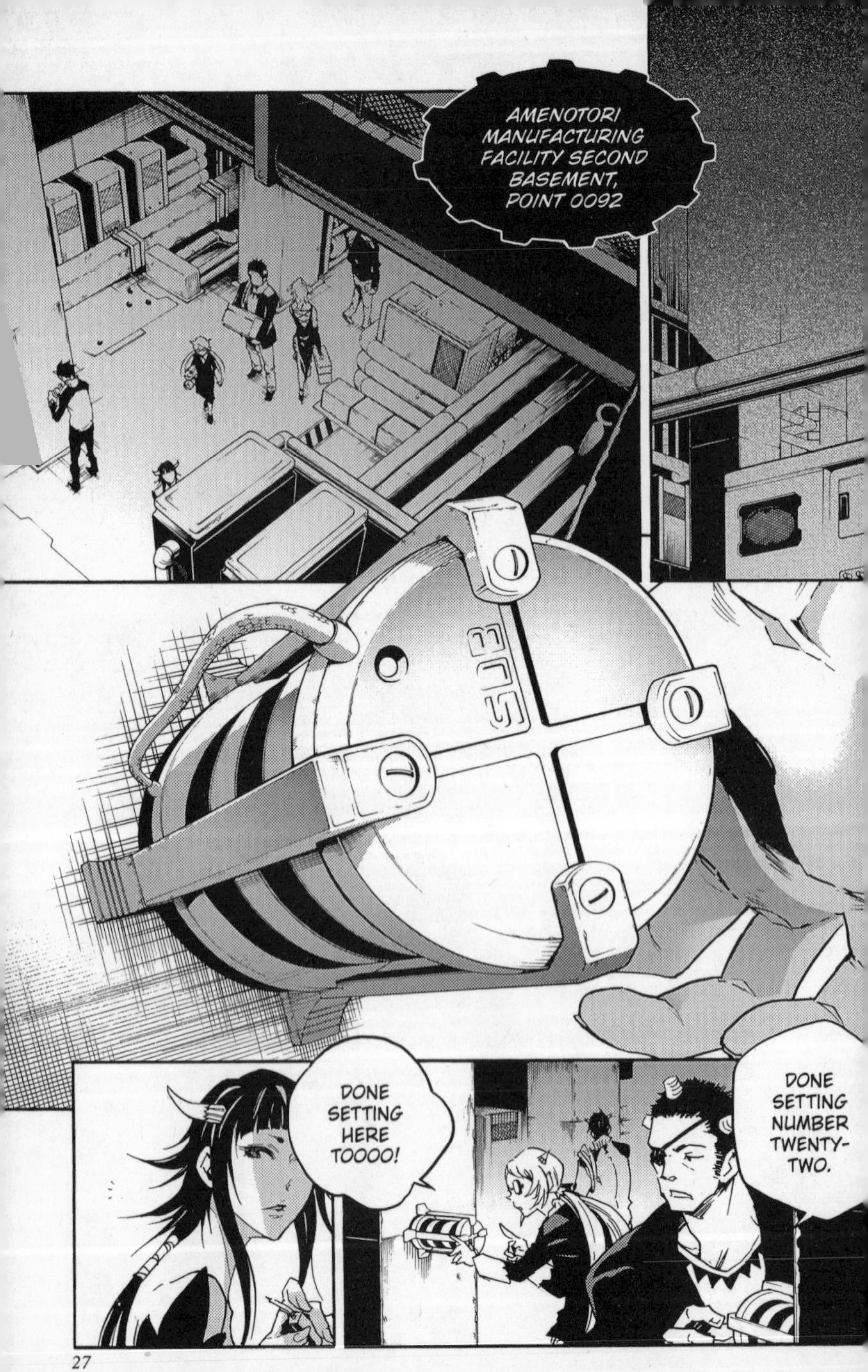
AMENOTORI MANUFACTURING FACILITY SECOND BASEMENT, POINT 0092
DONE SETTING NUMBER TWENTY-TWO.
DONE SETTING HERE TOOOO!

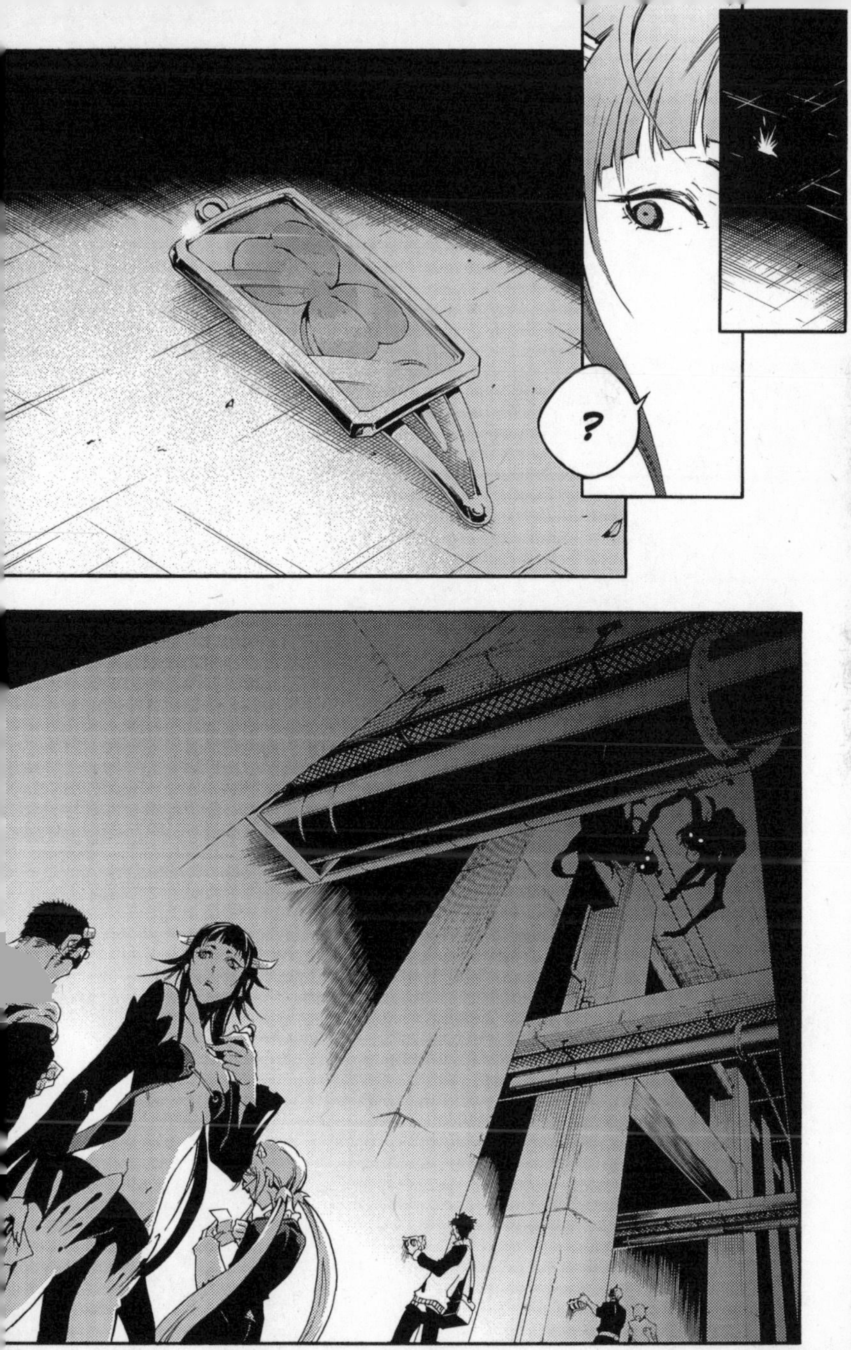
?

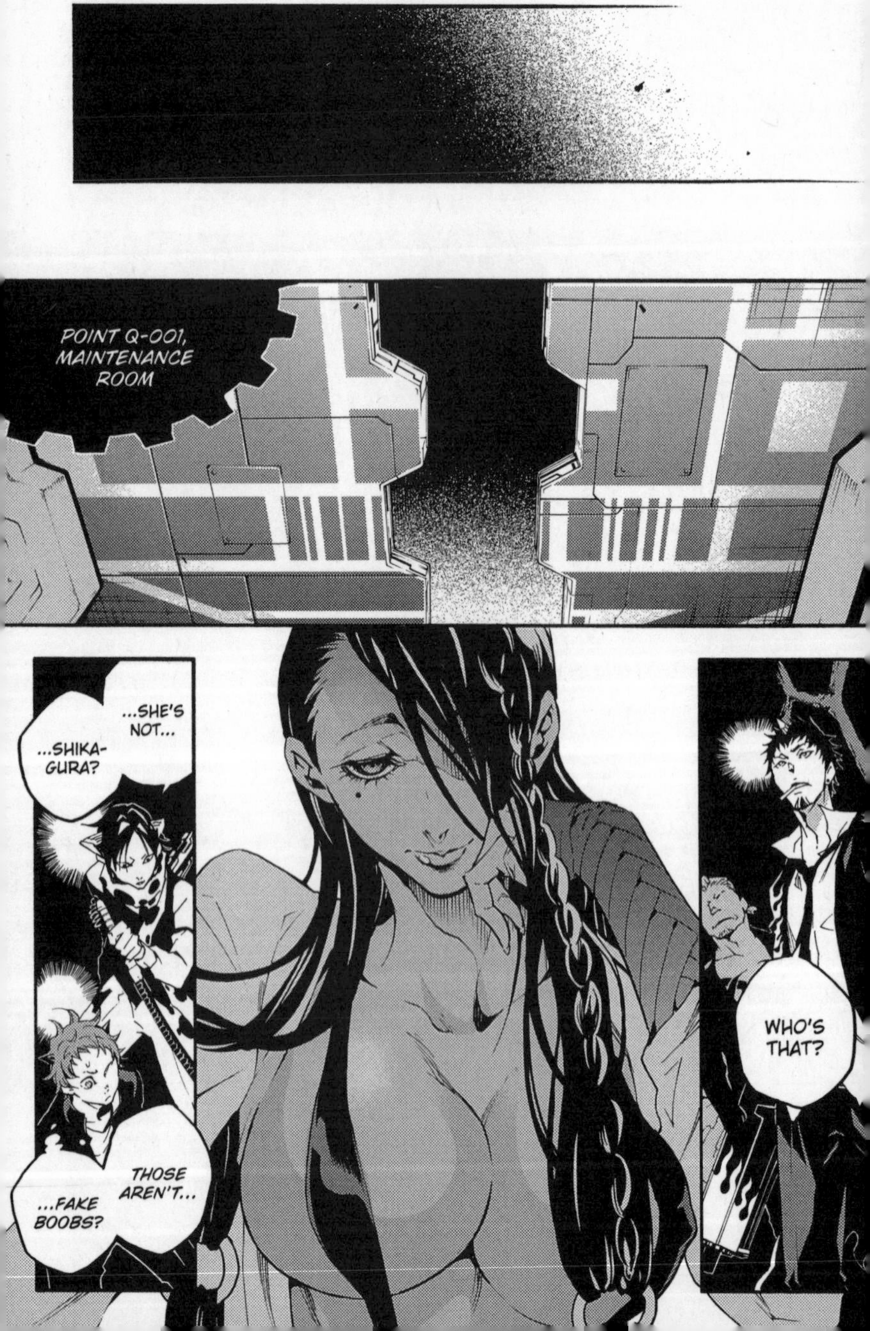
POINT Q-001, MAINTENANCE ROOM
WHO'S THAT?
...SHE'S NOT...
...SHIKA-GURA?
THOSE AREN'T...
...FAKE BOOBS?

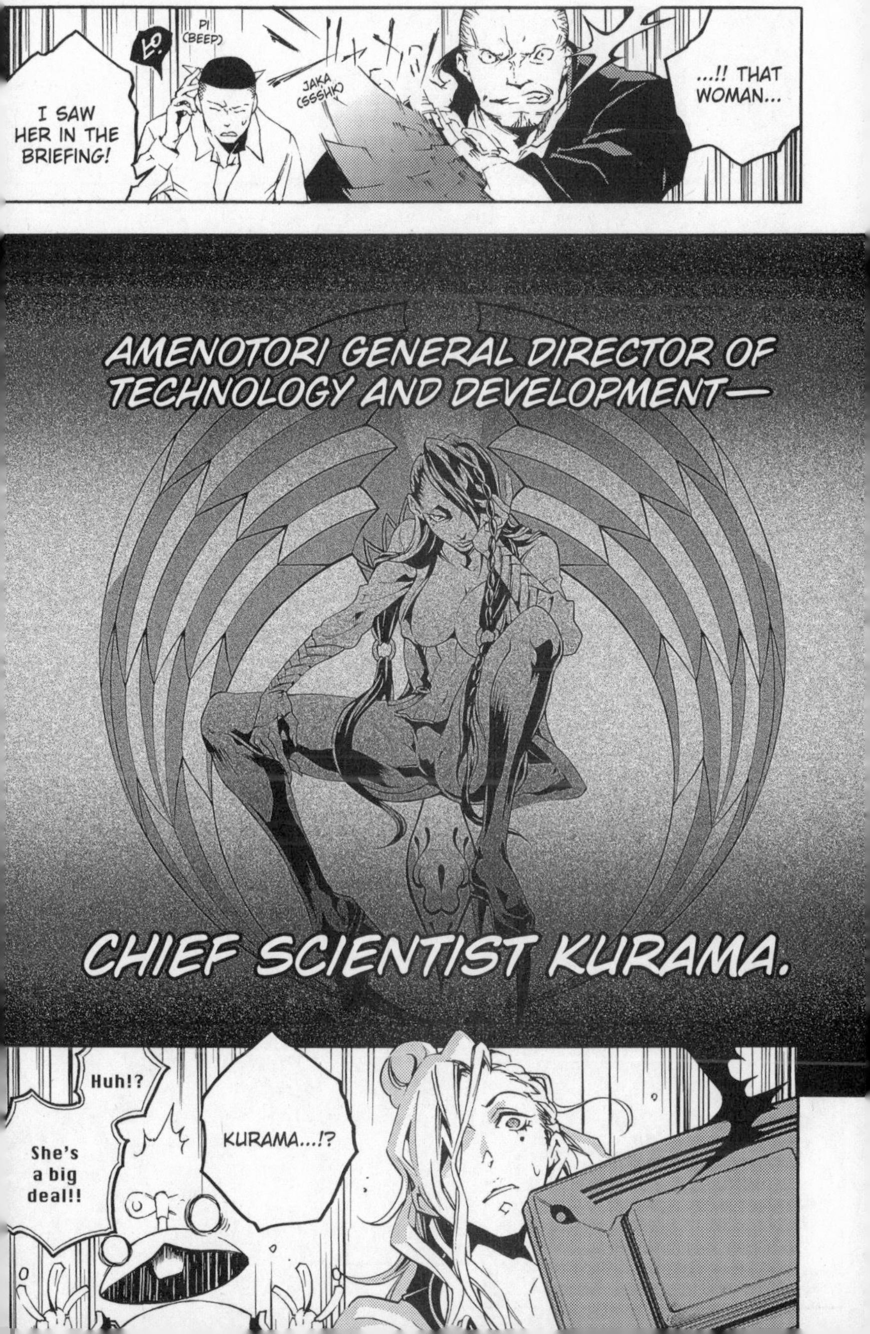
...!! THAT WOMAN...
JAKA (SSSHK)
PI (BEEP)
I SAW HER IN THE BRIEFING!
AMENOTORI GENERAL DIRECTOR OF TECHNOLOGY AND DEVELOPMENT—
CHIEF SCIENTIST KURAMA.
KURAMA...!?
Huh!?
She's a big deal!!

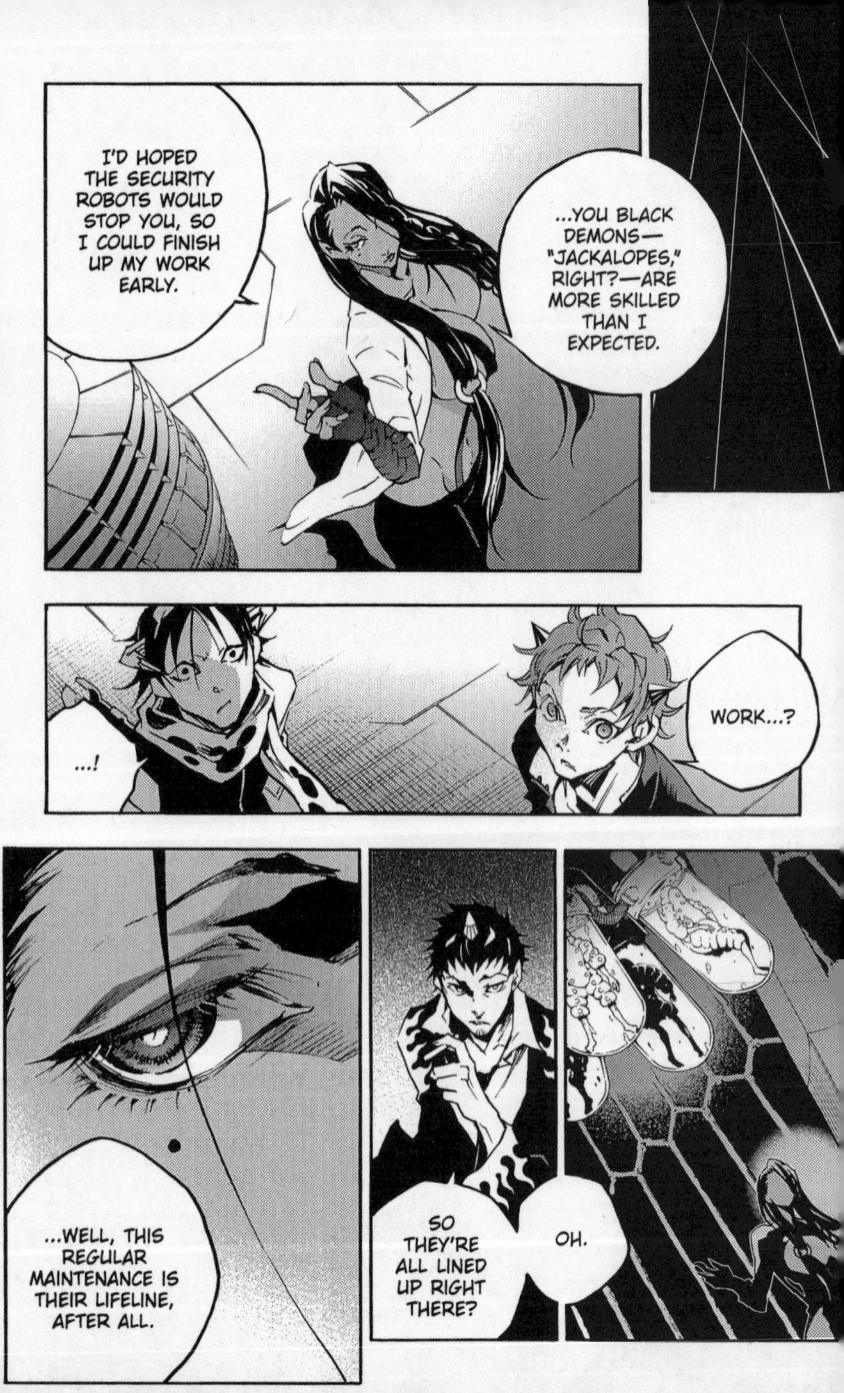
I'D HOPED THE SECURITY ROBOTS WOULD STOP YOU, SO I COULD FINISH UP MY WORK EARLY.
...YOU BLACK DEMONS—"JACKALOPES," RIGHT?—ARE MORE SKILLED THAN I EXPECTED.
WORK...?
...!
OH.
SO THEY'RE ALL LINED UP RIGHT THERE?
...WELL, THIS REGULAR MAINTENANCE IS THEIR LIFELINE, AFTER ALL.

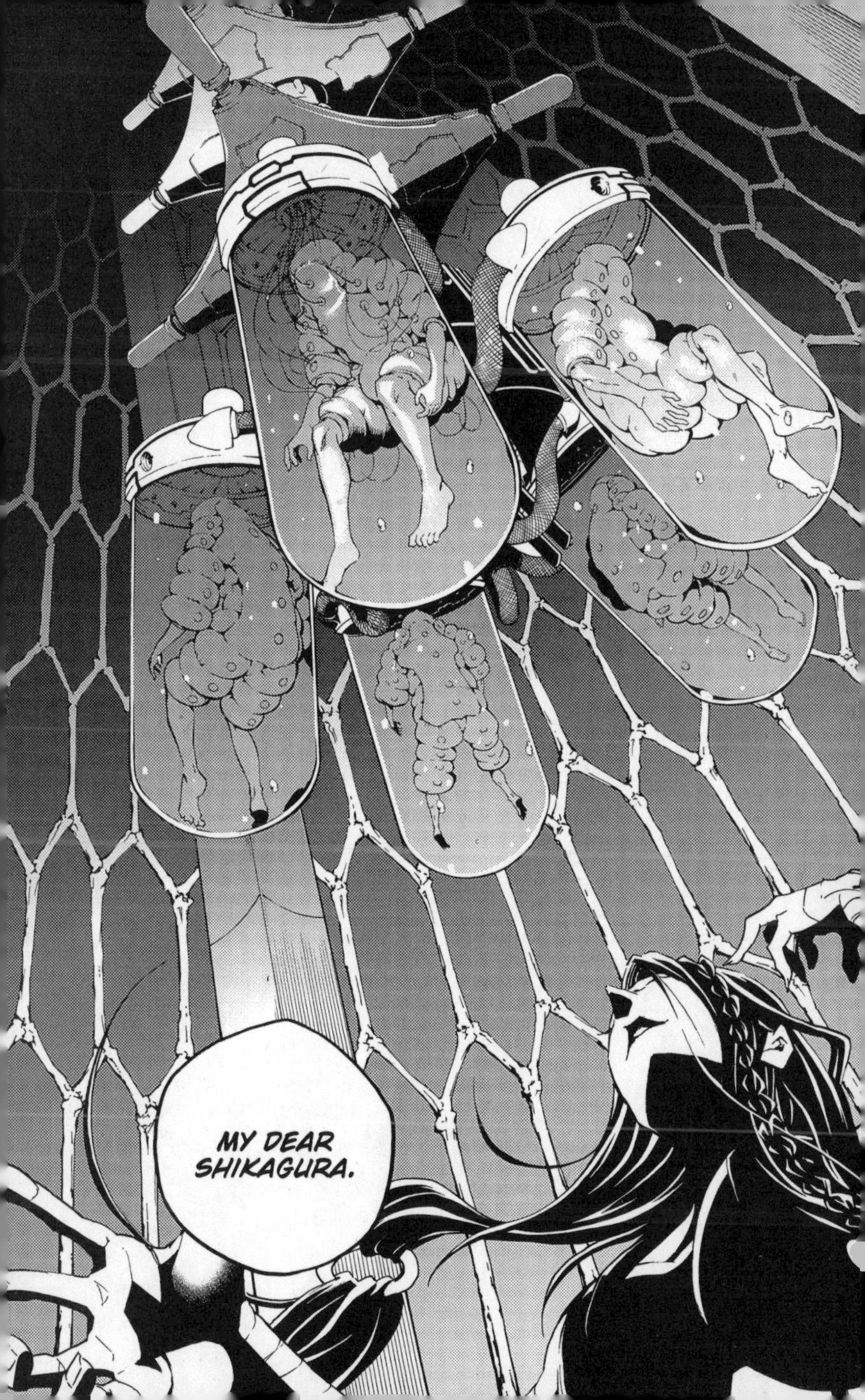
MY DEAR SHIKAGURA.

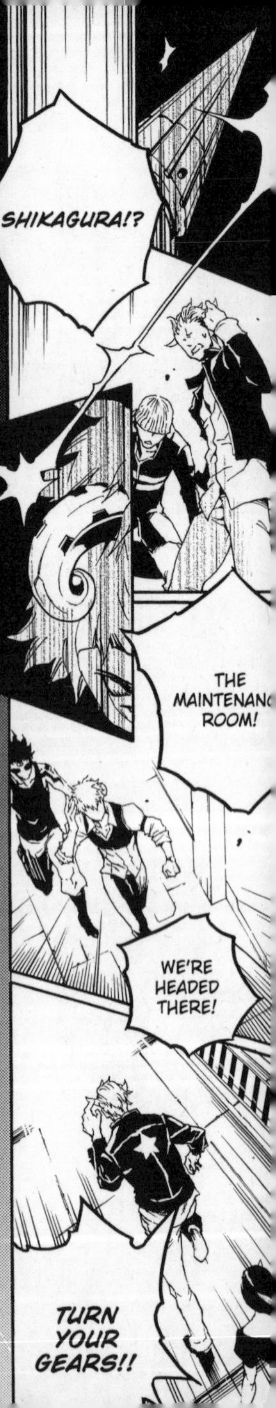
SHIKAGURA!?
THE MAINTENANC ROOM!
WE'RE HEADED THERE!
TURN YOUR GEARS!!
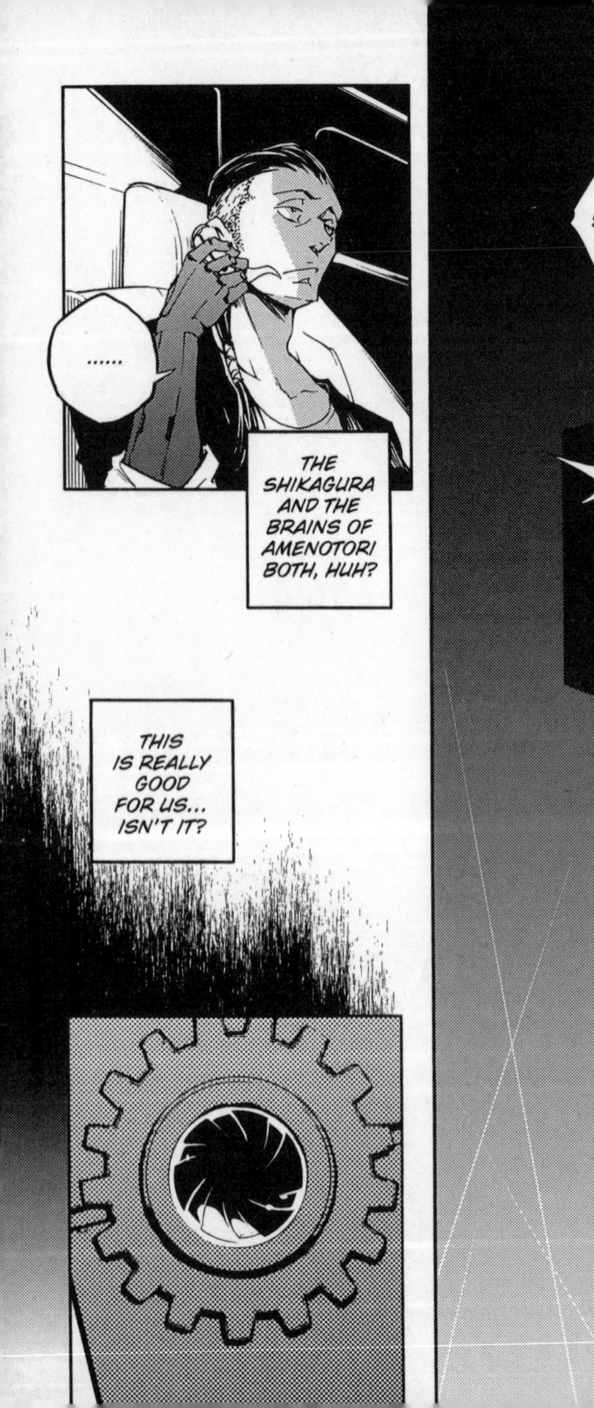
......
THE SHIKAGURA AND THE BRAINS OF AMENOTORI BOTH, HUH?
THIS IS REALLY GOOD FOR US... ISN'T IT?

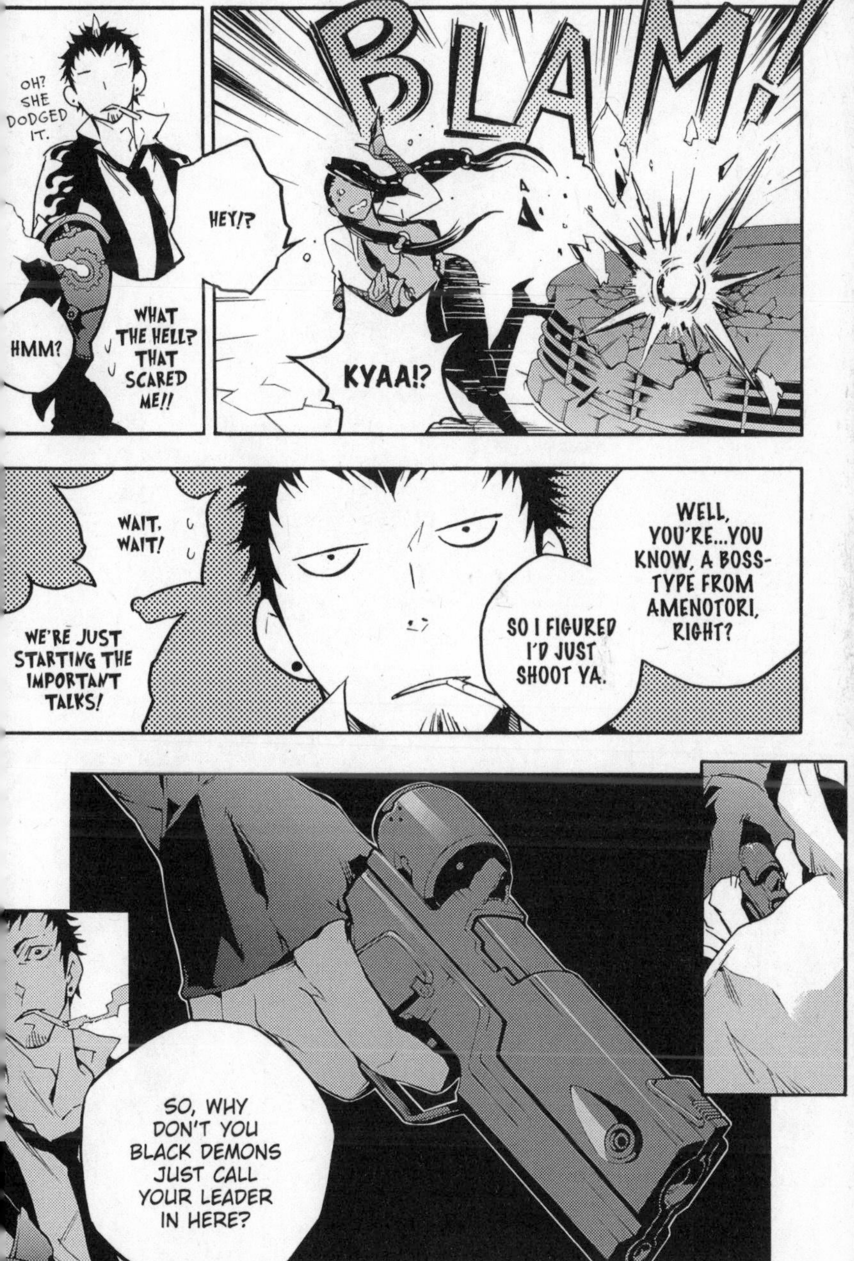
BLAM!
HEY!?
KYAA!?
OH? SHE DODGED IT.
WHAT THE HELL? THAT SCARED ME!!
HMM?
WELL, YOU'RE...YOU KNOW, A BOSS-TYPE FROM AMENOTORI, RIGHT?
SO I FIGURED I'D JUST SHOOT YA.
WAIT, WAIT!
WE'RE JUST STARTING THE IMPORTANT TALKS!
SO, WHY DON'T YOU BLACK DEMONS JUST CALL YOUR LEADER IN HERE?

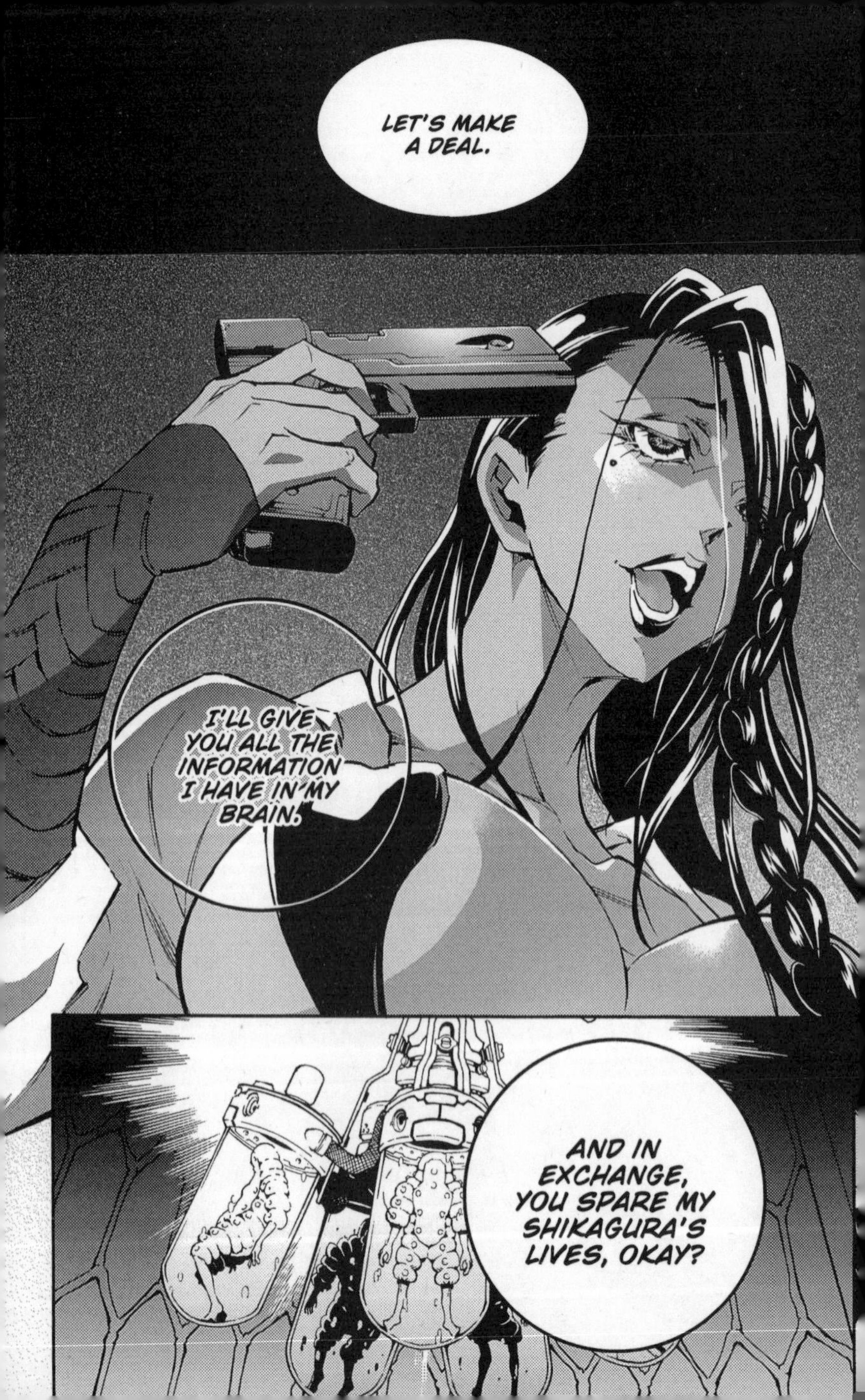
LET'S MAKE A DEAL.
I'LL GIVE YOU ALL THE INFORMATION I HAVE IN MY BRAIN.
AND IN EXCHANGE, YOU SPARE MY SHIKAGURA'S LIVES, OKAY?

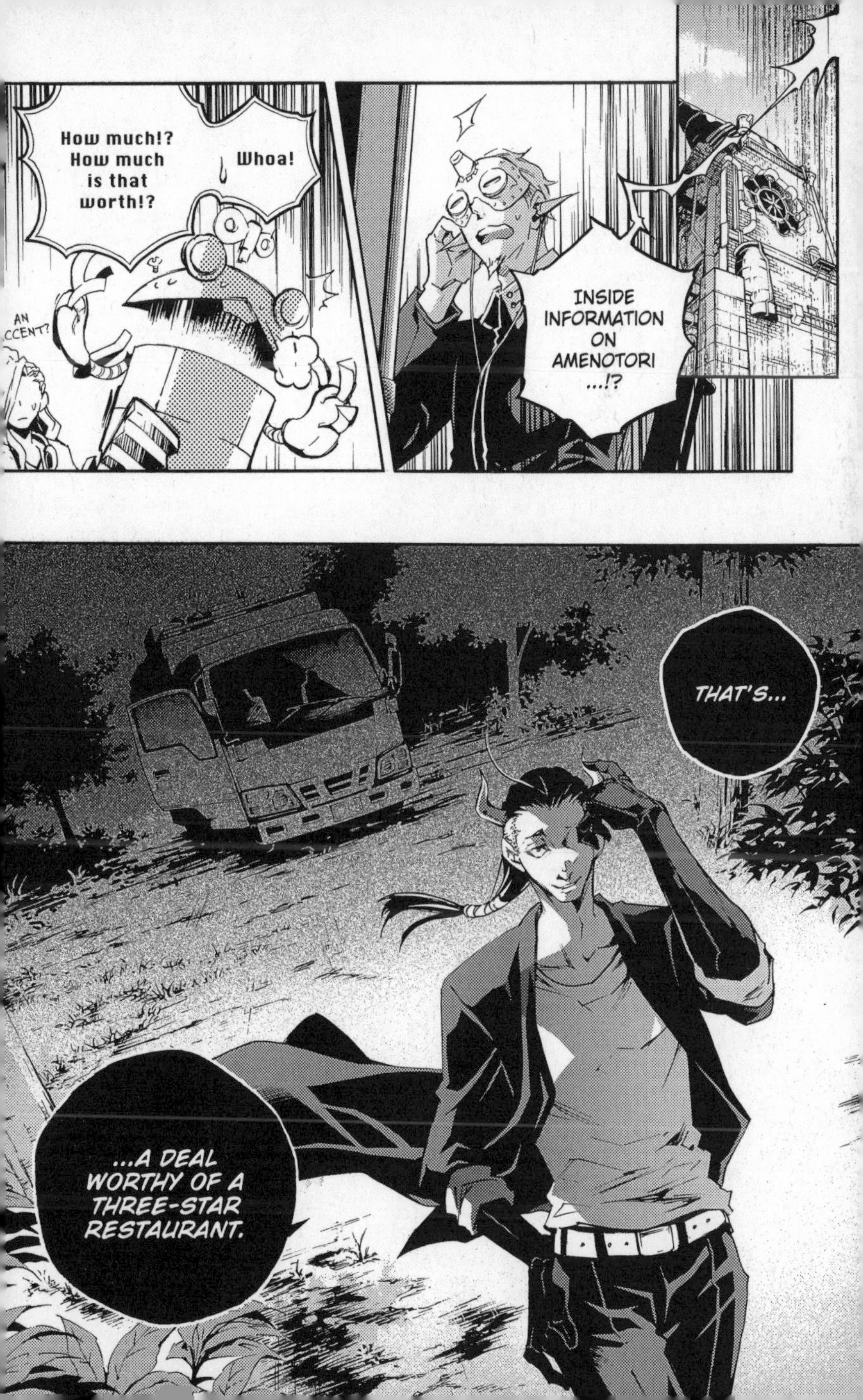
INSIDE INFORMATION ON AMENOTORI ...!?
Whoa!
How much!? How much is that worth!?
AN CCENT?
THAT'S...
...A DEAL WORTHY OF A THREE-STAR RESTAURANT.

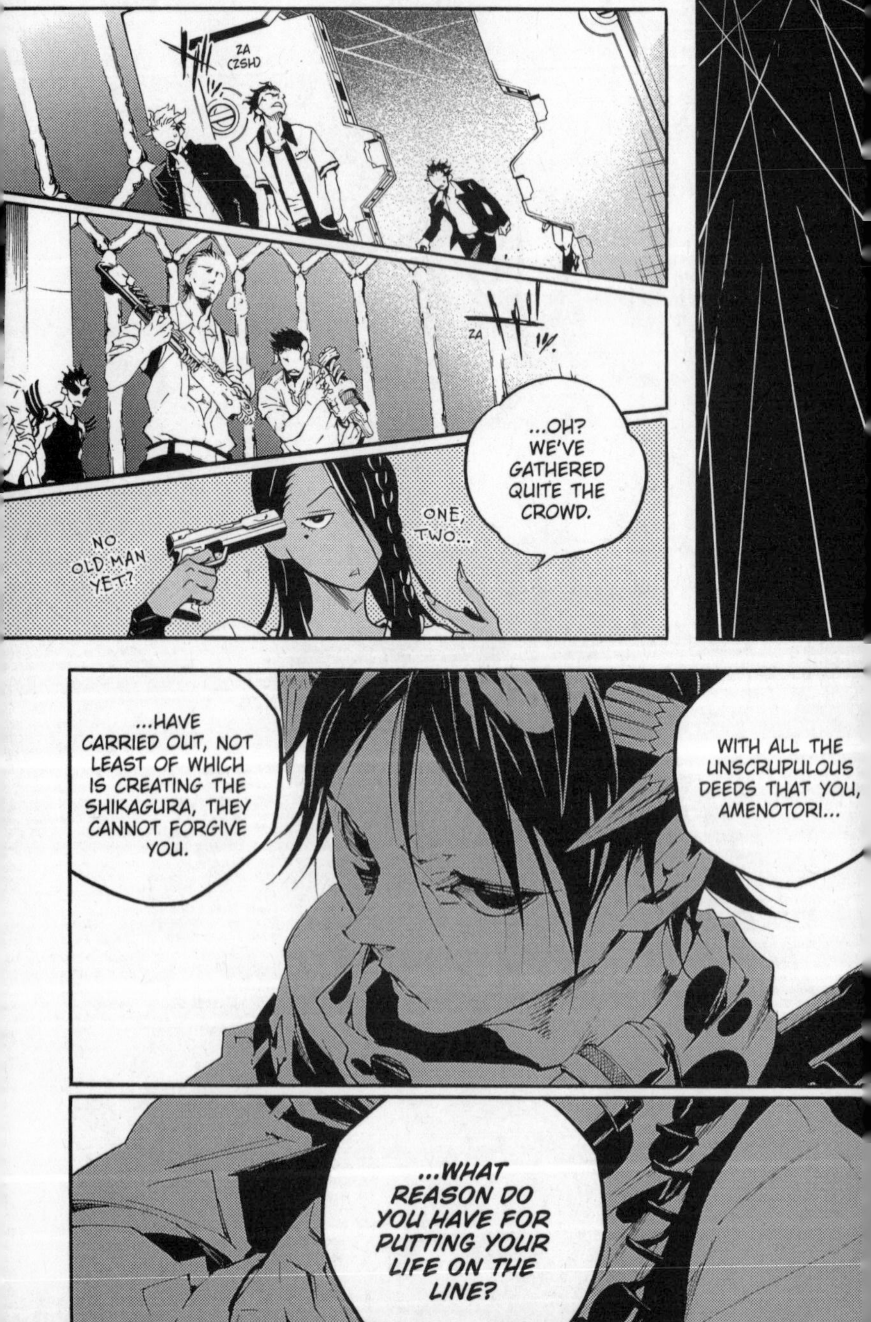
ZA (ZSH)
ZA
...OH? WE'VE GATHERED QUITE THE CROWD.
ONE, TWO...
NO OLD MAN YET?
WITH ALL THE UNSCRUPULOUS DEEDS THAT YOU, AMENOTORI...
...HAVE CARRIED OUT, NOT LEAST OF WHICH IS CREATING THE SHIKAGURA, THEY CANNOT FORGIVE YOU.
...WHAT REASON DO YOU HAVE FOR PUTTING YOUR LIFE ON THE LINE?

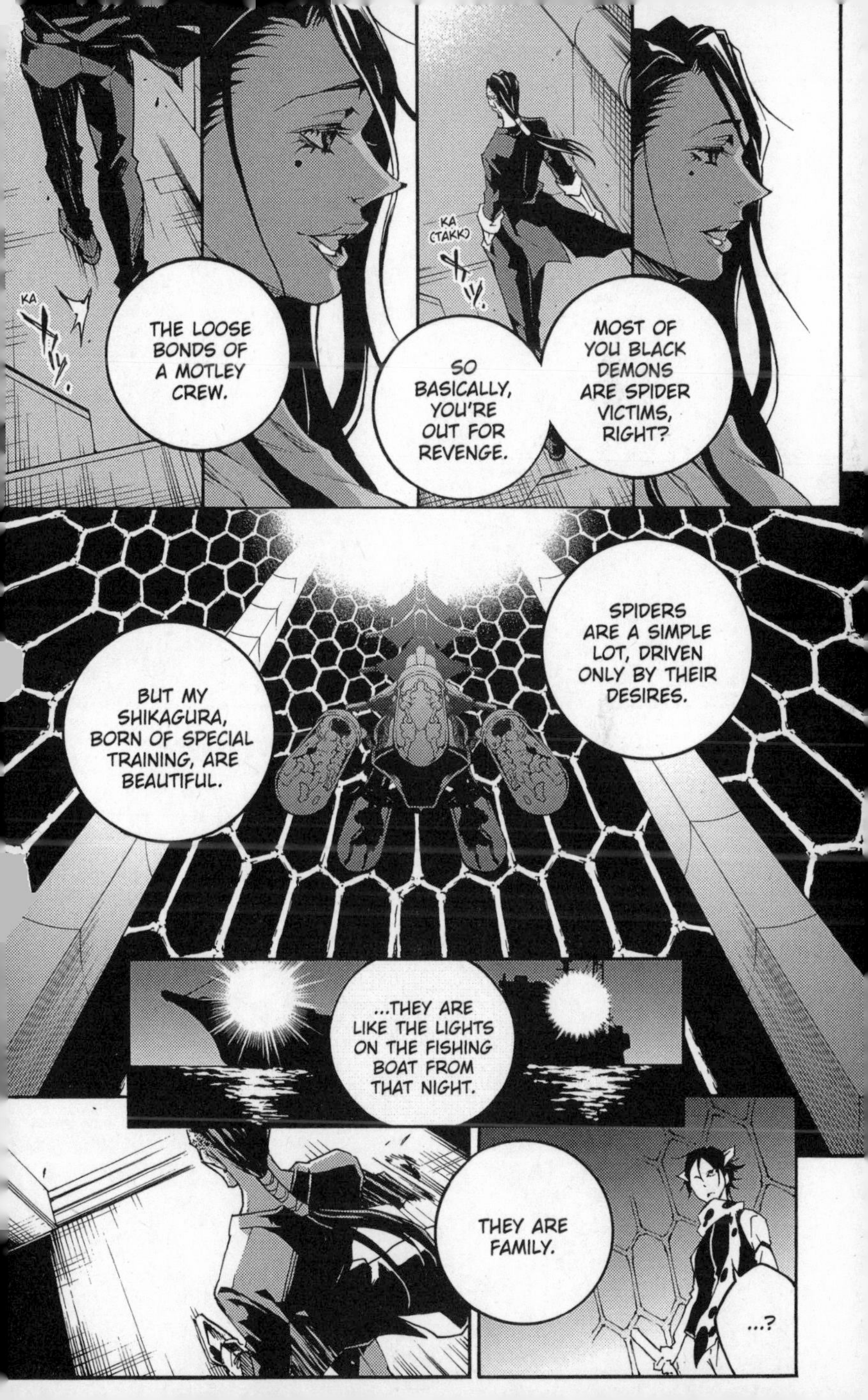
MOST OF YOU BLACK DEMONS ARE SPIDER VICTIMS, RIGHT?
KA (TAKK)
SO BASICALLY, YOU'RE OUT FOR REVENGE.
THE LOOSE BONDS OF A MOTLEY CREW.
KA
SPIDERS ARE A SIMPLE LOT, DRIVEN ONLY BY THEIR DESIRES.
BUT MY SHIKAGURA, BORN OF SPECIAL TRAINING, ARE BEAUTIFUL.
...THEY ARE LIKE THE LIGHTS ON THE FISHING BOAT FROM THAT NIGHT.
THEY ARE FAMILY.
...?

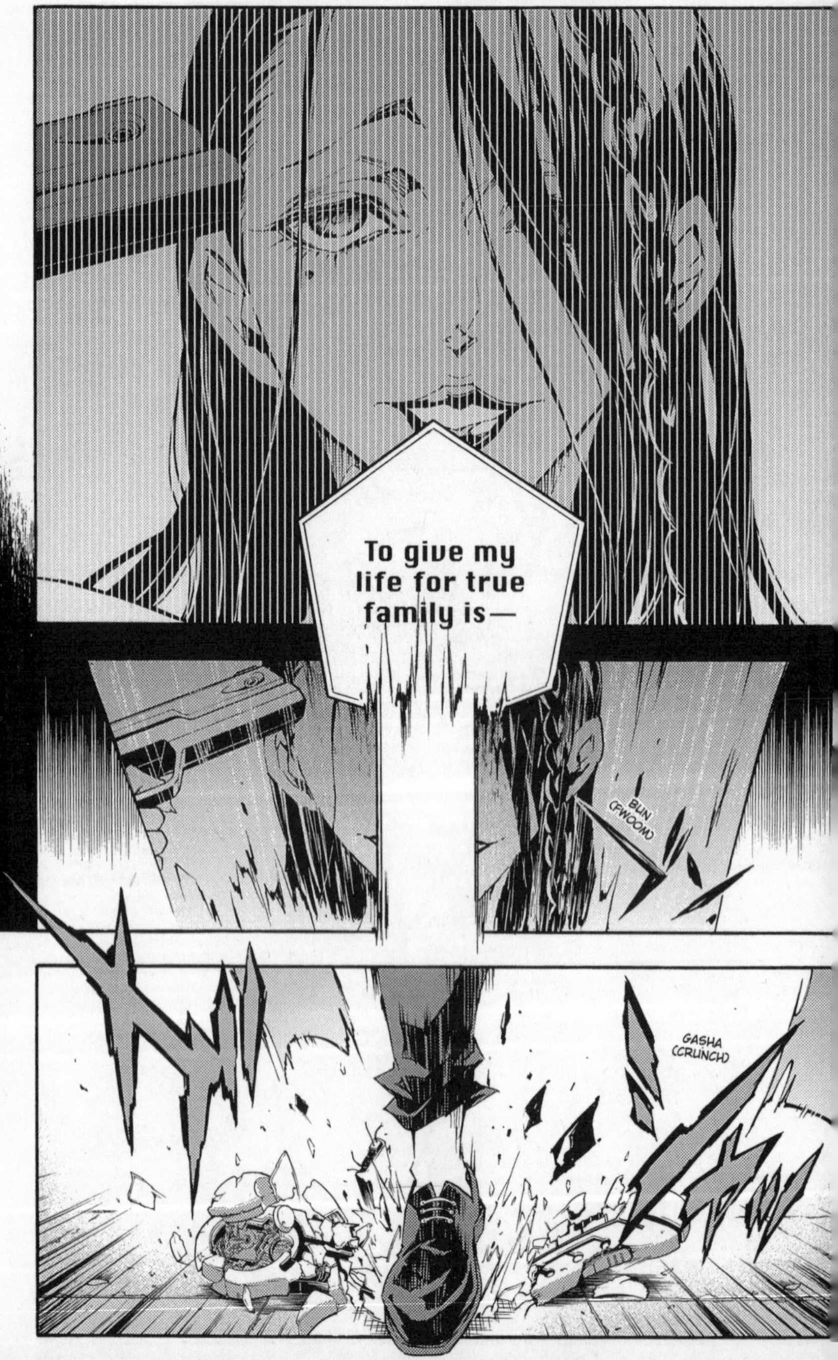
To give my life for true family is—
BUN (FWOOM)
GASHA (CRUNCH)

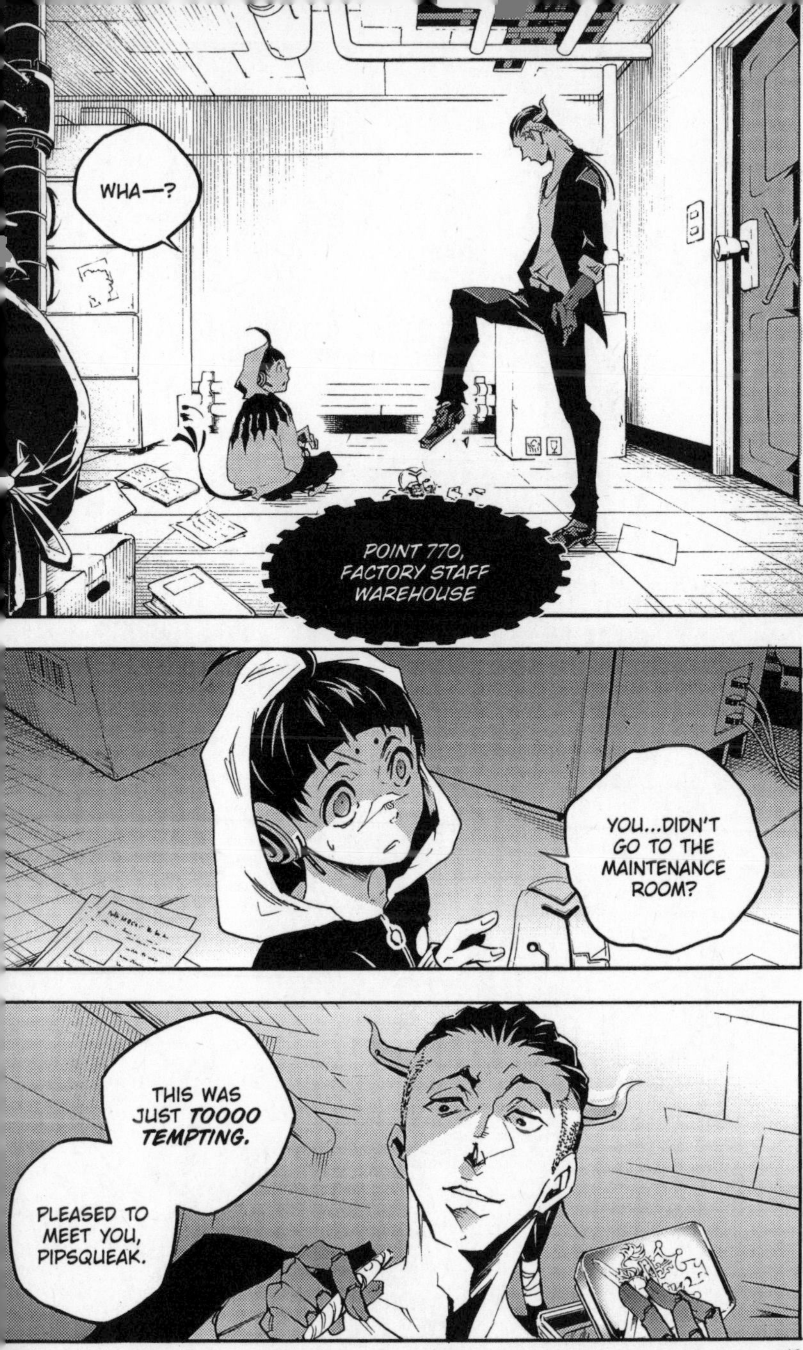
WHA—?
POINT 770, FACTORY STAFF WAREHOUSE
YOU...DIDN'T GO TO THE MAINTENANCE ROOM?
THIS WAS JUST *TOOOO TEMPTING*.
PLEASED TO MEET YOU, PIPSQUEAK.

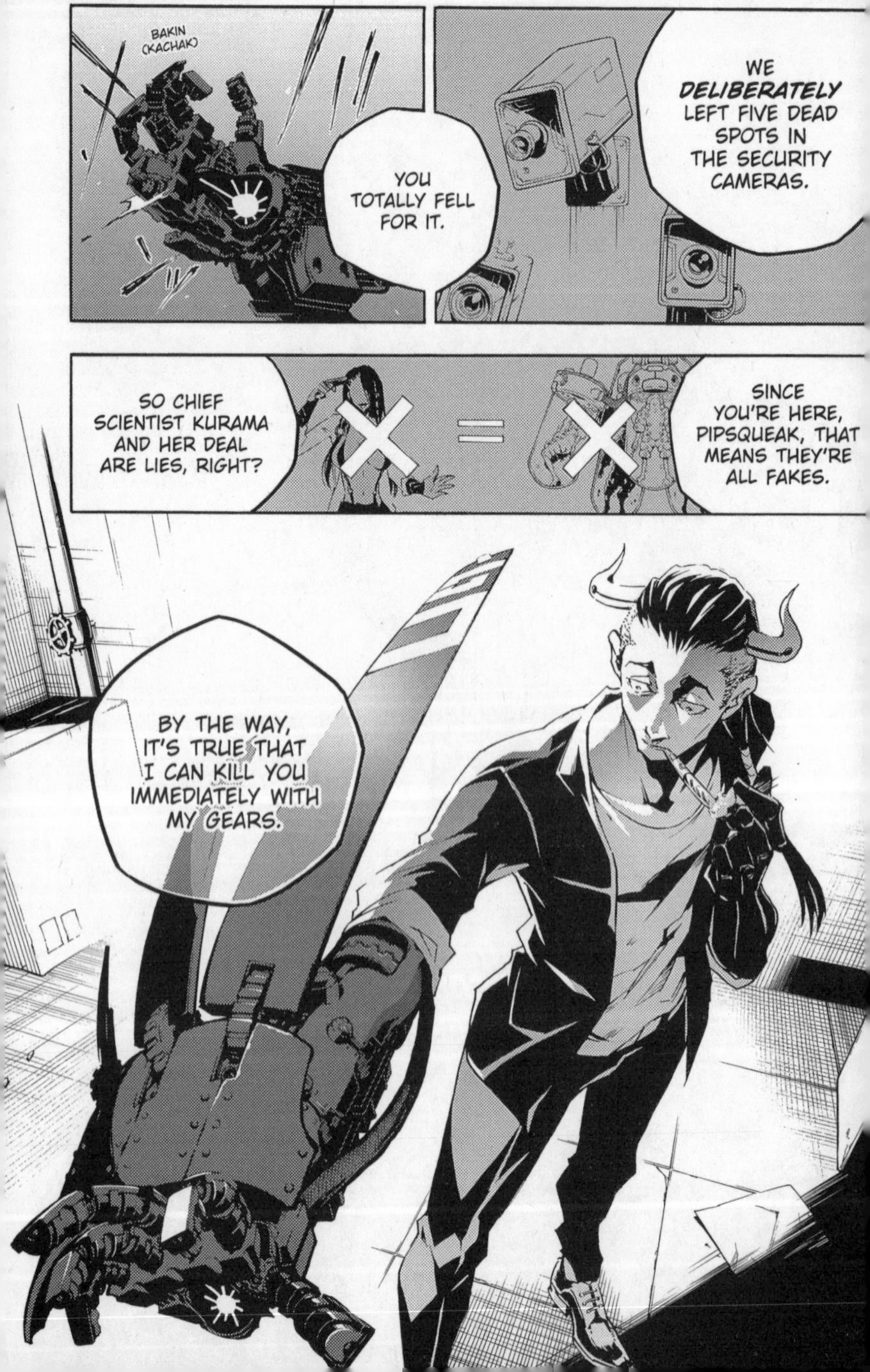
WE DELIBERATELY LEFT FIVE DEAD SPOTS IN THE SECURITY CAMERAS.
BAKIN (KACHAK)
YOU TOTALLY FELL FOR IT.
SINCE YOU'RE HERE, PIPSQUEAK, THAT MEANS THEY'RE ALL FAKES.
SO CHIEF SCIENTIST KURAMA AND HER DEAL ARE LIES, RIGHT?
BY THE WAY, IT'S TRUE THAT I CAN KILL YOU IMMEDIATELY WITH MY GEARS.

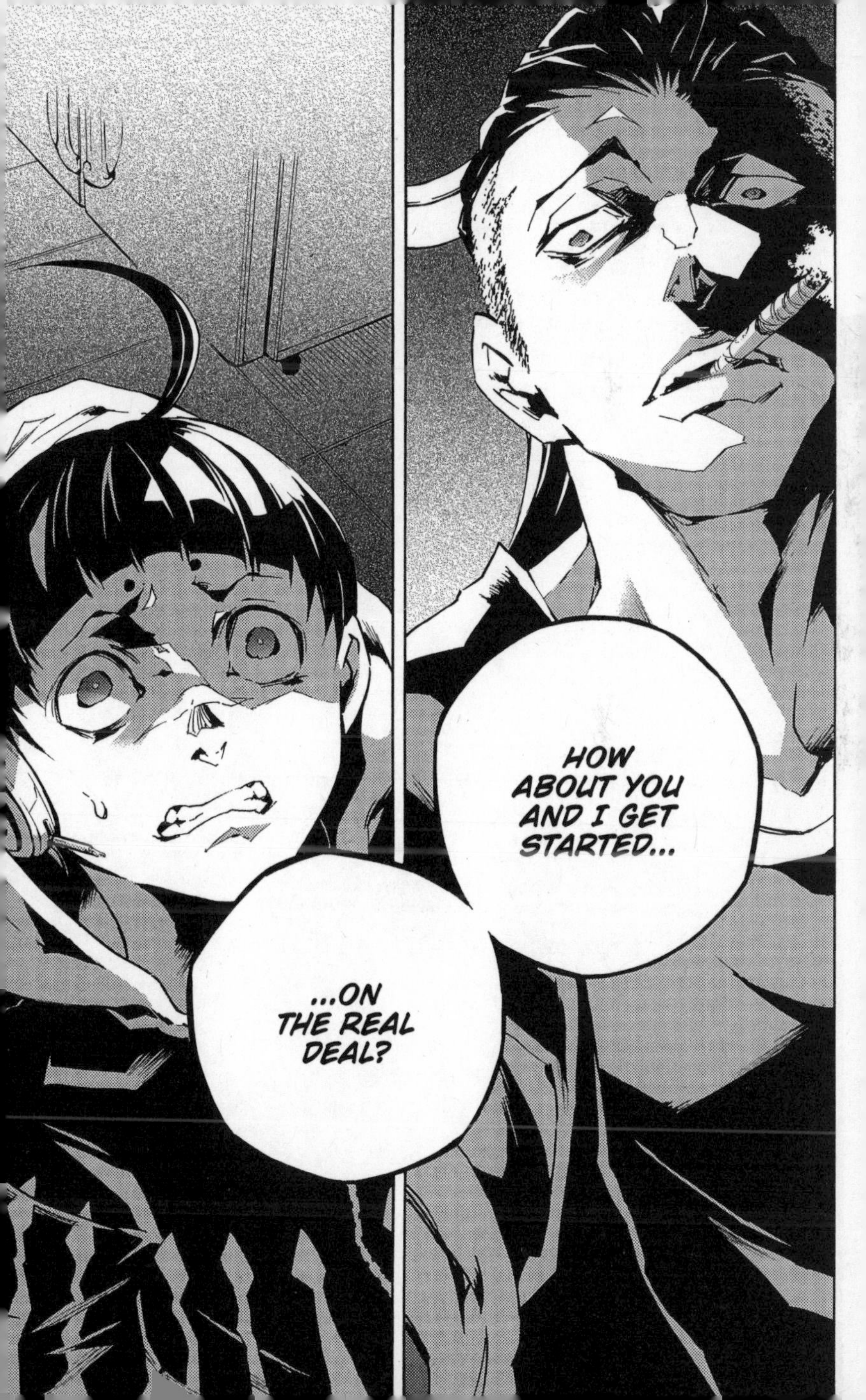
HOW ABOUT YOU AND I GET STARTED...
...ON THE REAL DEAL?

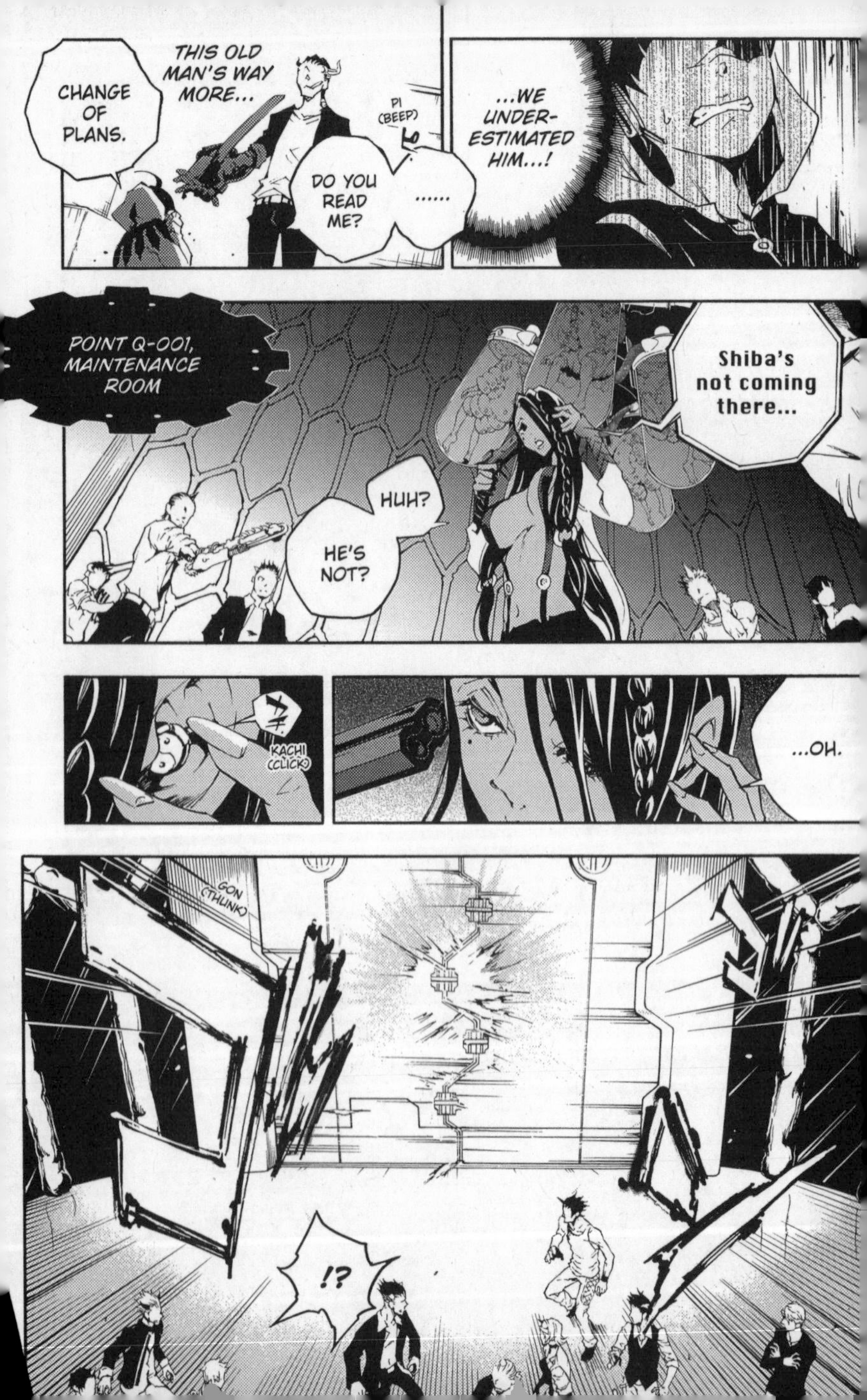

...WE UNDER-ESTIMATED HIM...!
PI (BEEP)
......
DO YOU READ ME?
THIS OLD MAN'S WAY MORE...
CHANGE OF PLANS.
Shiba's not coming there...
POINT Q-001, MAINTENANCE ROOM
HUH?
HE'S NOT?
...OH.
KACHI (CLICK)
GON (THUNK)
!?

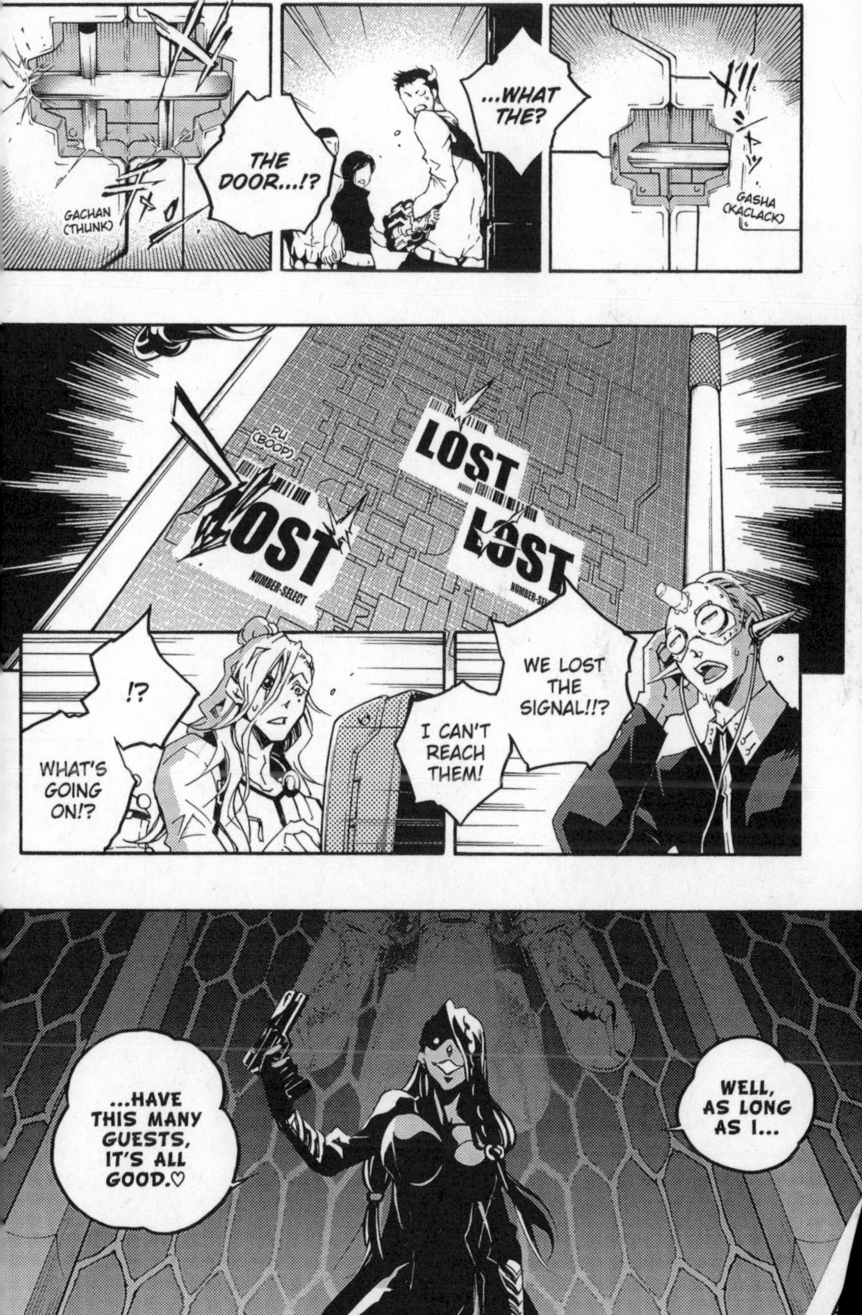
GASHA (KACLACK)
...WHAT THE?
THE DOOR...!?
GACHAN (THUNK)
PU (BOOP)
LOST
LOST
NUMBER-SELECT
LOST
NUMBER-SELECT
WE LOST THE SIGNAL!!?
I CAN'T REACH THEM!
!?
WHAT'S GOING ON!?
WELL, AS LONG AS I...
...HAVE THIS MANY GUESTS, IT'S ALL GOOD.♡

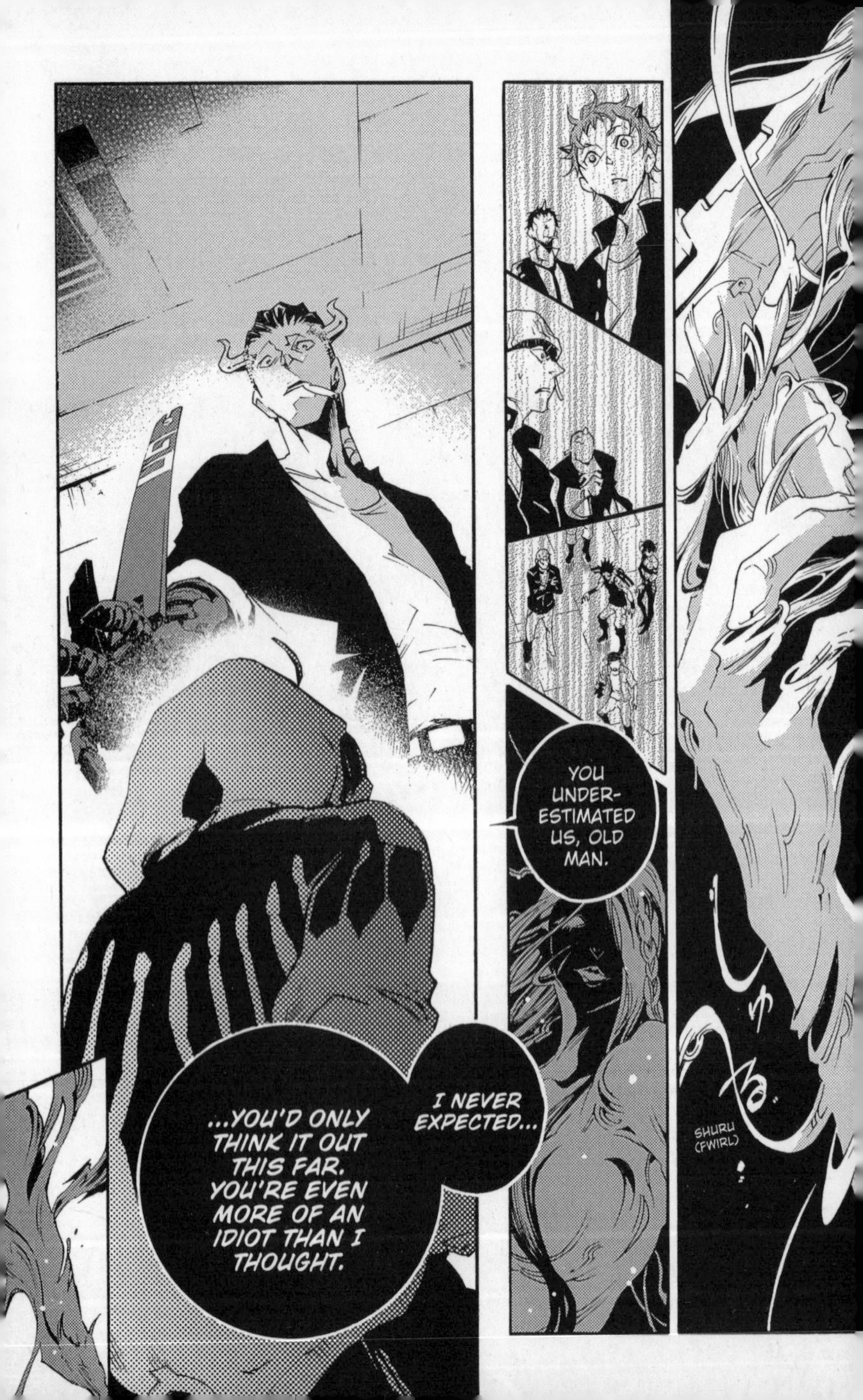
SHURU (FWIRL)
YOU UNDER-ESTIMATED US, OLD MAN.
I NEVER EXPECTED...
...YOU'D ONLY THINK IT OUT THIS FAR. YOU'RE EVEN MORE OF AN IDIOT THAN I THOUGHT.

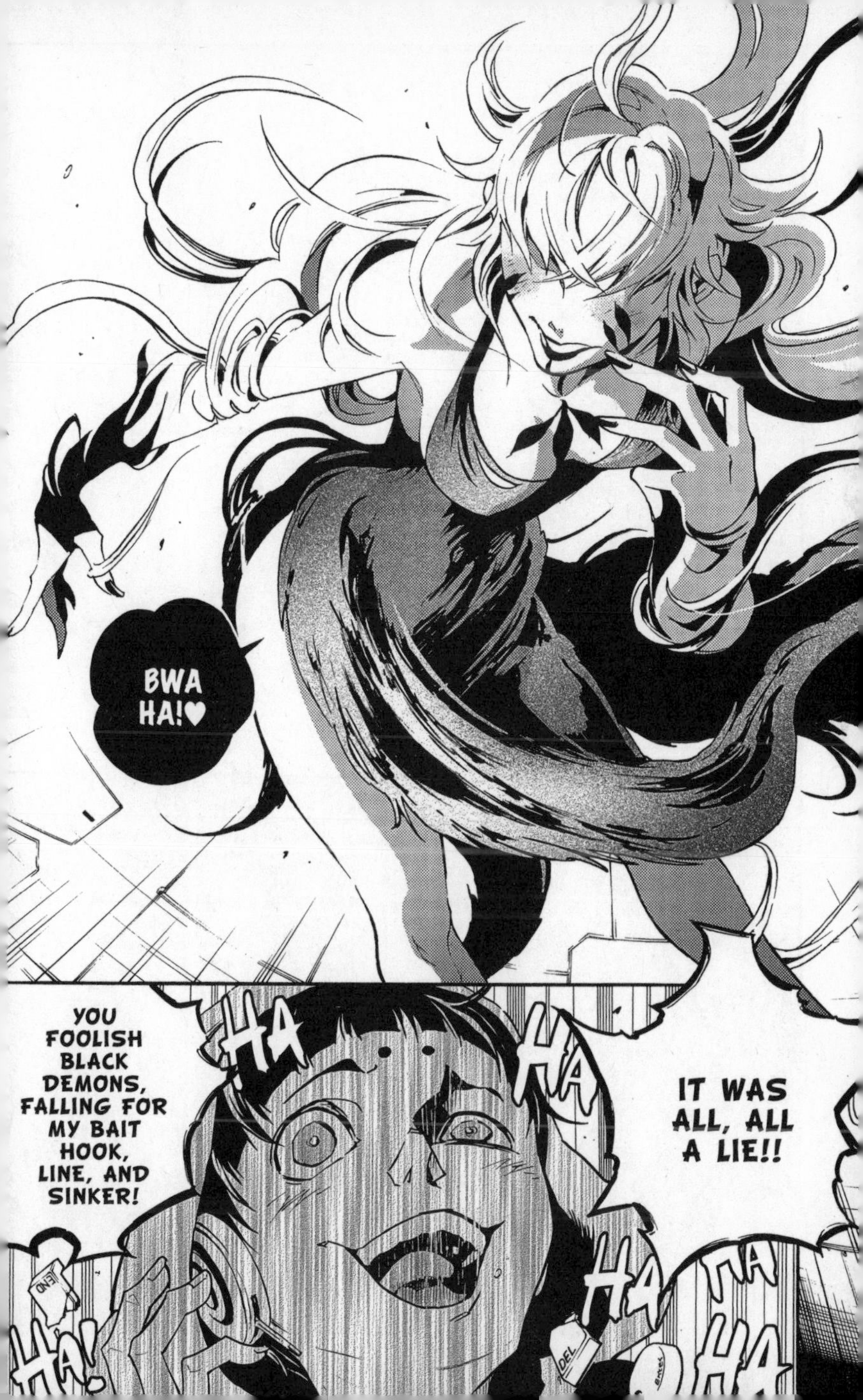
BWA HA!♥
HA
HA
IT WAS ALL, ALL A LIE!!
YOU FOOLISH BLACK DEMONS, FALLING FOR MY BAIT HOOK, LINE, AND SINKER!
HA HA
HA HA
HA!

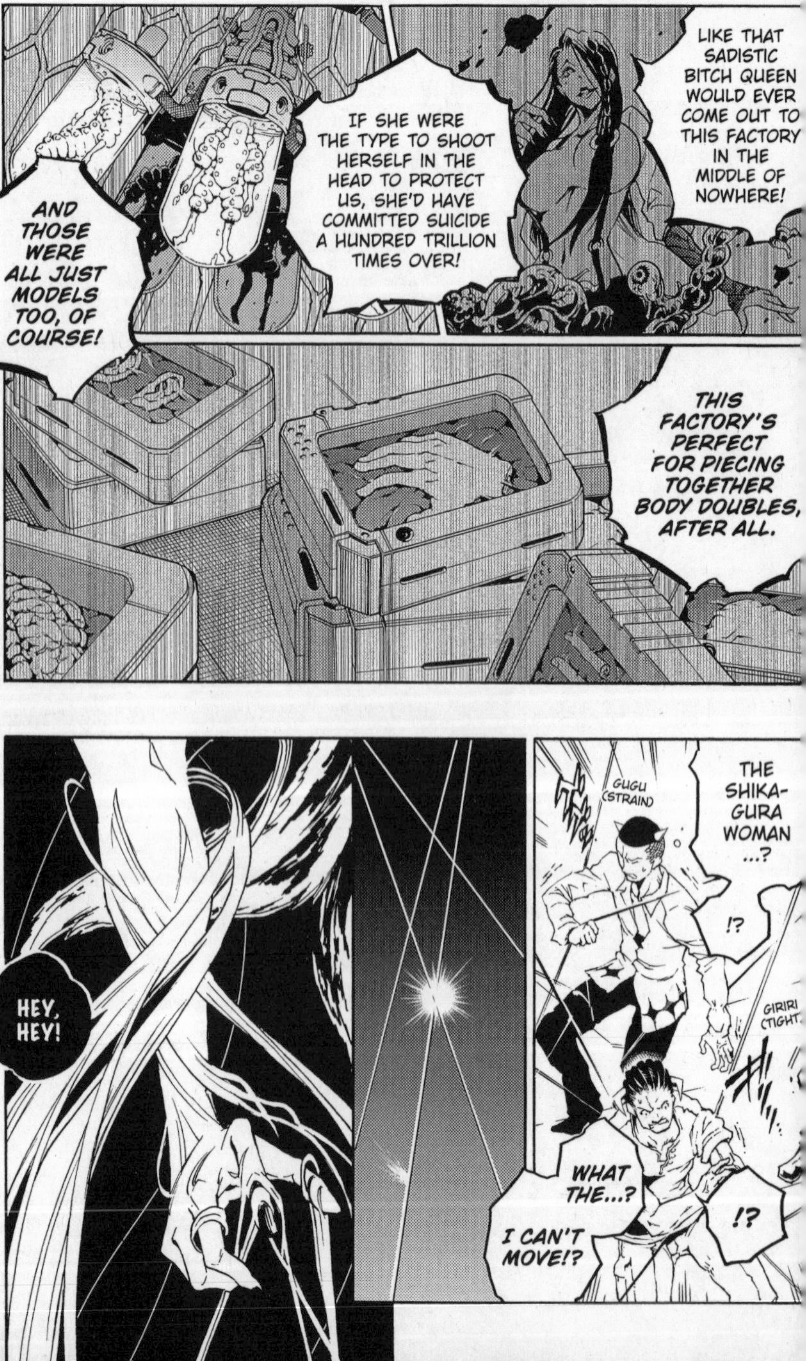
LIKE THAT SADISTIC BITCH QUEEN WOULD EVER COME OUT TO THIS FACTORY IN THE MIDDLE OF NOWHERE!
IF SHE WERE THE TYPE TO SHOOT HERSELF IN THE HEAD TO PROTECT US, SHE'D HAVE COMMITTED SUICIDE A HUNDRED TRILLION TIMES OVER!
AND THOSE WERE ALL JUST MODELS TOO, OF COURSE!
THIS FACTORY'S PERFECT FOR PIECING TOGETHER BODY DOUBLES, AFTER ALL.
THE SHIKA-GURA WOMAN ...?
GUGU (STRAIN)
!?
GIRIRI (TIGHT
!?
WHAT THE...?
I CAN'T MOVE!?
HEY, HEY!

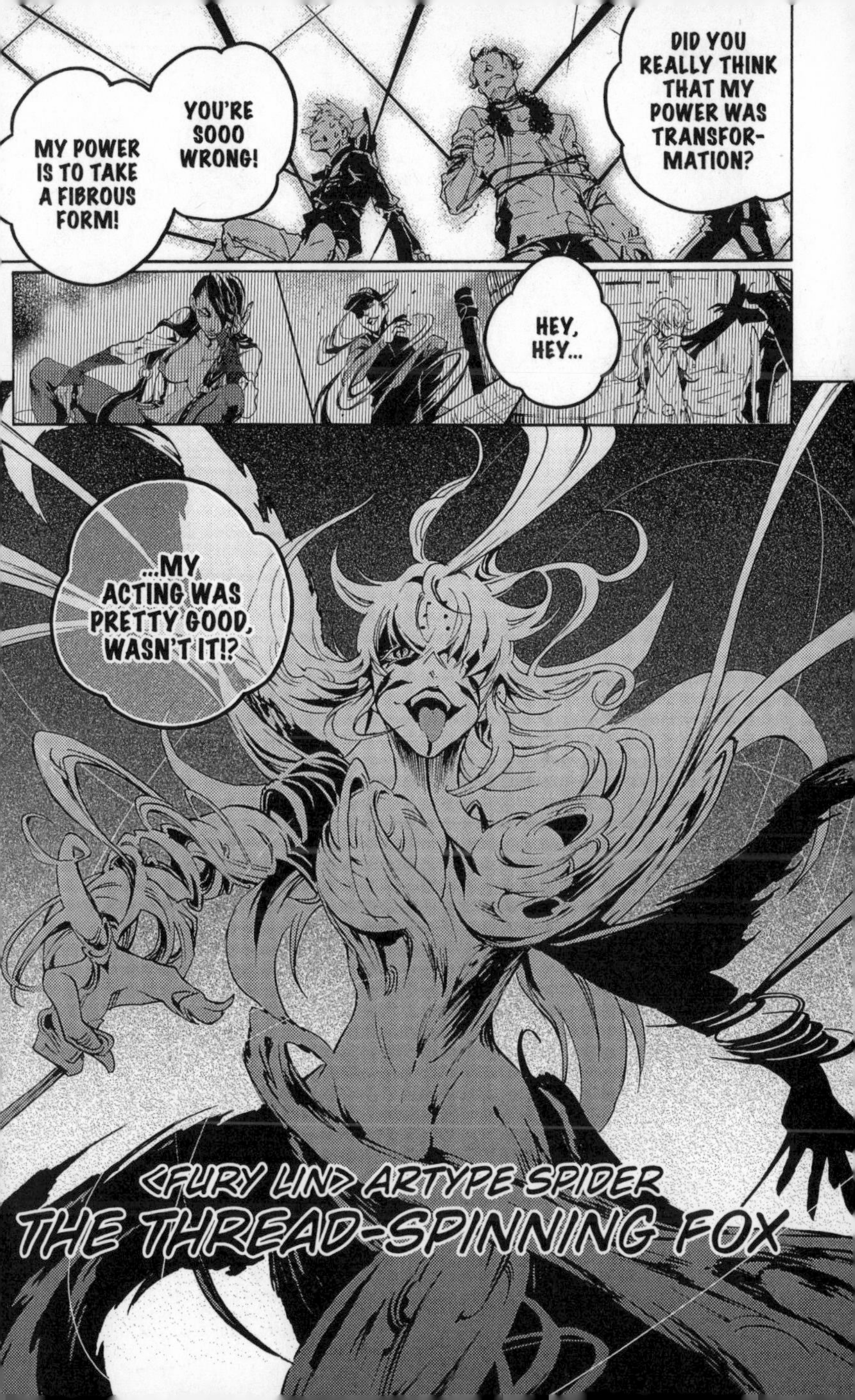
DID YOU REALLY THINK THAT MY POWER WAS TRANSFOR-MATION?
YOU'RE SOOO WRONG!
MY POWER IS TO TAKE A FIBROUS FORM!
HEY, HEY...
...MY ACTING WAS PRETTY GOOD, WASN'T IT!?
<FURY LIN> ARTYPE SPIDER
THE THREAD-SPINNING FOX

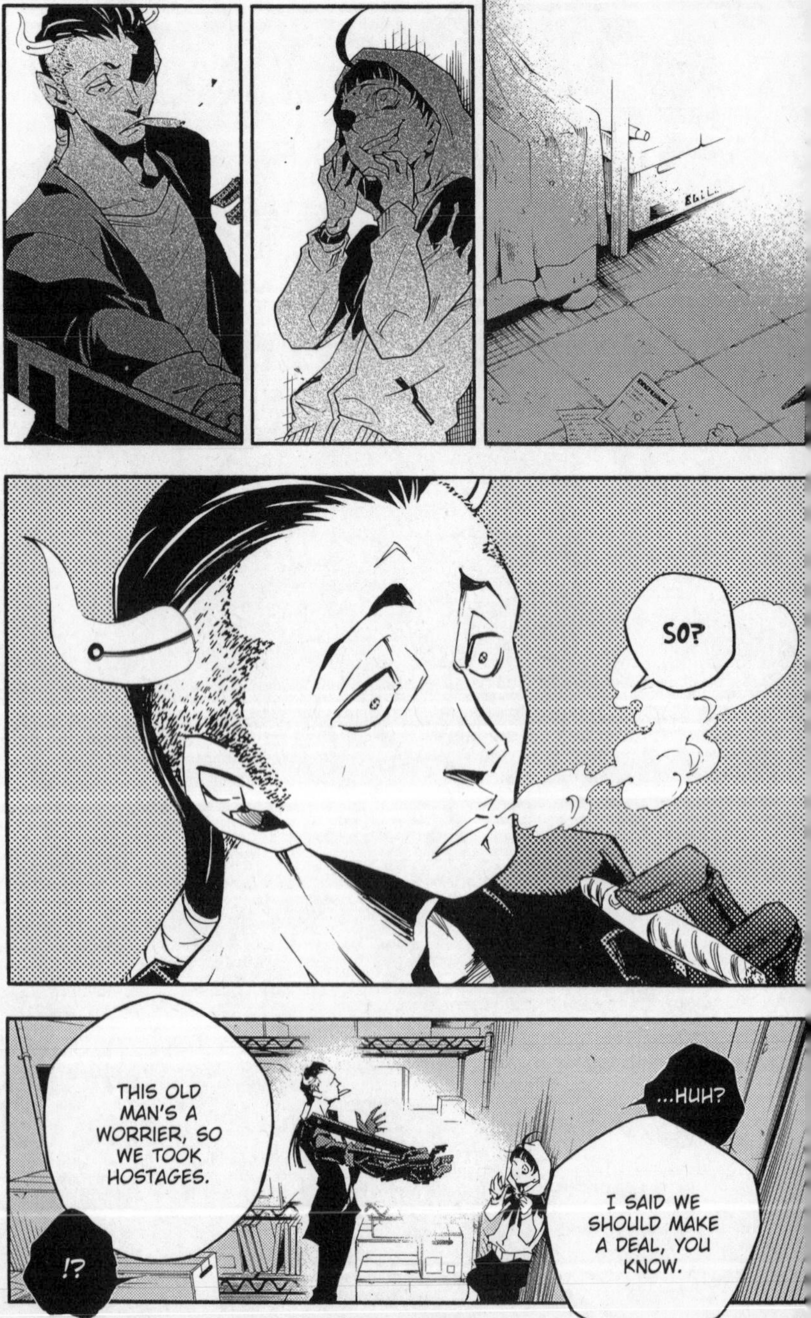
SO?
...HUH?
I SAID WE SHOULD MAKE A DEAL, YOU KNOW.
THIS OLD MAN'S A WORRIER, SO WE TOOK HOSTAGES.
!?

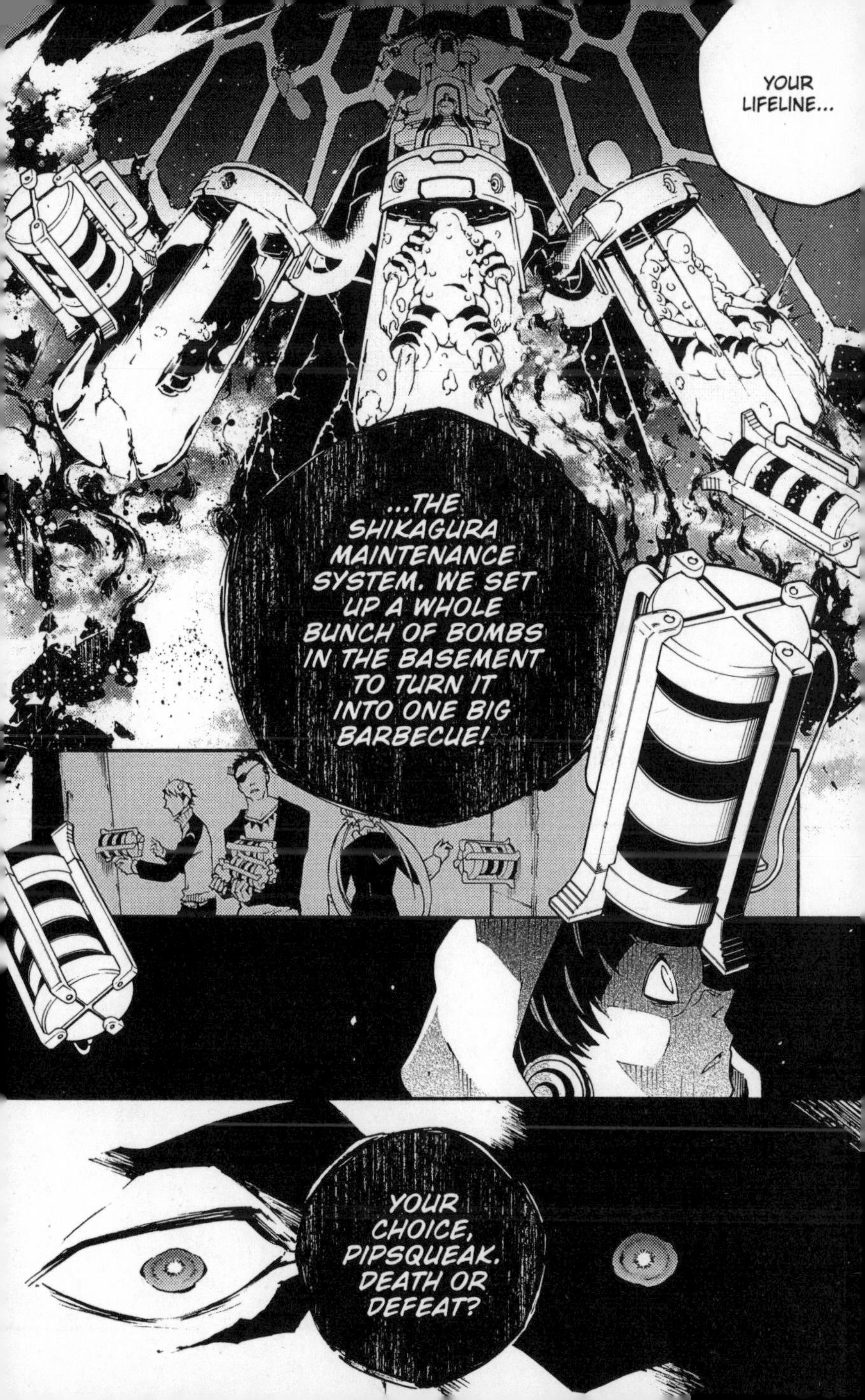
YOUR LIFELINE...
...THE SHIKAGURA MAINTENANCE SYSTEM. WE SET UP A WHOLE BUNCH OF BOMBS IN THE BASEMENT TO TURN IT INTO ONE BIG BARBECUE!☆
YOUR CHOICE, PIPSQUEAK. DEATH OR DEFEAT?

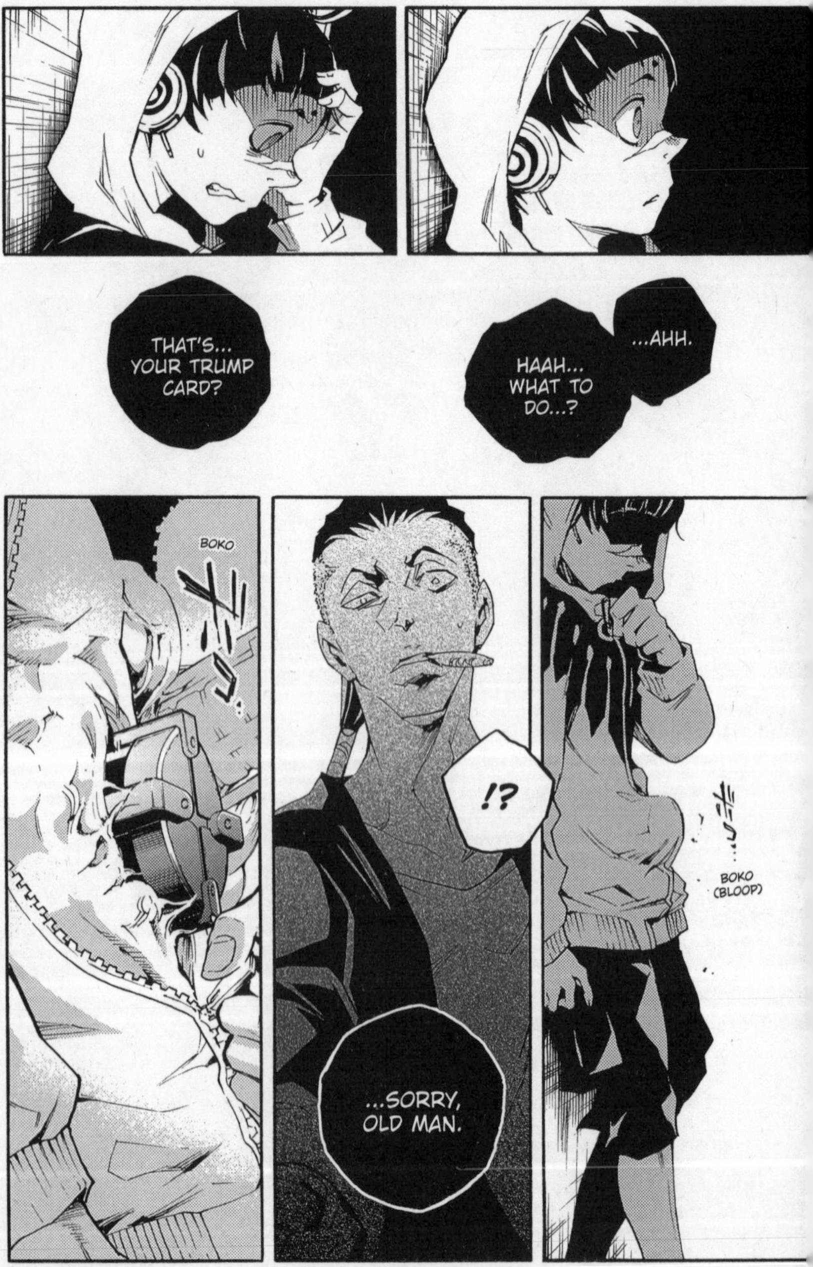
...AHH.
HAAH... WHAT TO DO...?
THAT'S... YOUR TRUMP CARD?
BOKO (BLOOP)
!?
...SORRY, OLD MAN.
BOKO

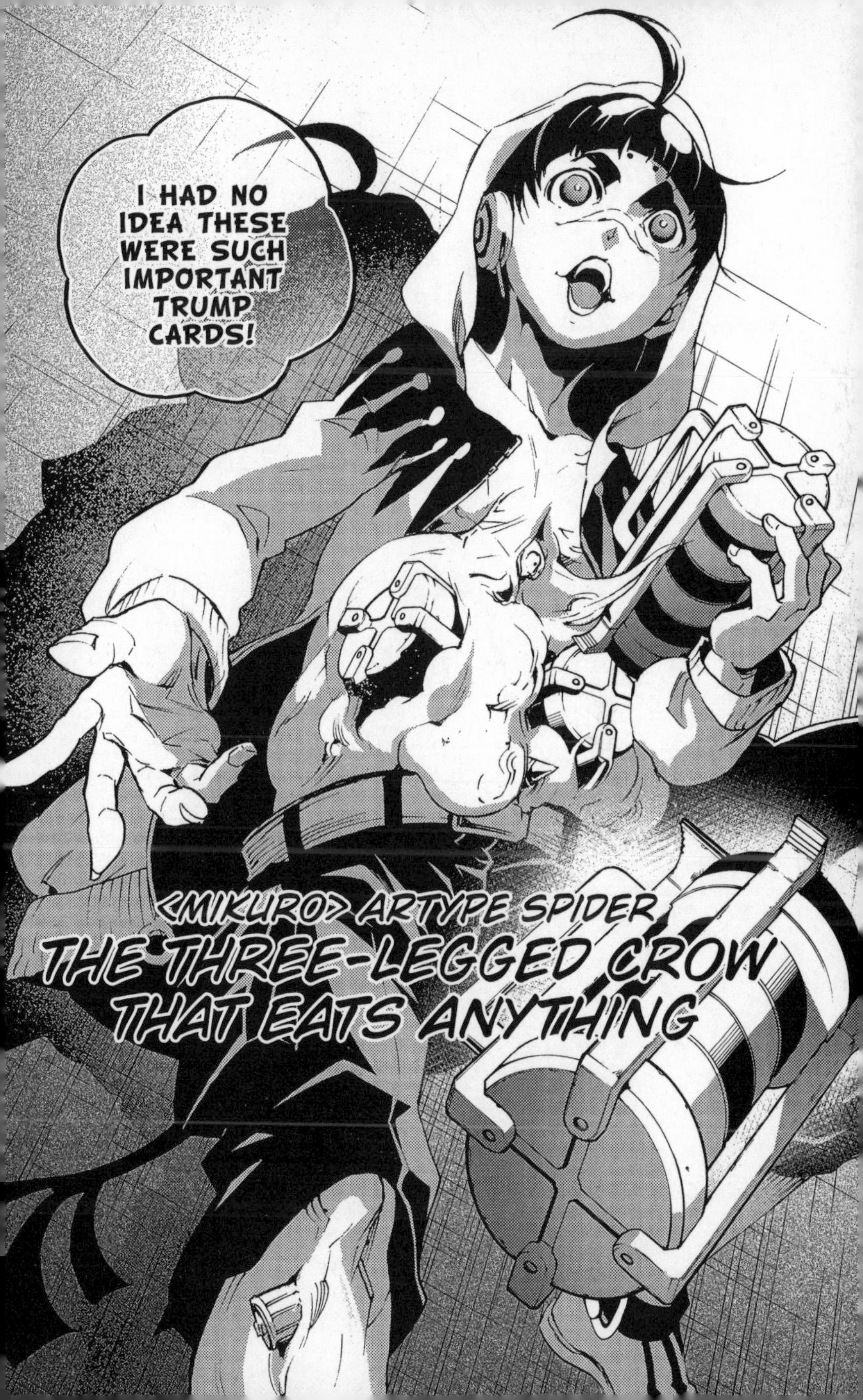
I HAD NO IDEA THESE WERE SUCH IMPORTANT TRUMP CARDS!
<MIKURO> ARTYPE SPIDER
THE THREE-LEGGED CROW THAT EATS ANYTHING

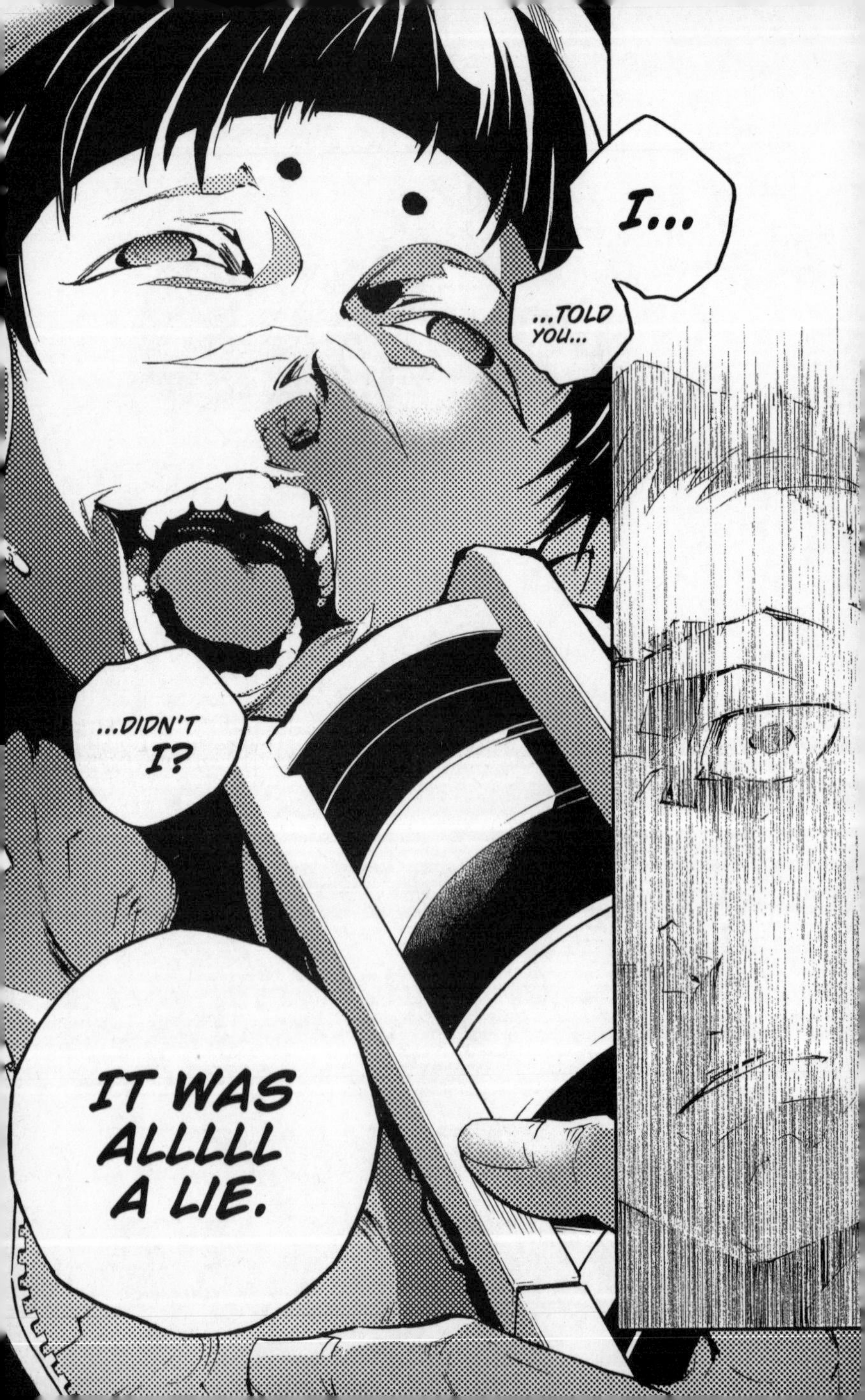
I...
...TOLD YOU...
...DIDN'T I?
IT WAS ALLLLL A LIE.

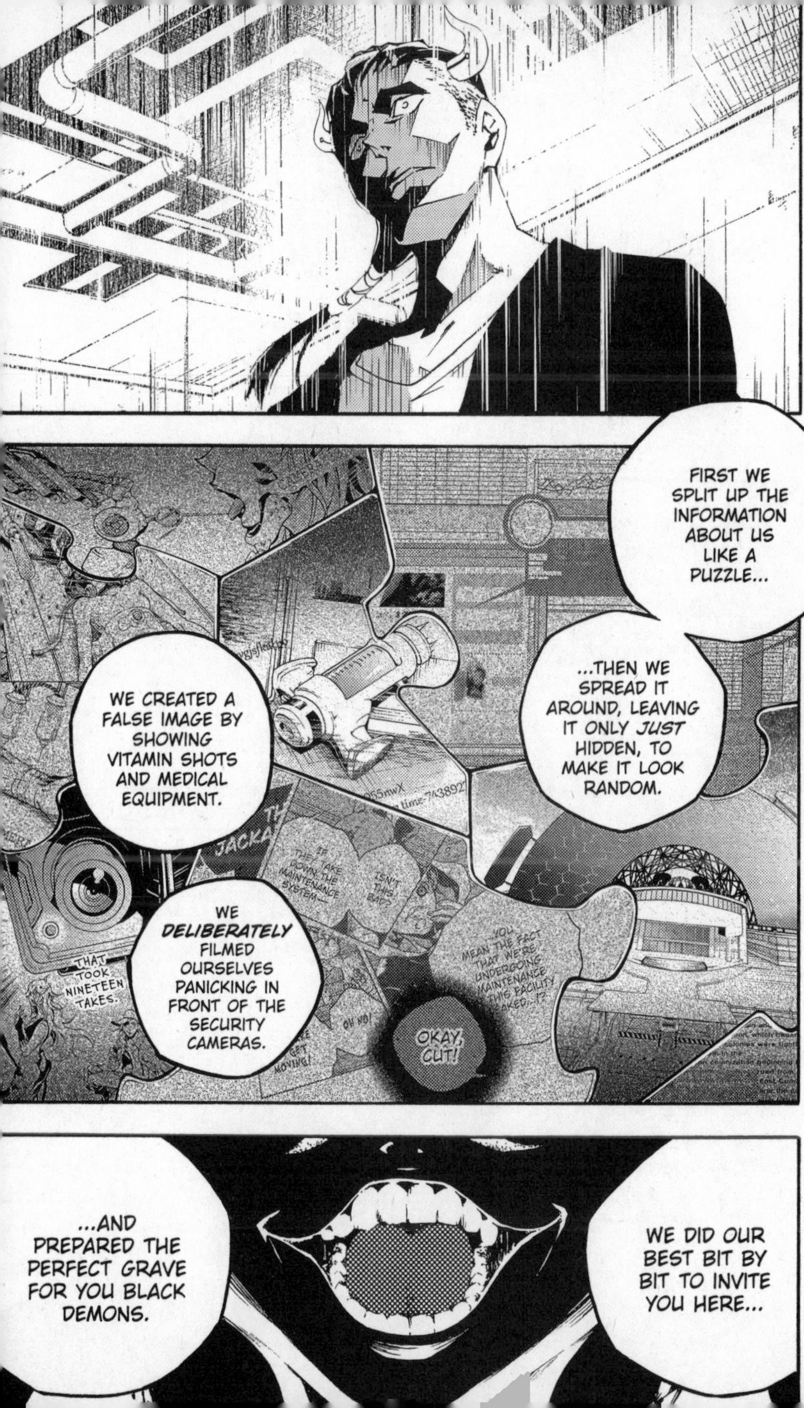
FIRST WE SPLIT UP THE INFORMATION ABOUT US LIKE A PUZZLE...
...THEN WE SPREAD IT AROUND, LEAVING IT ONLY *JUST* HIDDEN, TO MAKE IT LOOK RANDOM.
WE CREATED A FALSE IMAGE BY SHOWING VITAMIN SHOTS AND MEDICAL EQUIPMENT.
ISN'T THIS BAD?
WE ***DELIBERATELY*** FILMED OURSELVES PANICKING IN FRONT OF THE SECURITY CAMERAS.
OKAY, CUT!
OH NO!
THAT TOOK NINETEEN TAKES.
WE DID OUR BEST BIT BY BIT TO INVITE YOU HERE...
...AND PREPARED THE PERFECT GRAVE FOR YOU BLACK DEMONS.

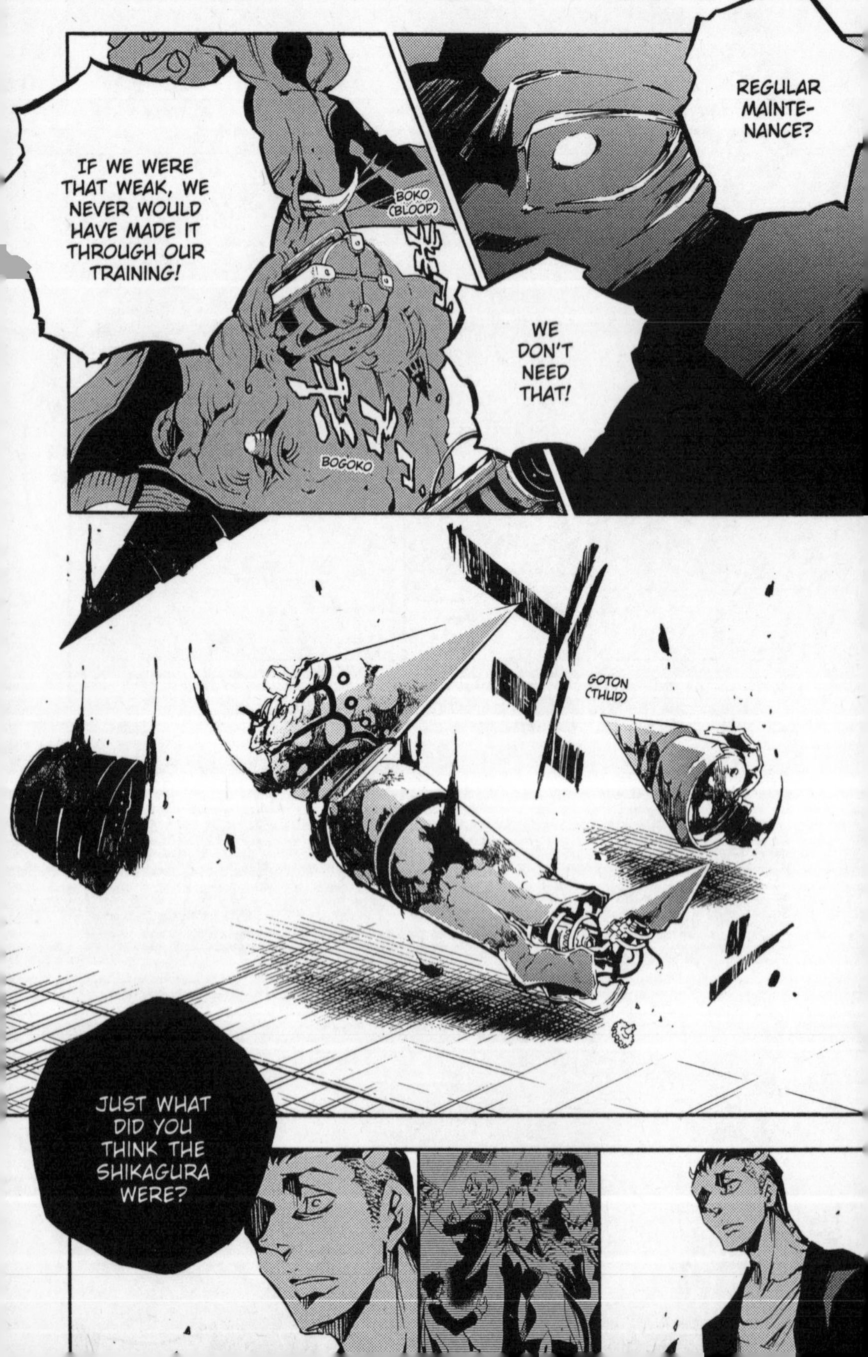
REGULAR MAINTE-NANCE?
BOKO (BLOOP)
WE DON'T NEED THAT!
IF WE WERE THAT WEAK, WE NEVER WOULD HAVE MADE IT THROUGH OUR TRAINING!
BOGOKO
GOTON (THUD)
JUST WHAT DID YOU THINK THE SHIKAGURA WERE?

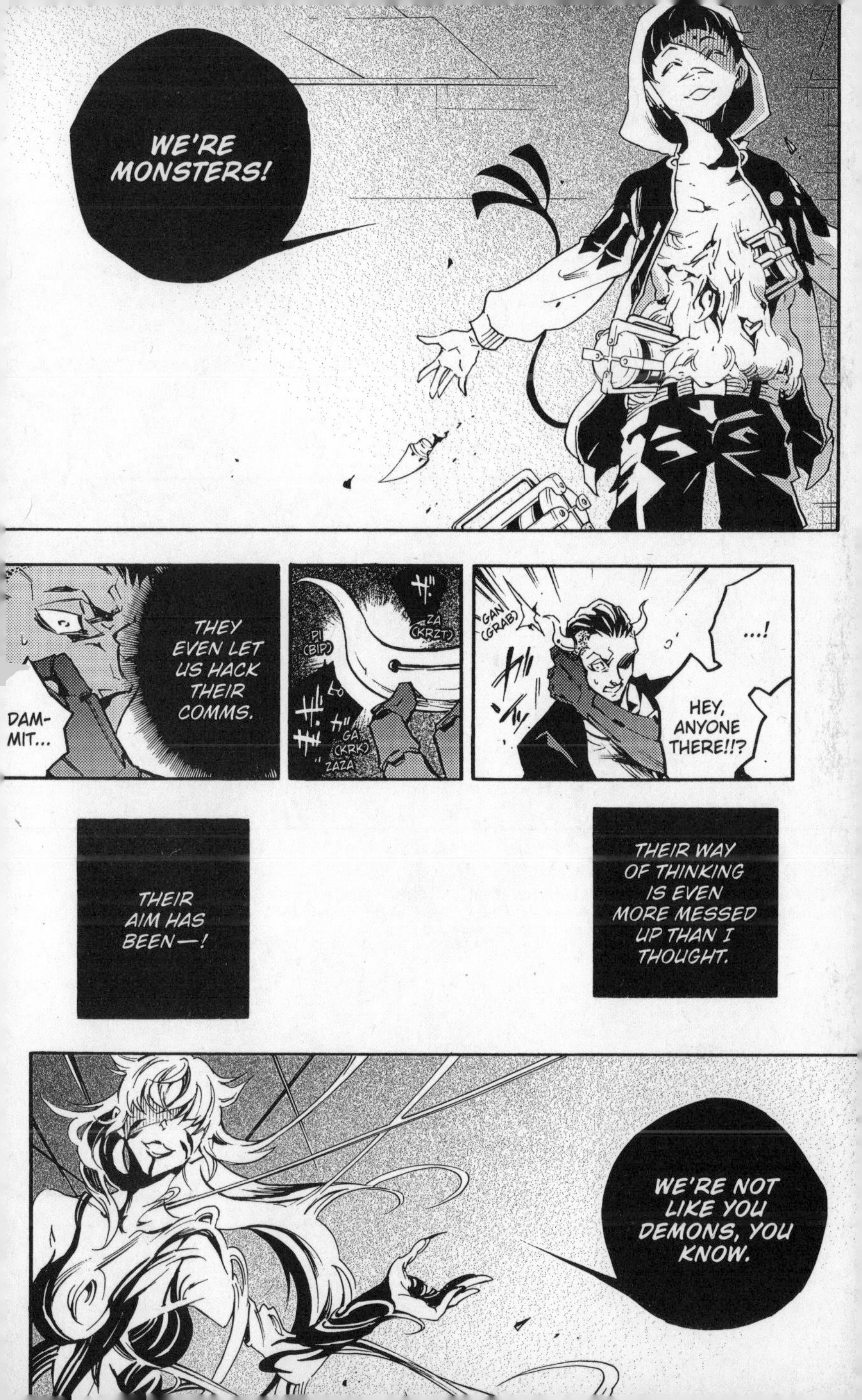
WE'RE MONSTERS!
GAN (GRAB)
...!
HEY, ANYONE THERE!!?
ZA (KRZT)
PI (BIP)
GA (KRK)
ZAZA
THEY EVEN LET US HACK THEIR COMMS.
DAM-MIT...
THEIR WAY OF THINKING IS EVEN MORE MESSED UP THAN I THOUGHT.
THEIR AIM HAS BEEN—!
WE'RE NOT LIKE YOU DEMONS, YOU KNOW.

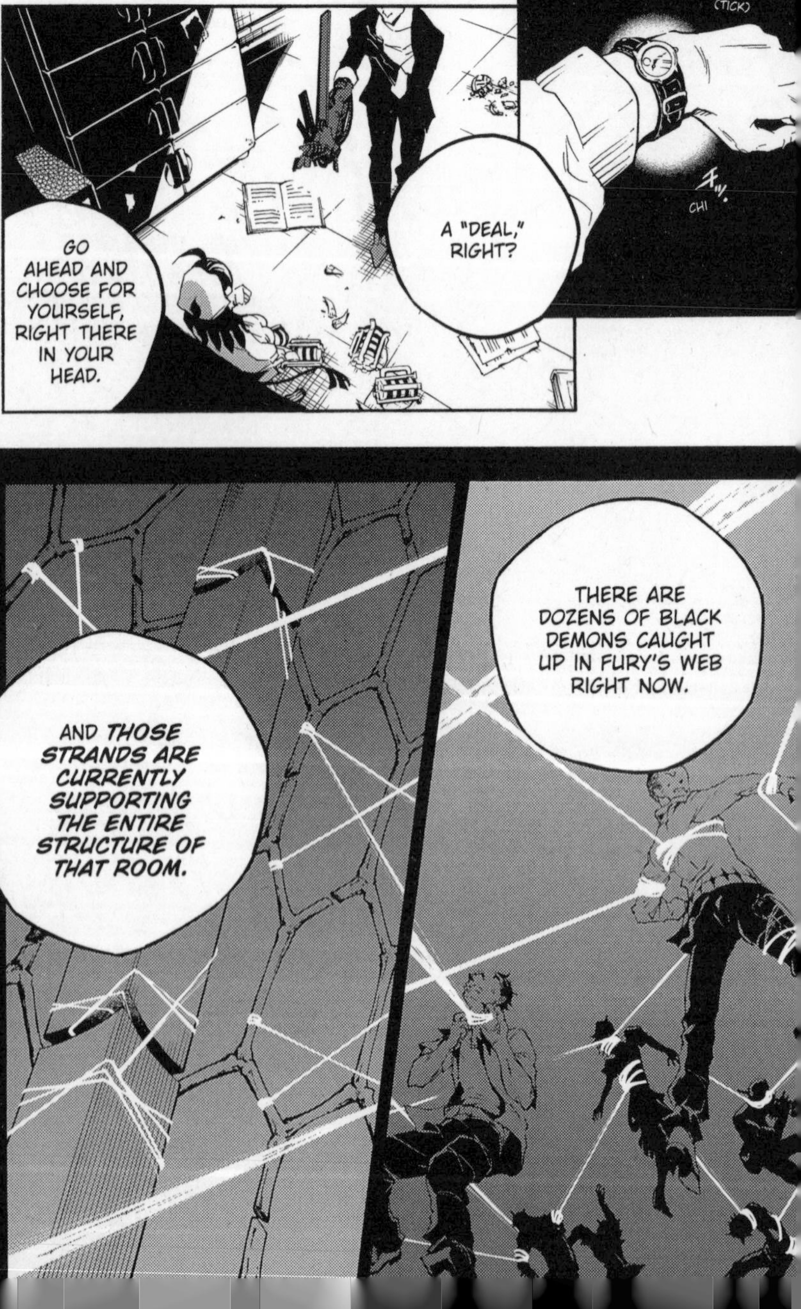
CHI
(TICK)
CHI
A "DEAL," RIGHT?
GO AHEAD AND CHOOSE FOR YOURSELF, RIGHT THERE IN YOUR HEAD.
THERE ARE DOZENS OF BLACK DEMONS CAUGHT UP IN FURY'S WEB RIGHT NOW.
AND *THOSE STRANDS ARE CURRENTLY SUPPORTING THE ENTIRE STRUCTURE OF THAT ROOM.*

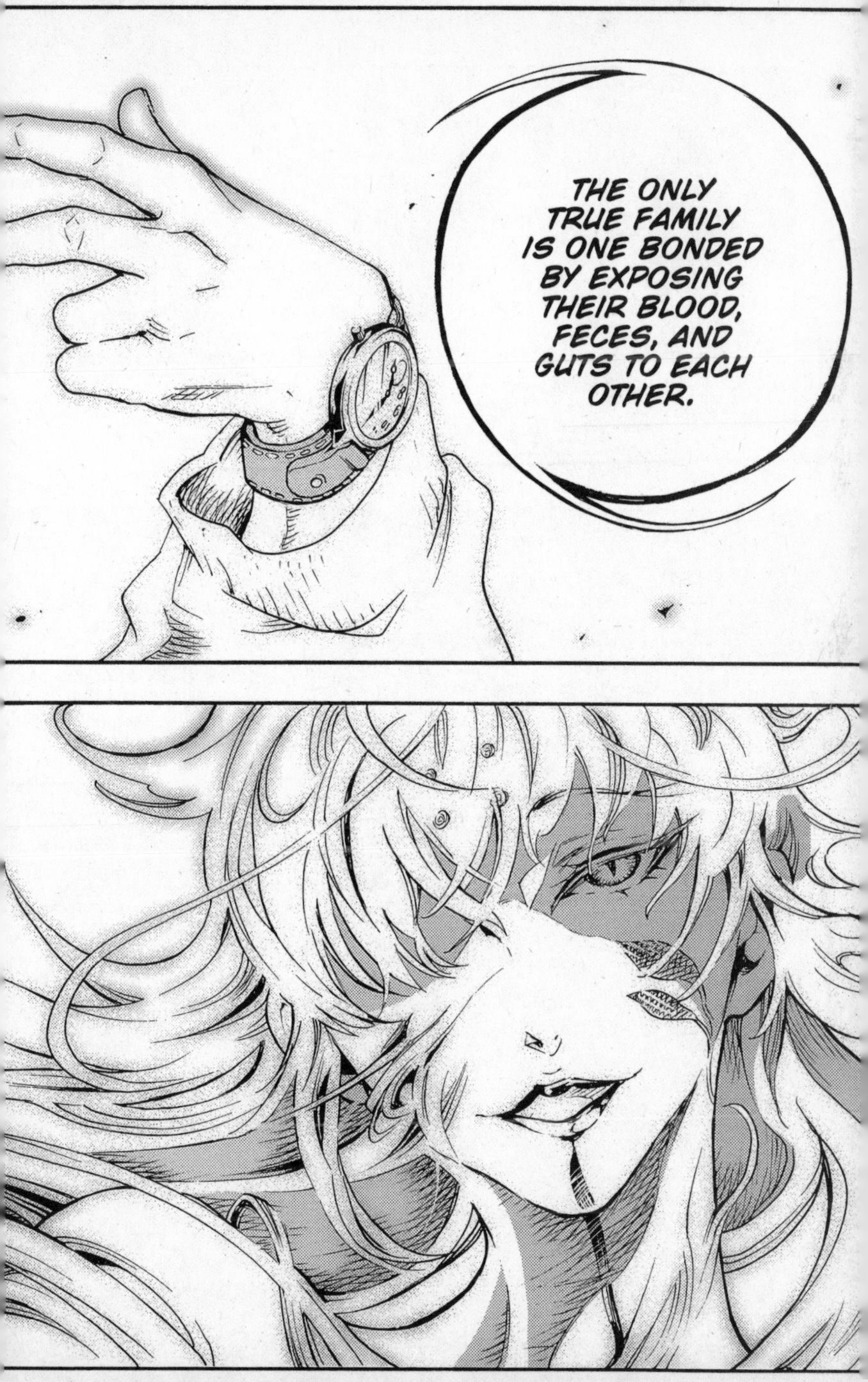
THE ONLY TRUE FAMILY IS ONE BONDED BY EXPOSING THEIR BLOOD, FECES, AND GUTS TO EACH OTHER.

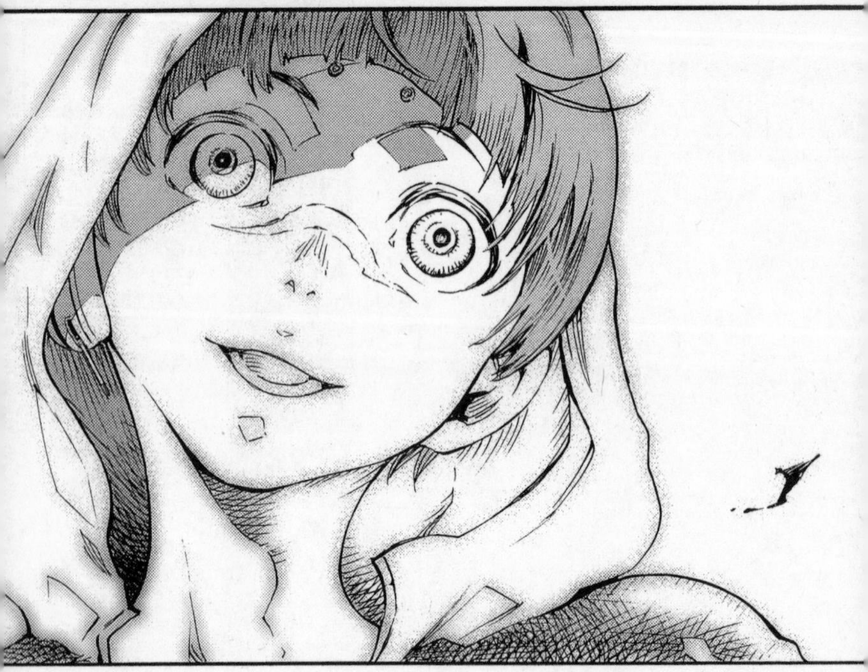
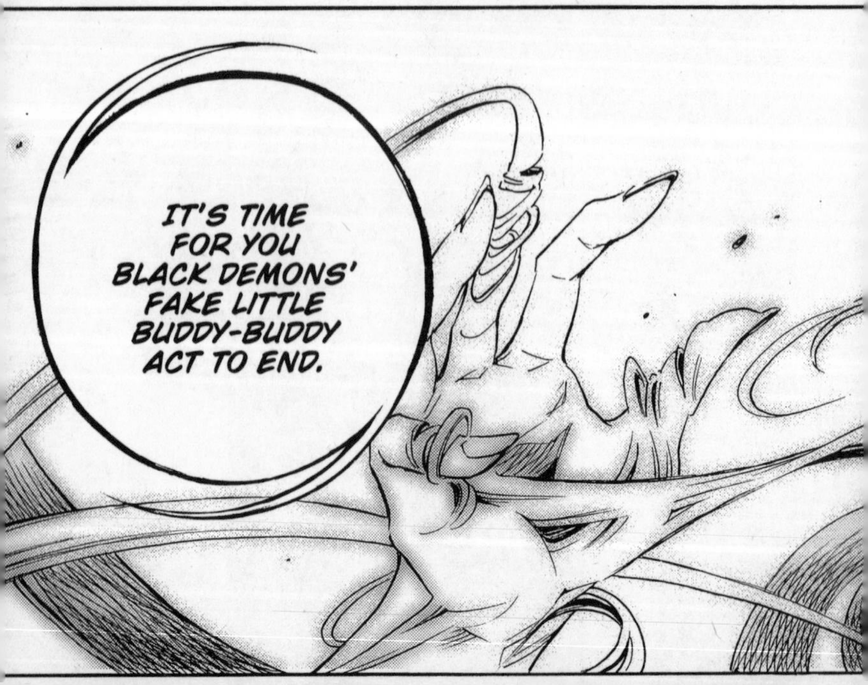
IT'S TIME FOR YOU BLACK DEMONS' FAKE LITTLE BUDDY-BUDDY ACT TO END.

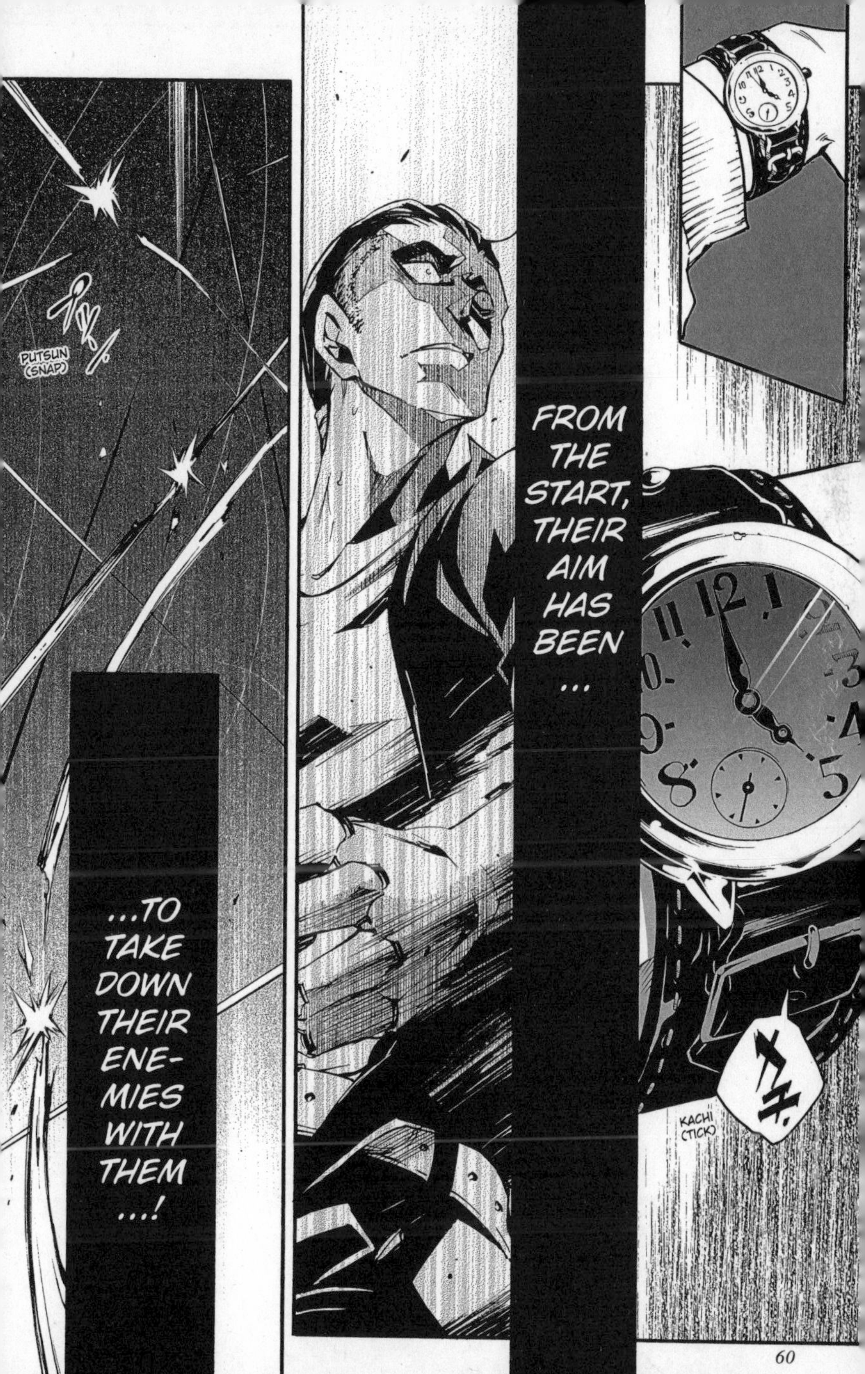
KACHI (TICK)
FROM THE START, THEIR AIM HAS BEEN...
PUTSUN (SNAP)
...TO TAKE DOWN THEIR ENE-MIES WITH THEM...!

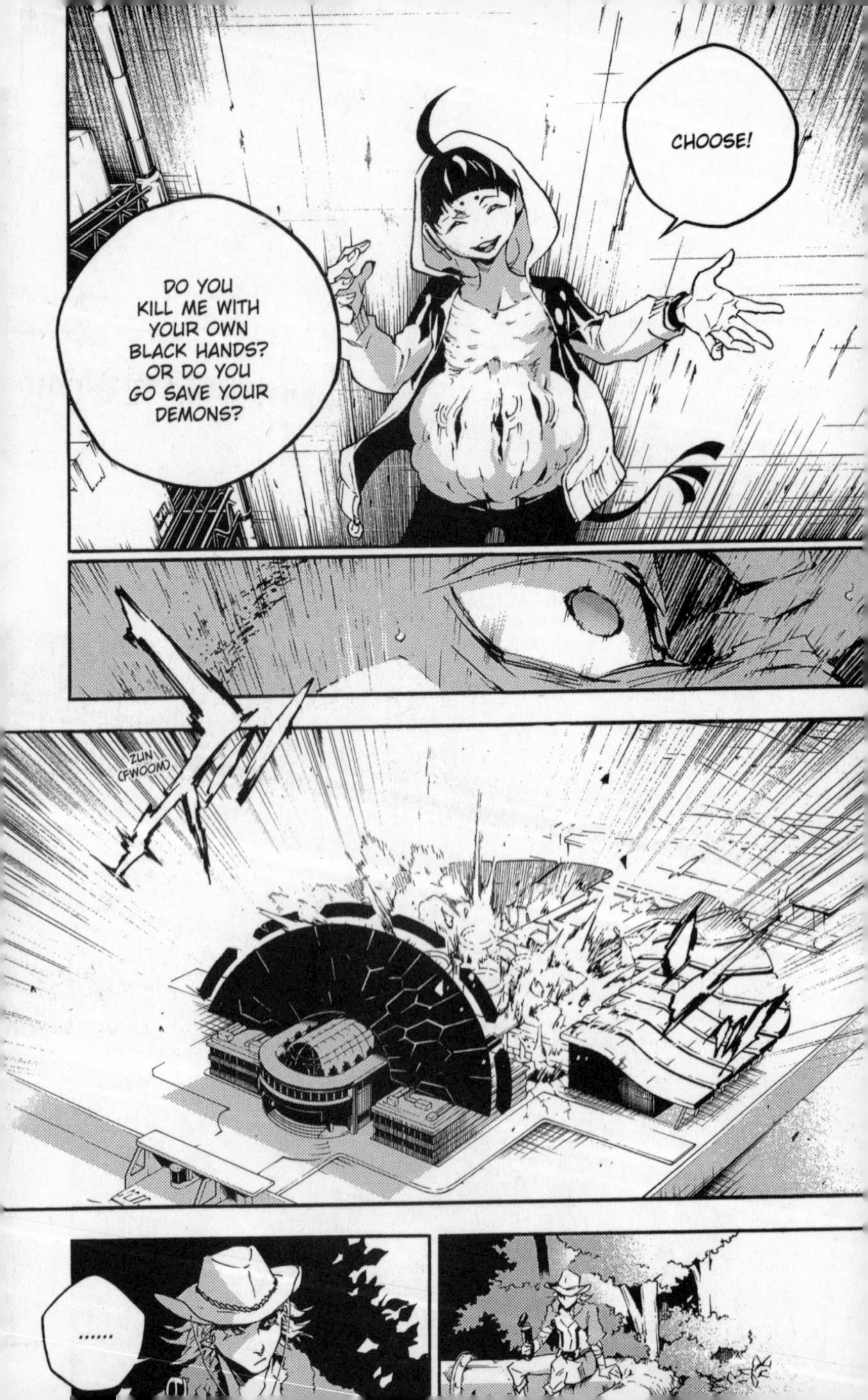
CHOOSE!
DO YOU KILL ME WITH YOUR OWN BLACK HANDS? OR DO YOU GO SAVE YOUR DEMONS?
ZUN (FWOOM)
......

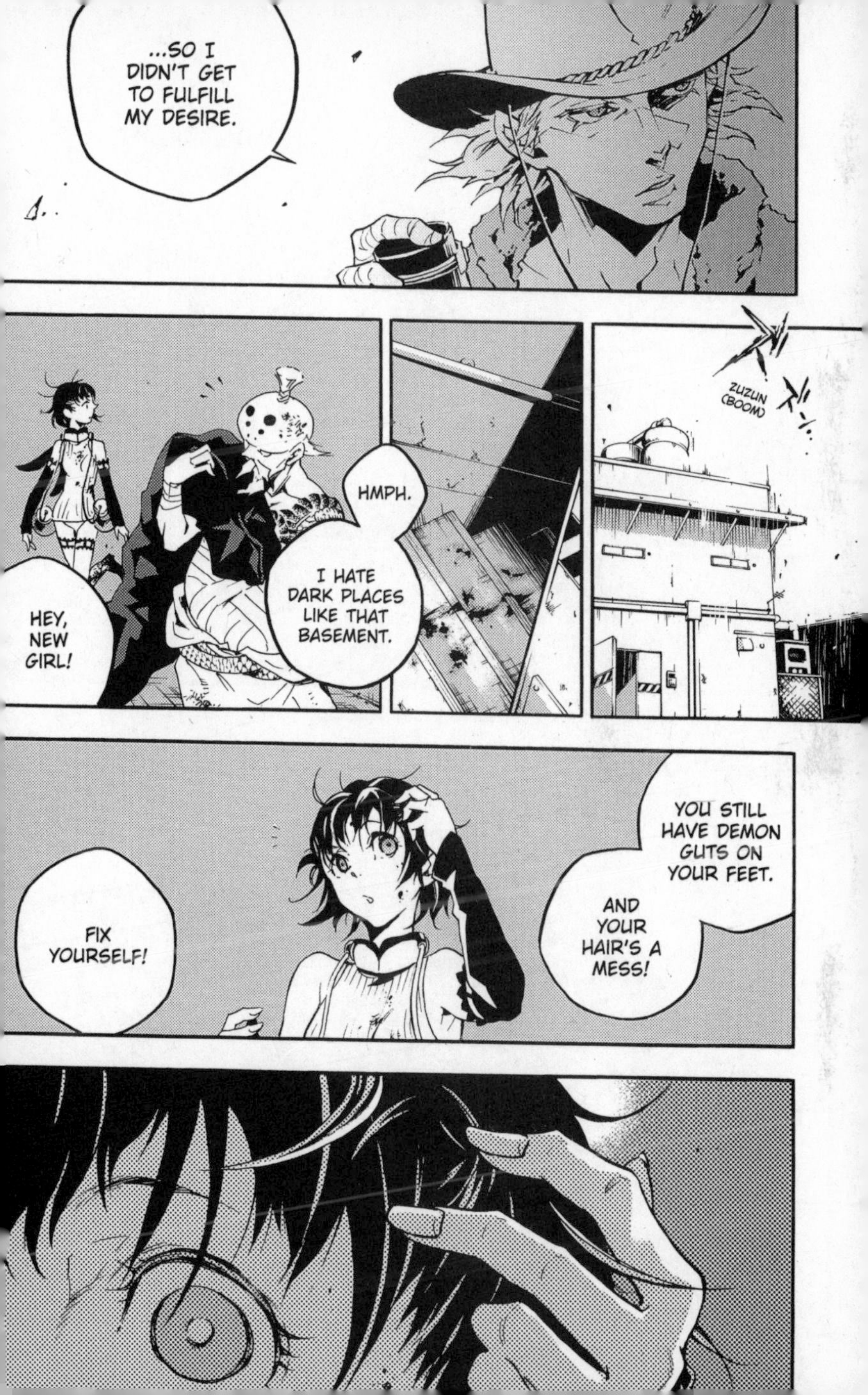
...SO I DIDN'T GET TO FULFILL MY DESIRE.
ZUZUN (BOOM)
HMPH.
I HATE DARK PLACES LIKE THAT BASEMENT.
HEY, NEW GIRL!
YOU STILL HAVE DEMON GUTS ON YOUR FEET.
AND YOUR HAIR'S A MESS!
FIX YOURSELF!

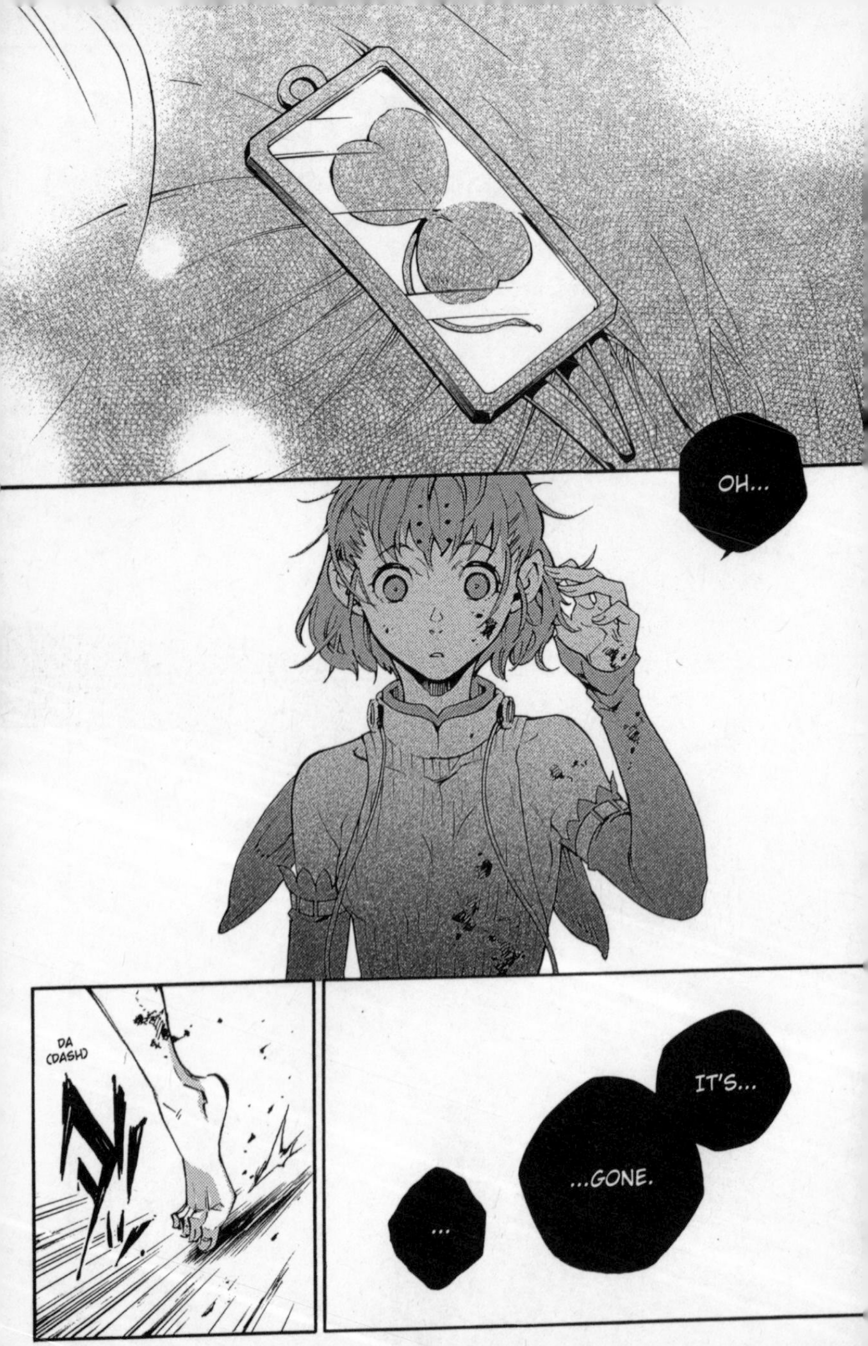
OH...
IT'S...
...GONE.
...
DA
(DASH)

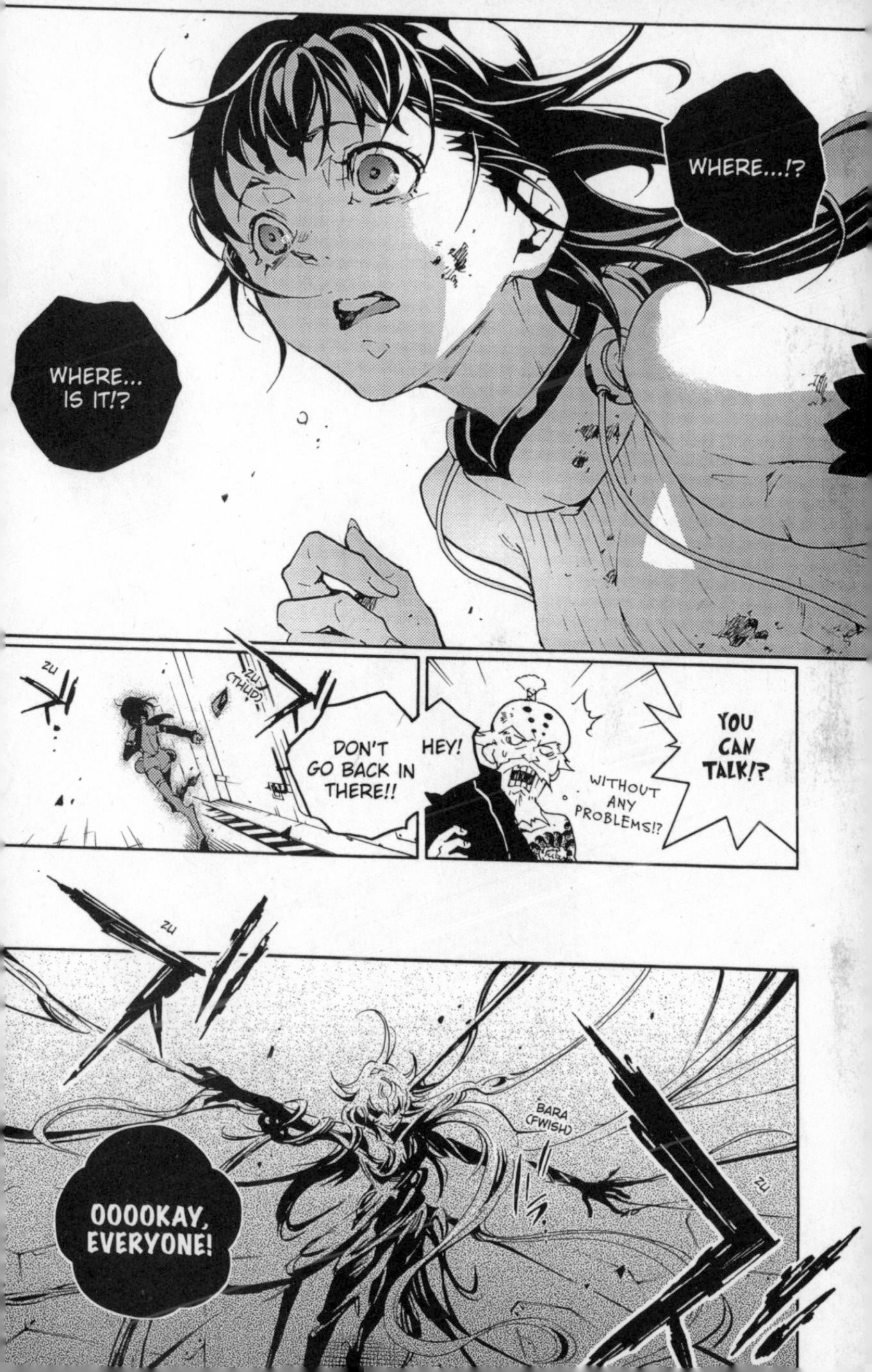
WHERE...!?
WHERE... IS IT!?
YOU CAN TALK!?
WITHOUT ANY PROBLEMS!?
HEY! DON'T GO BACK IN THERE!!
ZU (THUD)
ZU
ZU
BARA (FWISH)
ZU
OOOOKAY, EVERYONE!

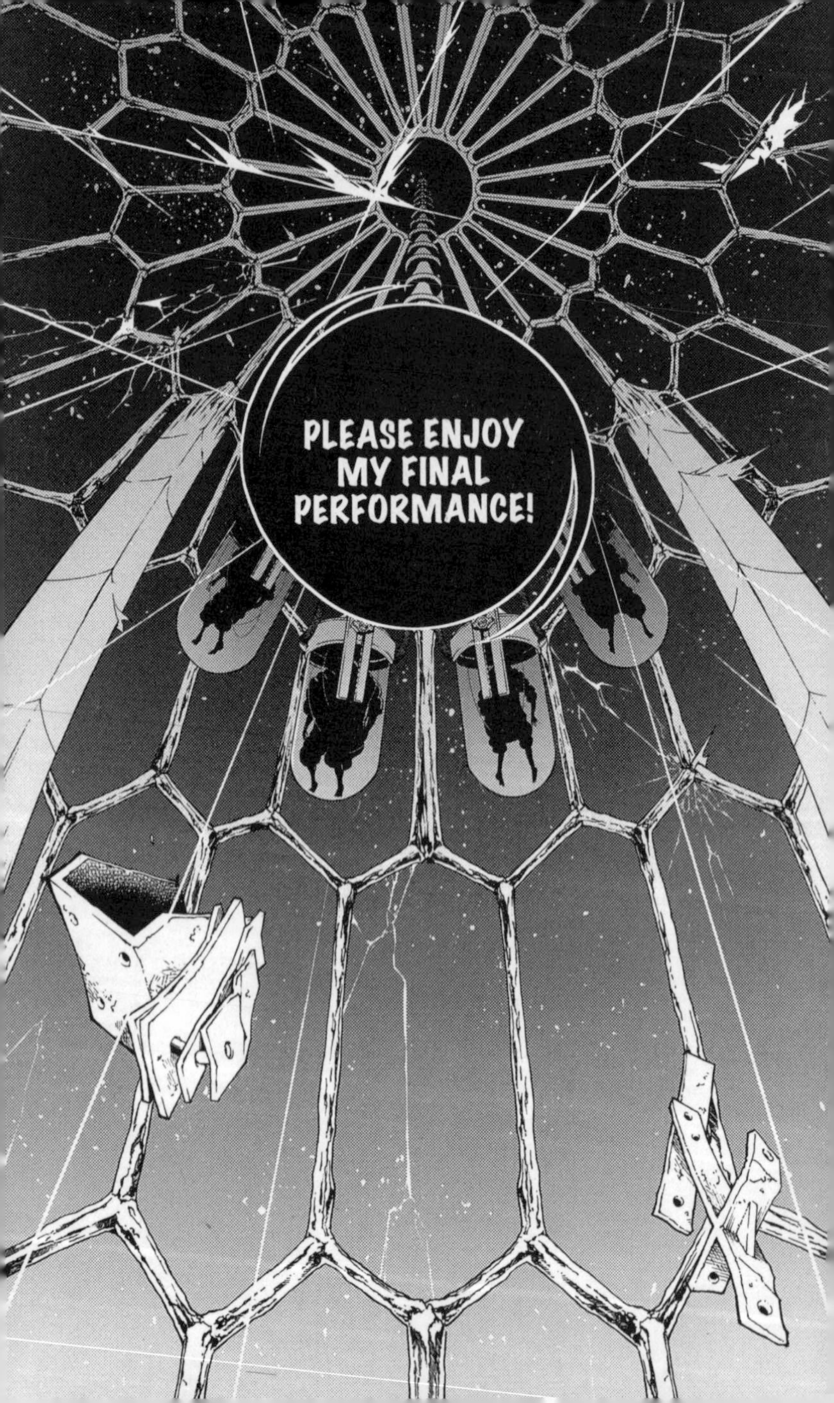
PLEASE ENJOY MY FINAL PERFORMANCE!

SMOKIN' PARADE

THE WORLD IS DEAD, THE PARADE WILL START.

JINSEI KATAOKA, KAZUMA KONDOU

SMOKIN' PARADE

THE WORLD IS DEAD, THE PARADE WILL START.

JINSEI KATAOKA, KAZUMA KONDOU

SMOKIN' PARADE

THE WORLD IS DEAD, THE PARADE WILL START.

JINSEI KATAOKA, KAZUMA KONDOU

SMOKIN' PARADE

THE WORLD IS DEAD, THE PARADE WILL START.

JINSEI KATAOKA, KAZUMA KONDOU

SMOKIN' PARADE

THE WORLD IS DEAD, THE PARADE WILL START.

JINSEI KATAOKA, KAZUMA KONDOU

SMOKIN' PARADE

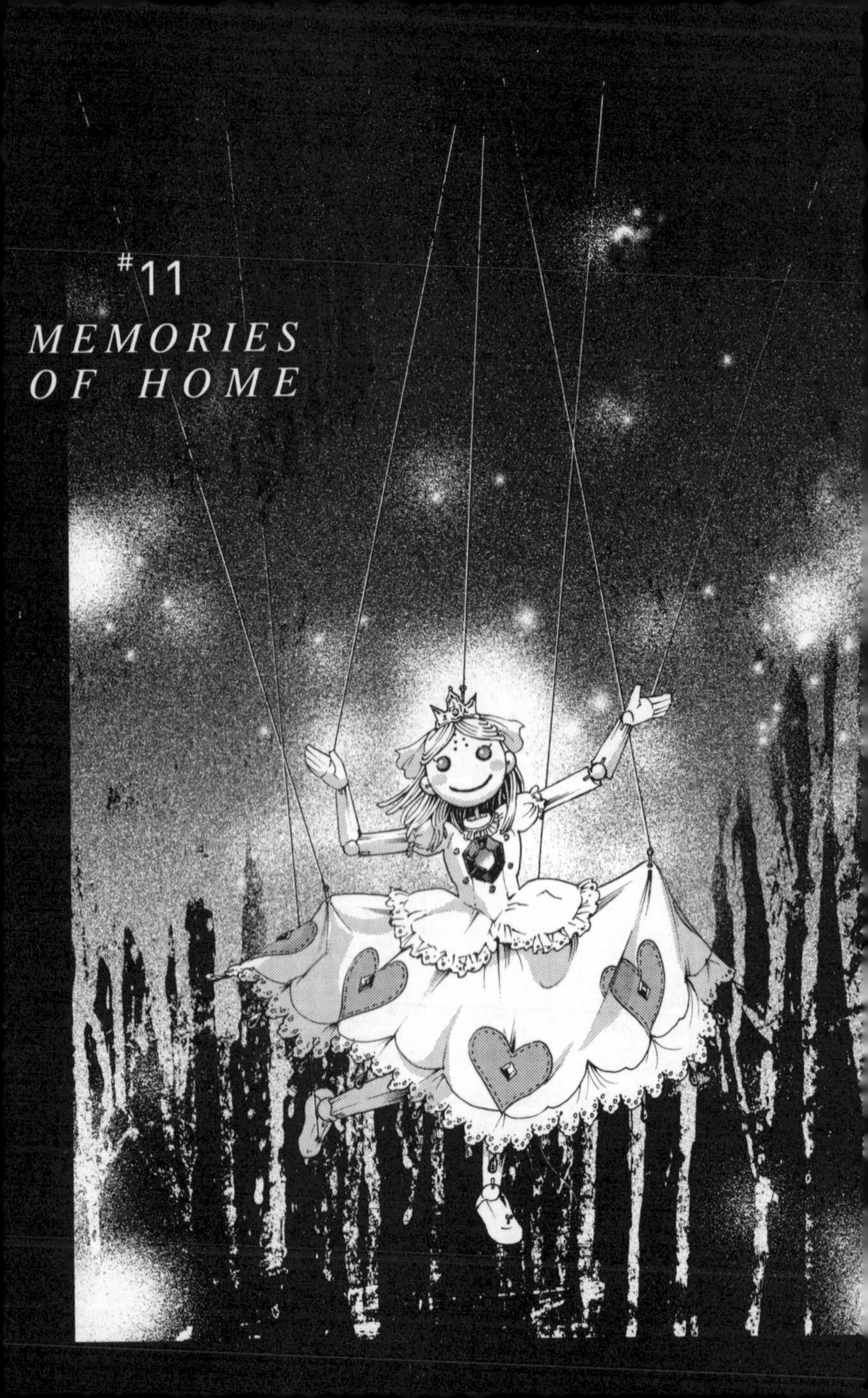
#11
MEMORIES OF HOME

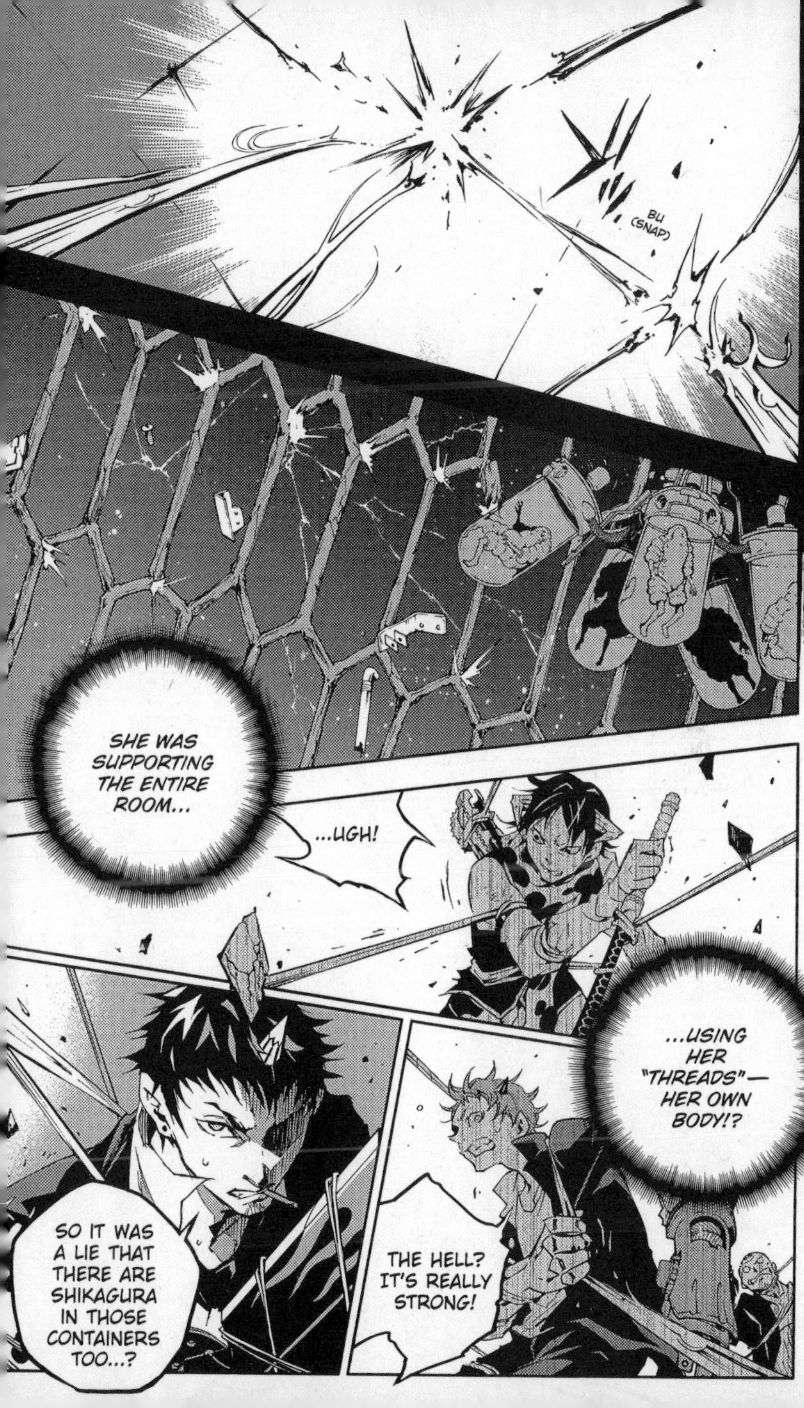
BU (SNAP)
SHE WAS SUPPORTING THE ENTIRE ROOM...
...UGH!
...USING HER "THREADS"— HER OWN BODY!?
THE HELL? IT'S REALLY STRONG!
SO IT WAS A LIE THAT THERE ARE SHIKAGURA IN THOSE CONTAINERS TOO...?

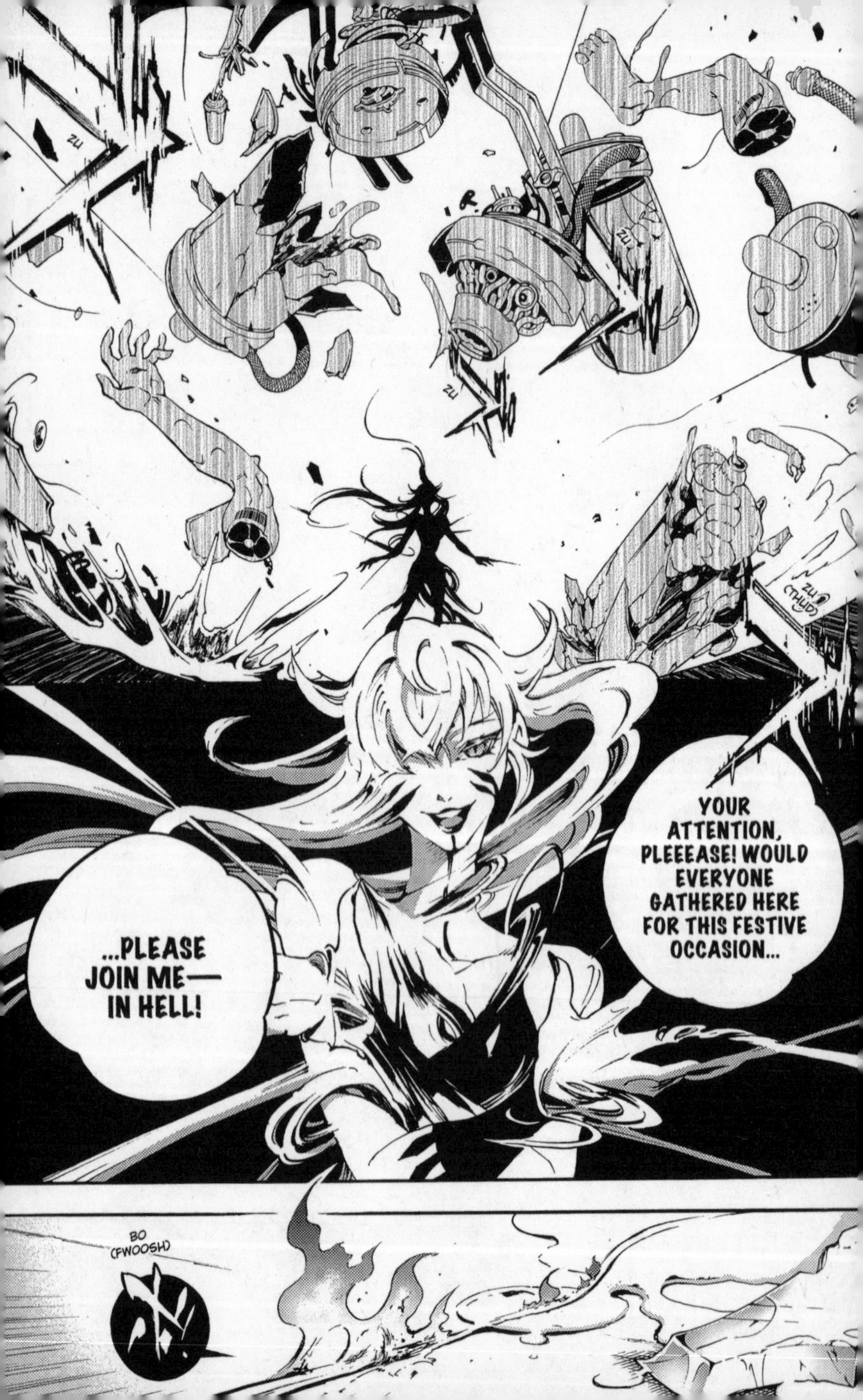
ZU
ZU
ZU
ZU
ZU (THUD)
YOUR ATTENTION, PLEEEASE! WOULD EVERYONE GATHERED HERE FOR THIS FESTIVE OCCASION...
...PLEASE JOIN ME—IN HELL!
BO (FWOOSH)

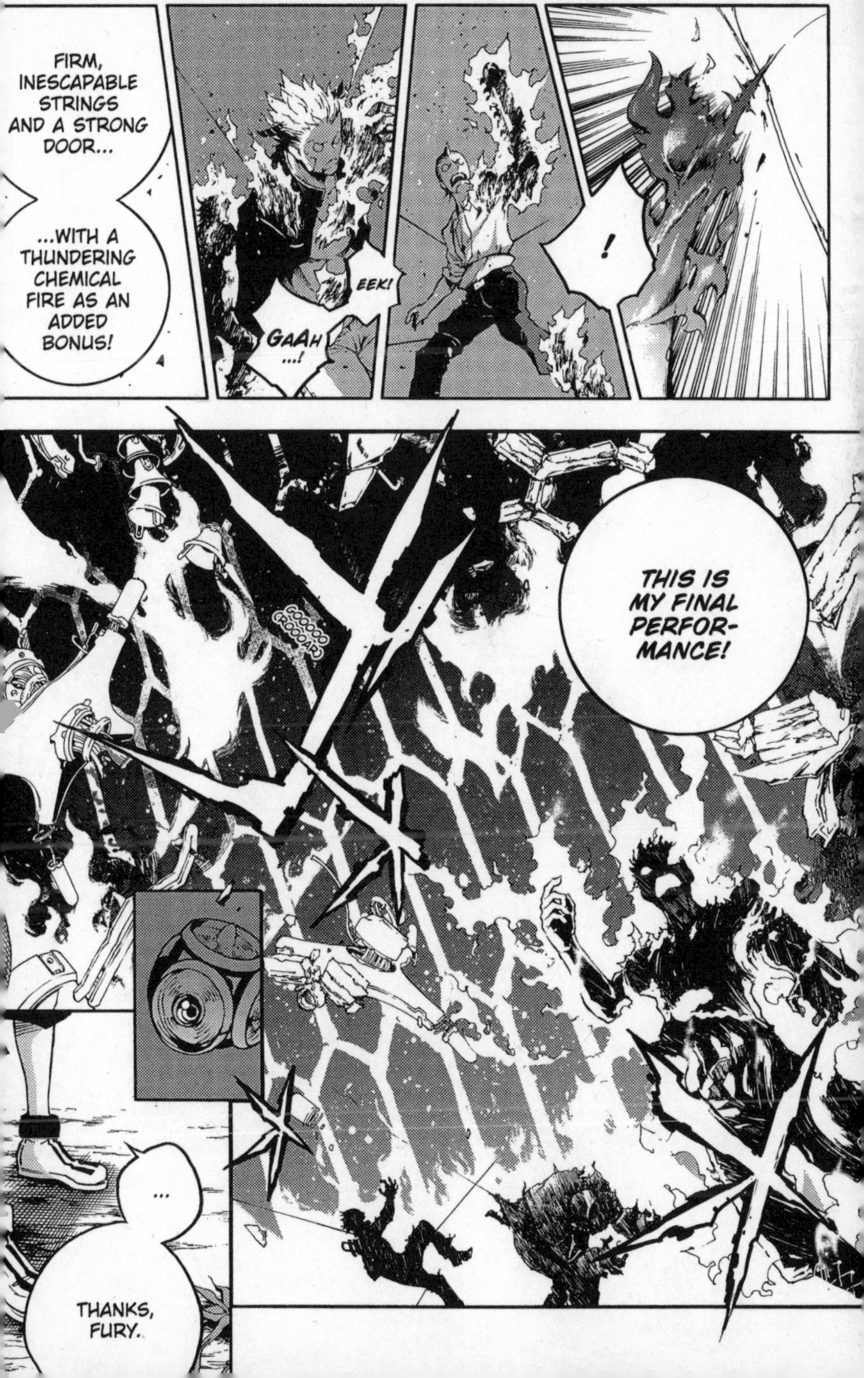
!
EEK!
GAAH ...!
FIRM, INESCAPABLE STRINGS AND A STRONG DOOR...
...WITH A THUNDERING CHEMICAL FIRE AS AN ADDED BONUS!
THIS IS MY FINAL PERFORMANCE!
GOOOOO (ROOOAR)
...
THANKS, FURY.

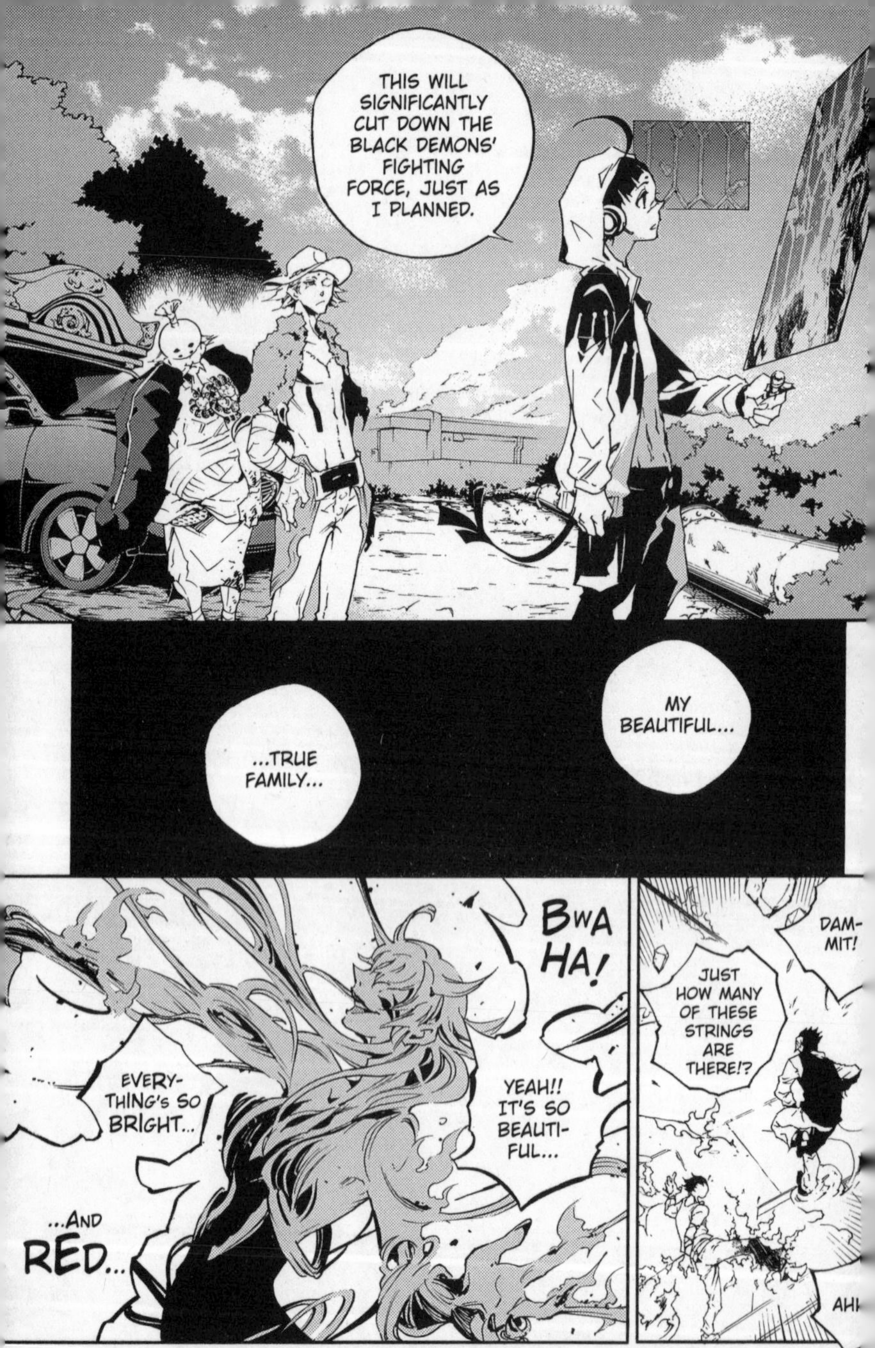
THIS WILL SIGNIFICANTLY CUT DOWN THE BLACK DEMONS' FIGHTING FORCE, JUST AS I PLANNED.
MY BEAUTIFUL...
...TRUE FAMILY...
DAM-MIT!
JUST HOW MANY OF THESE STRINGS ARE THERE!?
AH!
BWA HA!
YEAH!! IT'S SO BEAUTI-FUL...
EVERY-THING's SO BRIGHT...
...AND RED...

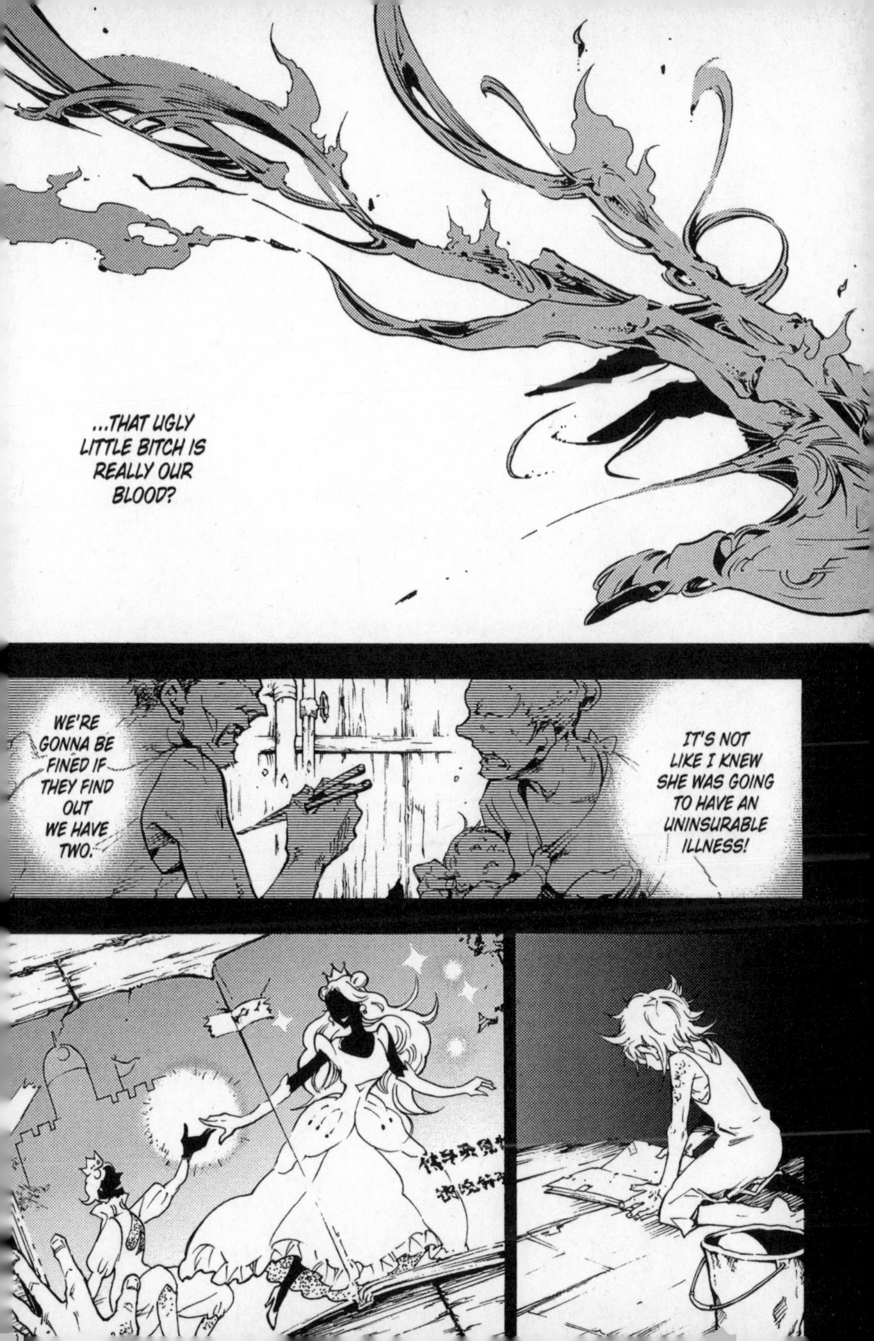
...THAT UGLY LITTLE BITCH IS REALLY OUR BLOOD?
IT'S NOT LIKE I KNEW SHE WAS GOING TO HAVE AN UNINSURABLE ILLNESS!
WE'RE GONNA BE FINED IF THEY FIND OUT WE HAVE TWO.

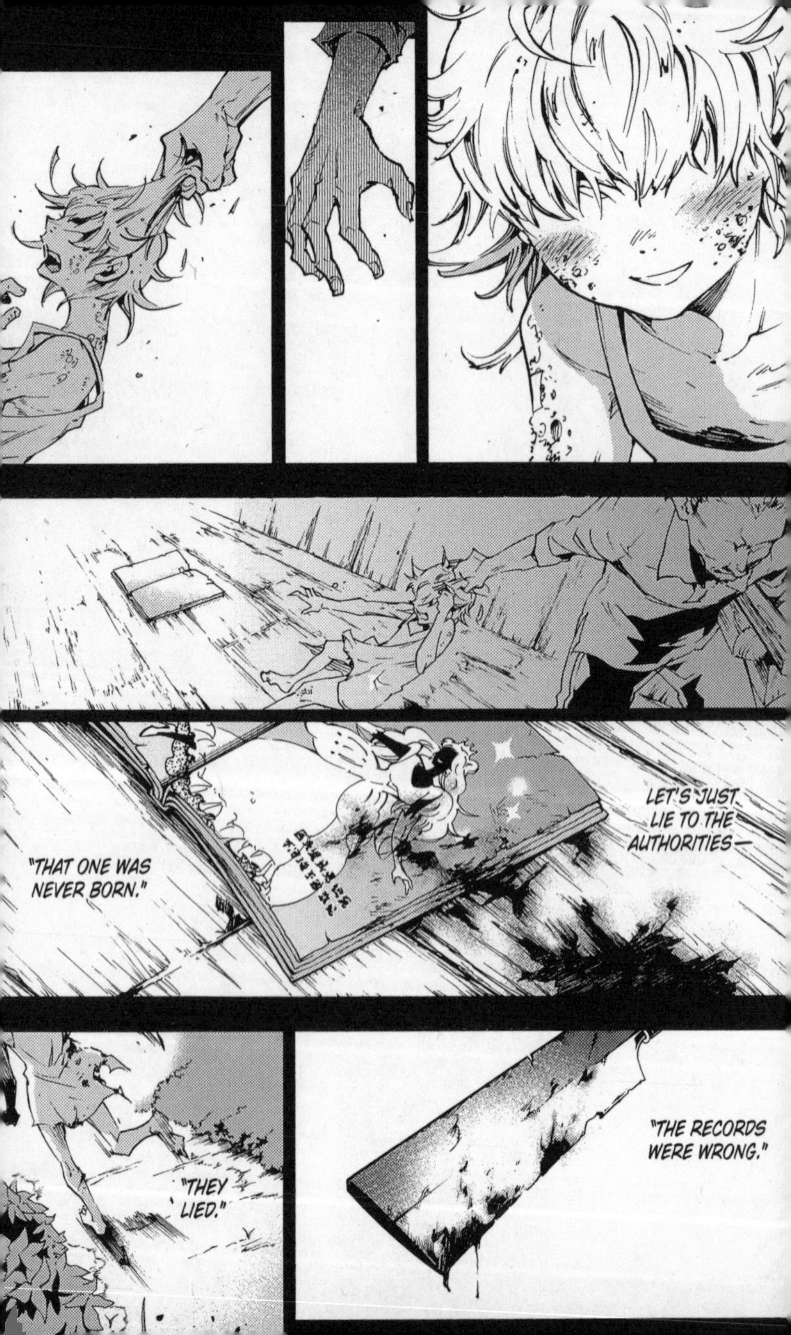
LET'S JUST LIE TO THE AUTHORITIES—
"THAT ONE WAS NEVER BORN."
"THE RECORDS WERE WRONG."
"THEY LIED."

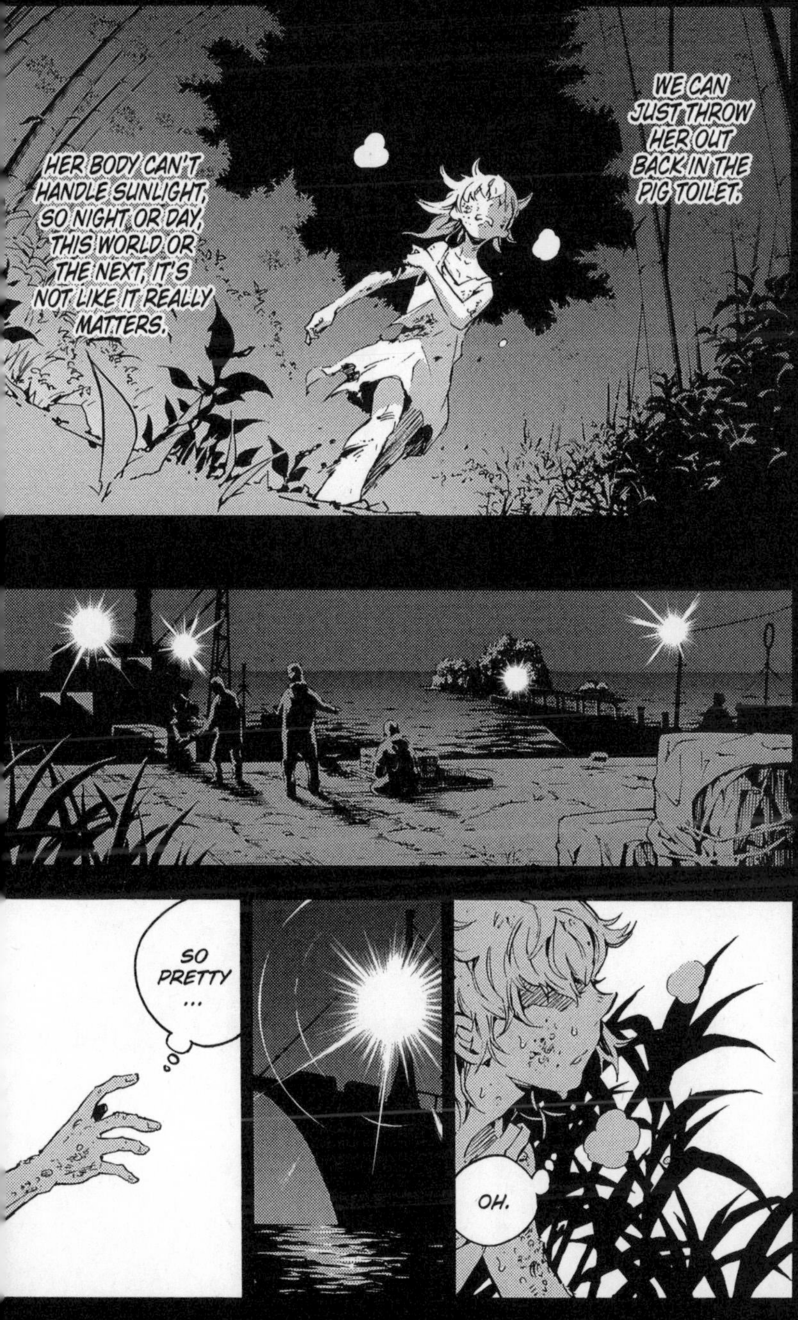
WE CAN JUST THROW HER OUT BACK IN THE PIG TOILET.
HER BODY CAN'T HANDLE SUNLIGHT, SO NIGHT OR DAY, THIS WORLD OR THE NEXT, IT'S NOT LIKE IT REALLY MATTERS.
OH.
SO PRETTY ...

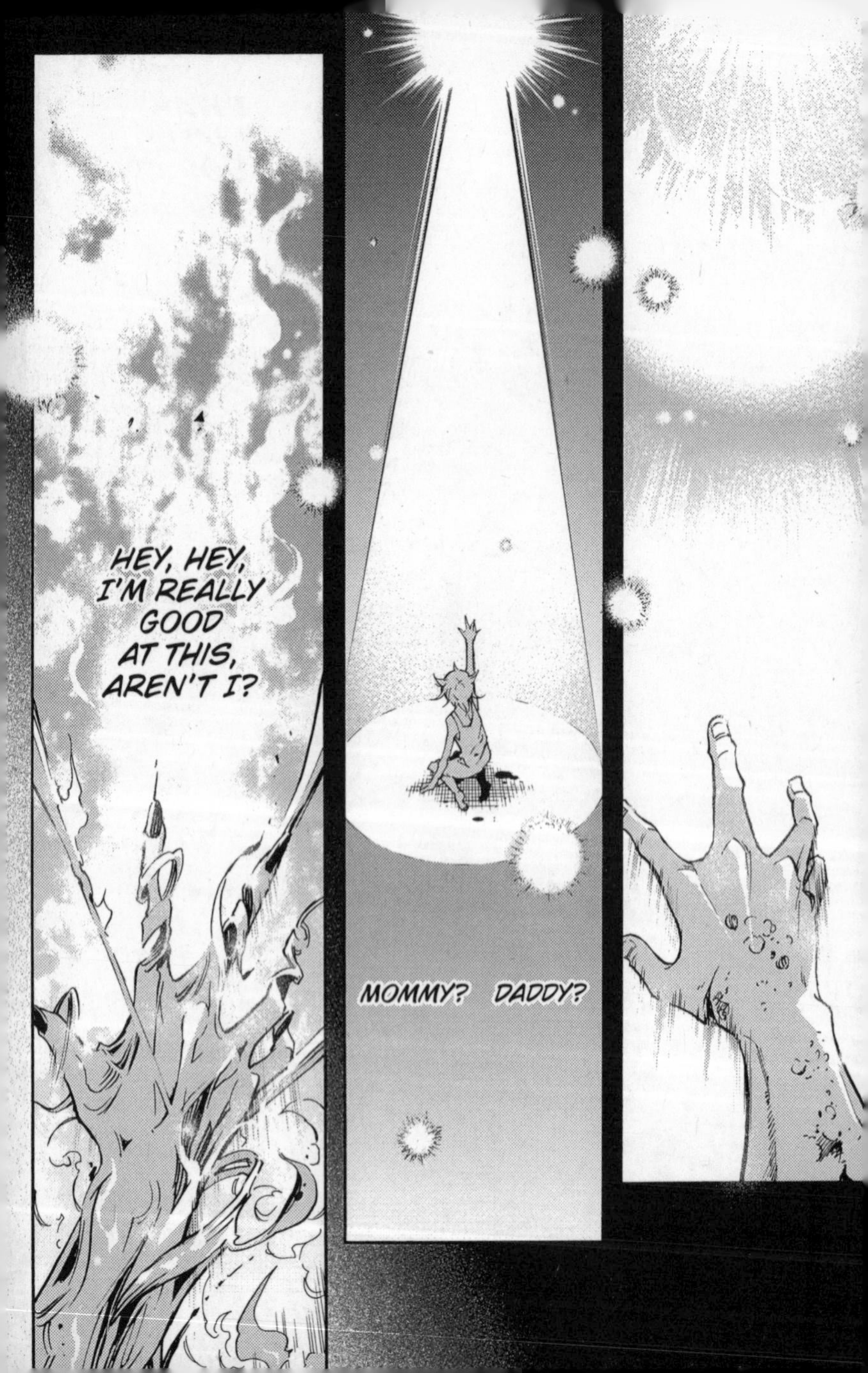
MOMMY? DADDY?
HEY, HEY, I'M REALLY GOOD AT THIS, AREN'T I?

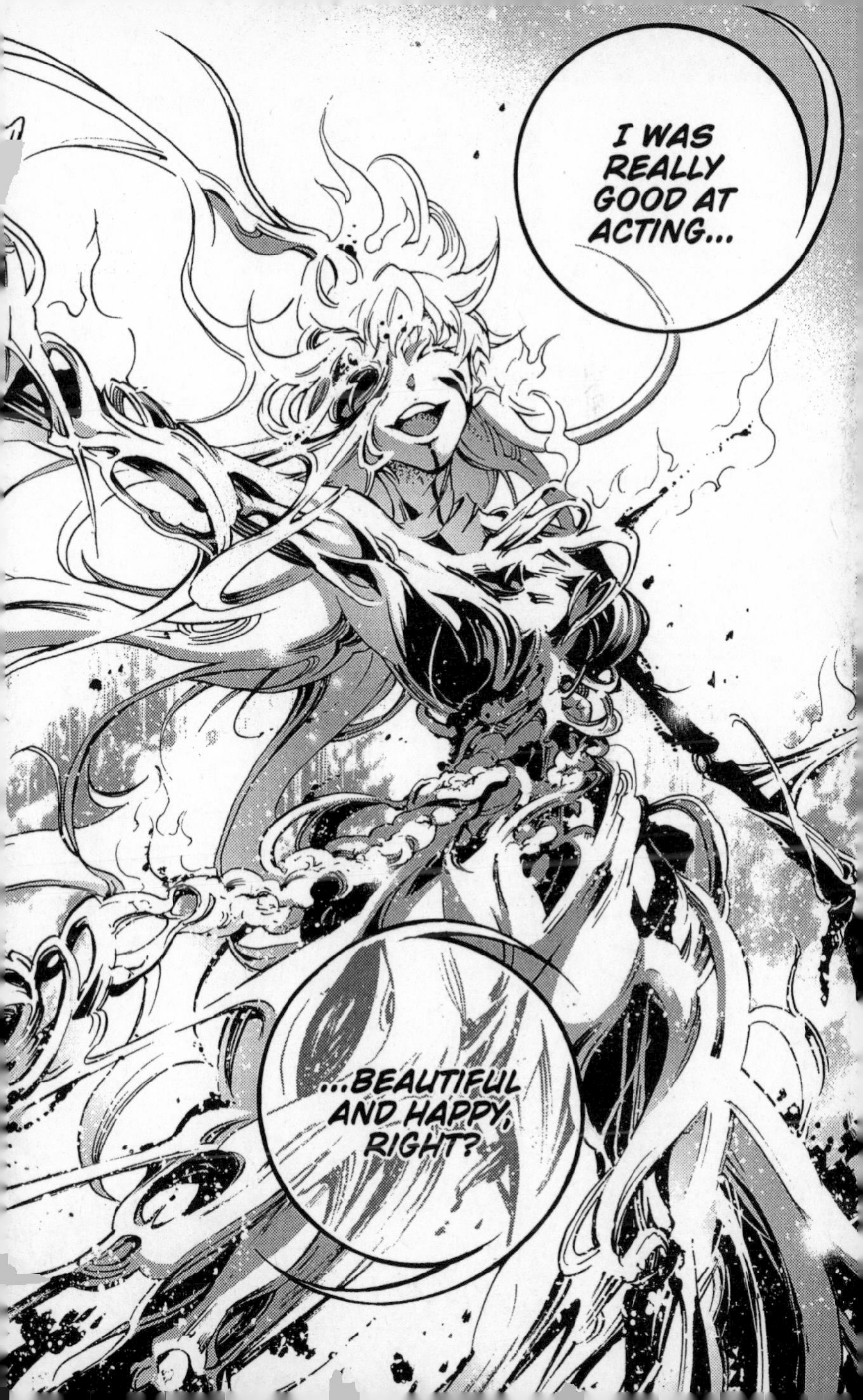
I WAS REALLY GOOD AT ACTING...
...BEAUTIFUL AND HAPPY, RIGHT?

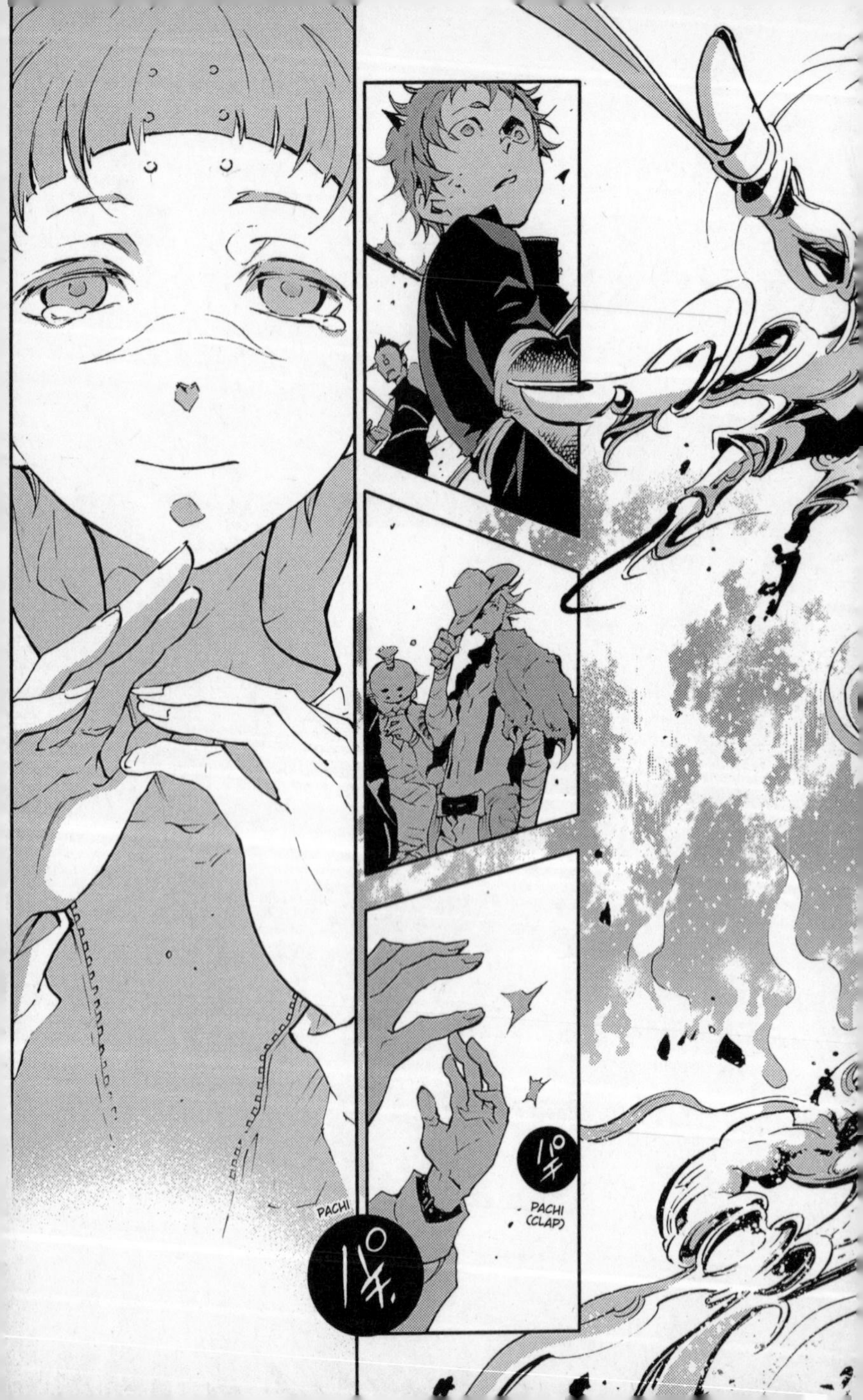
パチ
PACHI (CLAP)
パチ.
PACHI

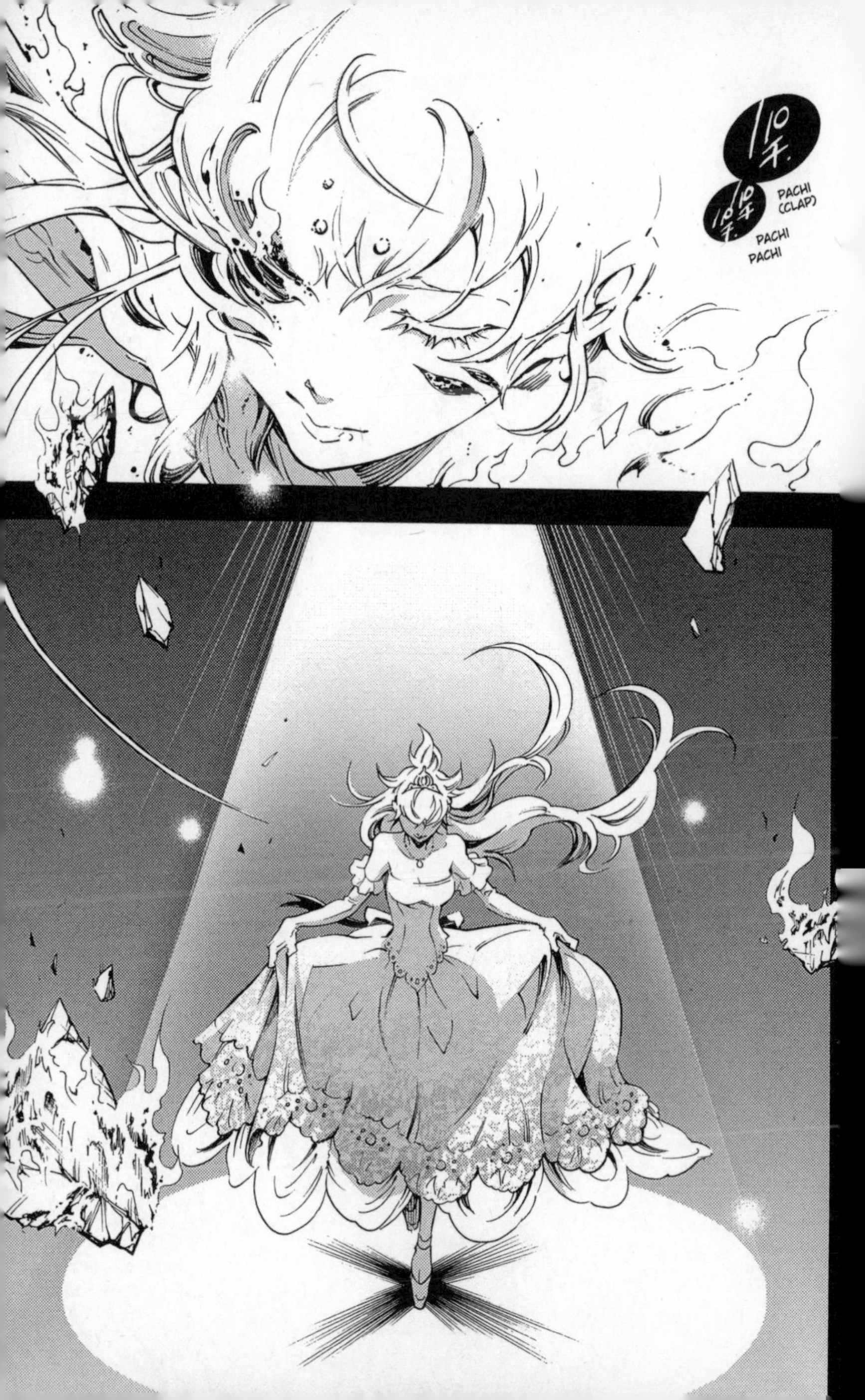
PACHI (CLAP)
PACHI
PACHI

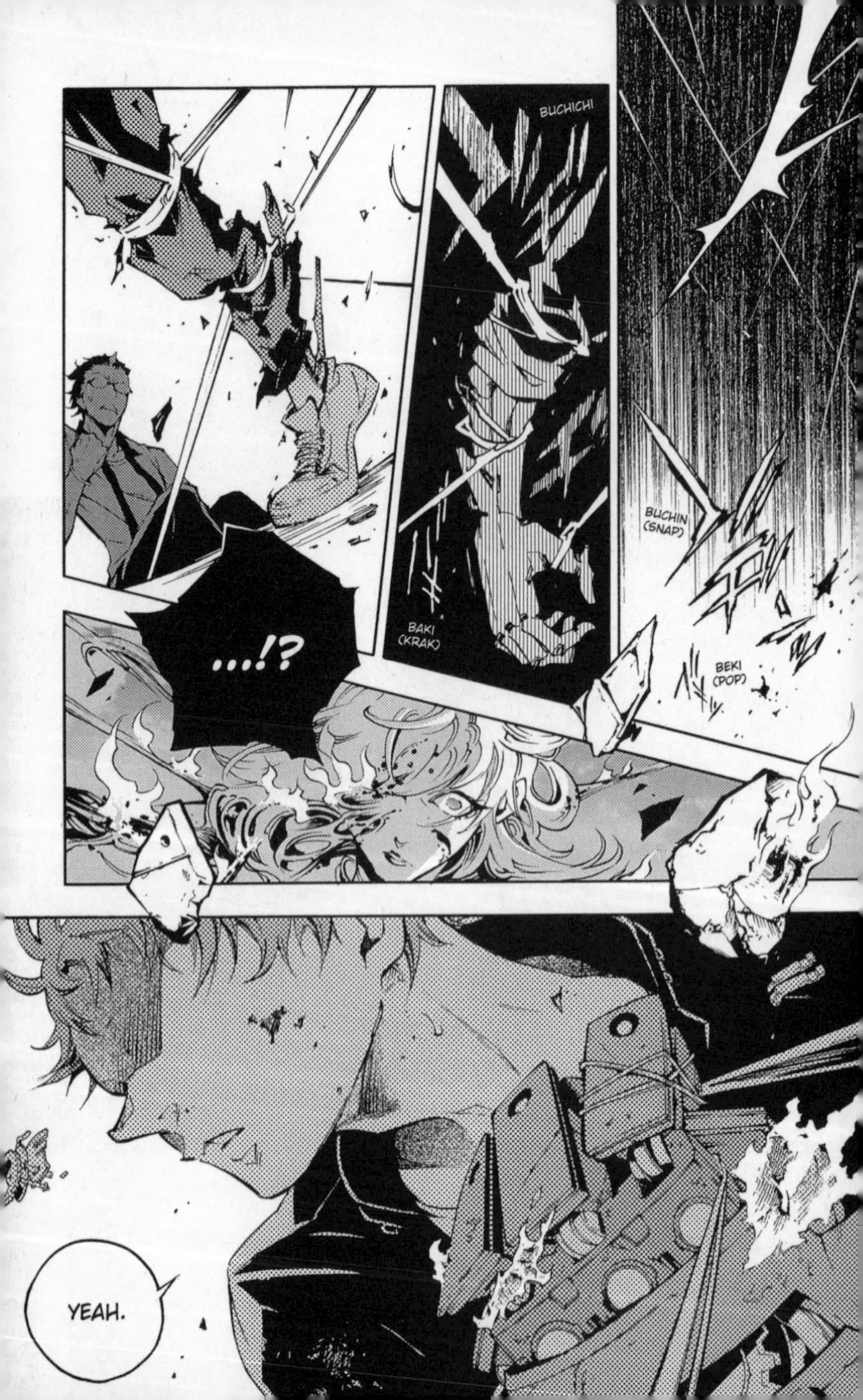

BUCHIN (SNAP)
BEKI (POP)
BUCHICHI
BAKI (KRAK)
...!?
YEAH.

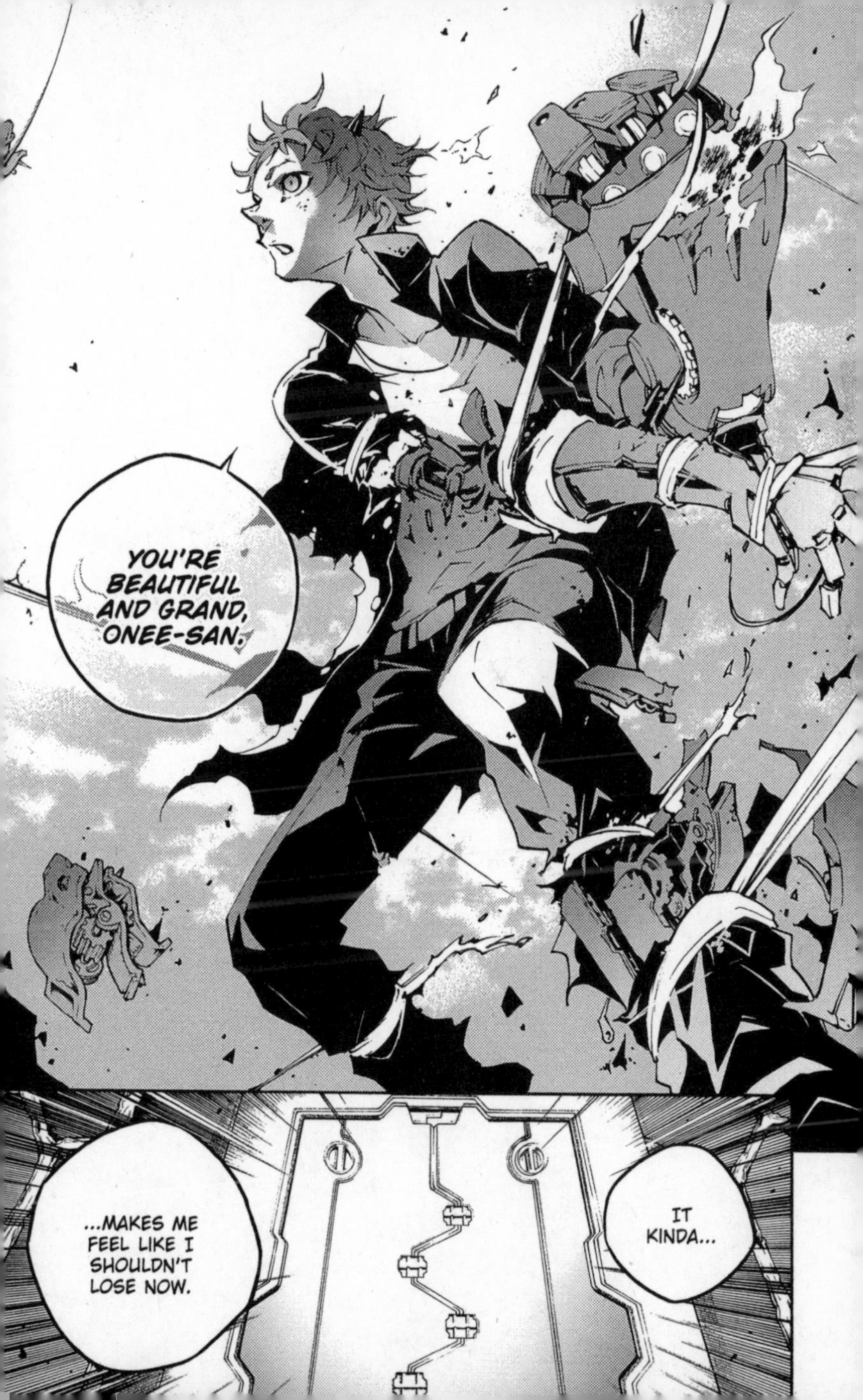
YOU'RE BEAUTIFUL AND GRAND, ONEE-SAN.
IT KINDA...
...MAKES ME FEEL LIKE I SHOULDN'T LOSE NOW.

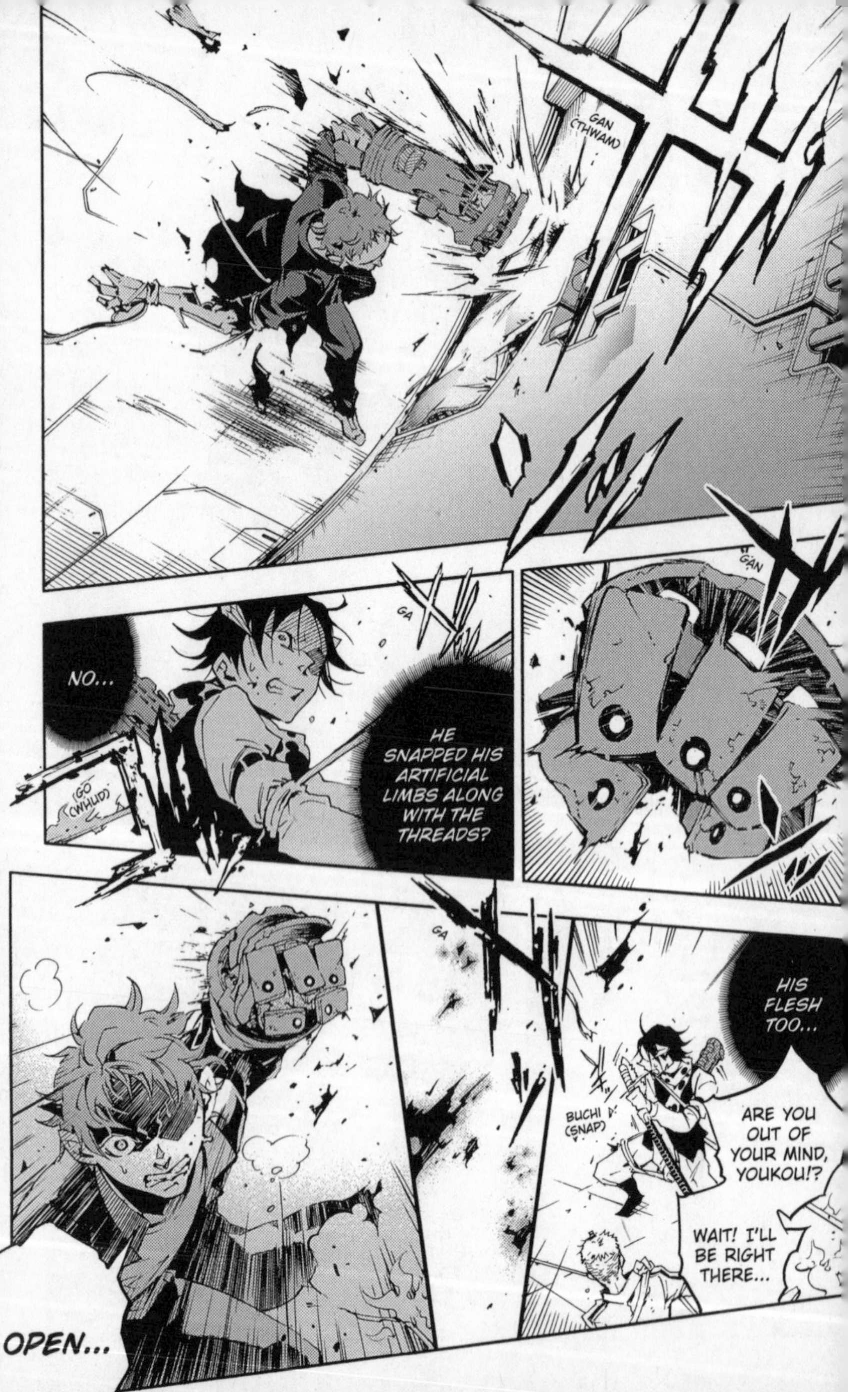
GAN (THWAM)
GAN
GA
NO...
HE SNAPPED HIS ARTIFICIAL LIMBS ALONG WITH THE THREADS?
(GO (WHUD))
GA
HIS FLESH TOO...
BUCHI (SNAP)
ARE YOU OUT OF YOUR MIND, YOUKOU!?
WAIT! I'LL BE RIGHT THERE...
OPEN...

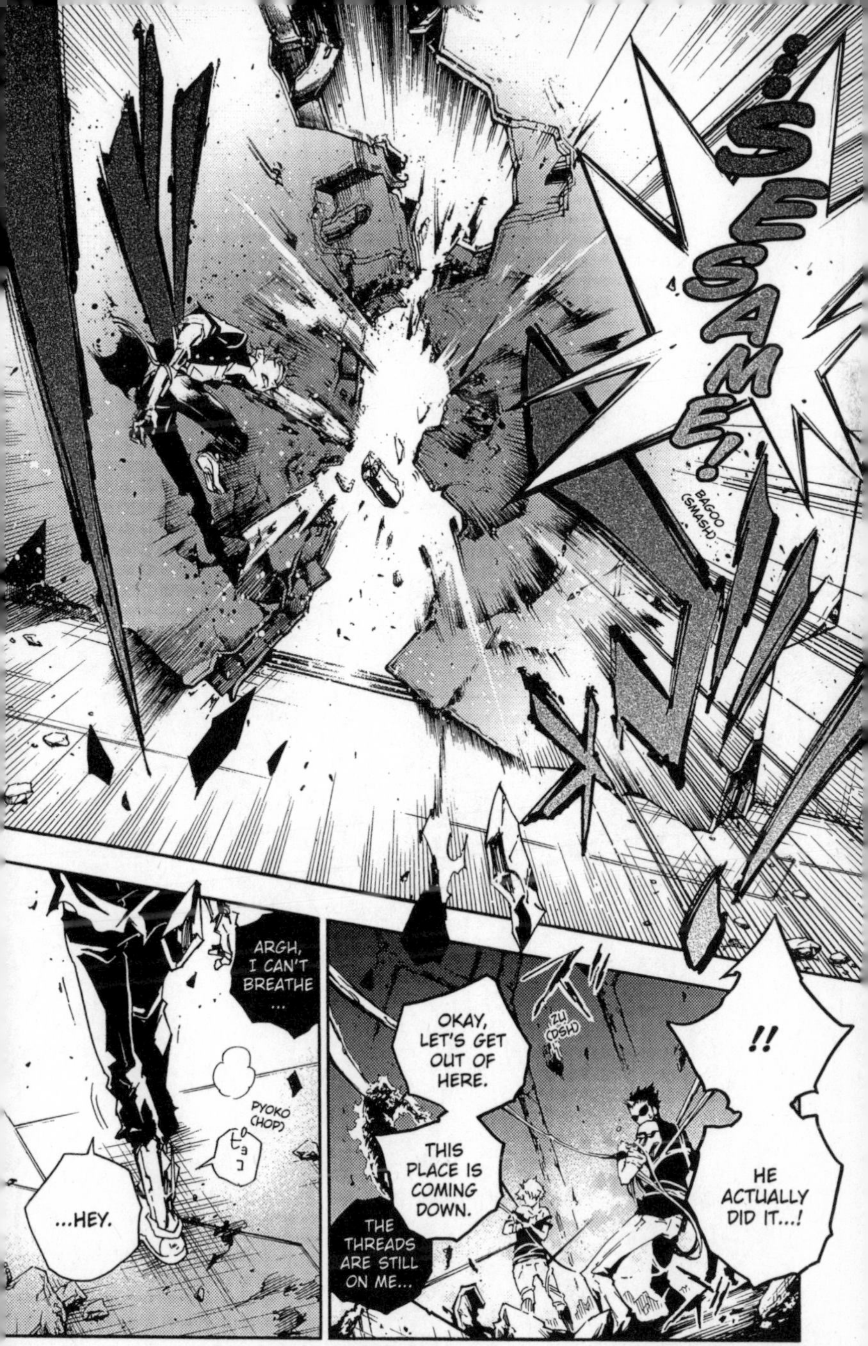
...SESAME!
BAGOO (SMASH)
!!
HE ACTUALLY DID IT...!
ZU (DSH)
OKAY, LET'S GET OUT OF HERE.
THIS PLACE IS COMING DOWN.
THE THREADS ARE STILL ON ME...
ARGH, I CAN'T BREATHE ...
PYOKO (HOP)
...HEY.

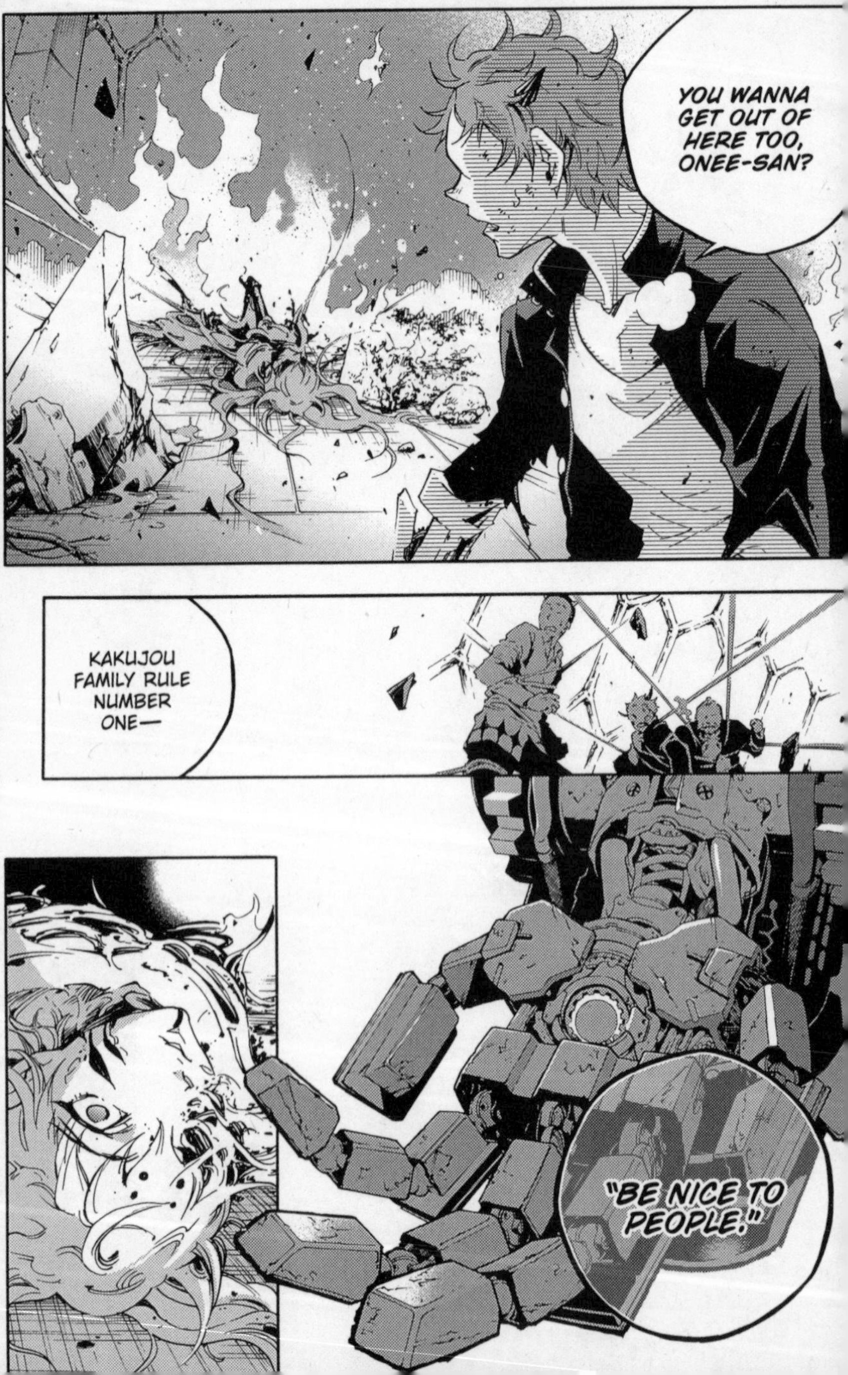
YOU WANNA GET OUT OF HERE TOO, ONEE-SAN?
KAKUJOU FAMILY RULE NUMBER ONE—
"BE NICE TO PEOPLE."

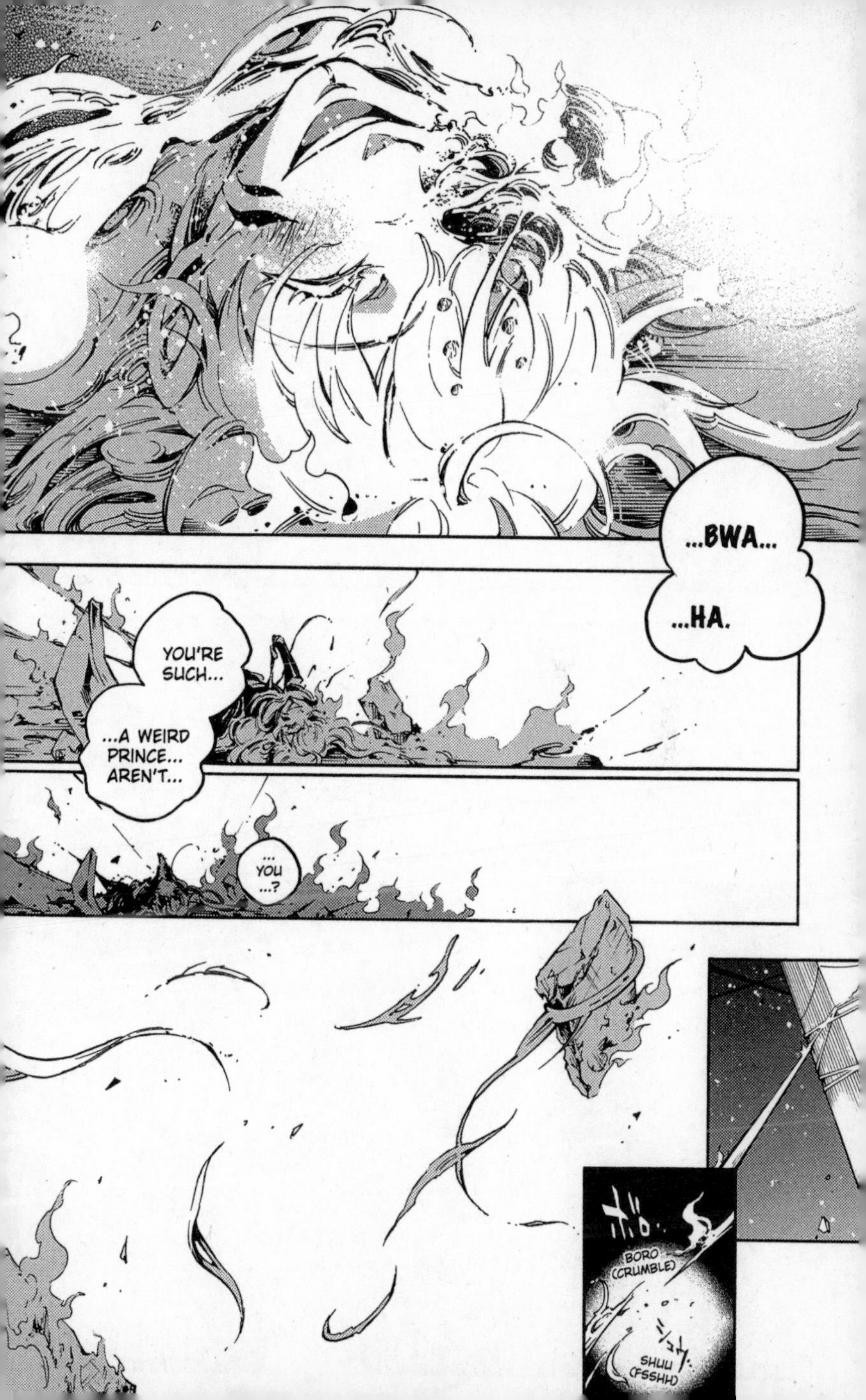
...BWA...
...HA.
YOU'RE SUCH...
...A WEIRD PRINCE... AREN'T...
...YOU...?
BORO (CRUMBLE)
SHUU (FSSHH)

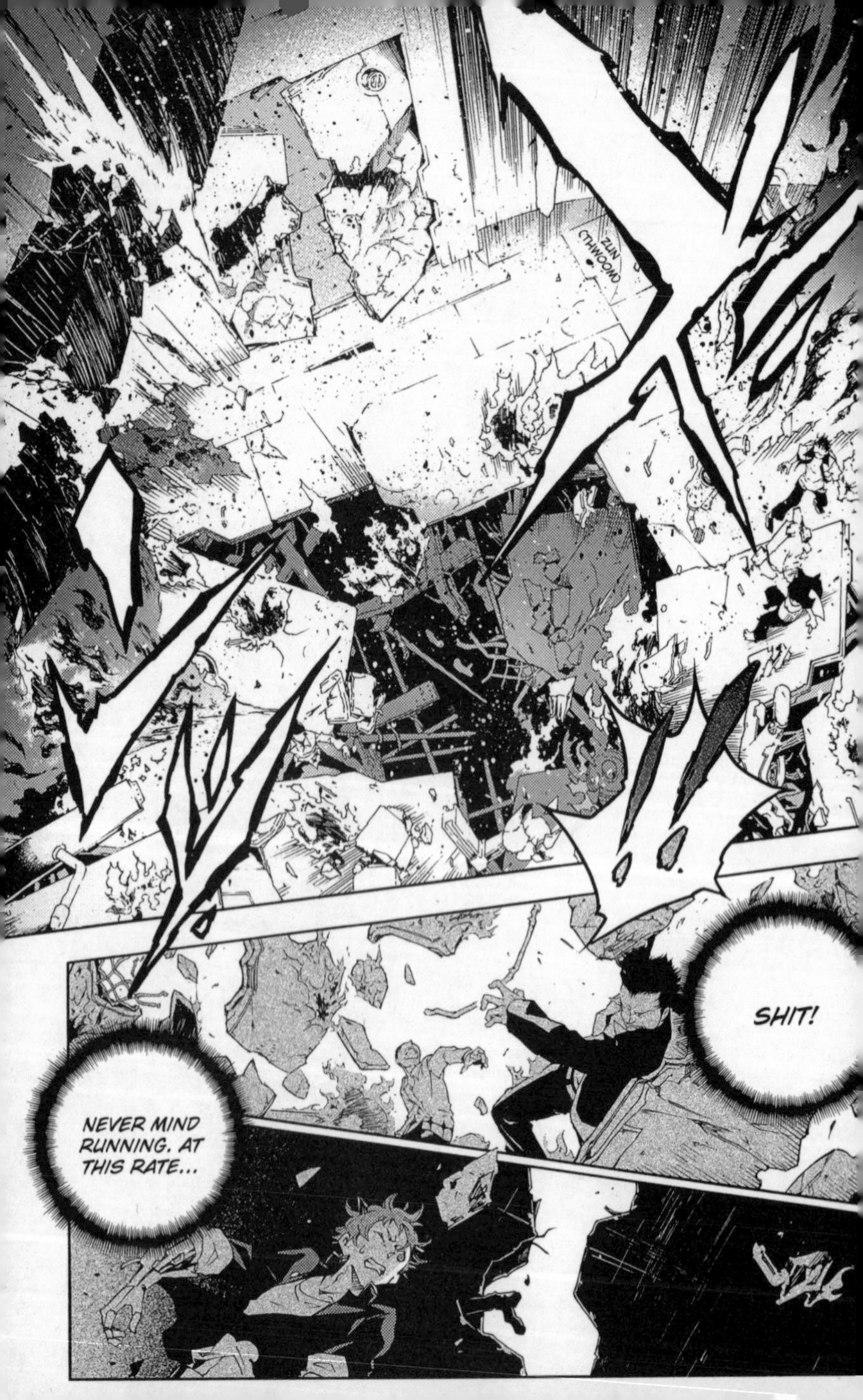
ZUN
CTHWOOM
SHIT!
NEVER MIND RUNNING. AT THIS RATE...

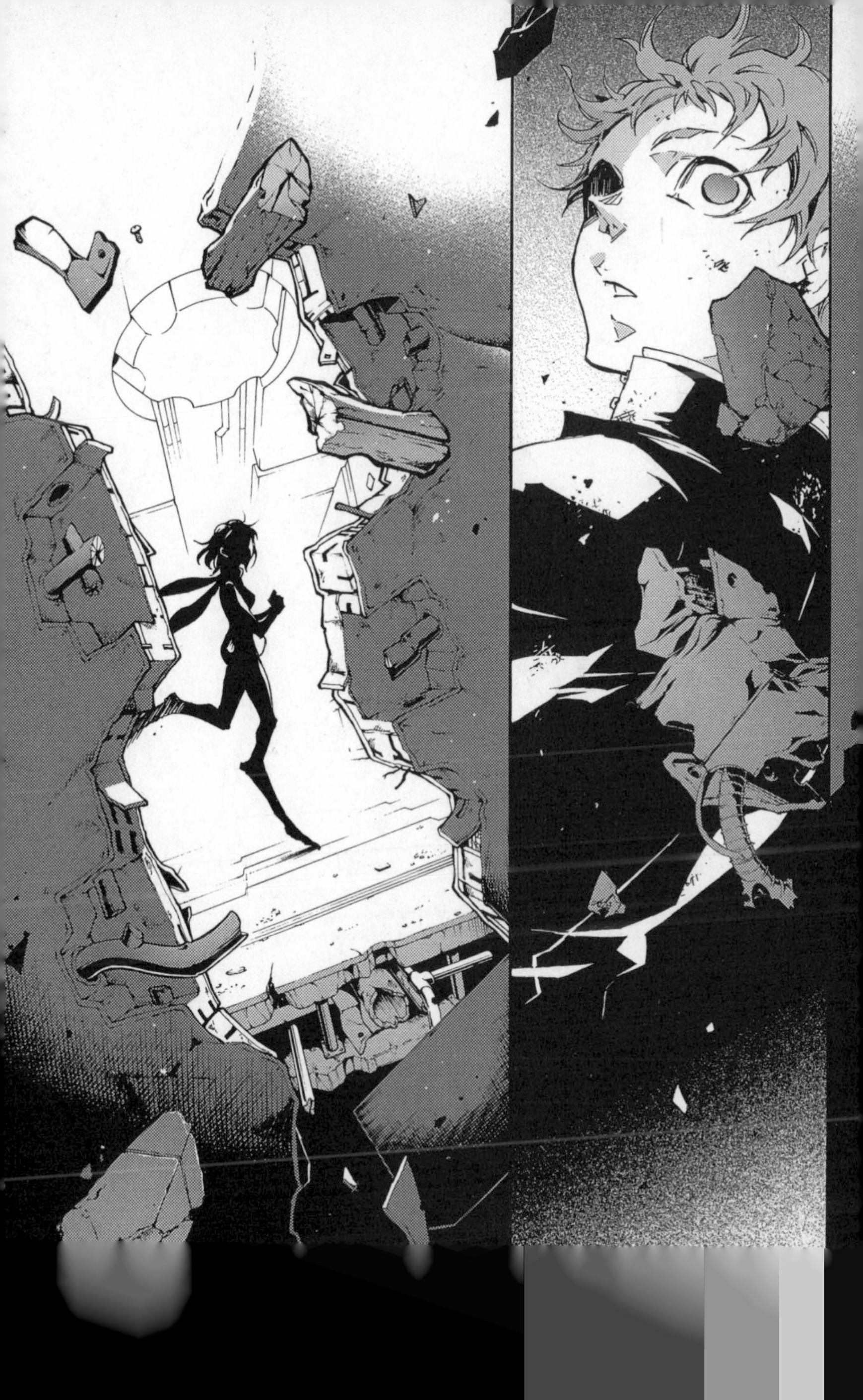

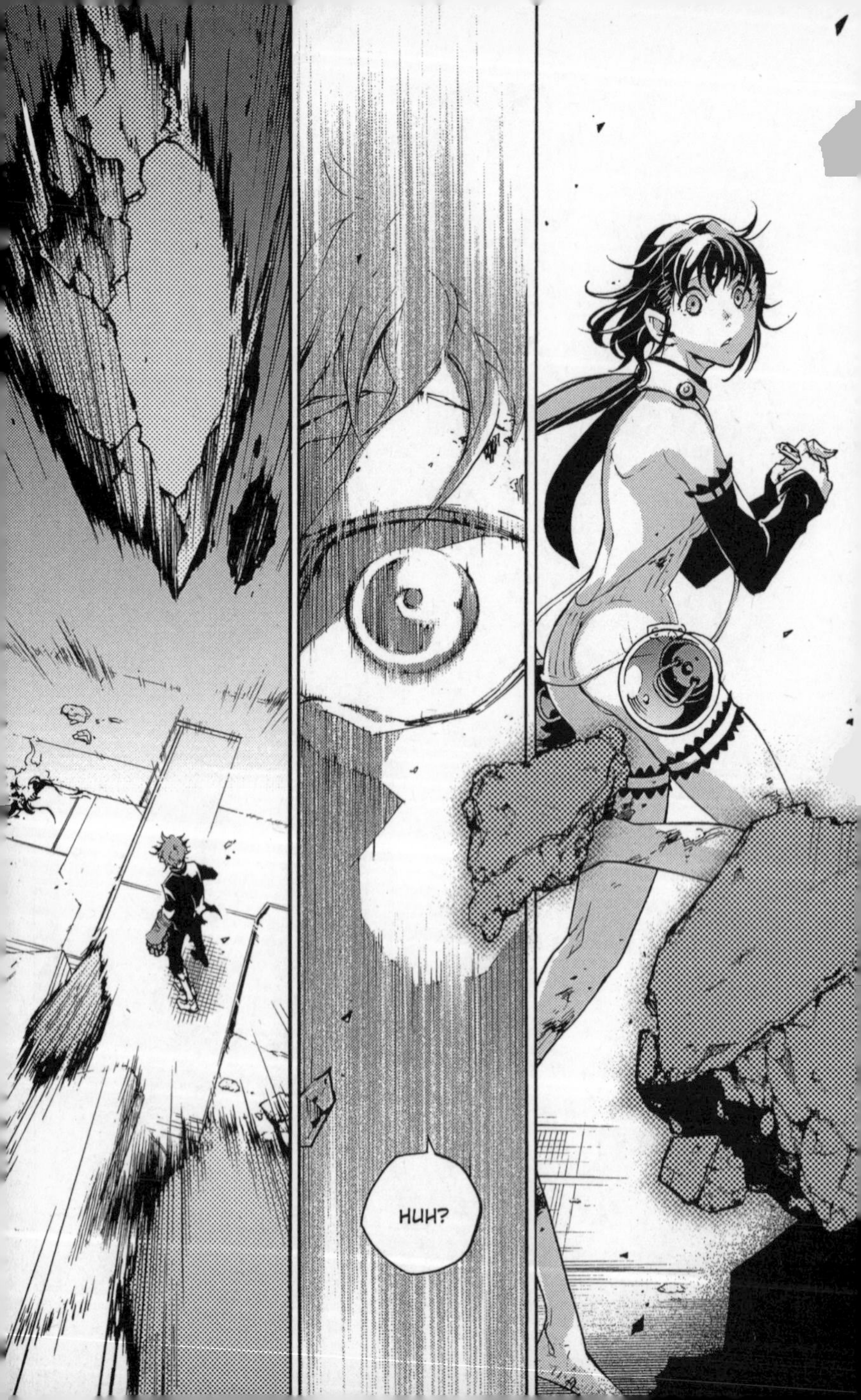
HUH?

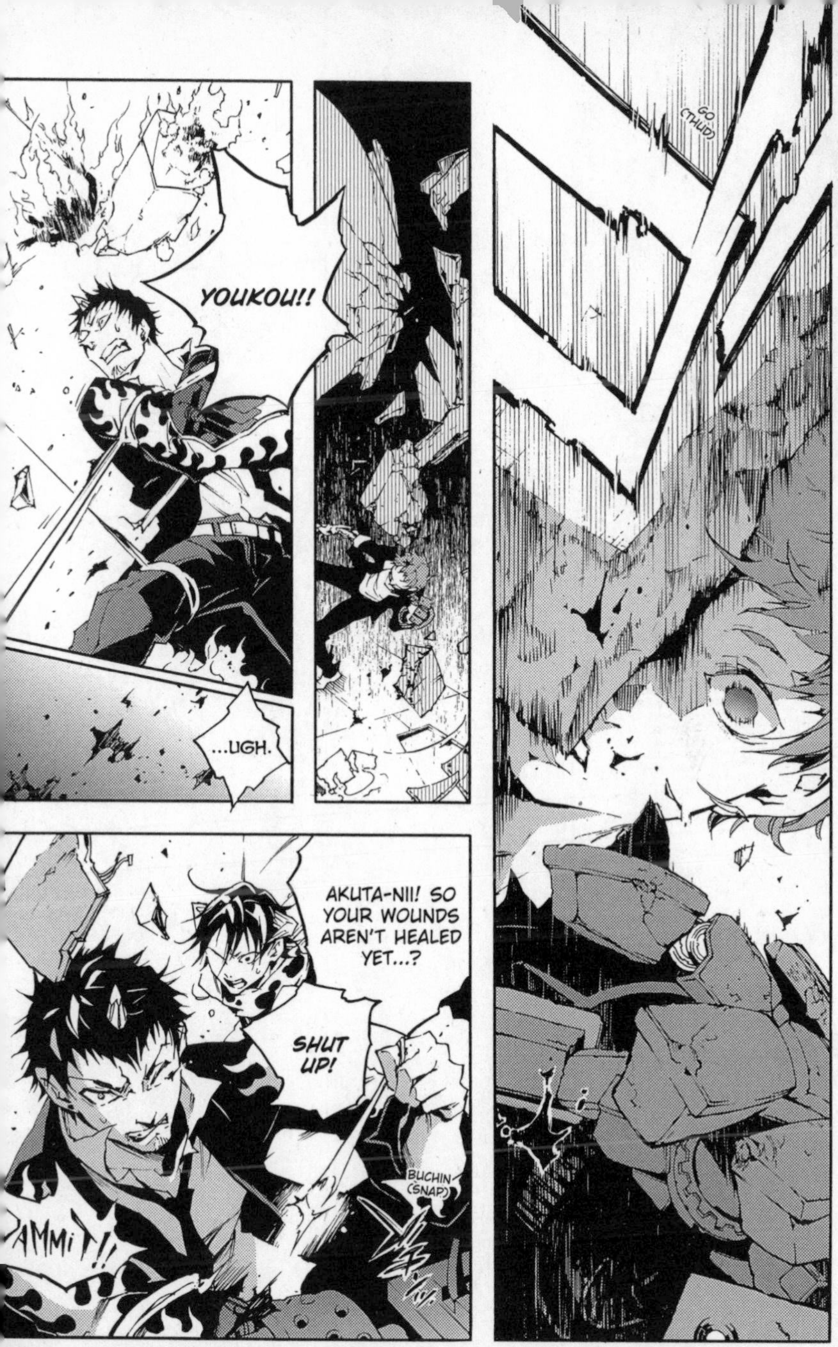
GO
(THUD)
YOUKOU!!
...UGH.
AKUTA-NII! SO YOUR WOUNDS AREN'T HEALED YET...?
SHUT UP!
BUCHIN
(SNAP)
DAMMIT!!

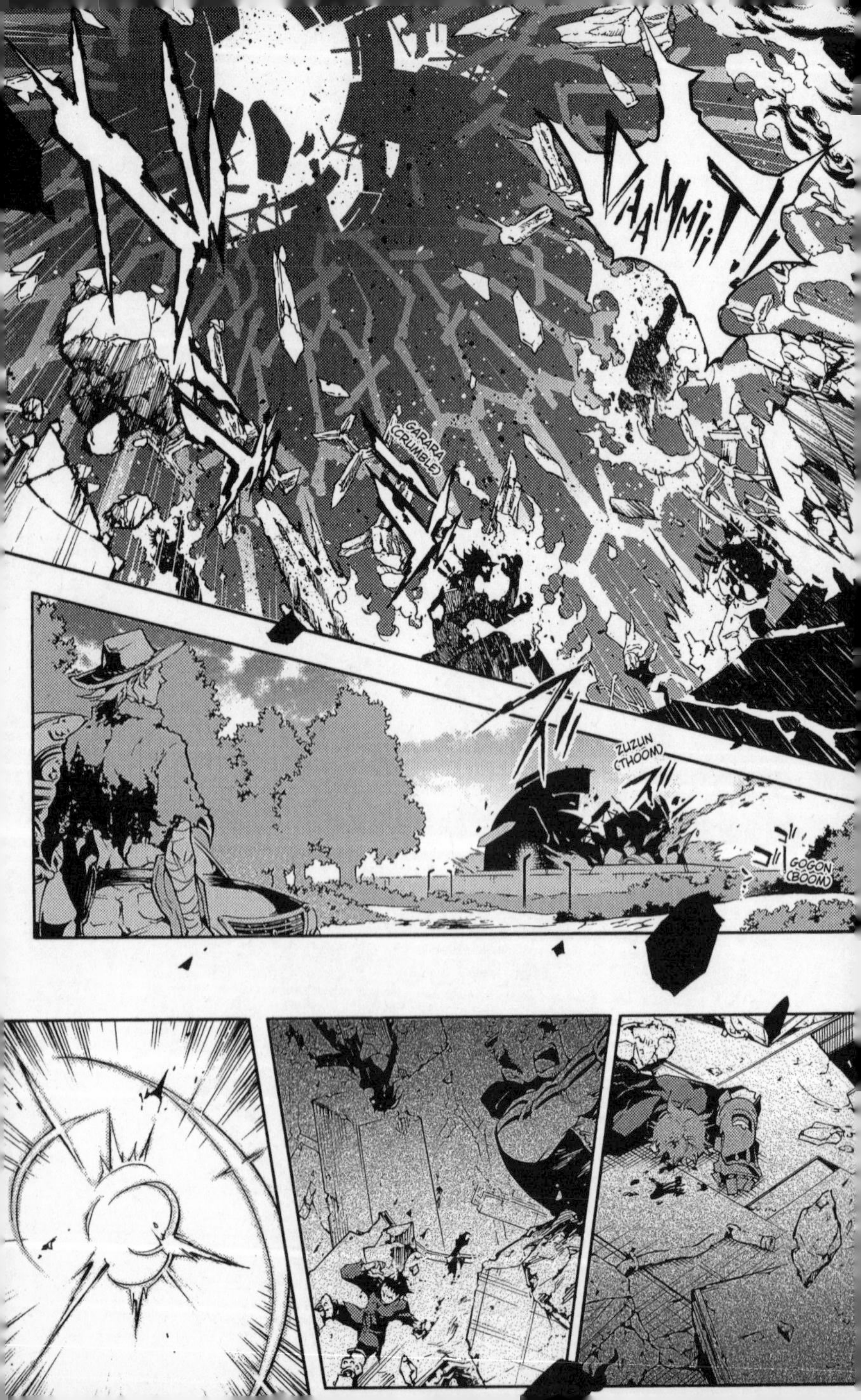
DAAMMIT!!
GARARA (CRUMBLE)
ZUZUN (THOOM)
GOGON (BOOM)

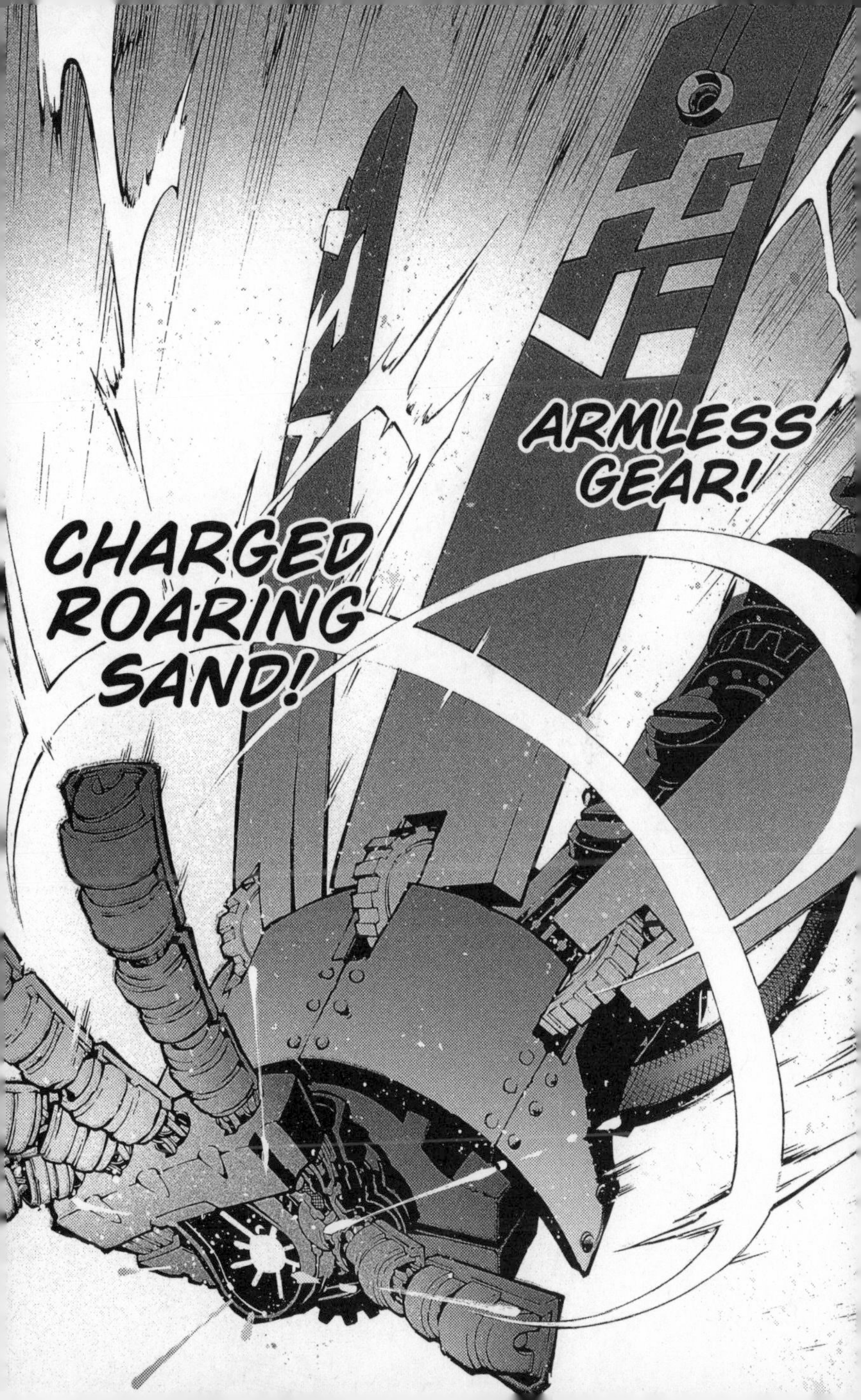
ARMLESS GEAR!
CHARGED ROARING SAND!

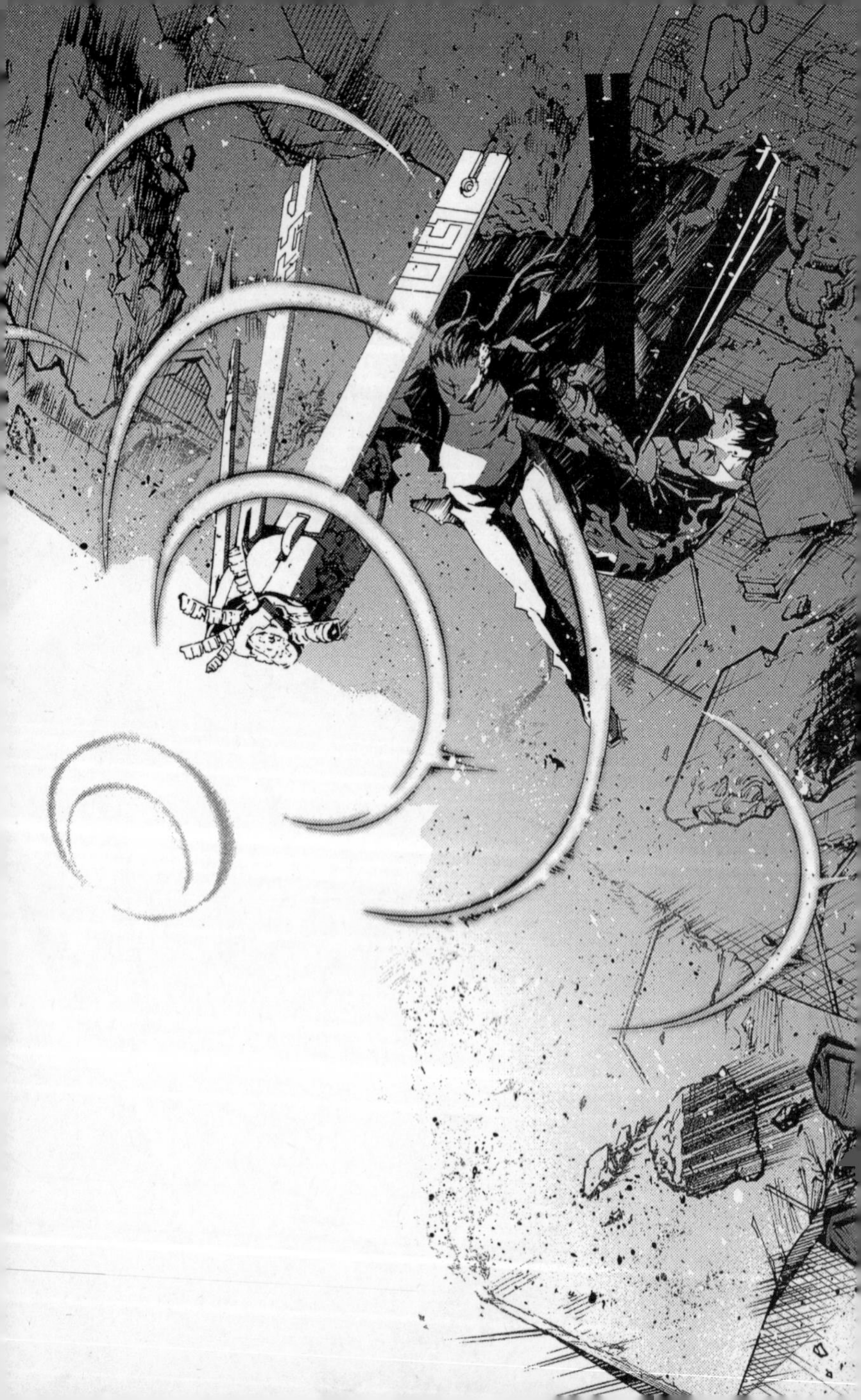

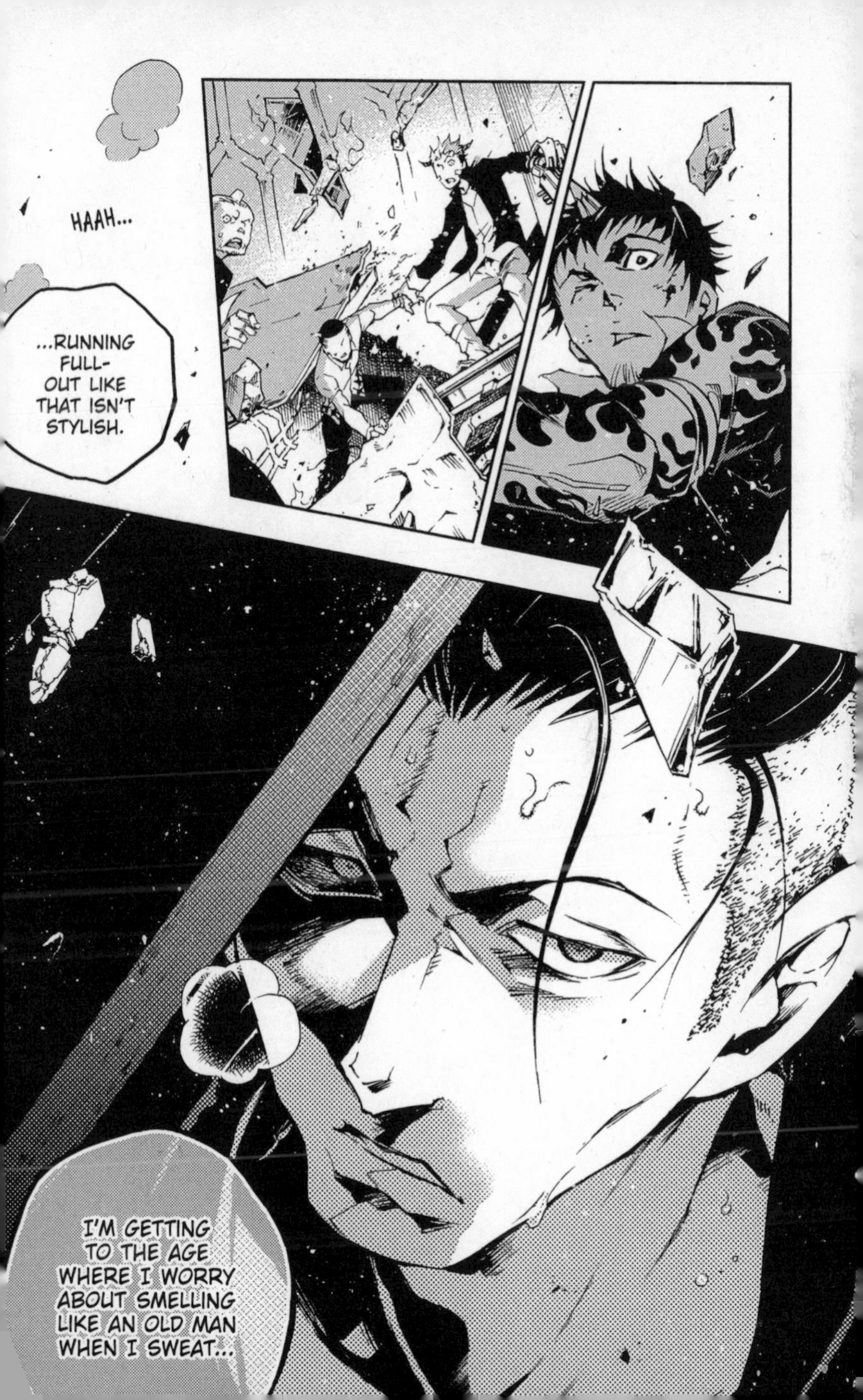
HAAH...
...RUNNING FULL-OUT LIKE THAT ISN'T STYLISH.
I'M GETTING TO THE AGE WHERE I WORRY ABOUT SMELLING LIKE AN OLD MAN WHEN I SWEAT...

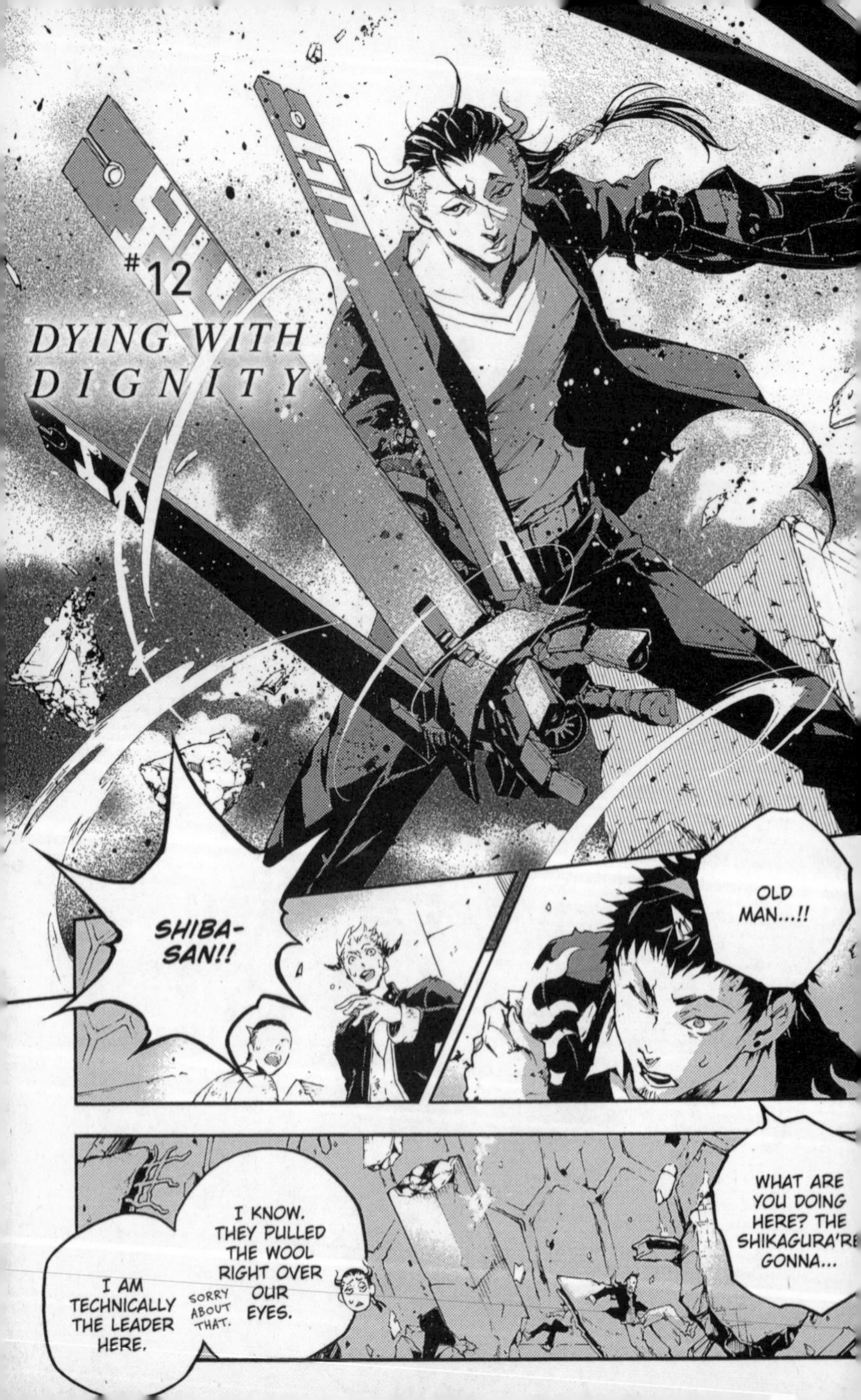
#12
DYING WITH DIGNITY
OLD MAN...!!
SHIBA-SAN!!
WHAT ARE YOU DOING HERE? THE SHIKAGURA'RE GONNA...
I KNOW. THEY PULLED THE WOOL RIGHT OVER OUR EYES.
SORRY ABOUT THAT.
I AM TECHNICALLY THE LEADER HERE.

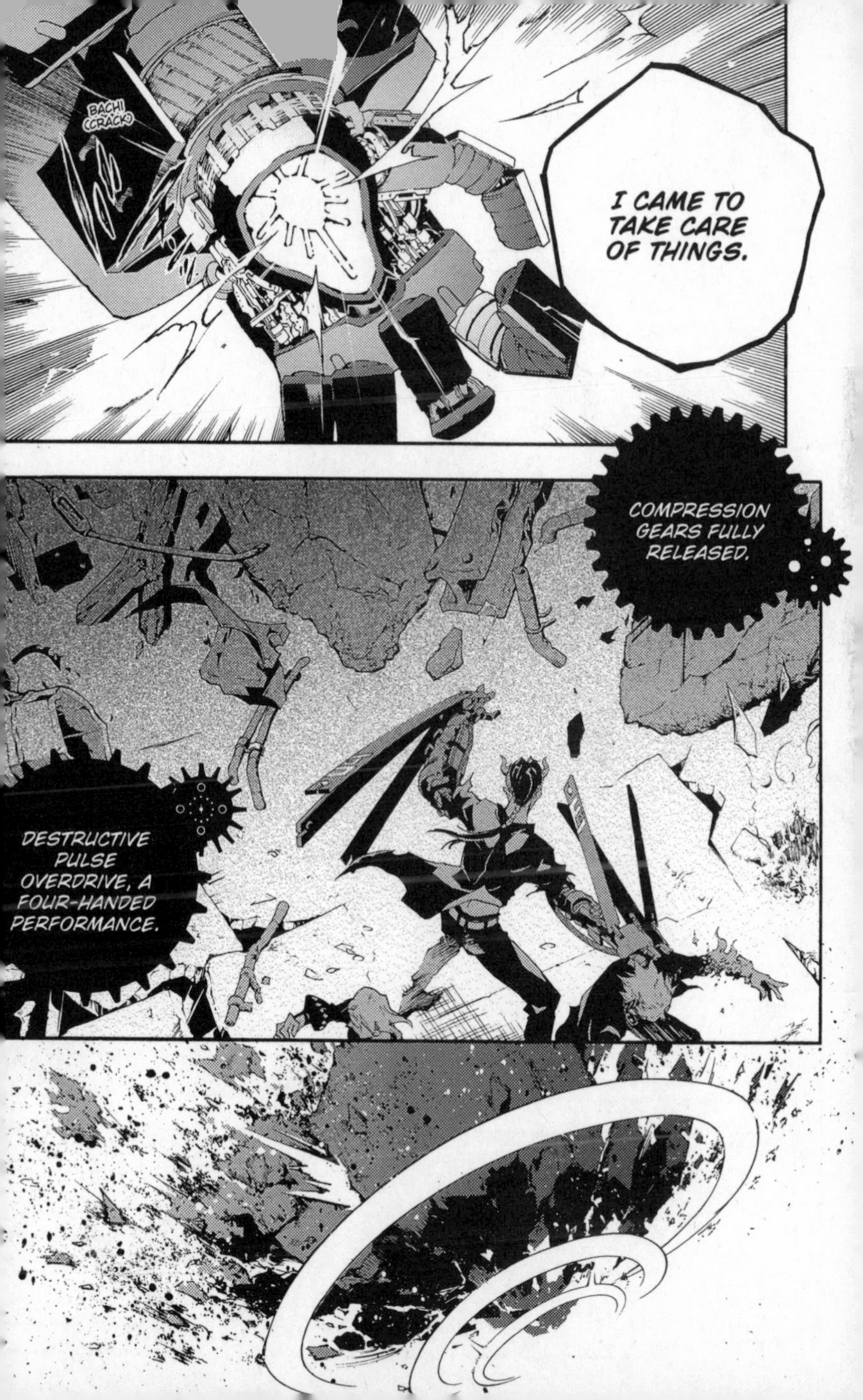
I CAME TO TAKE CARE OF THINGS.
BACHI (CRACK)
COMPRESSION GEARS FULLY RELEASED.
DESTRUCTIVE PULSE OVERDRIVE, A FOUR-HANDED PERFORMANCE.

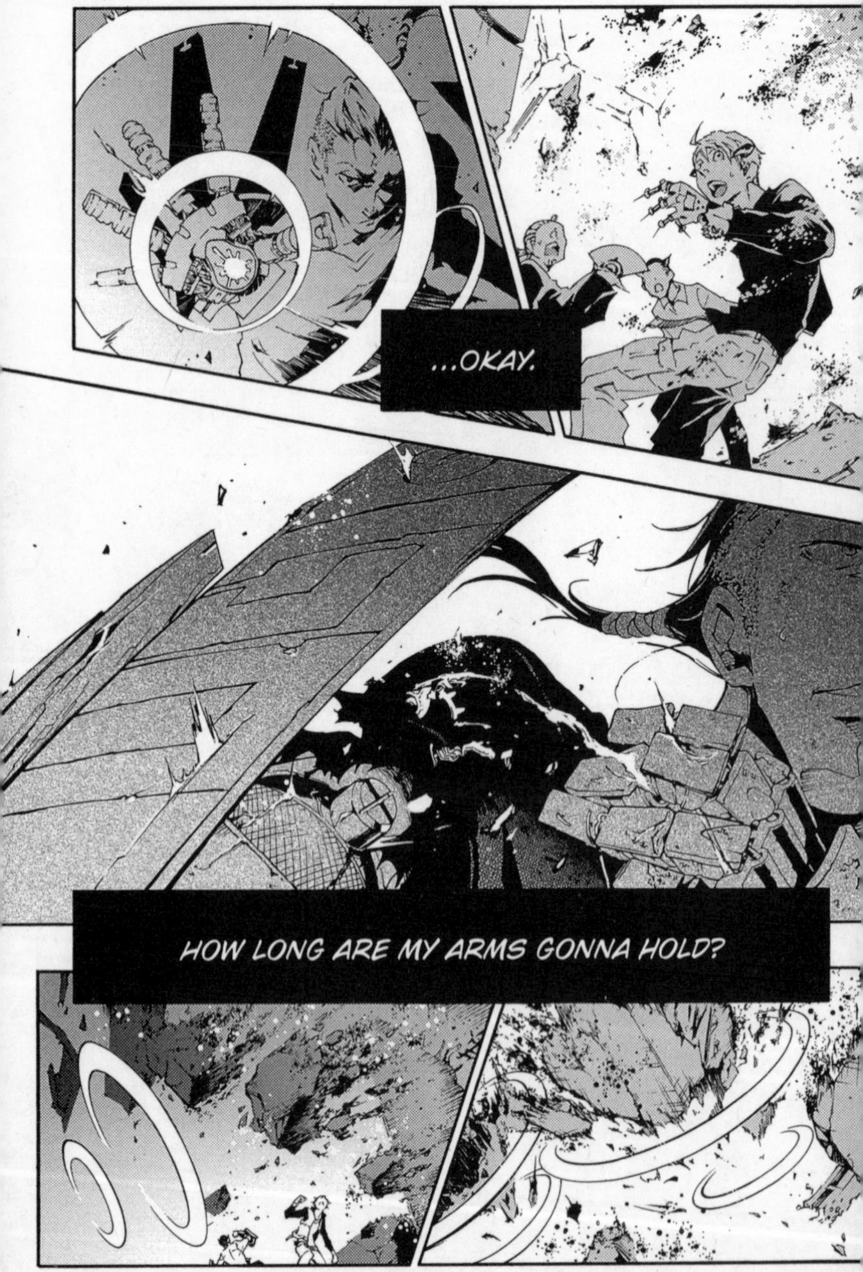
...OKAY.
HOW LONG ARE MY ARMS GONNA HOLD?

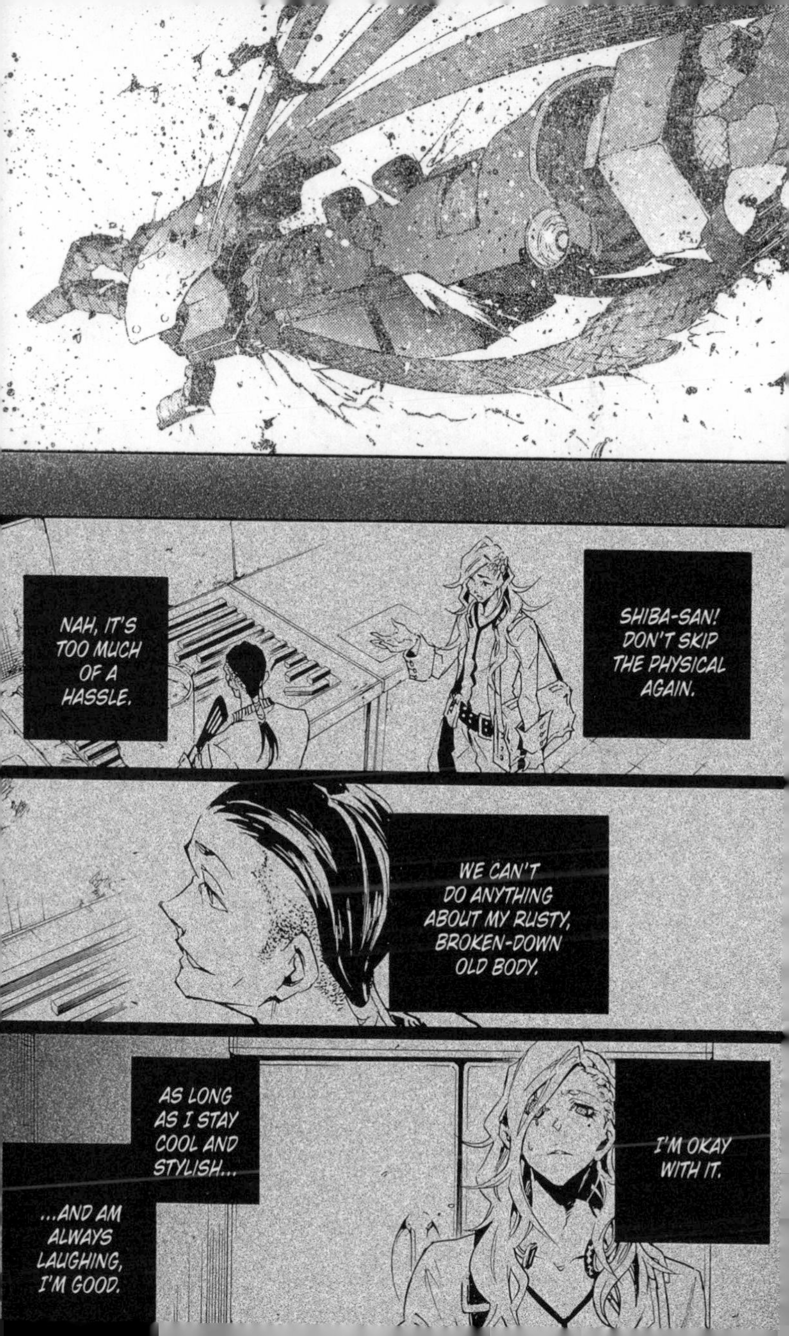
SHIBA-SAN! DON'T SKIP THE PHYSICAL AGAIN.
NAH, IT'S TOO MUCH OF A HASSLE.
WE CAN'T DO ANYTHING ABOUT MY RUSTY, BROKEN-DOWN OLD BODY.
I'M OKAY WITH IT.
AS LONG AS I STAY COOL AND STYLISH...
...AND AM ALWAYS LAUGHING, I'M GOOD.

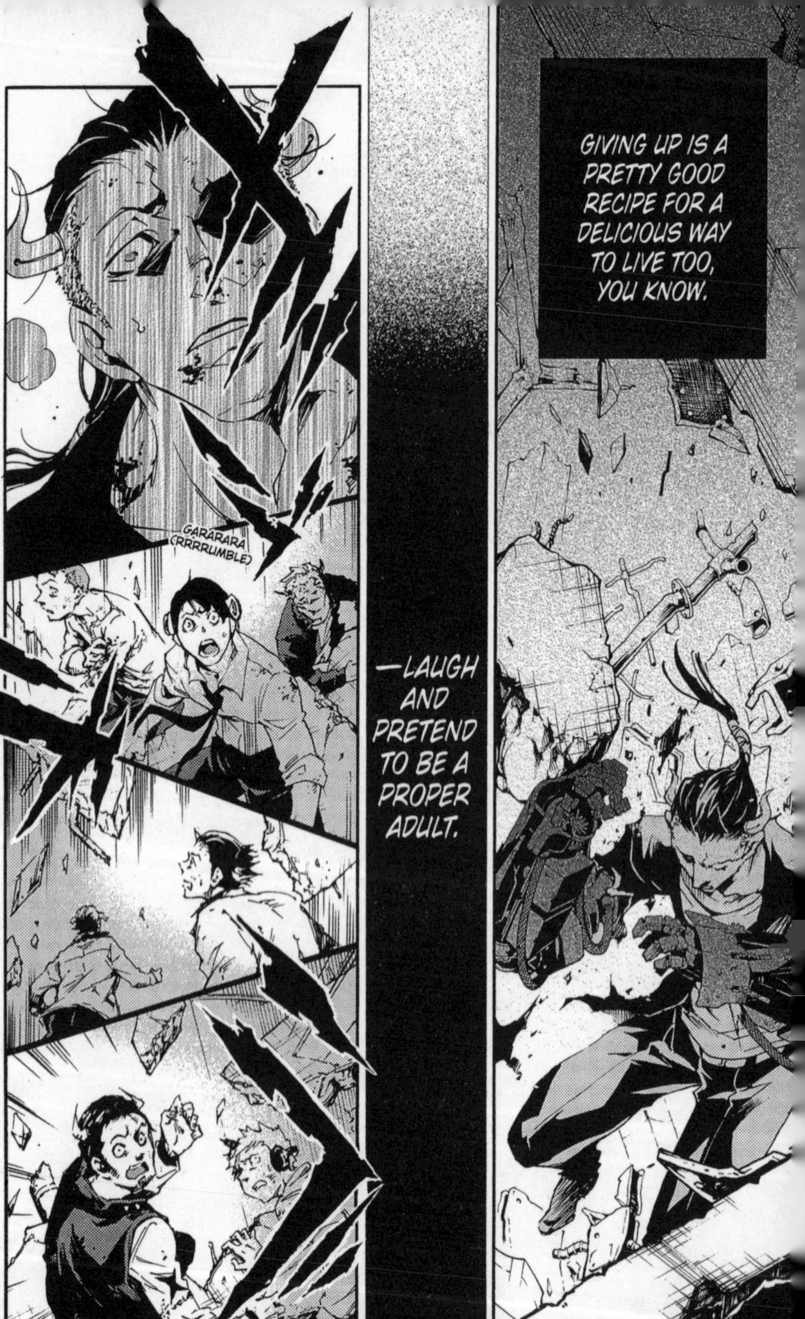
GIVING UP IS A PRETTY GOOD RECIPE FOR A DELICIOUS WAY TO LIVE TOO, YOU KNOW.
—LAUGH AND PRETEND TO BE A PROPER ADULT.
GARARARA (RRRRUMBLE)

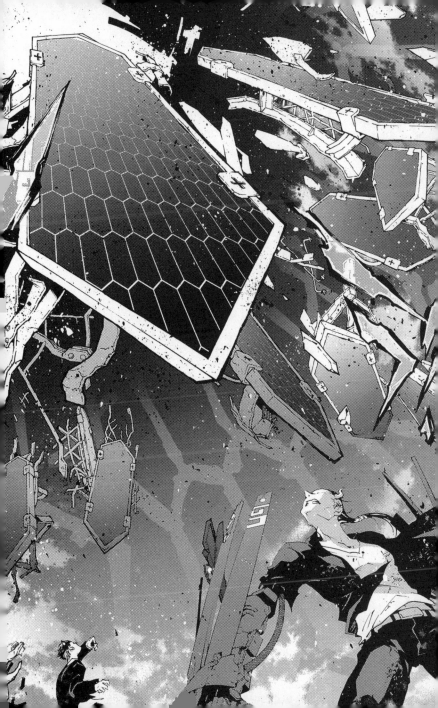

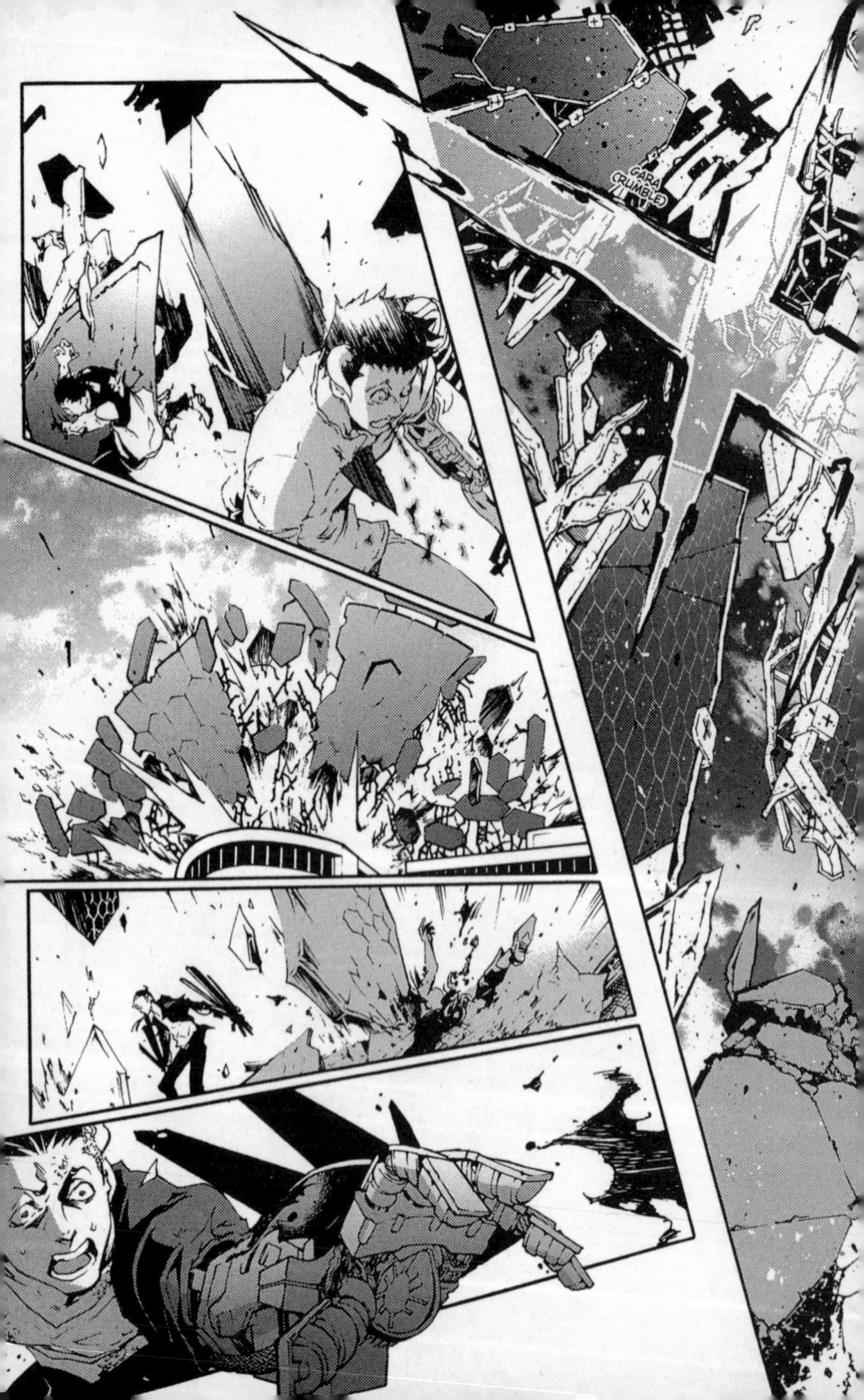
GARA (RUMBLE)

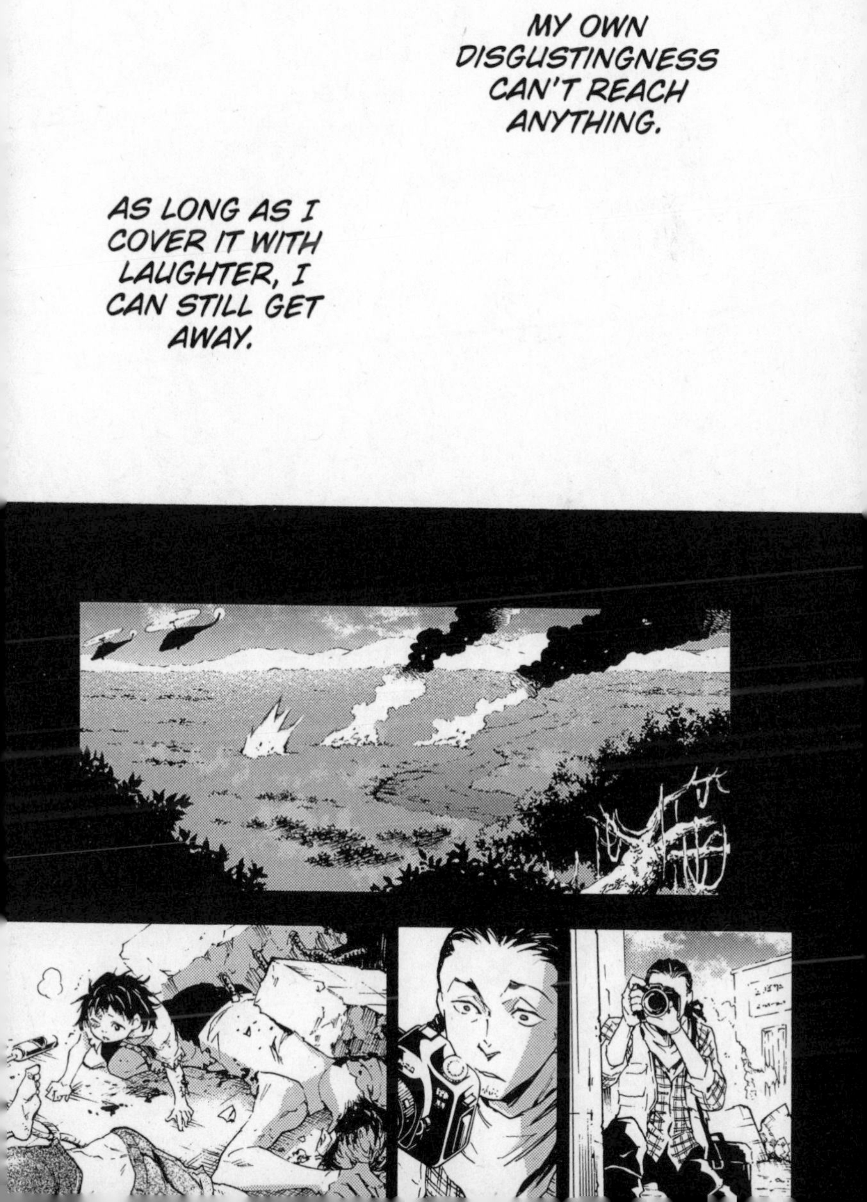
MY OWN DISGUSTINGNESS CAN'T REACH ANYTHING.
AS LONG AS I COVER IT WITH LAUGHTER, I CAN STILL GET AWAY.

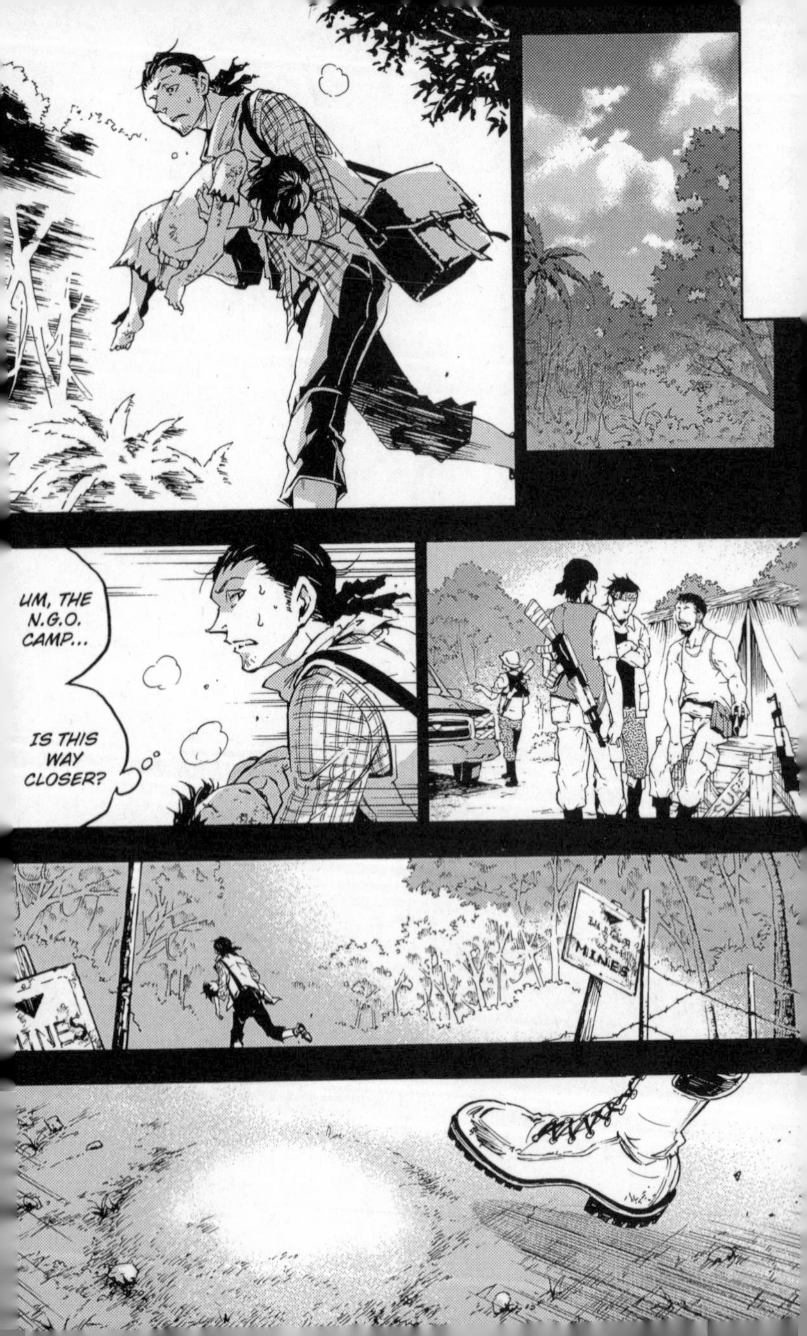
UM, THE N.G.O. CAMP...
IS THIS WAY CLOSER?
MINES

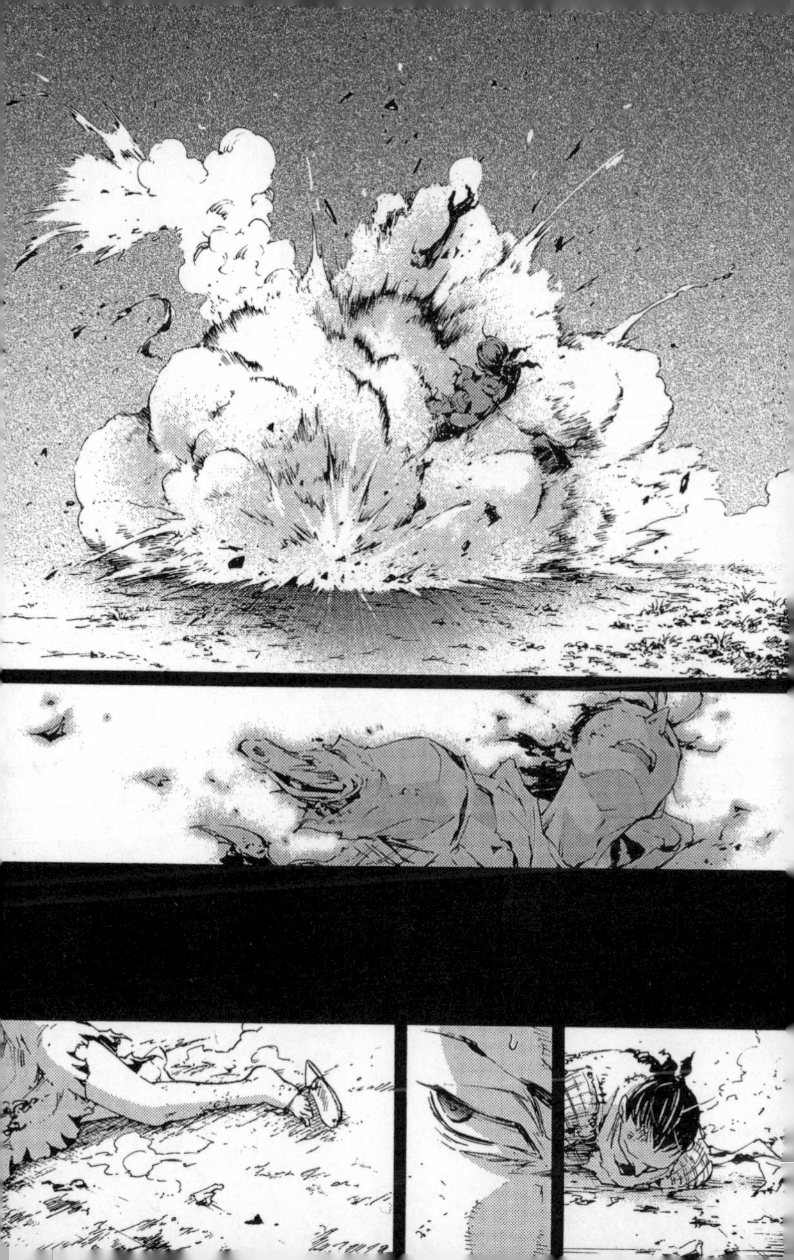

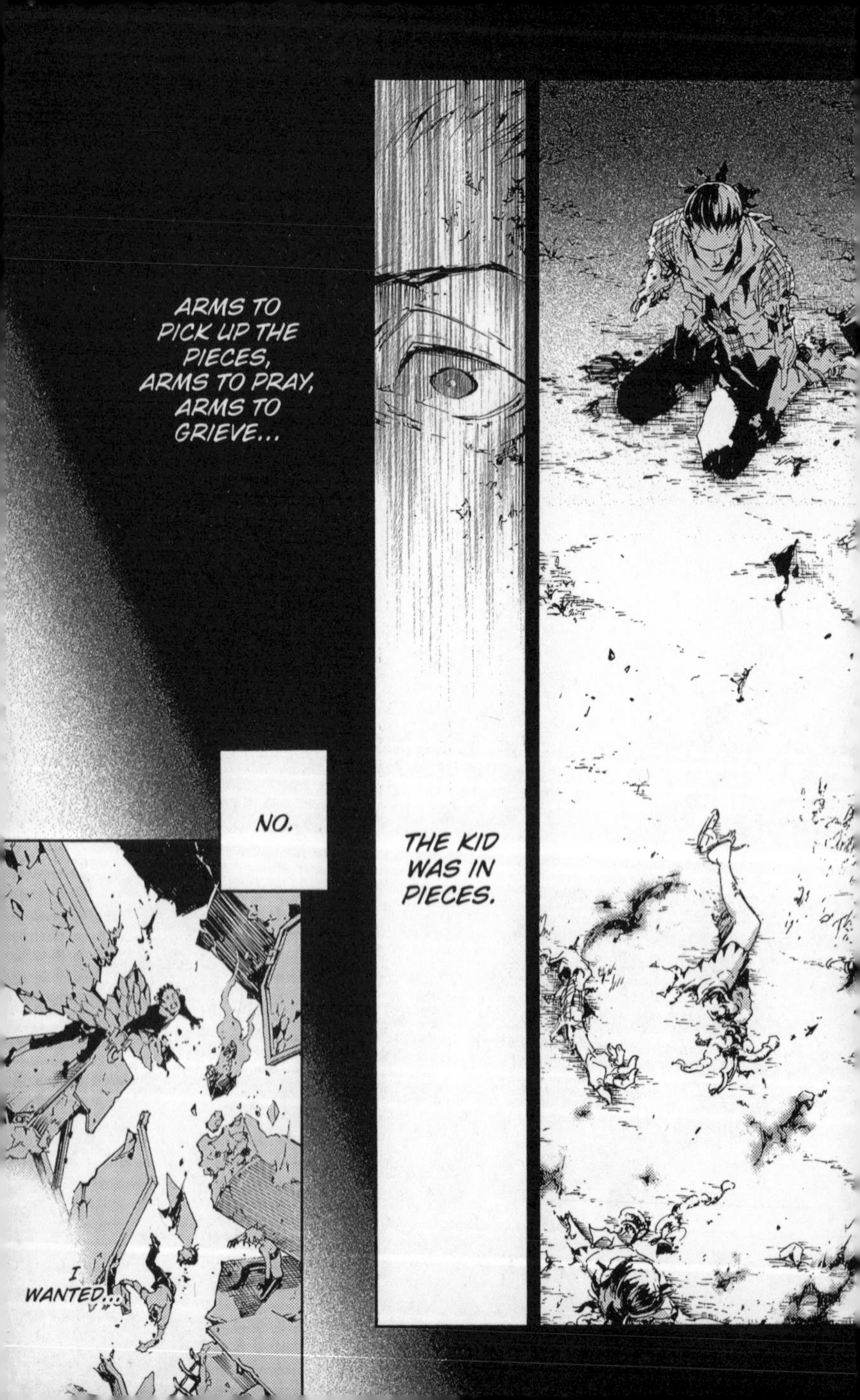
THE KID WAS IN PIECES.
ARMS TO PICK UP THE PIECES, ARMS TO PRAY, ARMS TO GRIEVE...
NO.
I WANTED...

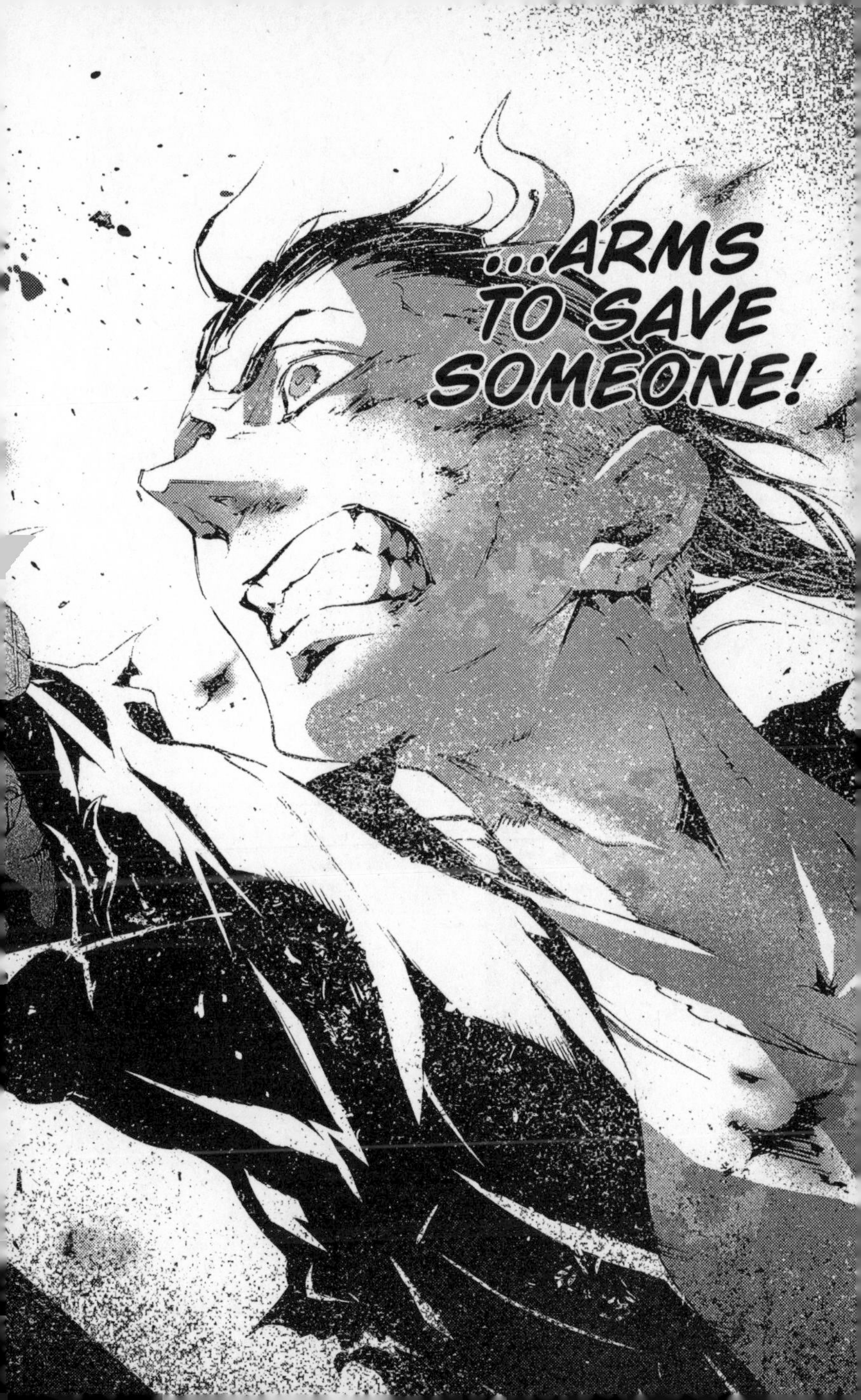
...ARMS TO SAVE SOMEONE!

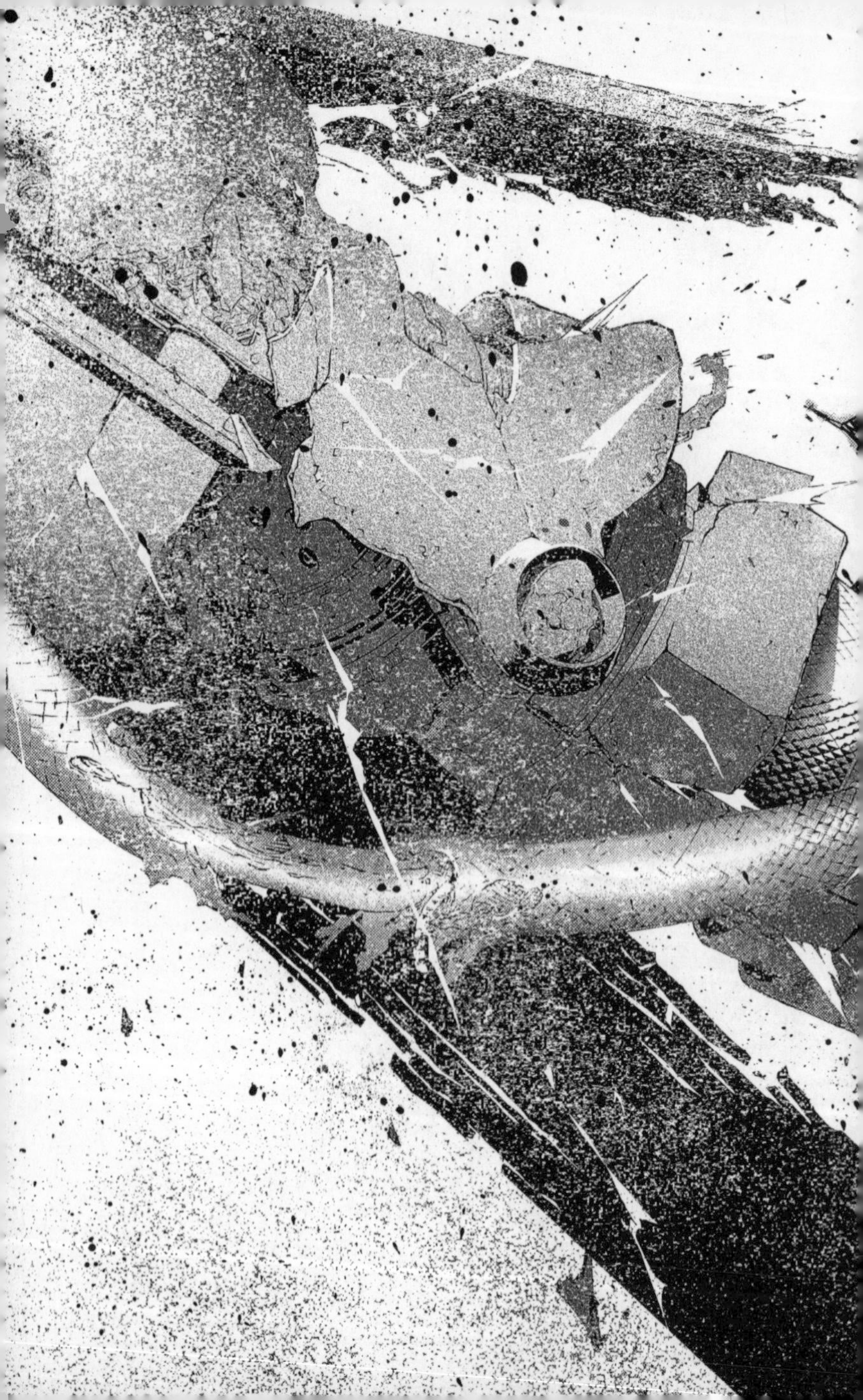

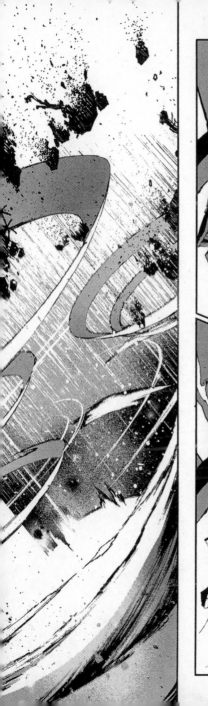
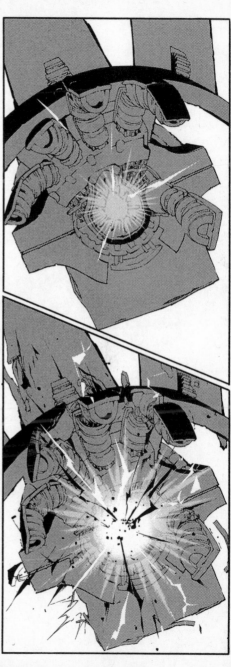

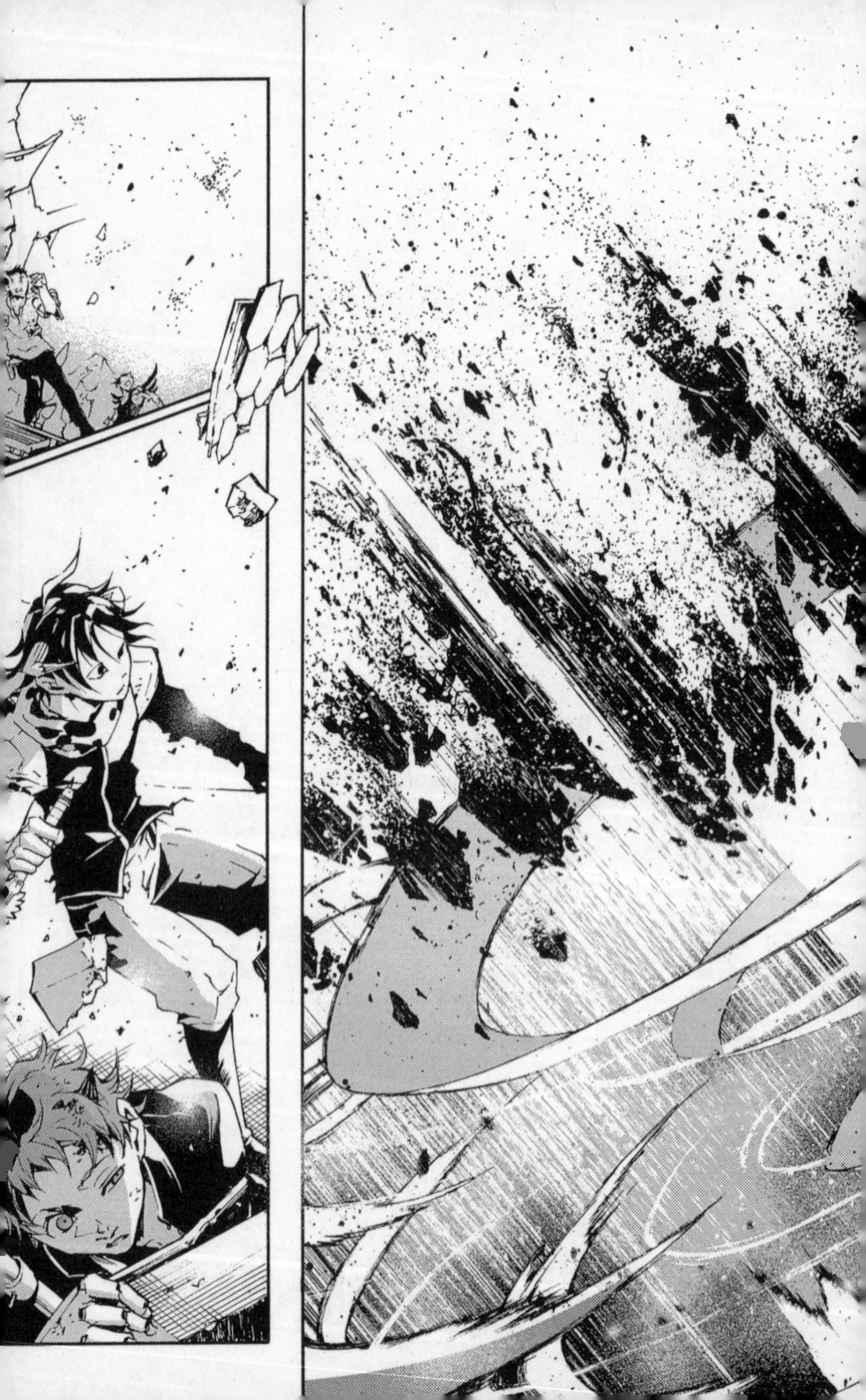

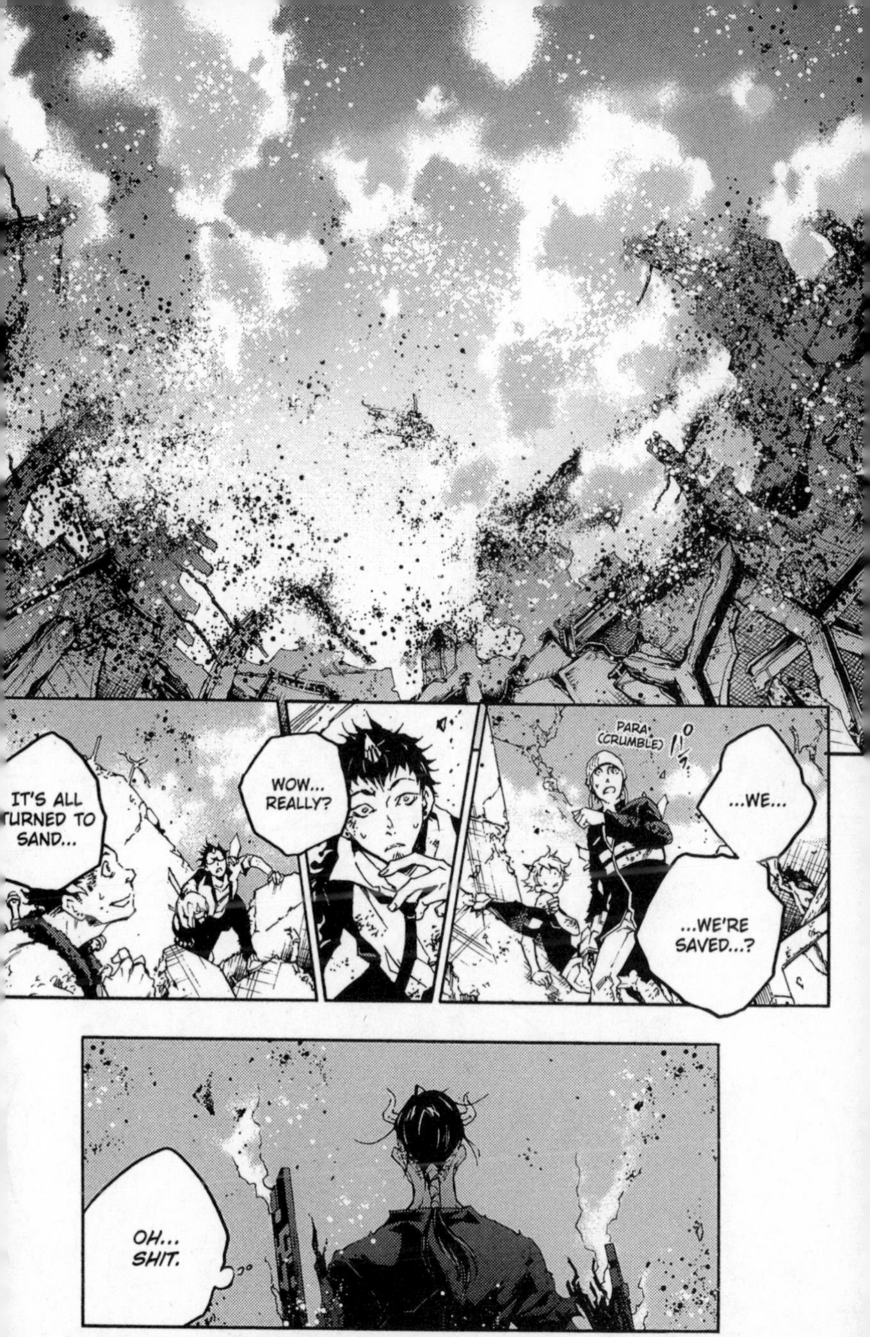
PARA (CRUMBLE)
...WE...
...WE'RE SAVED...?
WOW... REALLY?
IT'S ALL TURNED TO SAND...
OH... SHIT.

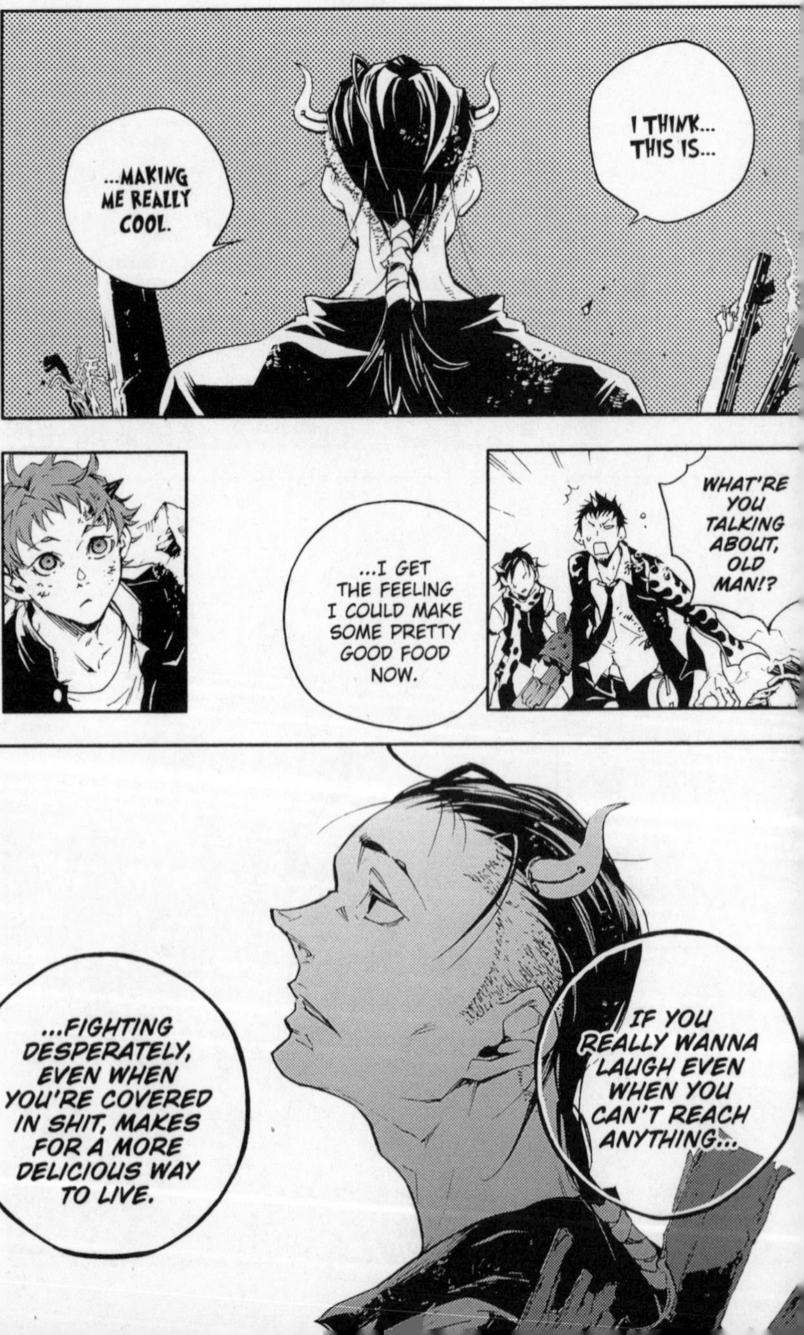
I THINK... THIS IS...
...MAKING ME REALLY COOL.
WHAT'RE YOU TALKING ABOUT, OLD MAN!?
...I GET THE FEELING I COULD MAKE SOME PRETTY GOOD FOOD NOW.
IF YOU REALLY WANNA LAUGH EVEN WHEN YOU CAN'T REACH ANYTHING...
...FIGHTING DESPERATELY, EVEN WHEN YOU'RE COVERED IN SHIT, MAKES FOR A MORE DELICIOUS WAY TO LIVE.

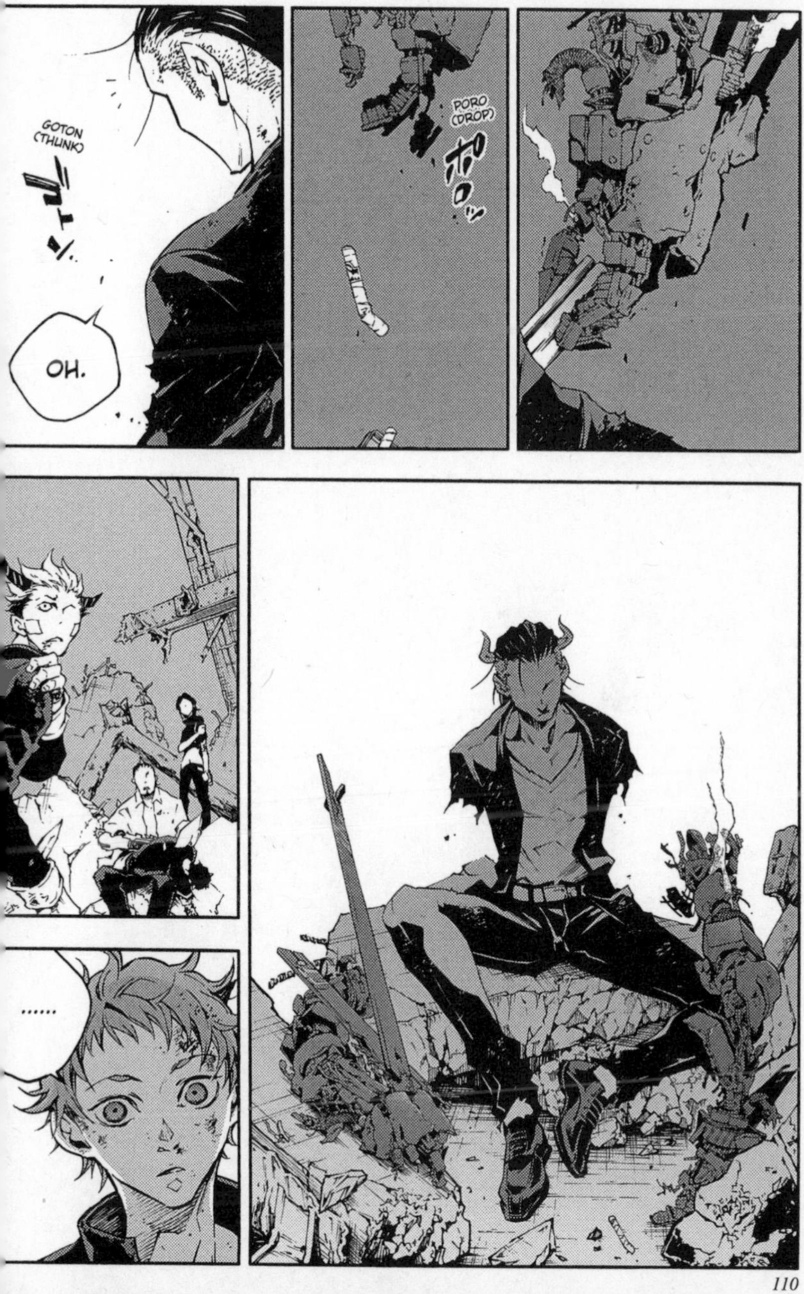
PORO (DROP)
GOTON (THUNK)
OH.
......

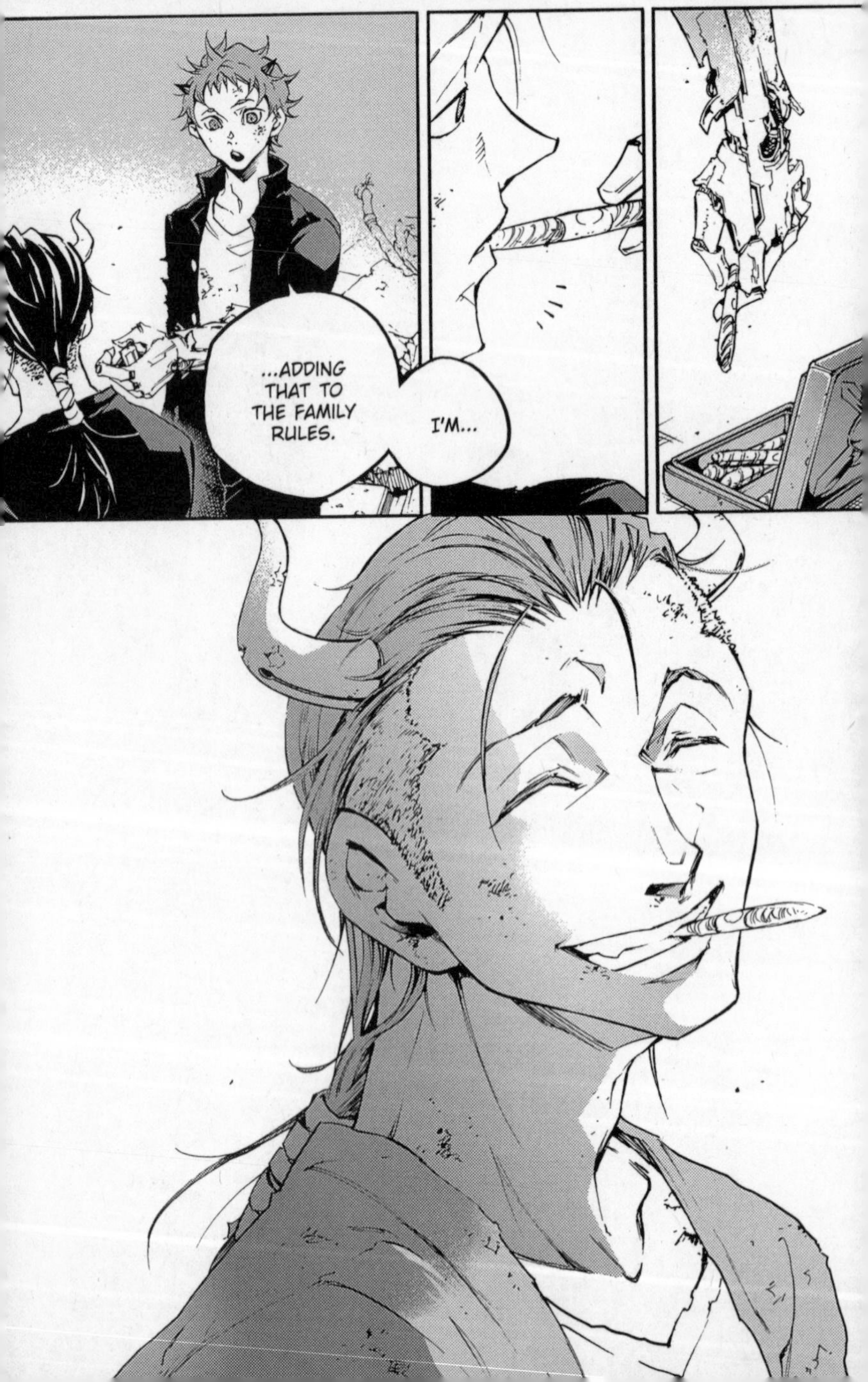
I'M...
...ADDING THAT TO THE FAMILY RULES.

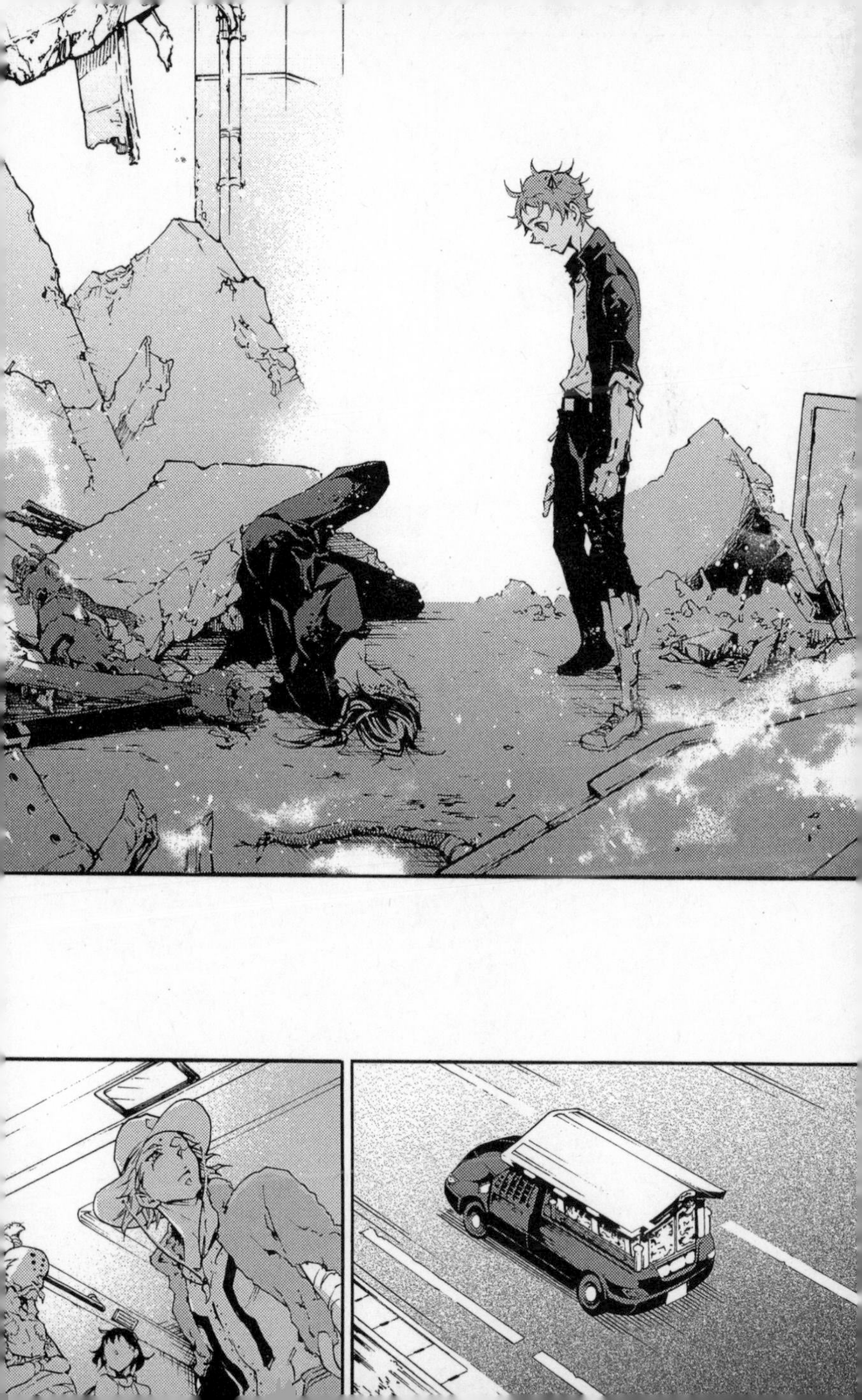

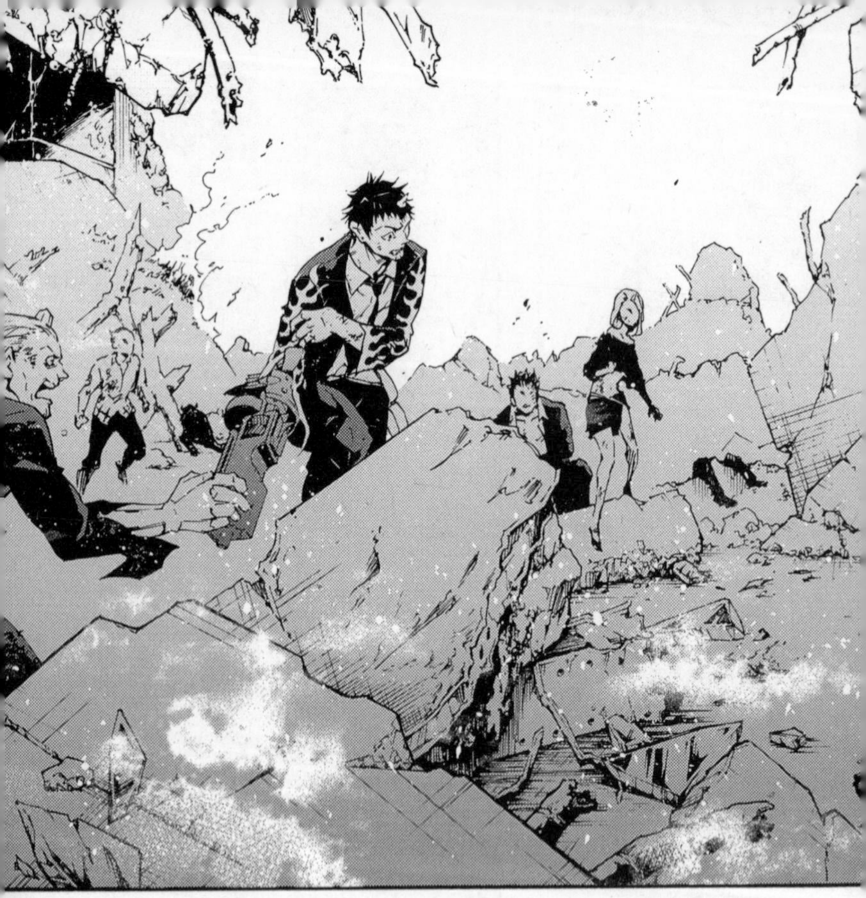
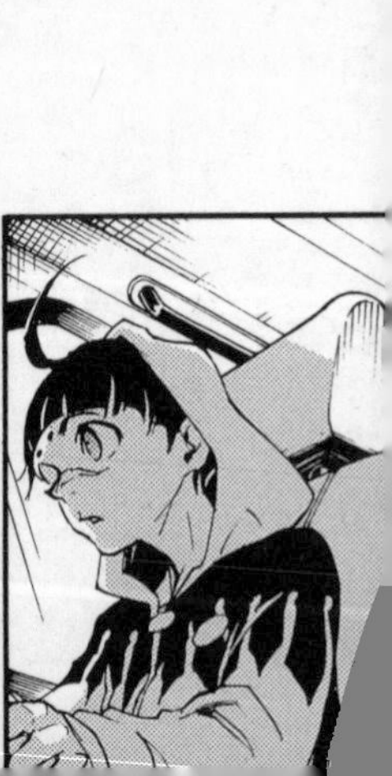
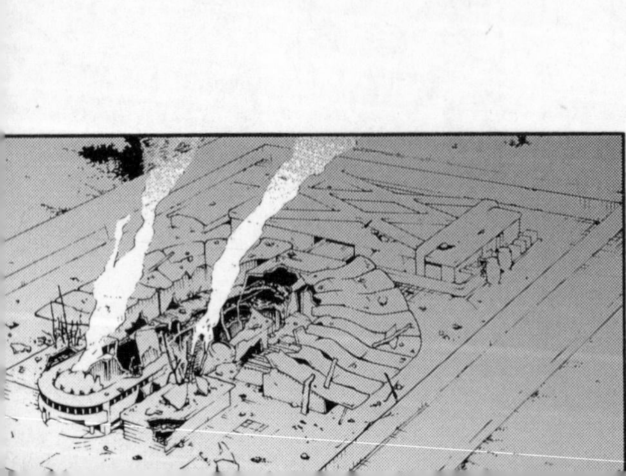

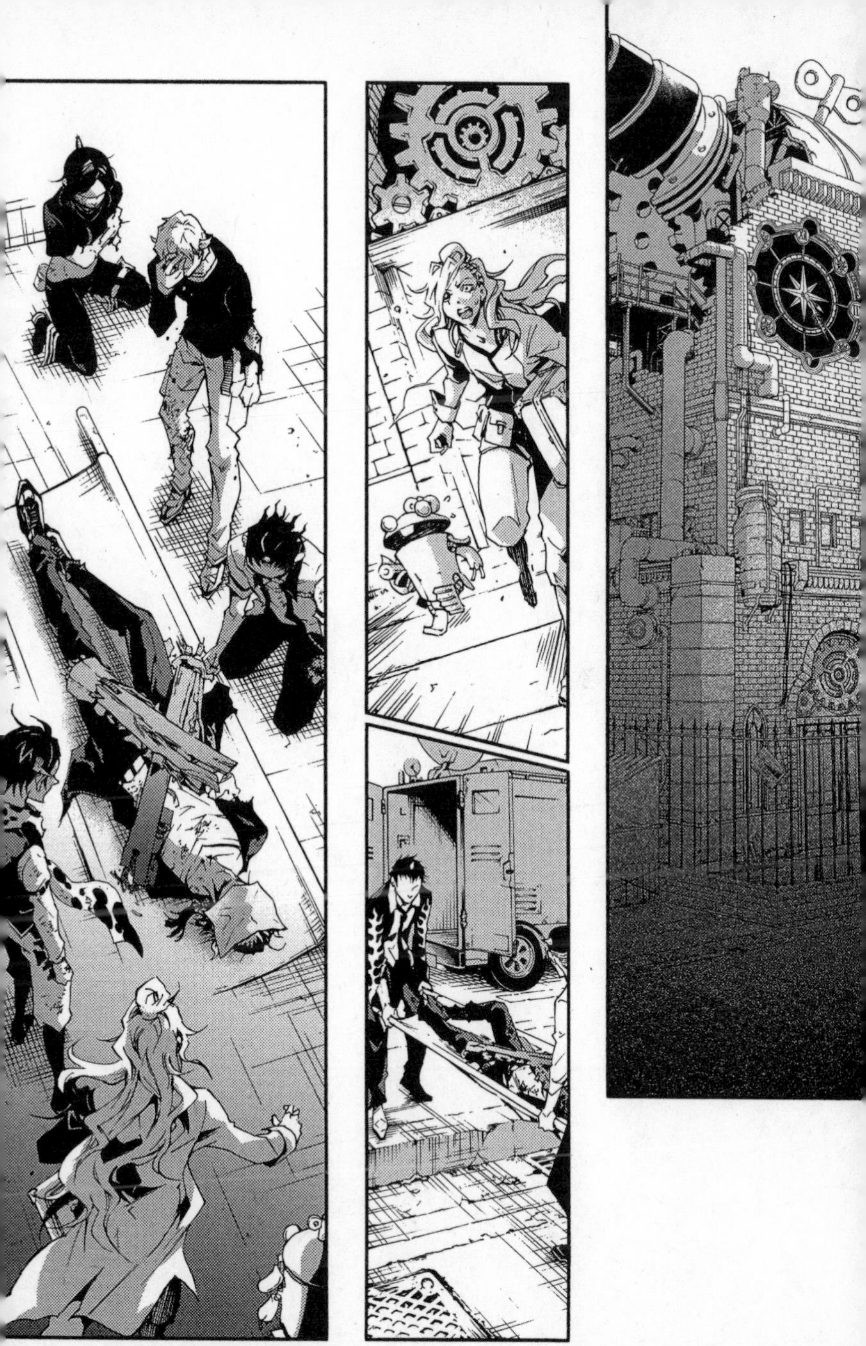

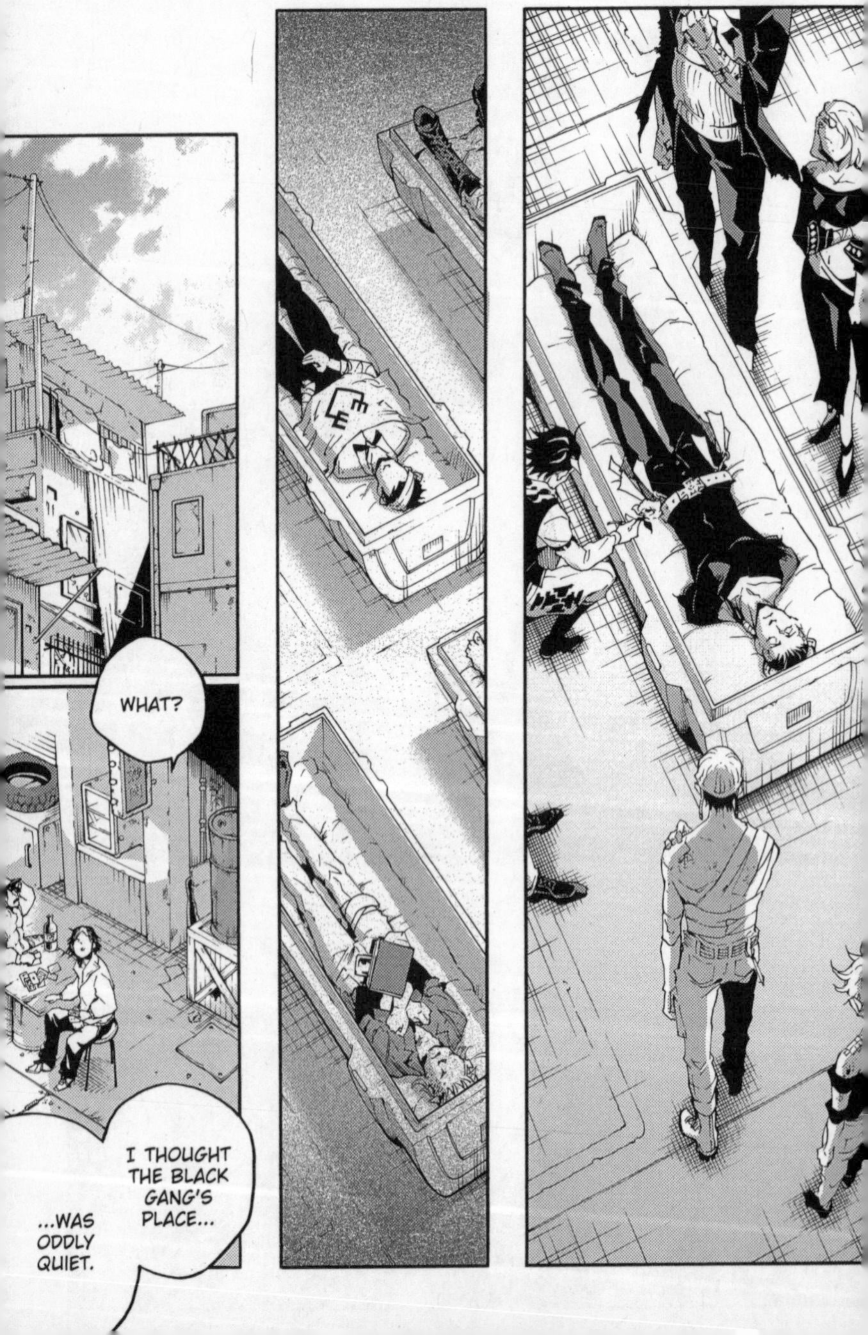
WHAT?
I THOUGHT THE BLACK GANG'S PLACE...
...WAS ODDLY QUIET.

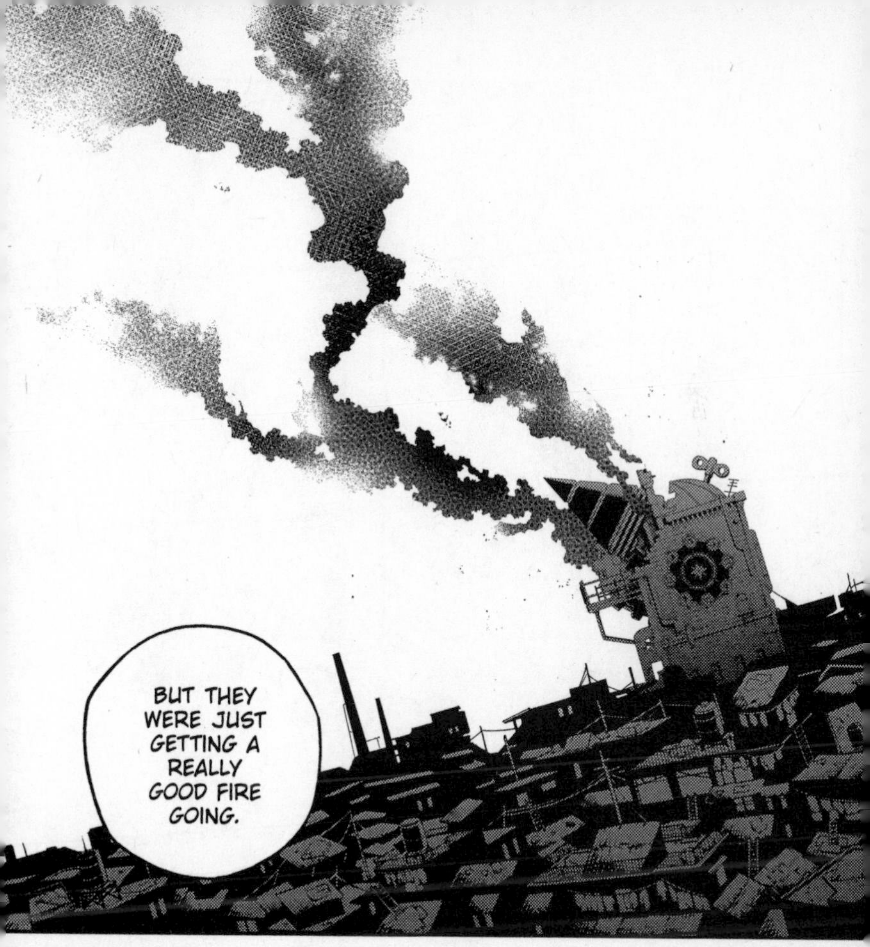
BUT THEY WERE JUST GETTING A REALLY GOOD FIRE GOING.

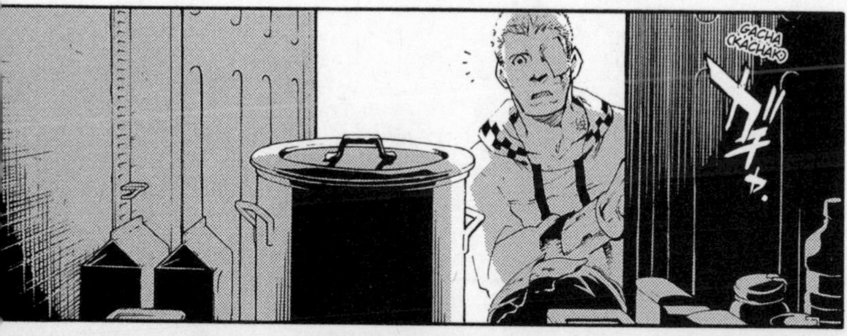
GACHA (KACHAK)

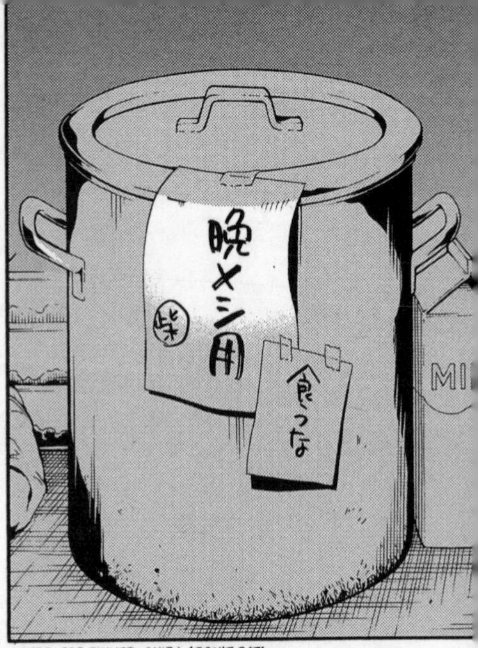
晩メシ用
柴
食うな
MI
NOTES: FOR DINNER–SHIBA / DON'T EAT!

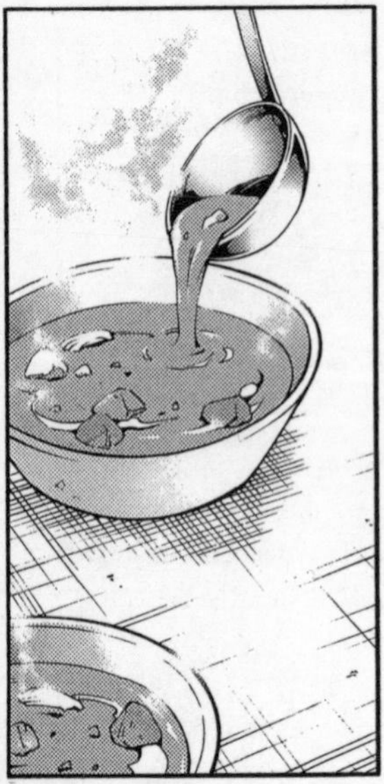

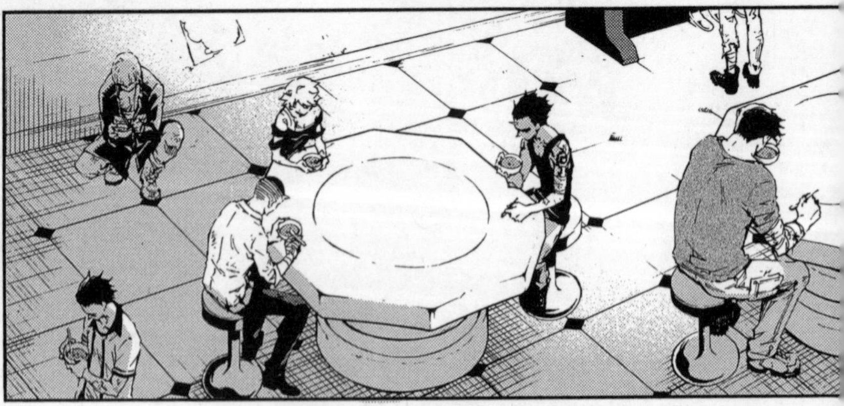

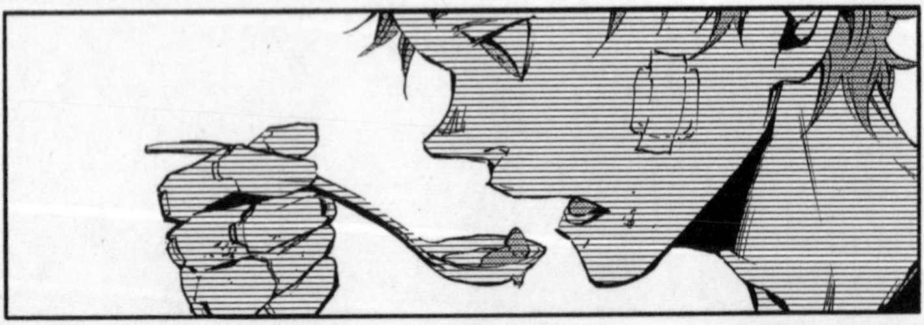

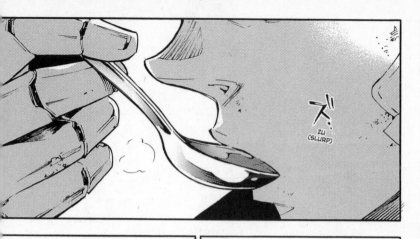

ズ
ZU
(SLURP)

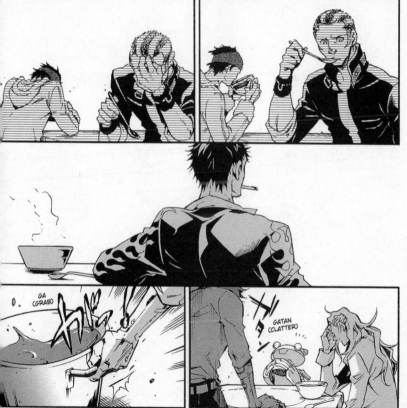

GA
(GRAB)

GATAN
(CLATTER)

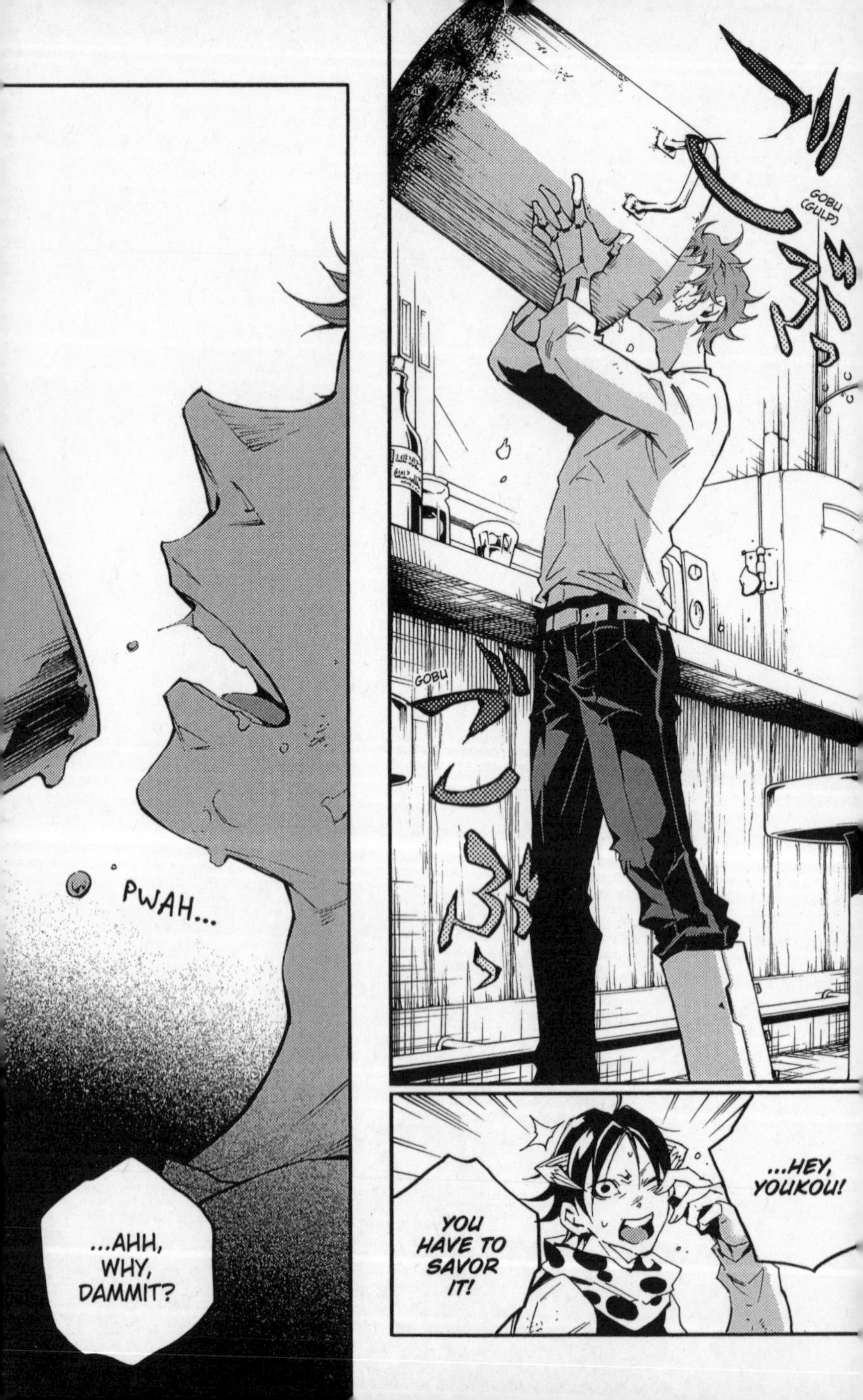
GOBU (GULP)
GOBU
...HEY, YOUKOU!
YOU HAVE TO SAVOR IT!
PWAH...
...AHH, WHY, DAMMIT?

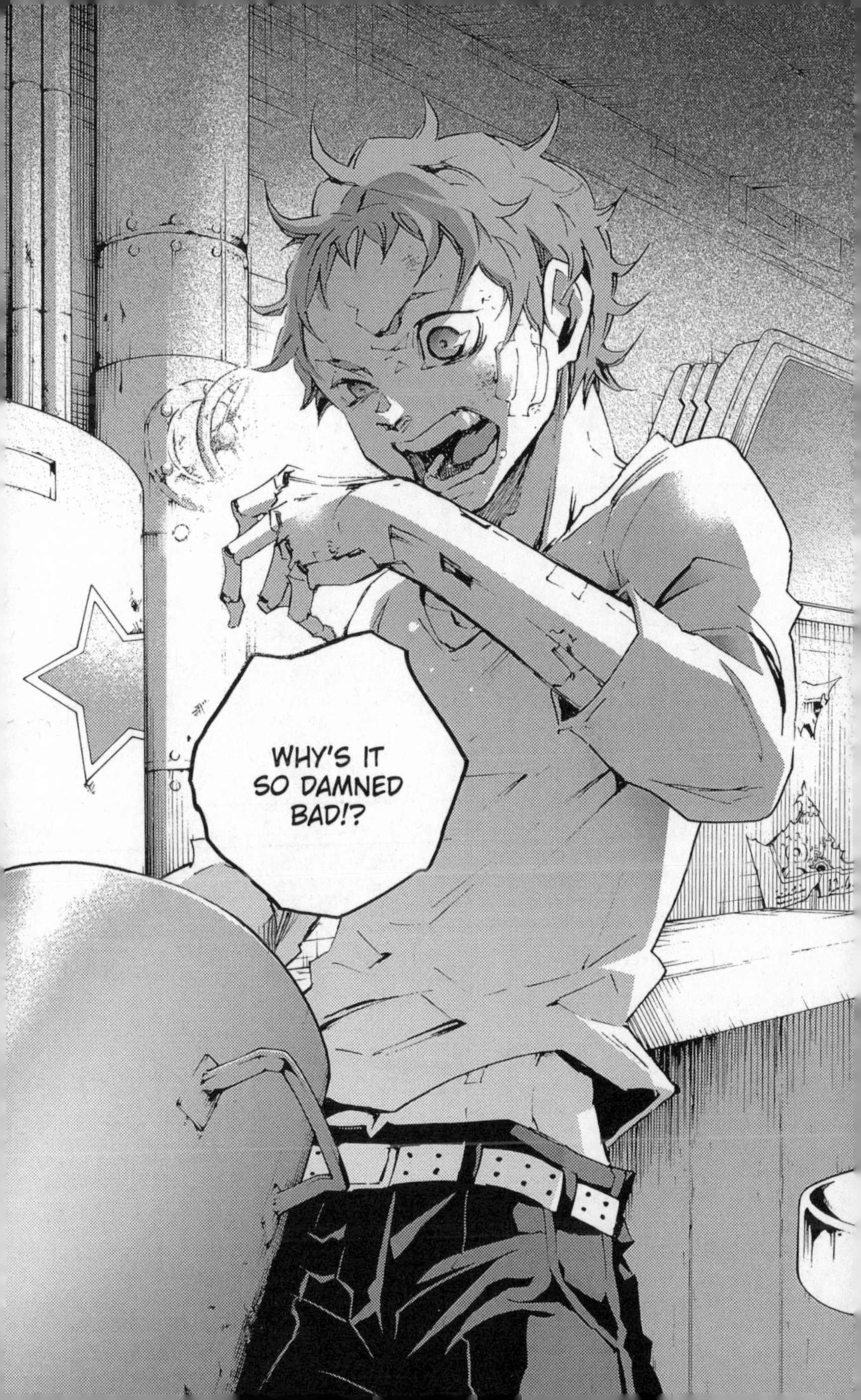
WHY'S IT SO DAMNED BAD!?

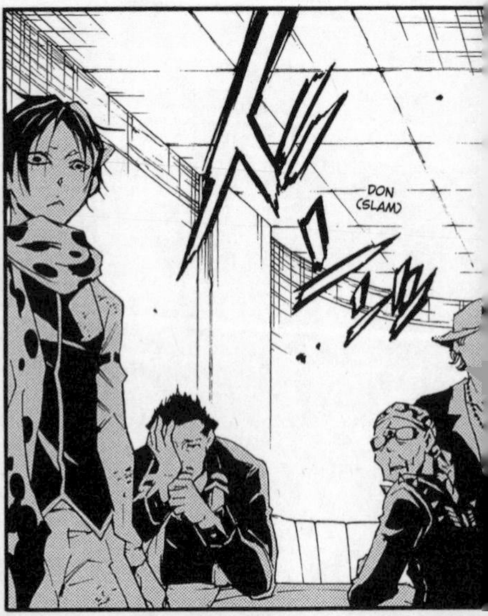
DON
(SLAM)

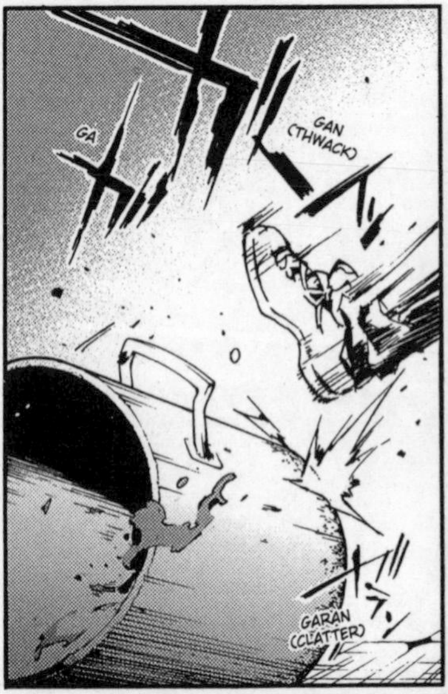
GAN
(THWACK)
GA
GARAN
(CLATTER)

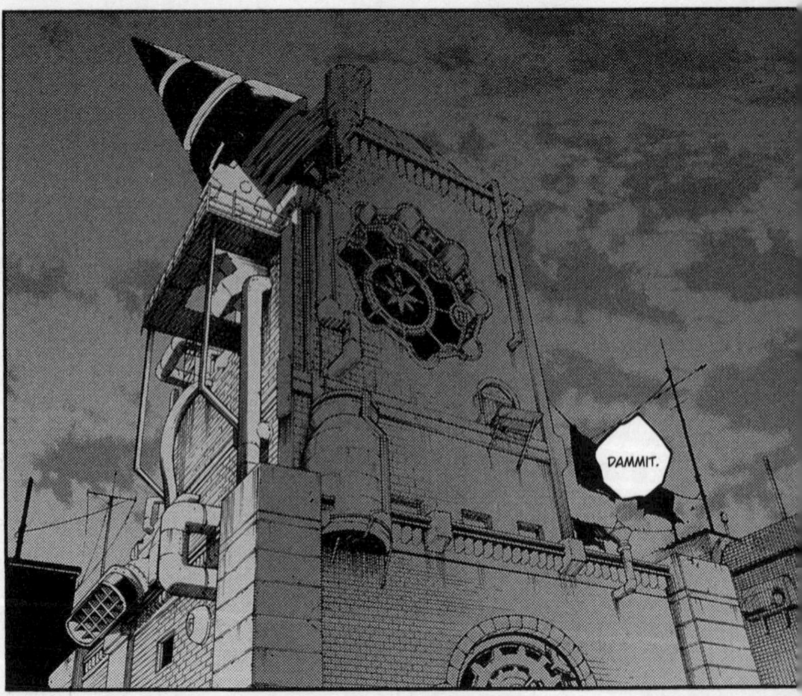
DAMMIT.

SMOKIN'

JINSEI KATAOKA
KAZUMA KONDOU

PARADE

THE WORLD IS DEAD.
THE PARADE WILL START.

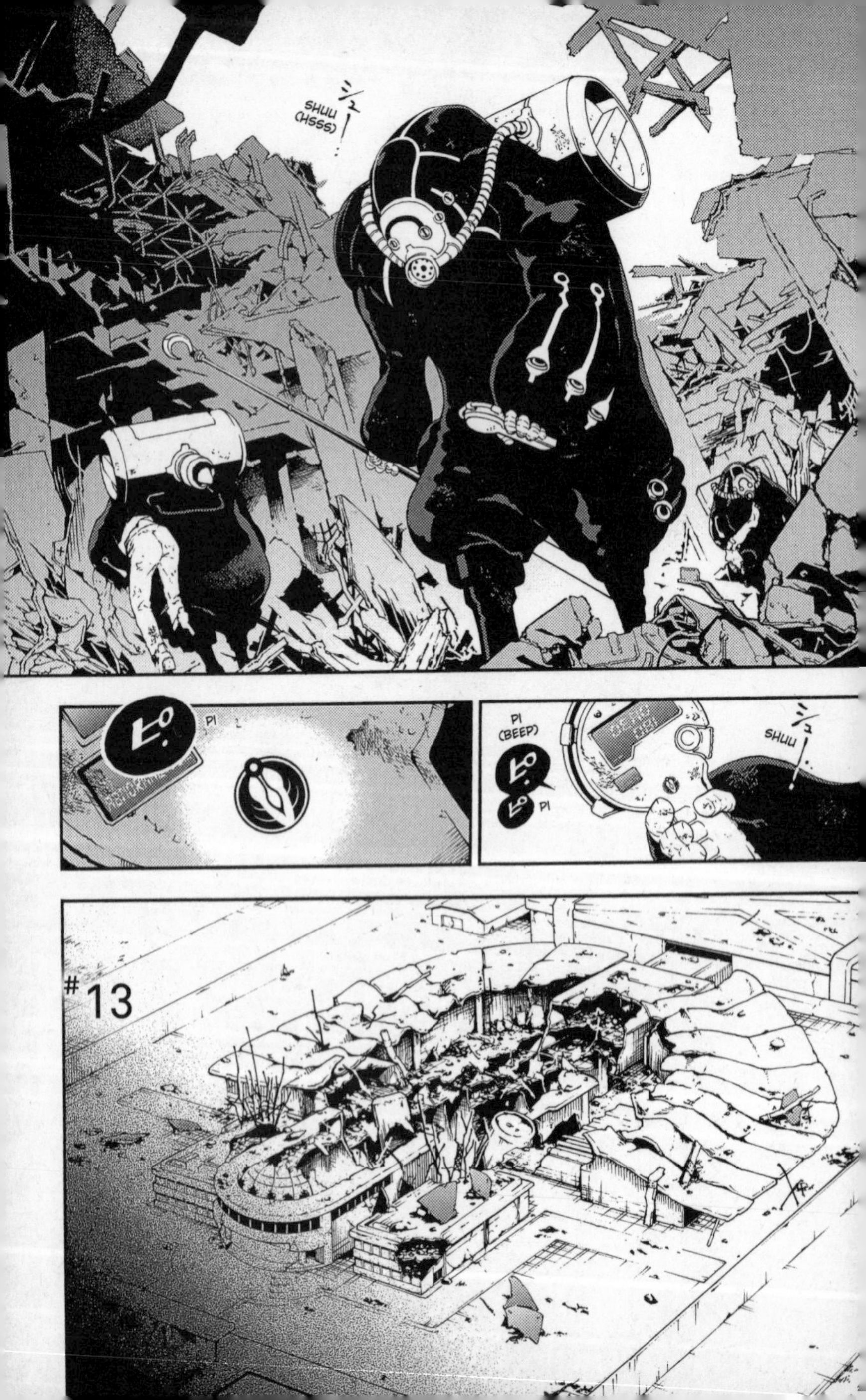

シュ
SHUU (HSSS)
シュ
SHUU
ピ
PI (BEEP)
ピ
PI
ピ
PI
#13

#13
OPPOSING WORLDS

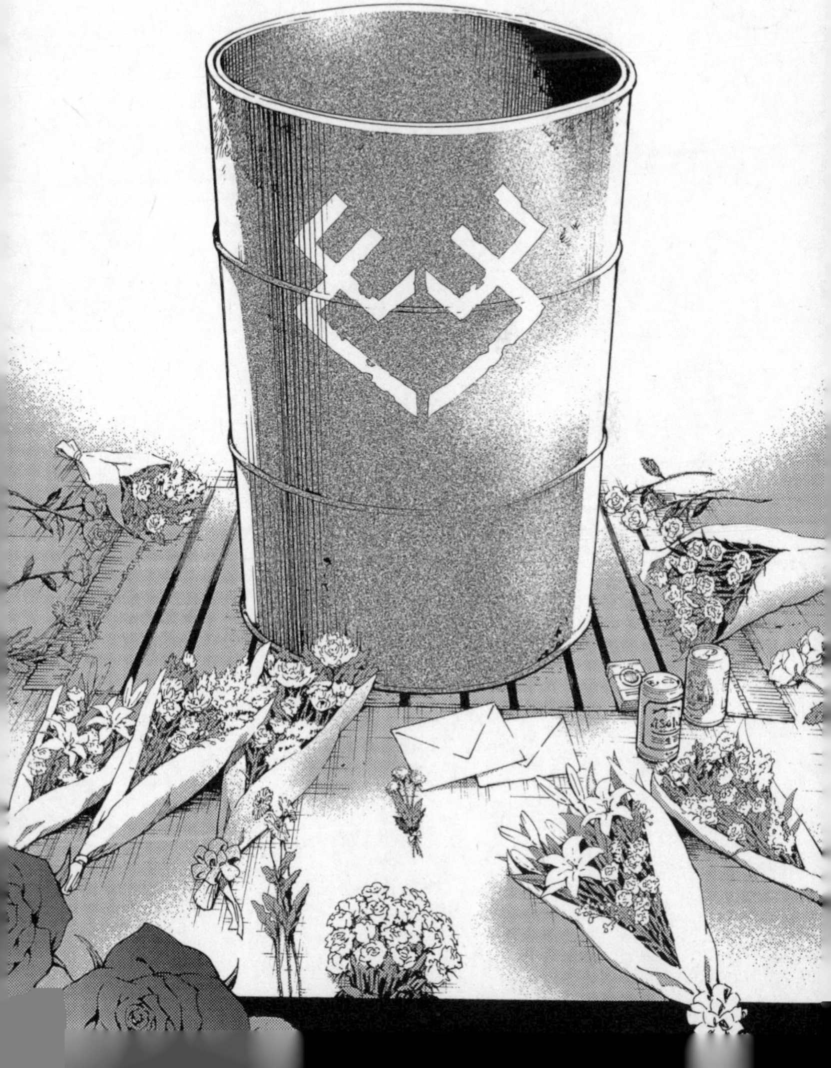

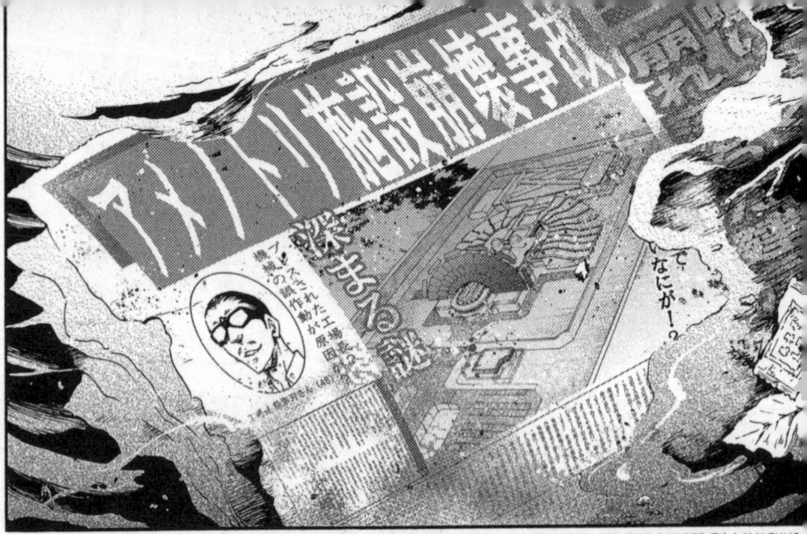
でなにが!?

PAPER: AMENOTORI FACILITY COLLAPSES / THE DEEPENING MYSTERY / FOREMAN CRUSHED? WAS THIS CAUSED BY A MALFUNCTION?

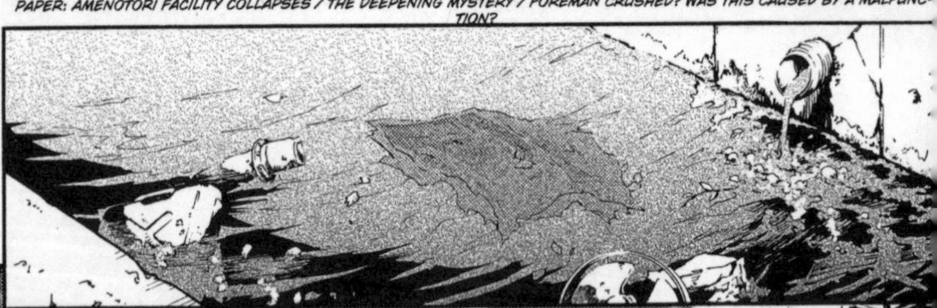

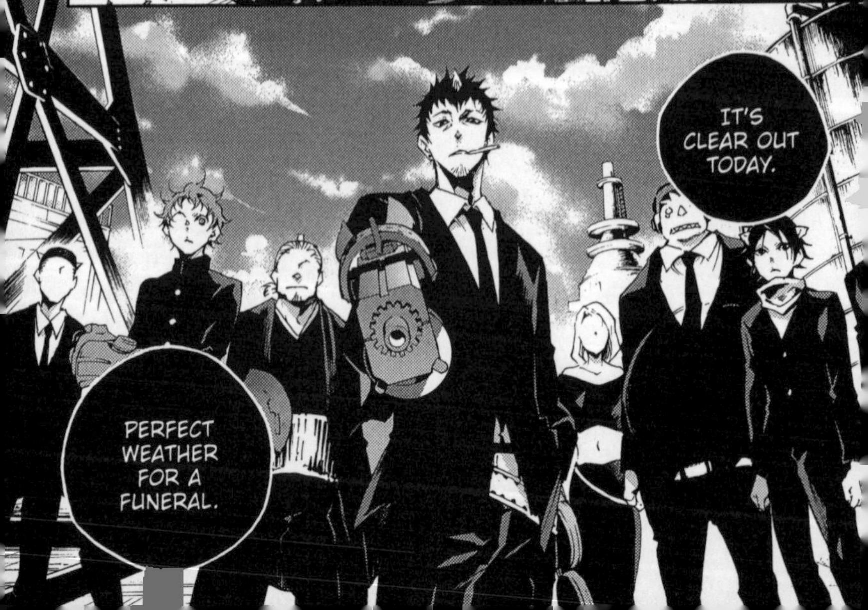
IT'S CLEAR OUT TODAY.
PERFECT WEATHER FOR A FUNERAL.

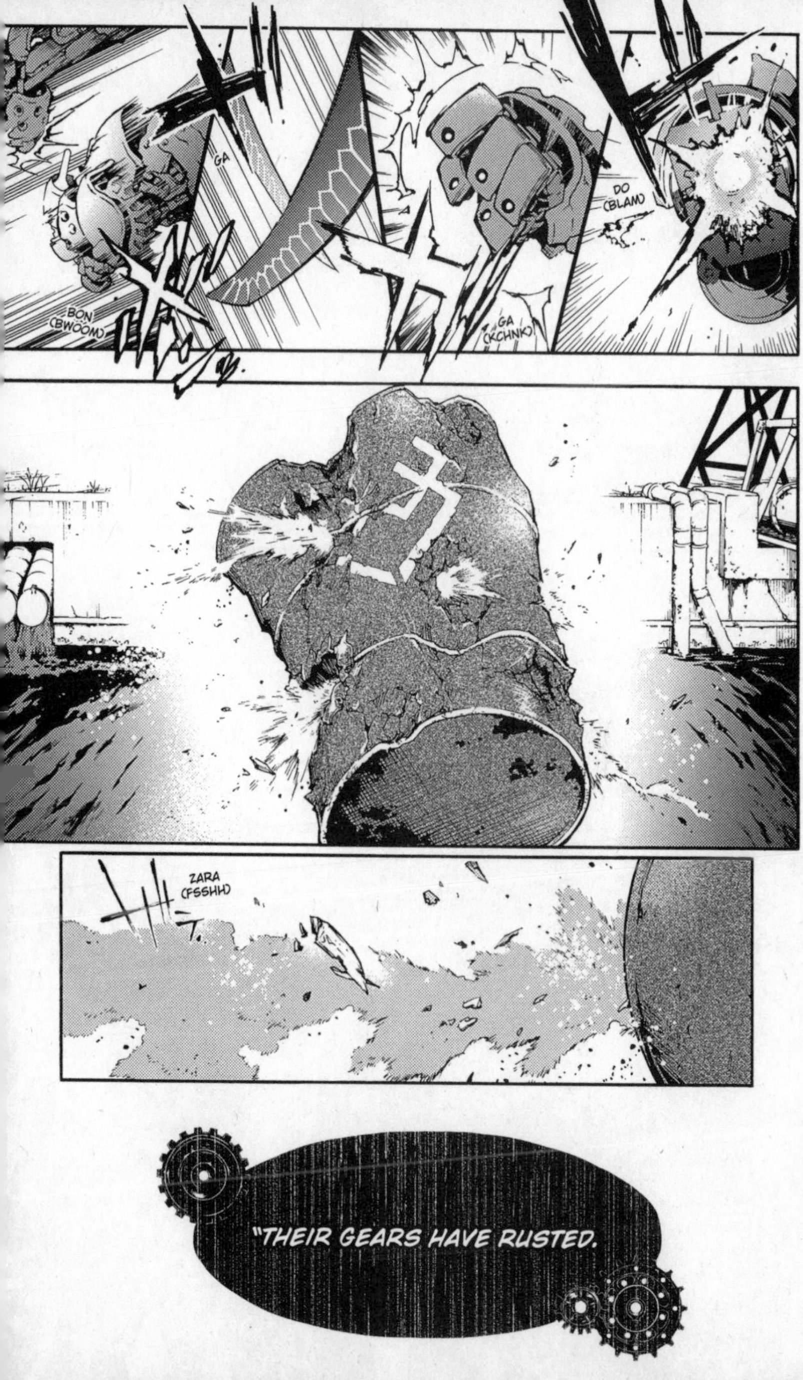
DO (BLAM)
GA (KCHNK)
GA
BON (BWOOM)
ZARA (FSSHH)
"THEIR GEARS HAVE RUSTED.

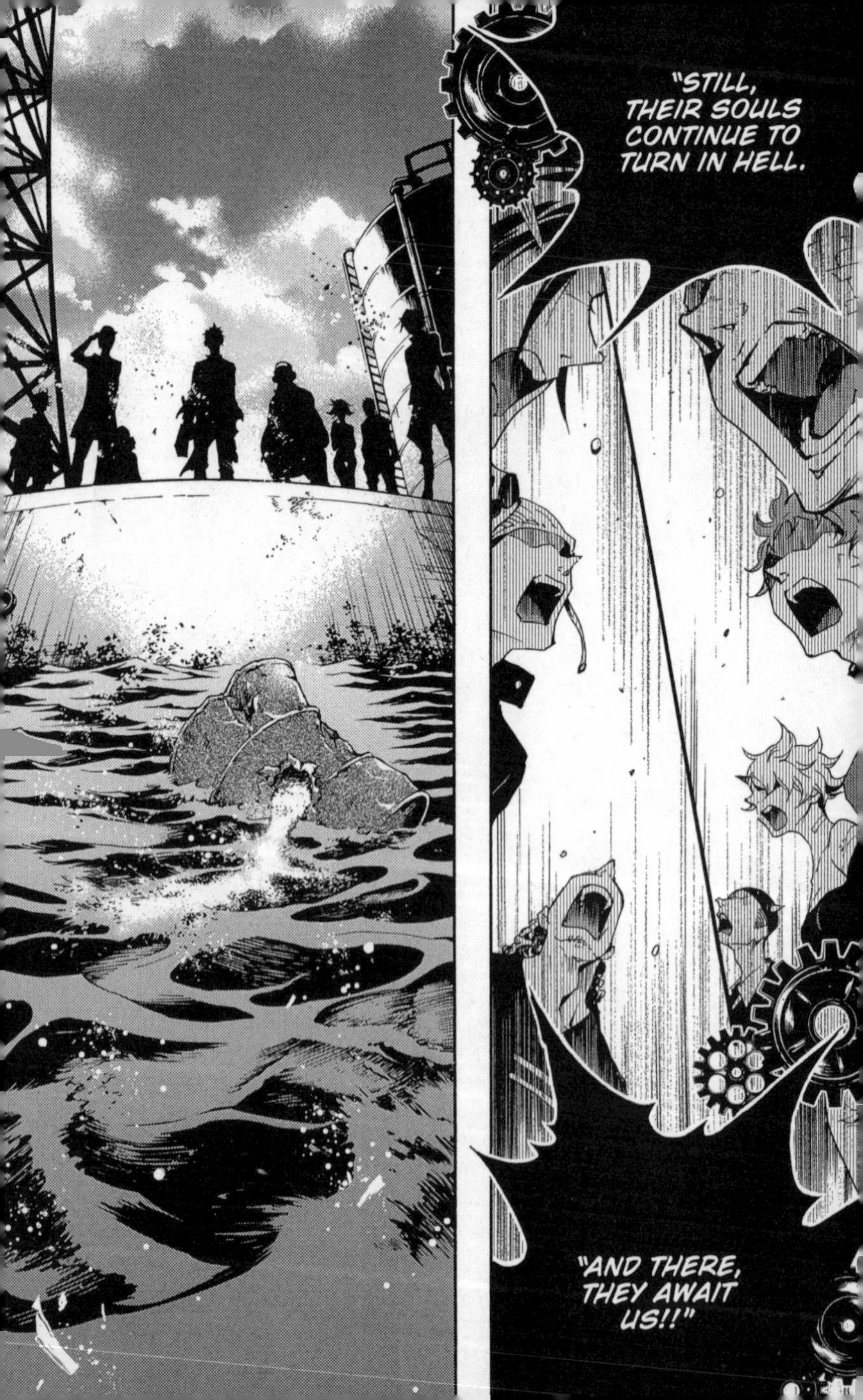
"STILL, THEIR SOULS CONTINUE TO TURN IN HELL.
"AND THERE, THEY AWAIT US!!"

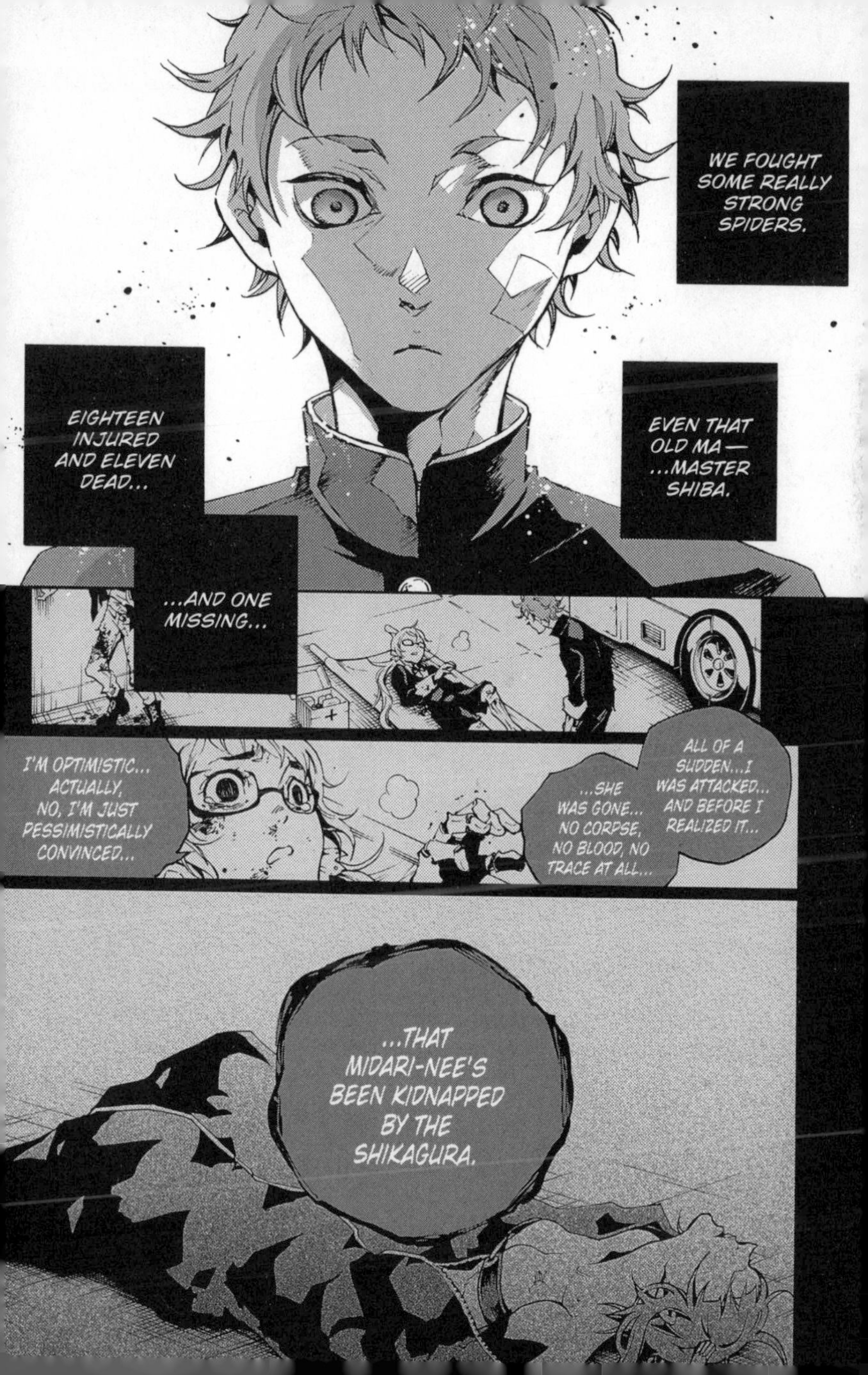
WE FOUGHT SOME REALLY STRONG SPIDERS.
EVEN THAT OLD MA— ...MASTER SHIBA.
EIGHTEEN INJURED AND ELEVEN DEAD...
...AND ONE MISSING...
ALL OF A SUDDEN...I WAS ATTACKED... AND BEFORE I REALIZED IT...
...SHE WAS GONE... NO CORPSE, NO BLOOD, NO TRACE AT ALL...
I'M OPTIMISTIC... ACTUALLY, NO, I'M JUST PESSIMISTICALLY CONVINCED...
...THAT MIDARI-NEE'S BEEN KIDNAPPED BY THE SHIKAGURA.

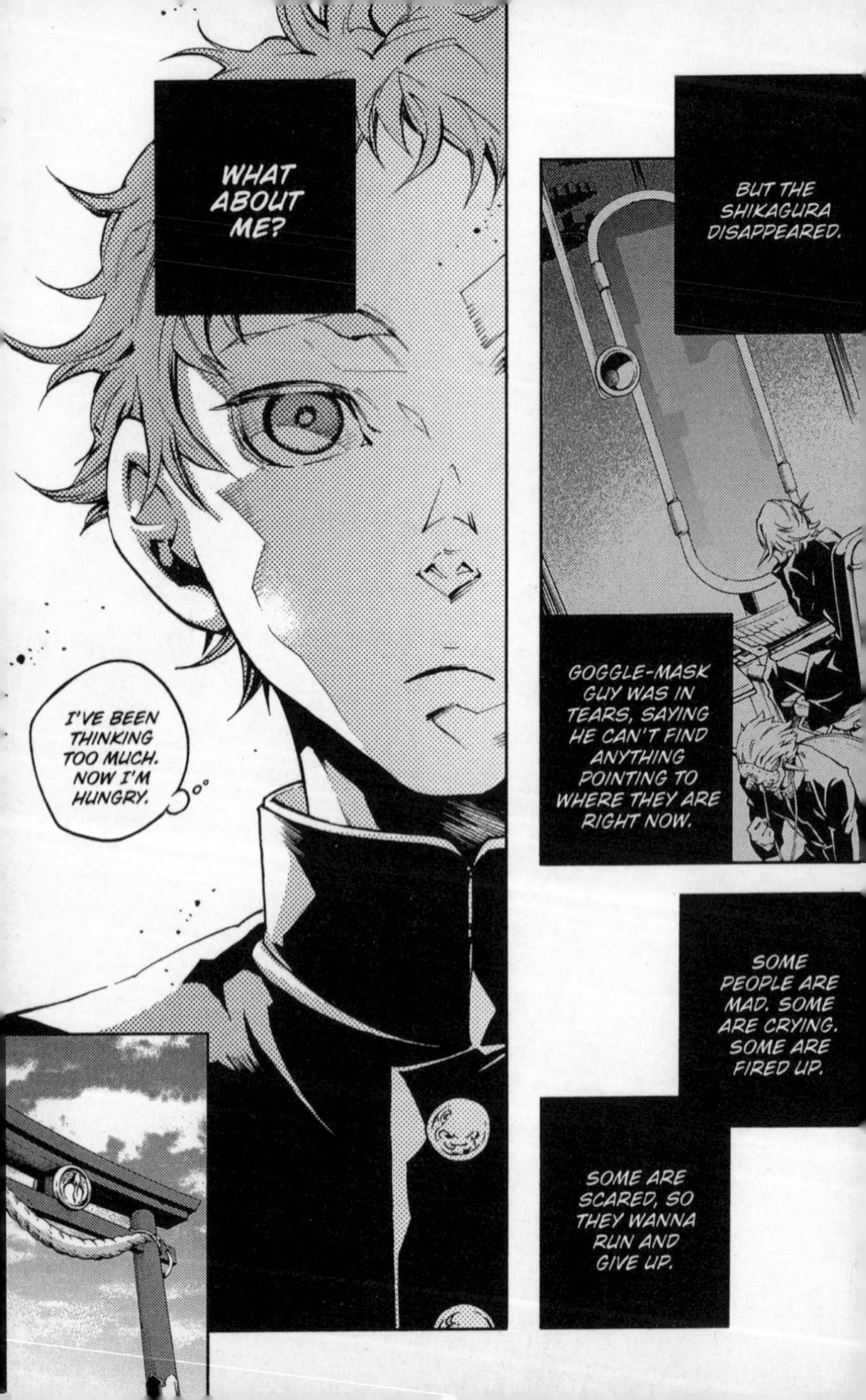
BUT THE SHIKAGURA DISAPPEARED.
GOGGLE-MASK GUY WAS IN TEARS, SAYING HE CAN'T FIND ANYTHING POINTING TO WHERE THEY ARE RIGHT NOW.
SOME PEOPLE ARE MAD. SOME ARE CRYING. SOME ARE FIRED UP.
SOME ARE SCARED, SO THEY WANNA RUN AND GIVE UP.
WHAT ABOUT ME?
I'VE BEEN THINKING TOO MUCH. NOW I'M HUNGRY.

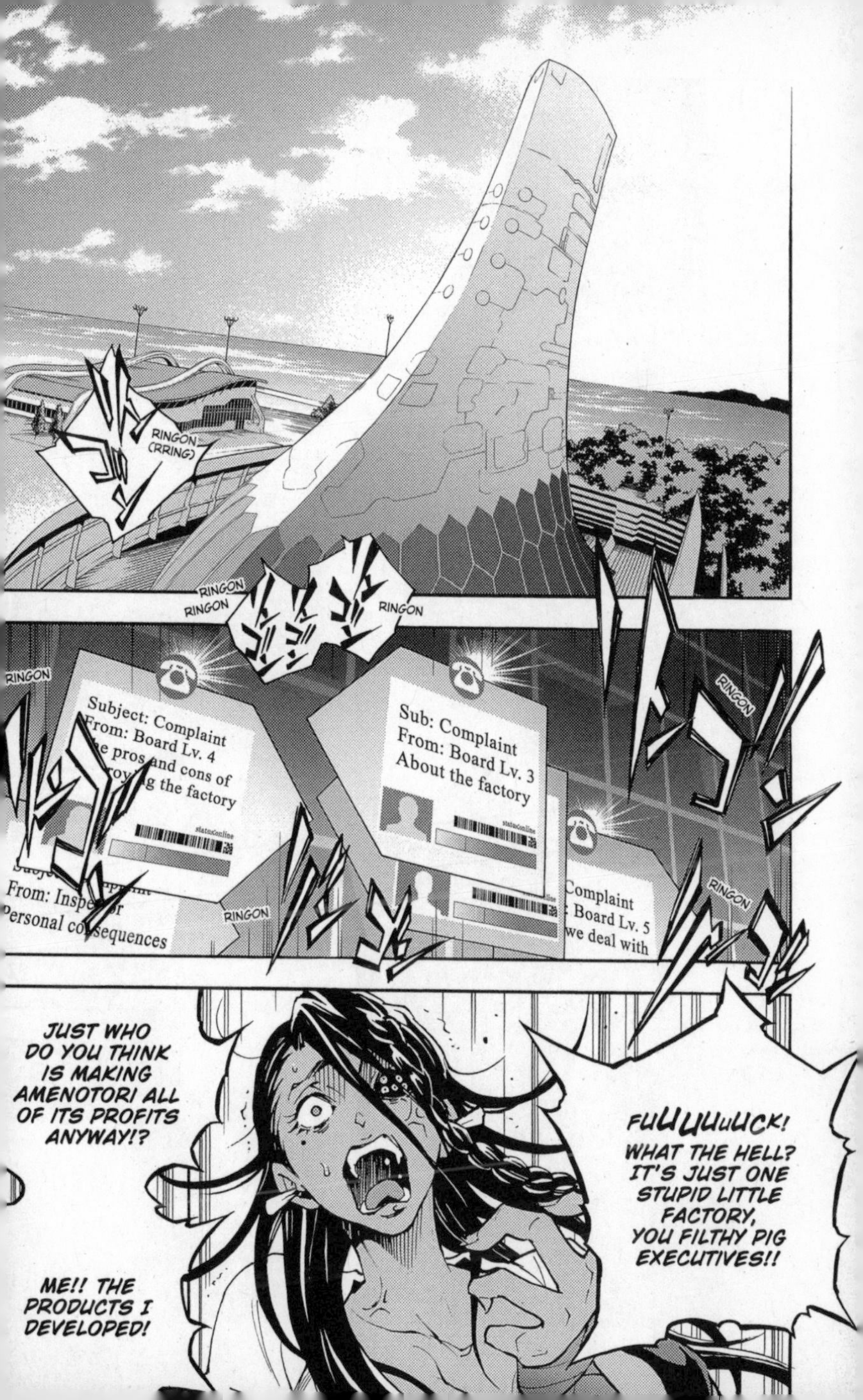
RINGON (RRING)
RINGON
RINGON
RINGON
RINGON
RINGON
Sub: Complaint
From: Board Lv. 3
About the factory
Subject: Complaint
From: Board Lv. 4
Complaint
Board Lv. 5
we deal with
From: Inspe
Personal co sequences
RINGON
RINGON
FUUUUUUCK! WHAT THE HELL? IT'S JUST ONE STUPID LITTLE FACTORY, YOU FILTHY PIG EXECUTIVES!!
JUST WHO DO YOU THINK IS MAKING AMENOTORI ALL OF ITS PROFITS ANYWAY!?
ME!! THE PRODUCTS I DEVELOPED!

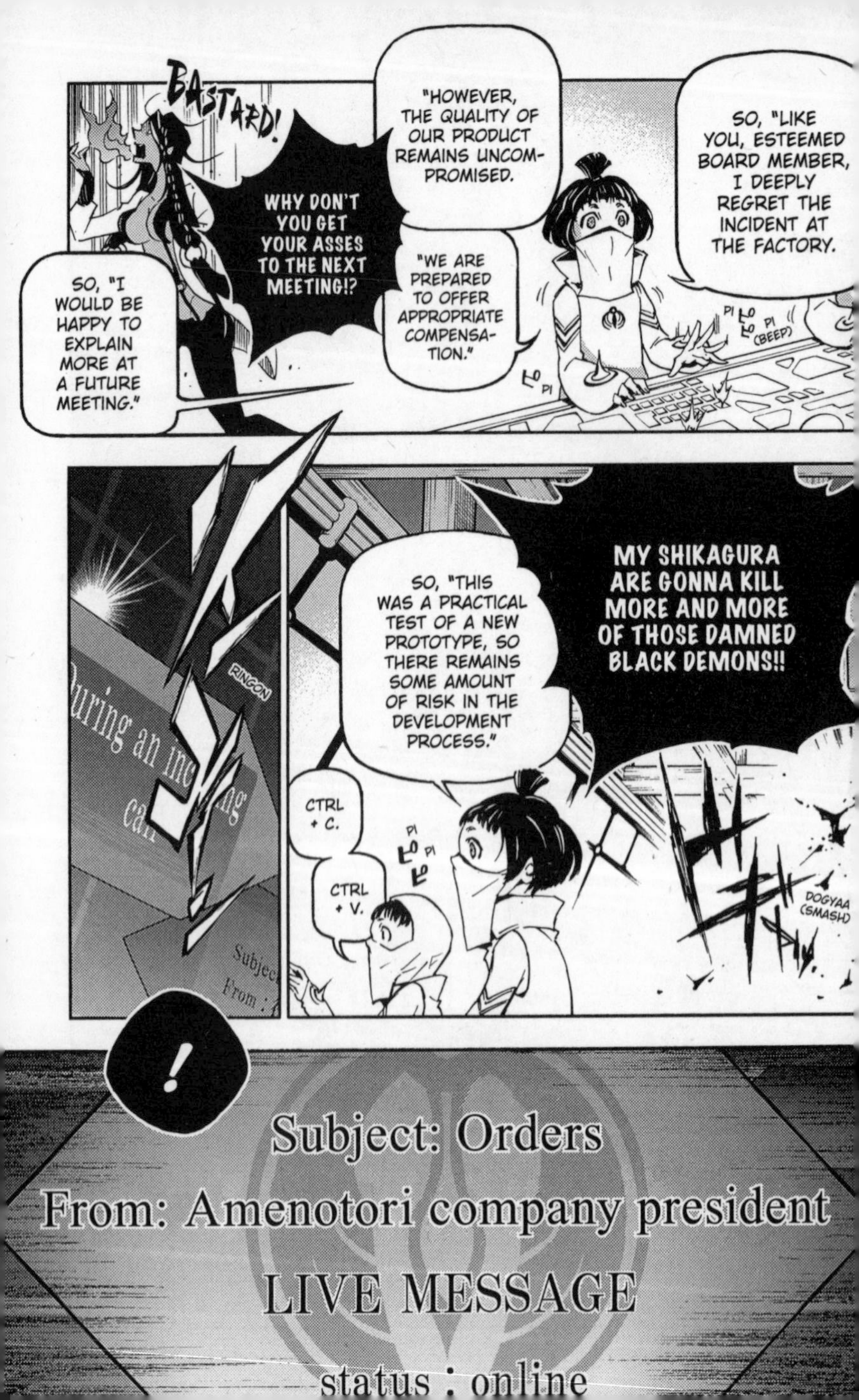

SO, "LIKE YOU, ESTEEMED BOARD MEMBER, I DEEPLY REGRET THE INCIDENT AT THE FACTORY.
"HOWEVER, THE QUALITY OF OUR PRODUCT REMAINS UNCOMPROMISED.
PI PI (BEEP)
"WE ARE PREPARED TO OFFER APPROPRIATE COMPENSATION."
PI
BASTARD!
WHY DON'T YOU GET YOUR ASSES TO THE NEXT MEETING!?
SO, "I WOULD BE HAPPY TO EXPLAIN MORE AT A FUTURE MEETING."
MY SHIKAGURA ARE GONNA KILL MORE AND MORE OF THOSE DAMNED BLACK DEMONS!!
SO, "THIS WAS A PRACTICAL TEST OF A NEW PROTOTYPE, SO THERE REMAINS SOME AMOUNT OF RISK IN THE DEVELOPMENT PROCESS."
DOGYAA (SMASH)
CTRL + C.
PI PI
CTRL + V.
RINGON
!
Subject: Orders
From: Amenotori company president
LIVE MESSAGE
status : online

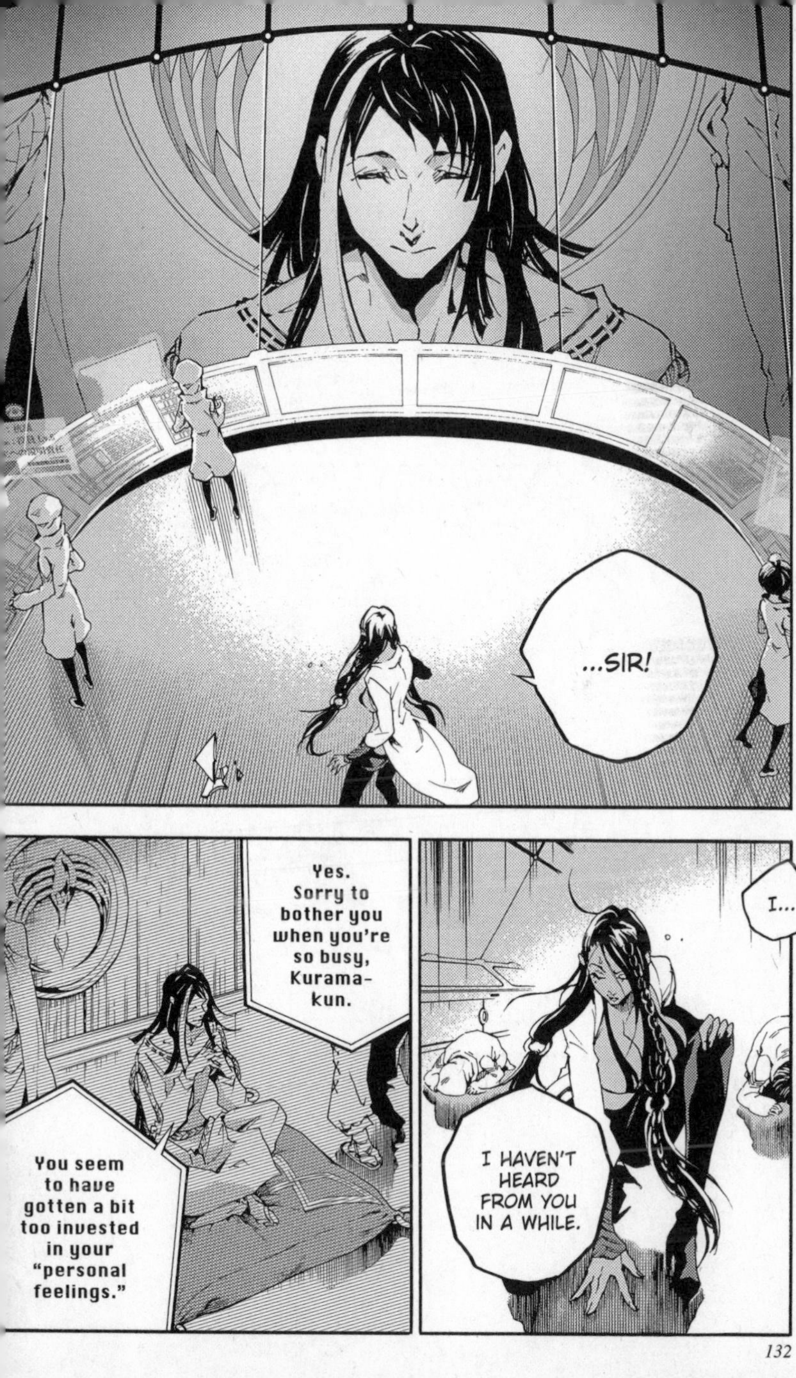
...SIR!
I...
I HAVEN'T HEARD FROM YOU IN A WHILE.
Yes. Sorry to bother you when you're so busy, Kurama-kun.
You seem to have gotten a bit too invested in your "personal feelings."

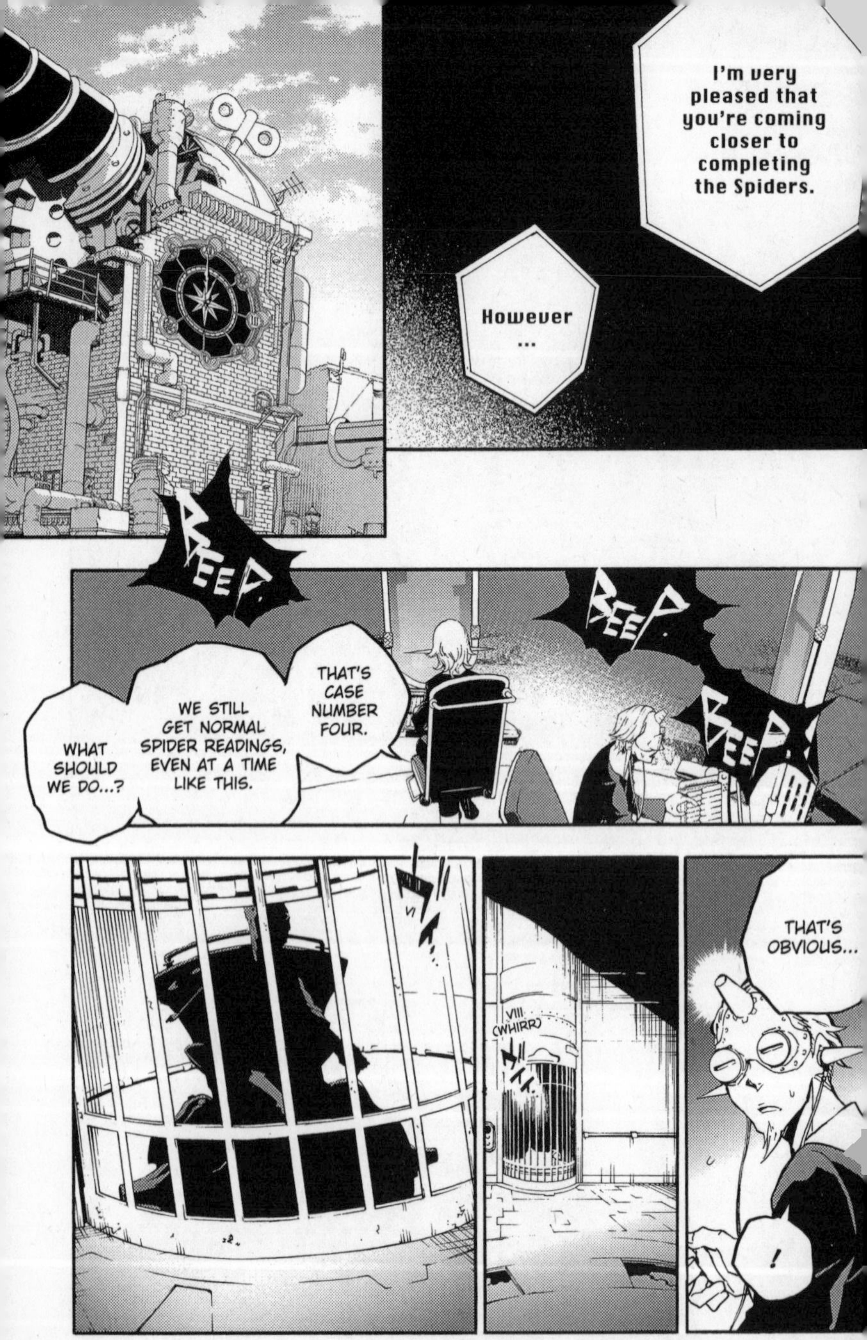

I'm very pleased that you're coming closer to completing the Spiders.
However ...
BEEP
BEEP
THAT'S CASE NUMBER FOUR.
WE STILL GET NORMAL SPIDER READINGS, EVEN AT A TIME LIKE THIS.
WHAT SHOULD WE DO...?
BEEP
THAT'S OBVIOUS...
!
(WHIRR)

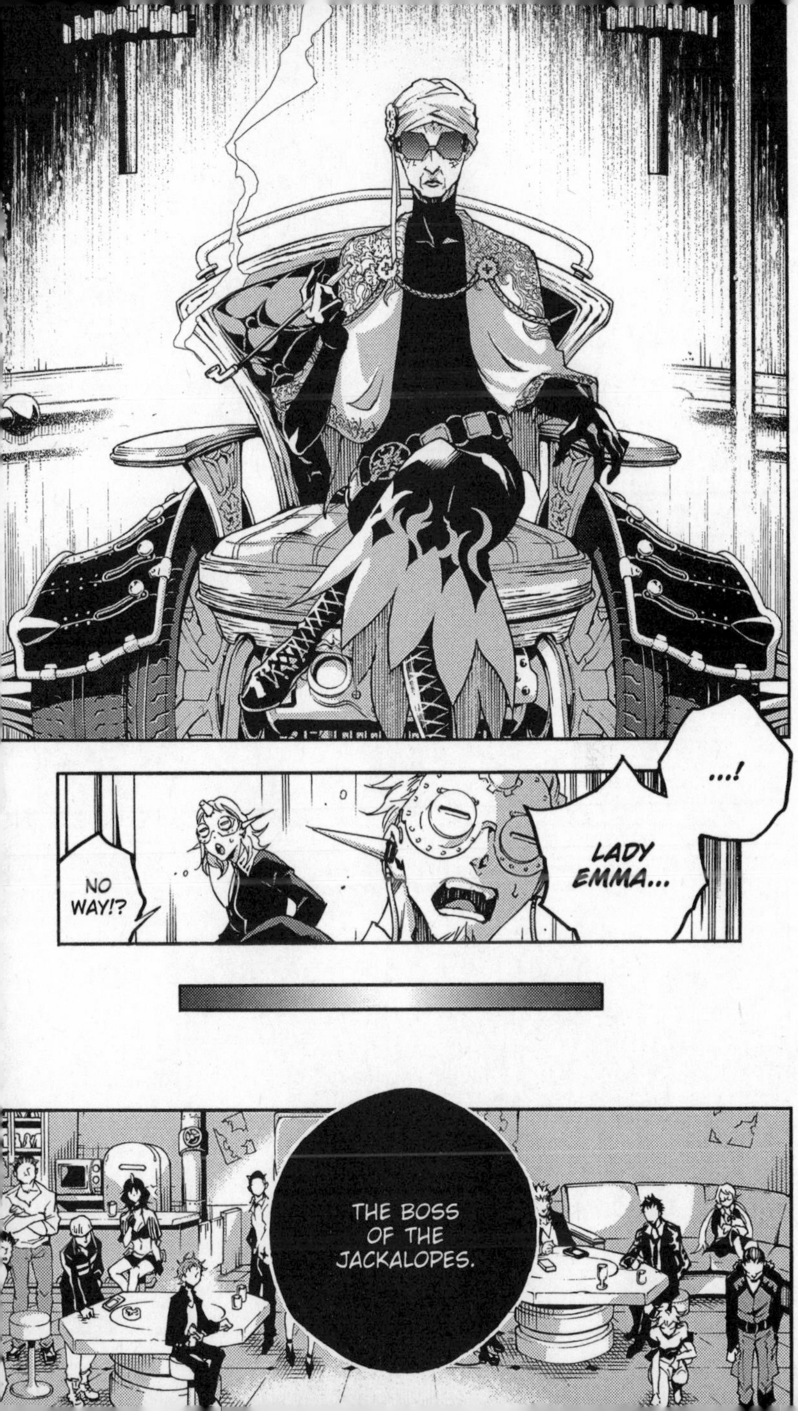
...!
LADY EMMA...
NO WAY!?
THE BOSS OF THE JACKALOPES.

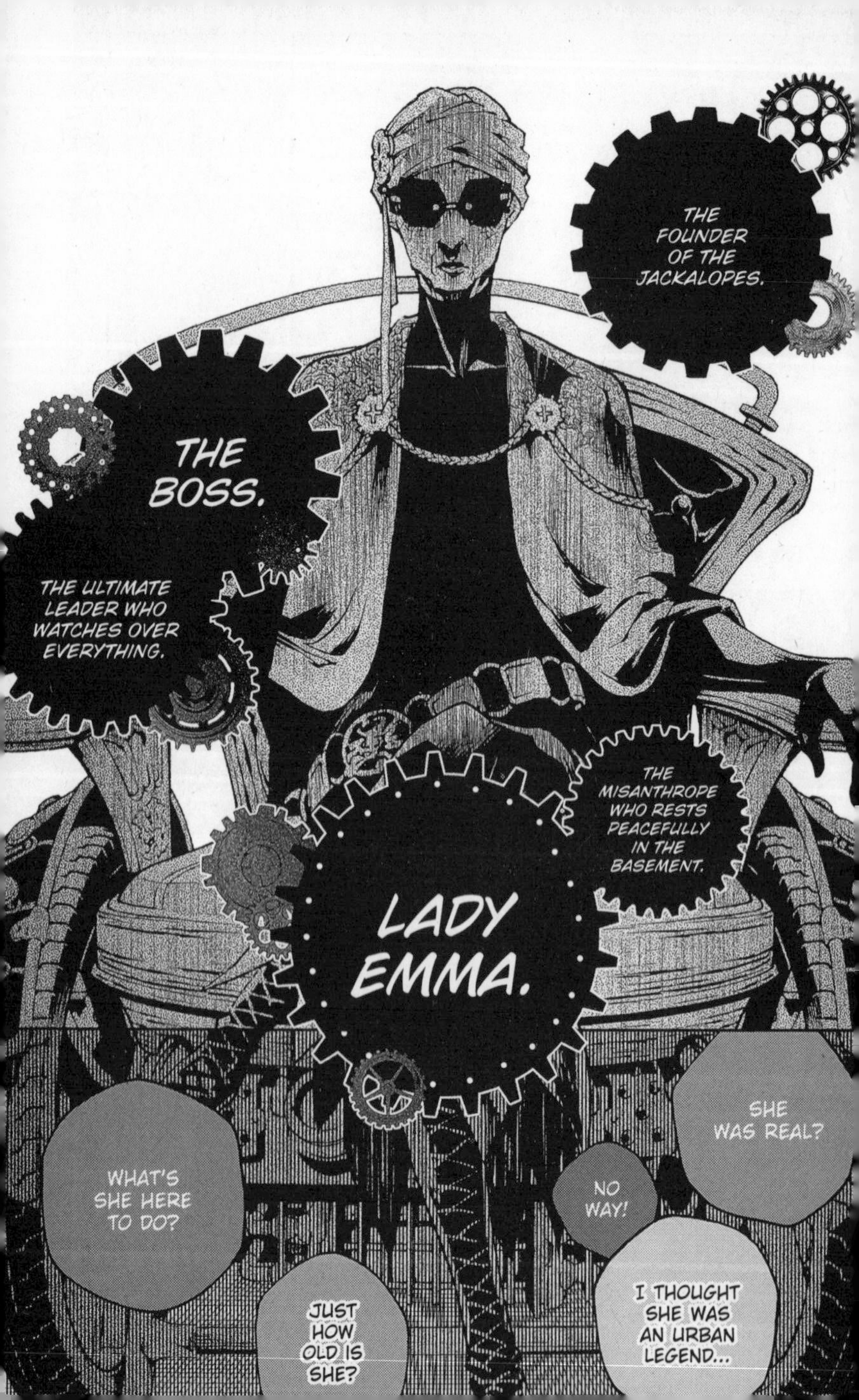
THE FOUNDER OF THE JACKALOPES.
THE BOSS.
THE ULTIMATE LEADER WHO WATCHES OVER EVERYTHING.
THE MISANTHROPE WHO RESTS PEACEFULLY IN THE BASEMENT.
LADY EMMA.
SHE WAS REAL?
NO WAY!
I THOUGHT SHE WAS AN URBAN LEGEND...
WHAT'S SHE HERE TO DO?
JUST HOW OLD IS SHE?

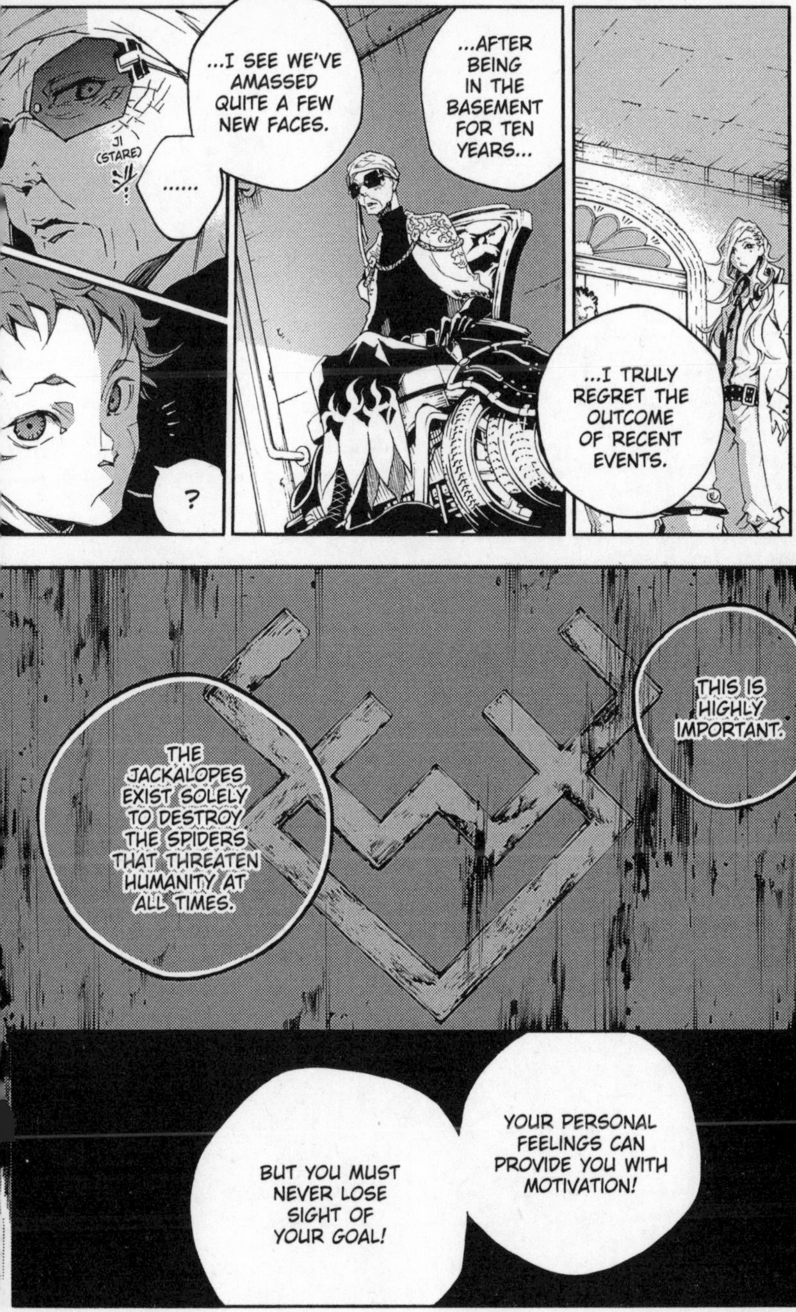
...I TRULY REGRET THE OUTCOME OF RECENT EVENTS.
...AFTER BEING IN THE BASEMENT FOR TEN YEARS...
...I SEE WE'VE AMASSED QUITE A FEW NEW FACES.
JI (STARE)
......
?
THIS IS HIGHLY IMPORTANT.
THE JACKALOPES EXIST SOLELY TO DESTROY THE SPIDERS THAT THREATEN HUMANITY AT ALL TIMES.
YOUR PERSONAL FEELINGS CAN PROVIDE YOU WITH MOTIVATION!
BUT YOU MUST NEVER LOSE SIGHT OF YOUR GOAL!

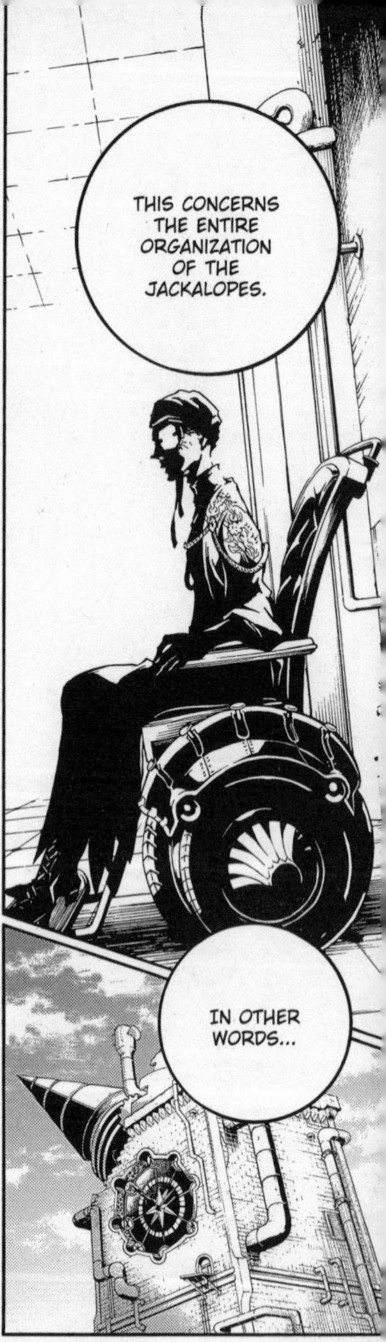
THIS CONCERNS THE ENTIRE ORGANIZATION OF THE JACKALOPES.
IN OTHER WORDS...

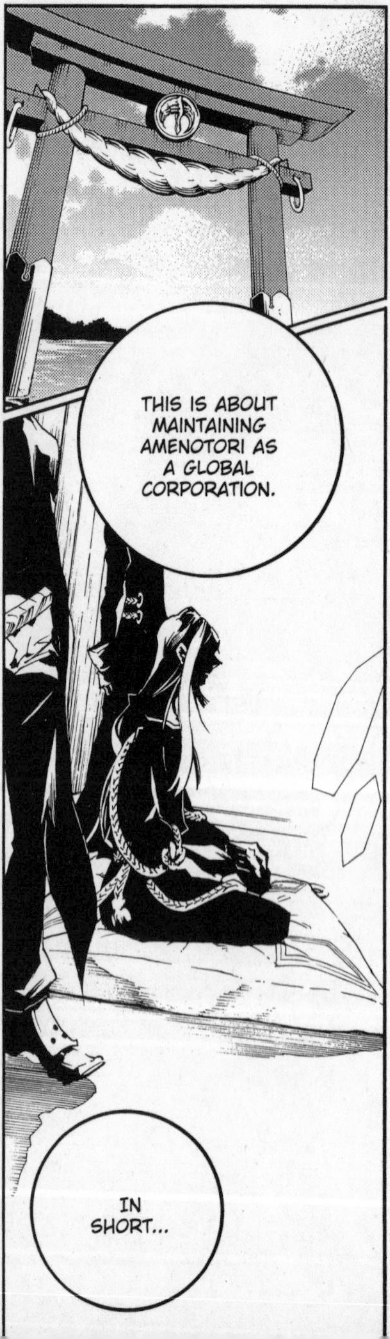
THIS IS ABOUT MAINTAINING AMENOTORI AS A GLOBAL CORPORATION.
IN SHORT...

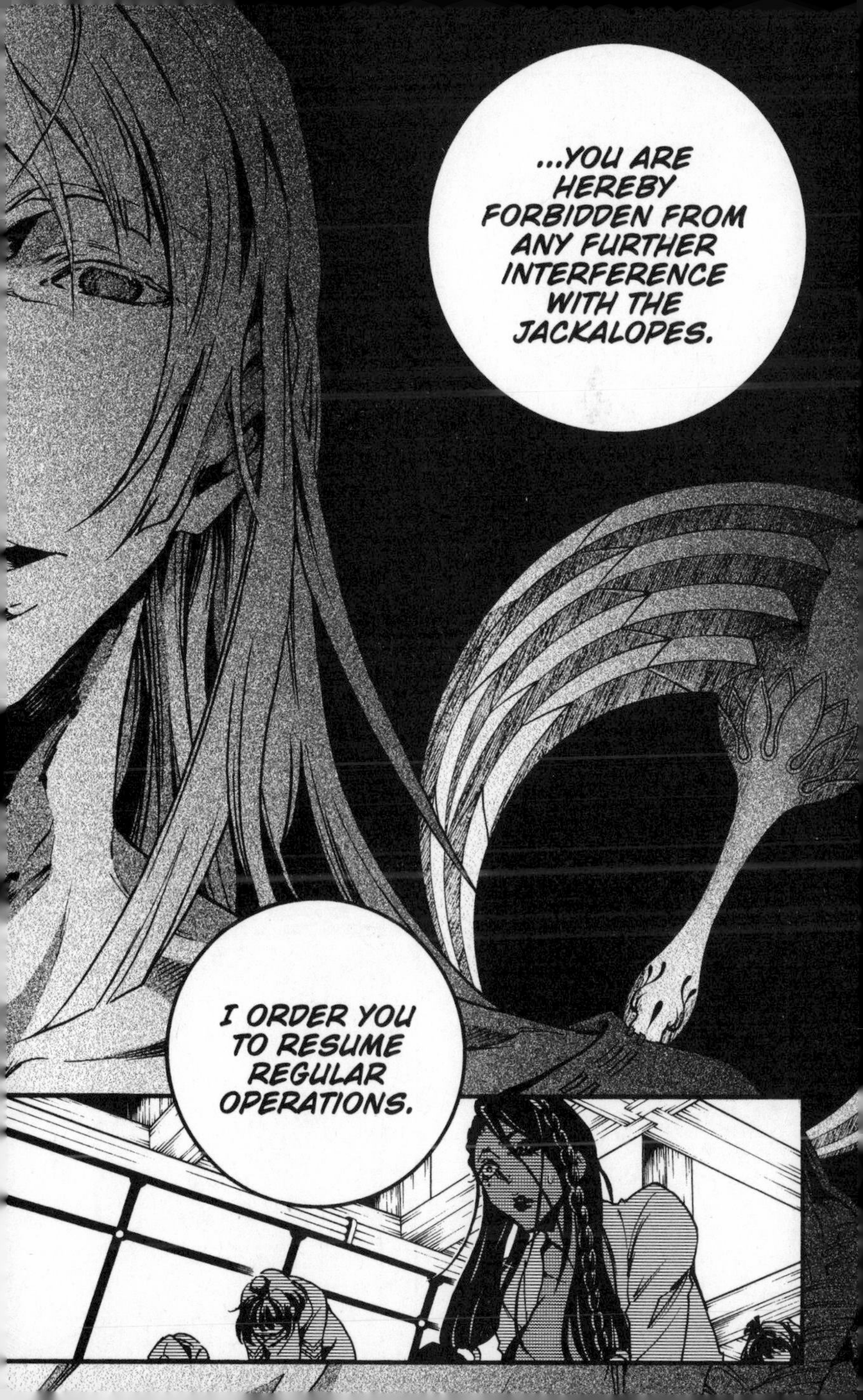
...YOU ARE HEREBY FORBIDDEN FROM ANY FURTHER INTERFERENCE WITH THE JACKALOPES.
I ORDER YOU TO RESUME REGULAR OPERATIONS.

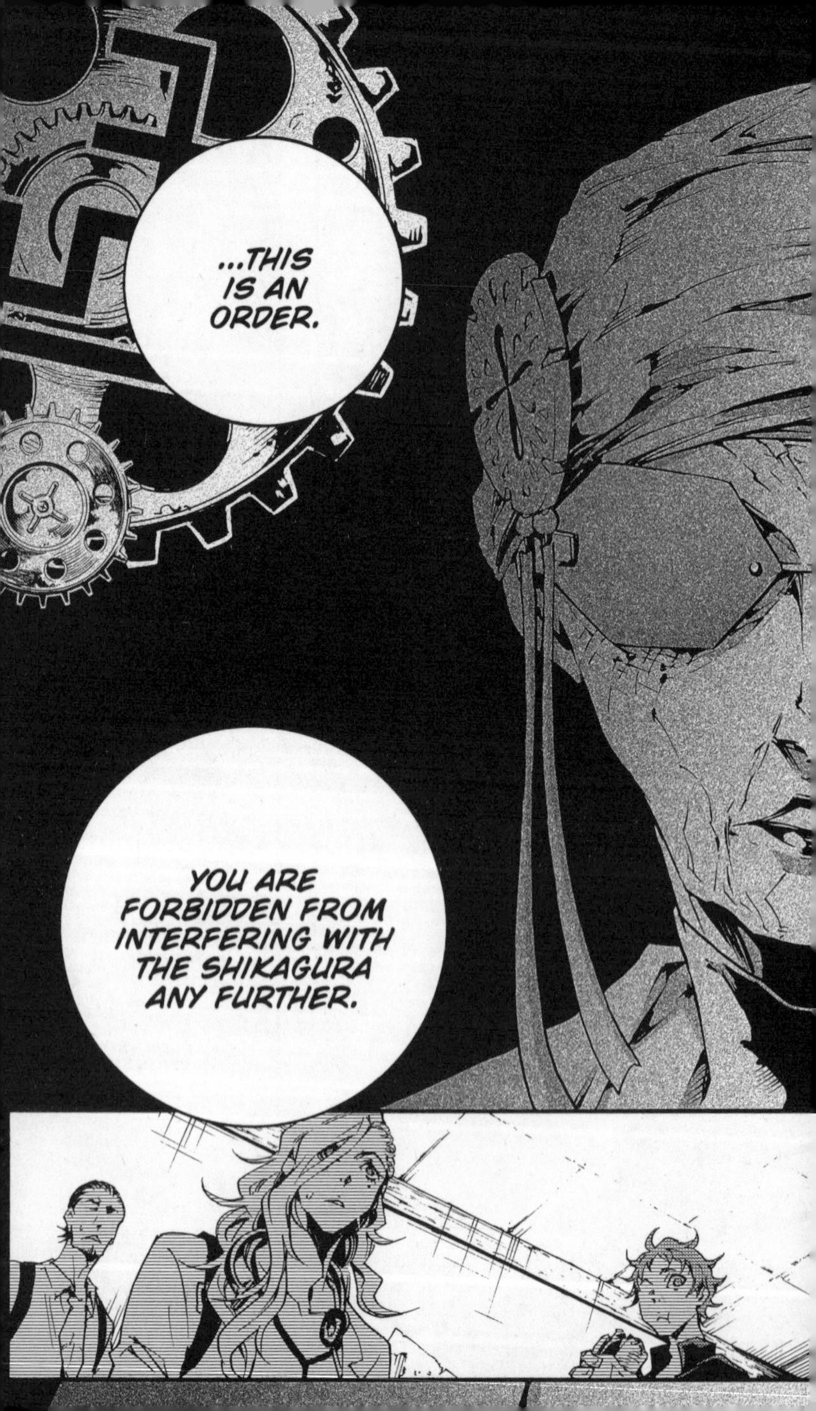
...THIS IS AN ORDER.
YOU ARE FORBIDDEN FROM INTERFERING WITH THE SHIKAGURA ANY FURTHER.

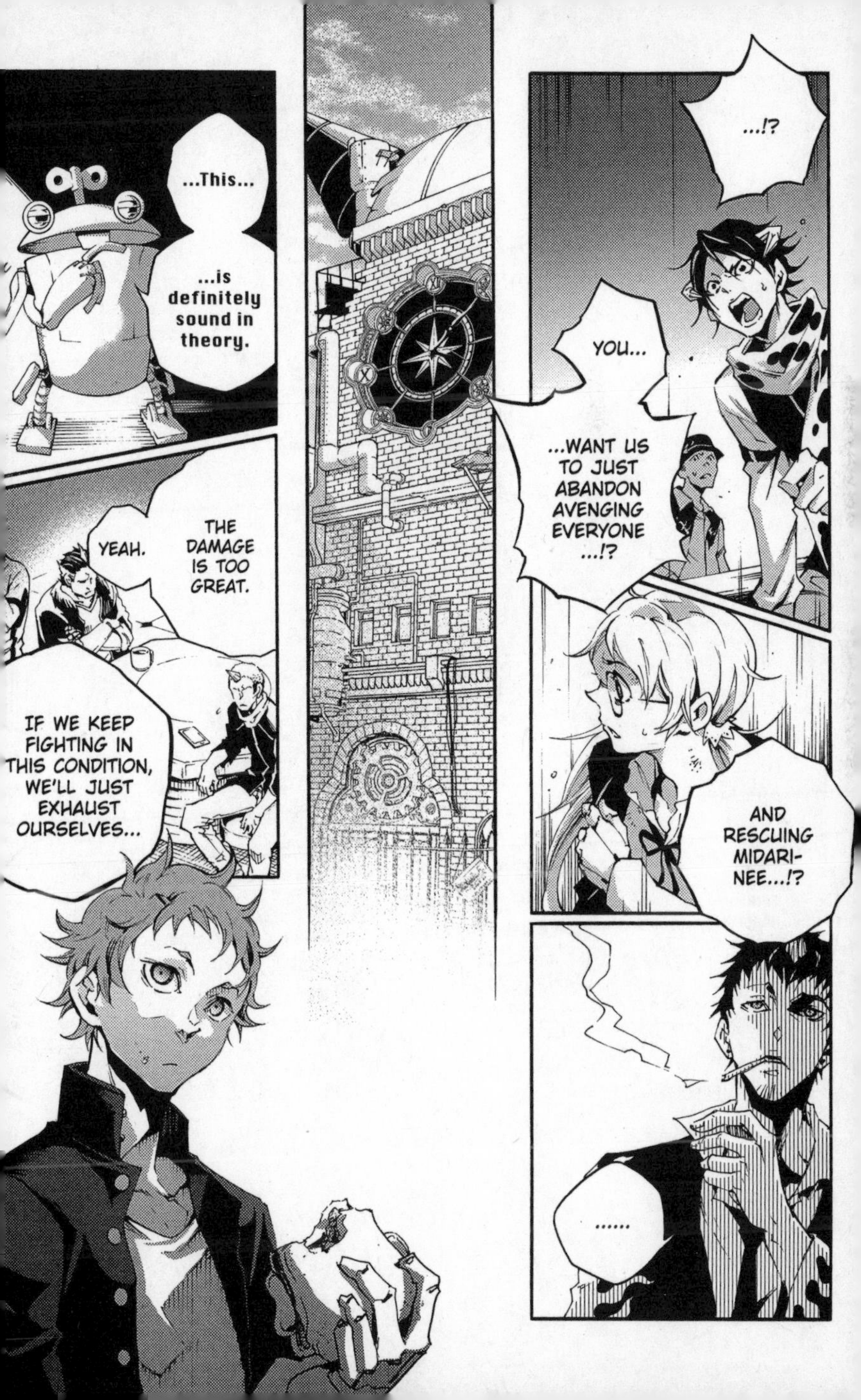
...This...
...is definitely sound in theory.
YEAH.
THE DAMAGE IS TOO GREAT.
IF WE KEEP FIGHTING IN THIS CONDITION, WE'LL JUST EXHAUST OURSELVES...
...!?
YOU...
...WANT US TO JUST ABANDON AVENGING EVERYONE ...!?
AND RESCUING MIDARI-NEE...!?
......

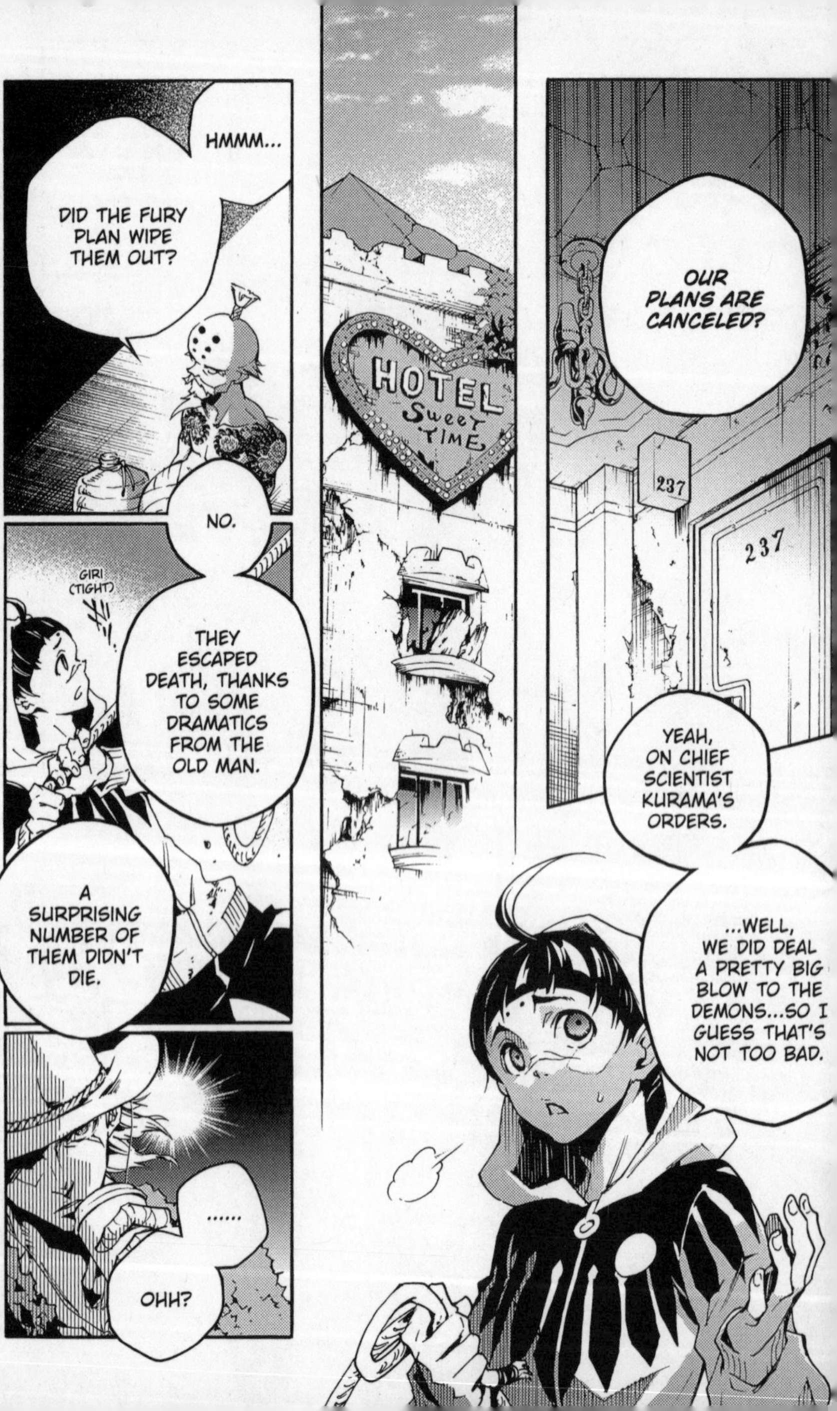
OUR PLANS ARE CANCELED?
237
237
YEAH, ON CHIEF SCIENTIST KURAMA'S ORDERS.
...WELL, WE DID DEAL A PRETTY BIG BLOW TO THE DEMONS...SO I GUESS THAT'S NOT TOO BAD.
HOTEL Sweet TIME
HMMM...
DID THE FURY PLAN WIPE THEM OUT?
NO.
GIRI (TIGHT)
THEY ESCAPED DEATH, THANKS TO SOME DRAMATICS FROM THE OLD MAN.
A SURPRISING NUMBER OF THEM DIDN'T DIE.
......
OHH?

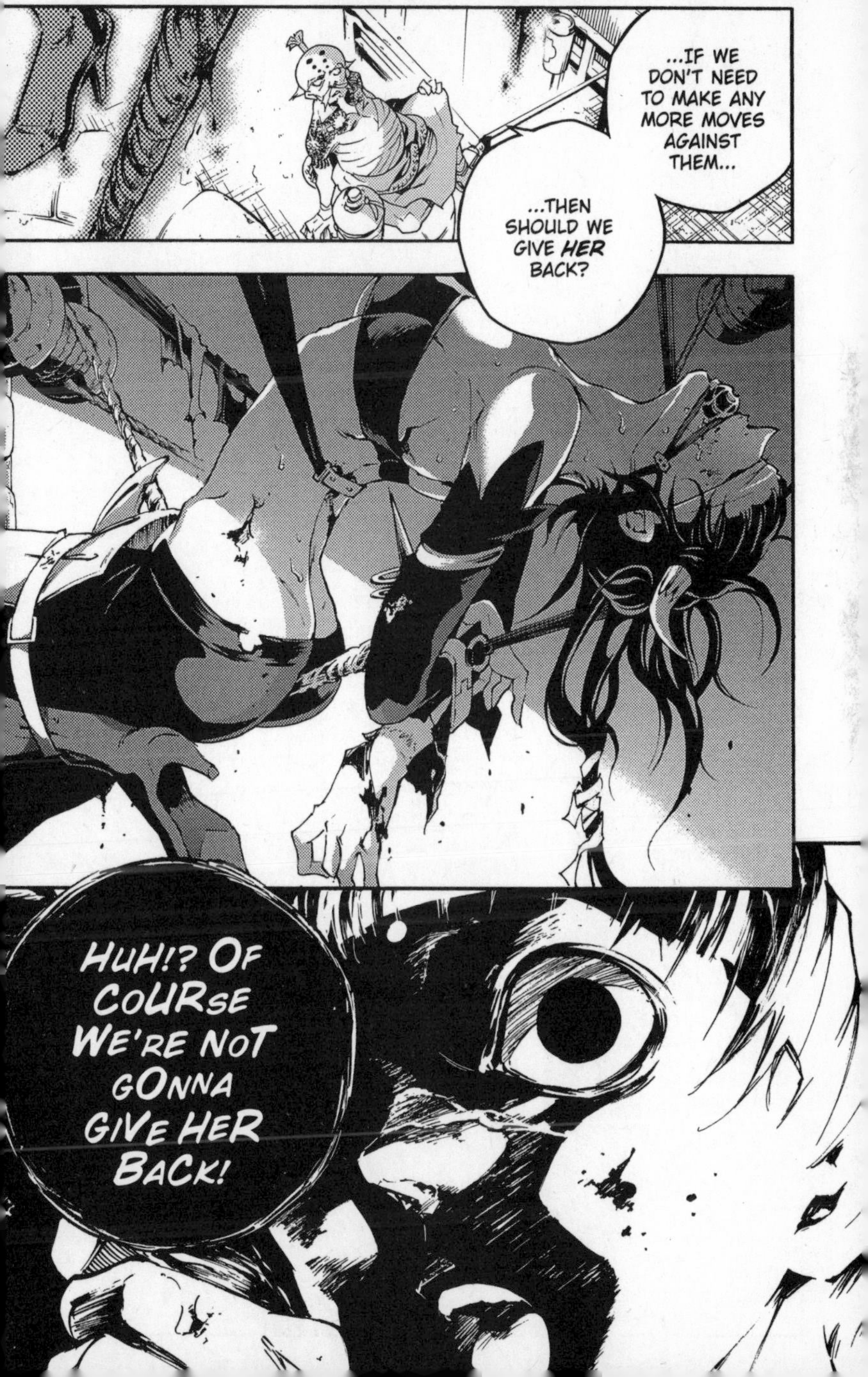
...IF WE DON'T NEED TO MAKE ANY MORE MOVES AGAINST THEM...
...THEN SHOULD WE GIVE HER BACK?
HUH!? OF COURSE WE'RE NOT GONNA GIVE HER BACK!

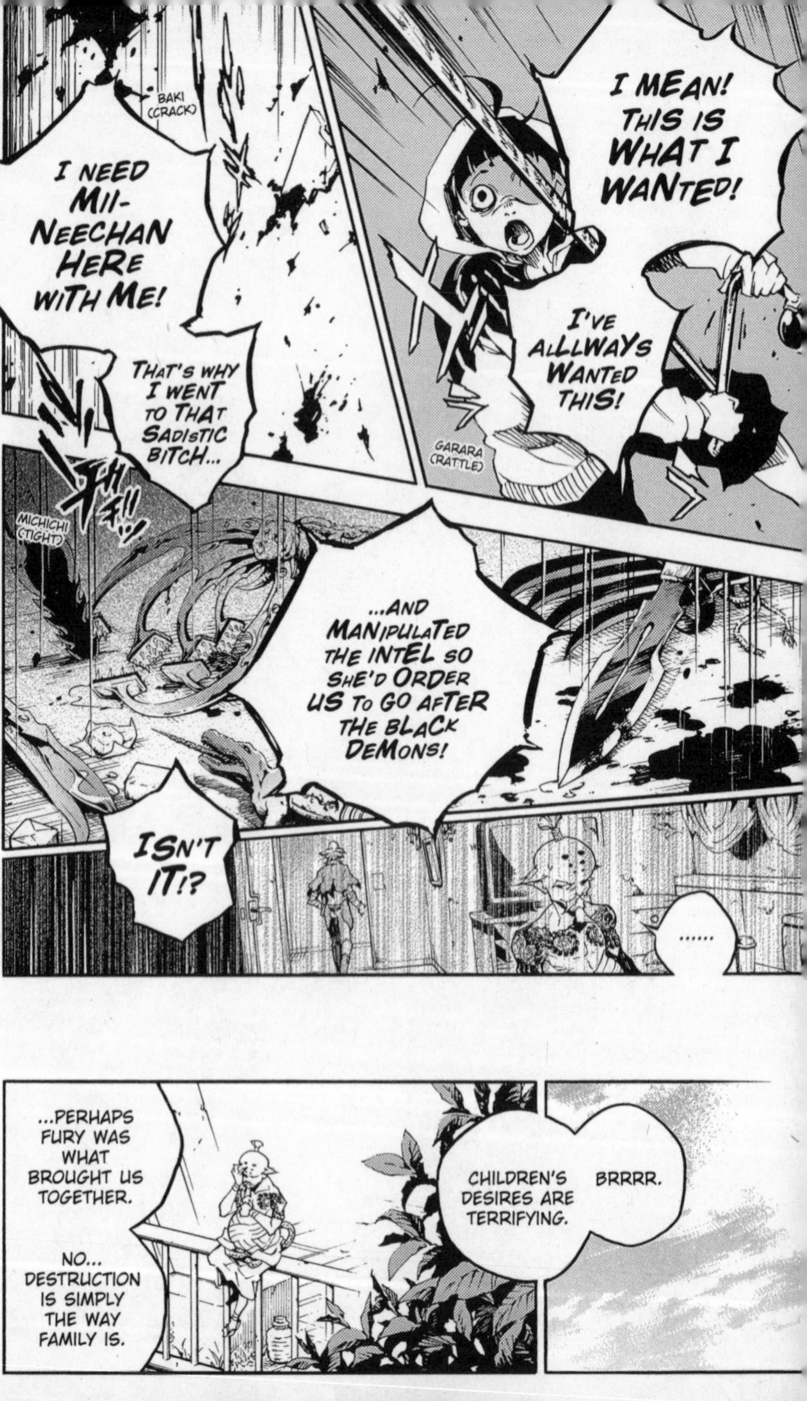
I MEAN! THIS IS WHAT I WANTED!
I'VE ALLWAYS WANTED THIS!
GARARA (RATTLE)
BAKI (CRACK)
I NEED MII-NEECHAN HERE WITH ME!
THAT'S WHY I WENT TO THAT SADISTIC BITCH...
MICHICHI (TIGHT)
...AND MANIPULATED THE INTEL SO SHE'D ORDER US TO GO AFTER THE BLACK DEMONS!
ISN'T IT!?
......
CHILDREN'S DESIRES ARE TERRIFYING.
BRRRR.
...PERHAPS FURY WAS WHAT BROUGHT US TOGETHER.
NO... DESTRUCTION IS SIMPLY THE WAY FAMILY IS.

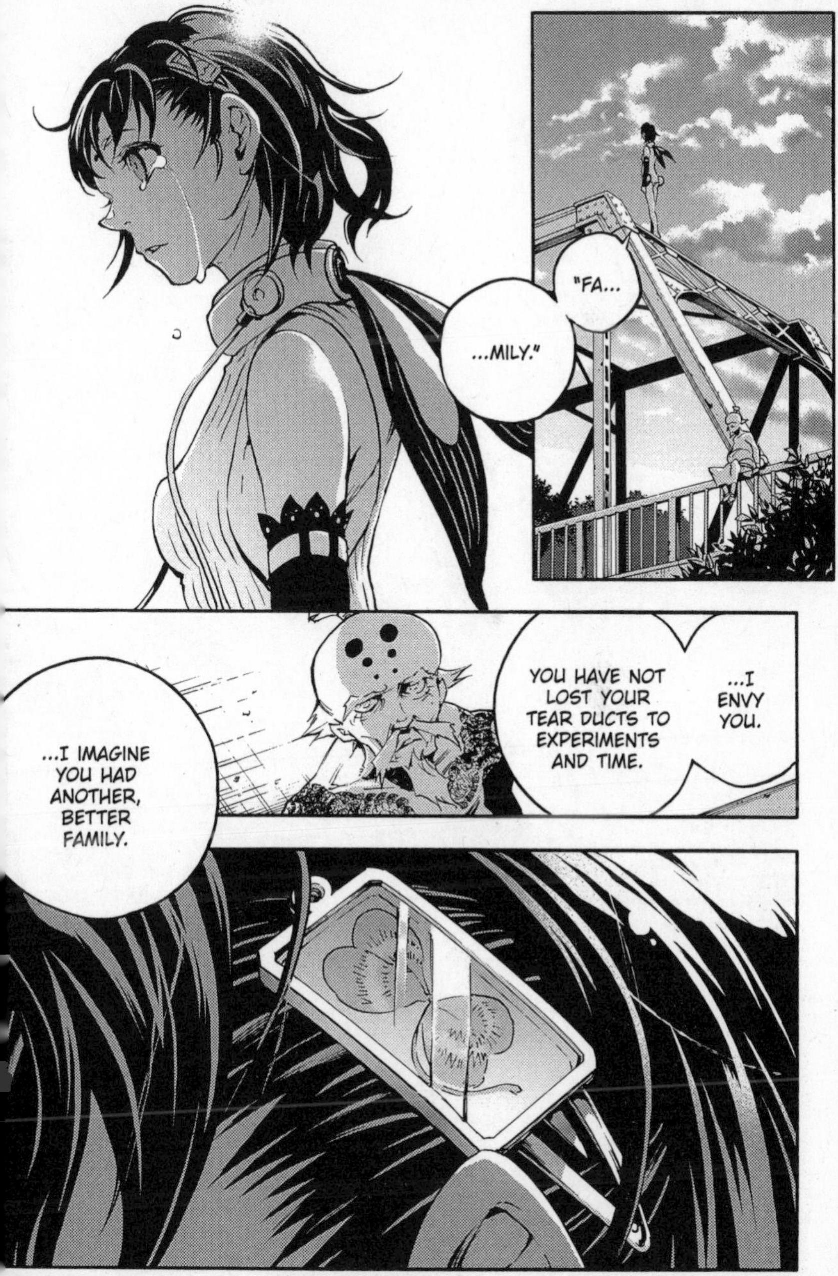
"FA...
...MILY."
...I ENVY YOU.
YOU HAVE NOT LOST YOUR TEAR DUCTS TO EXPERIMENTS AND TIME.
...I IMAGINE YOU HAD ANOTHER, BETTER FAMILY.

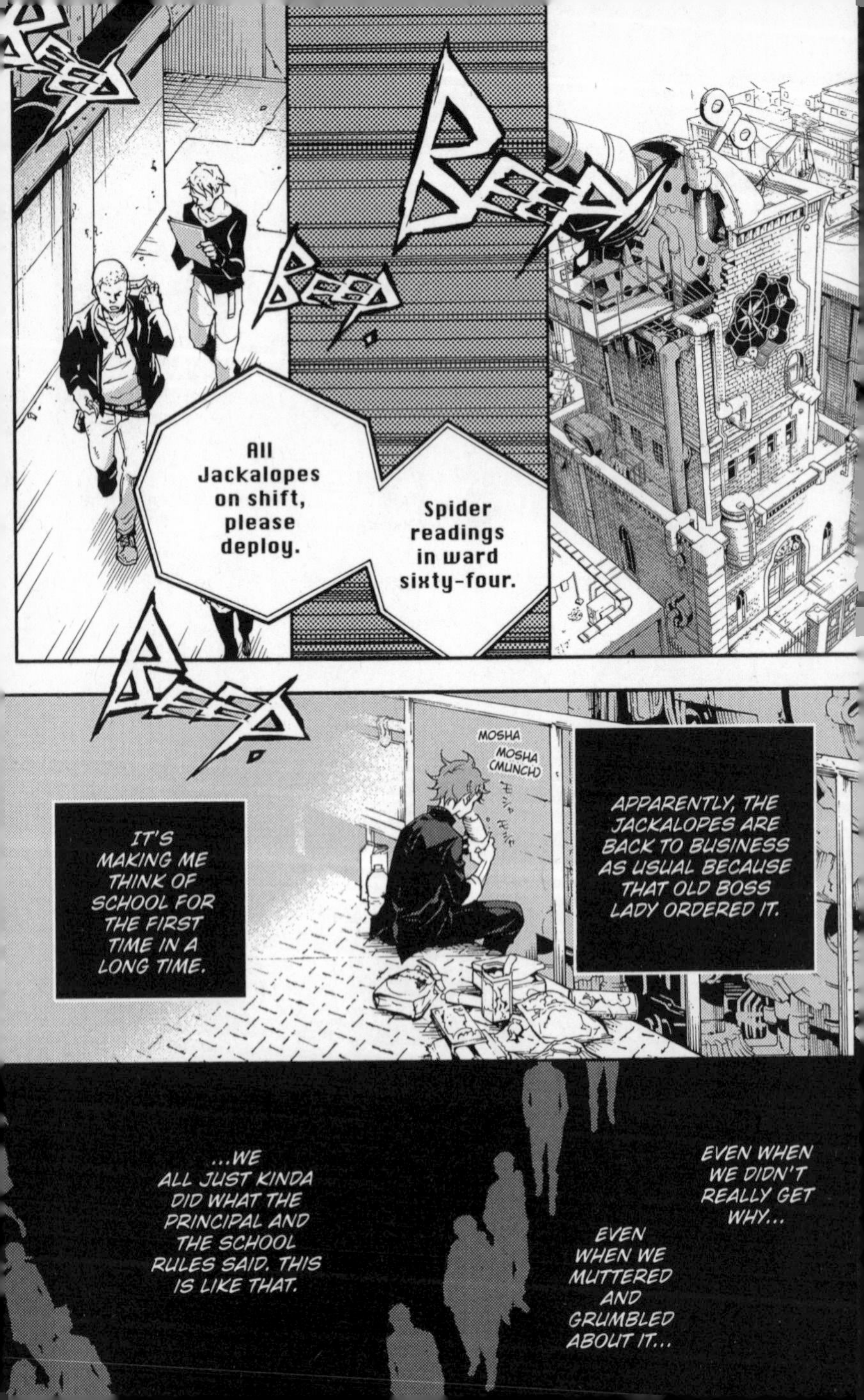
BEEP
BEEP
BEEP
Spider readings in ward sixty-four.
All Jackalopes on shift, please deploy.
BEEP
APPARENTLY, THE JACKALOPES ARE BACK TO BUSINESS AS USUAL BECAUSE THAT OLD BOSS LADY ORDERED IT.
MOSHA MOSHA (MUNCH)
IT'S MAKING ME THINK OF SCHOOL FOR THE FIRST TIME IN A LONG TIME.
EVEN WHEN WE DIDN'T REALLY GET WHY...
EVEN WHEN WE MUTTERED AND GRUMBLED ABOUT IT...
...WE ALL JUST KINDA DID WHAT THE PRINCIPAL AND THE SCHOOL RULES SAID. THIS IS LIKE THAT.

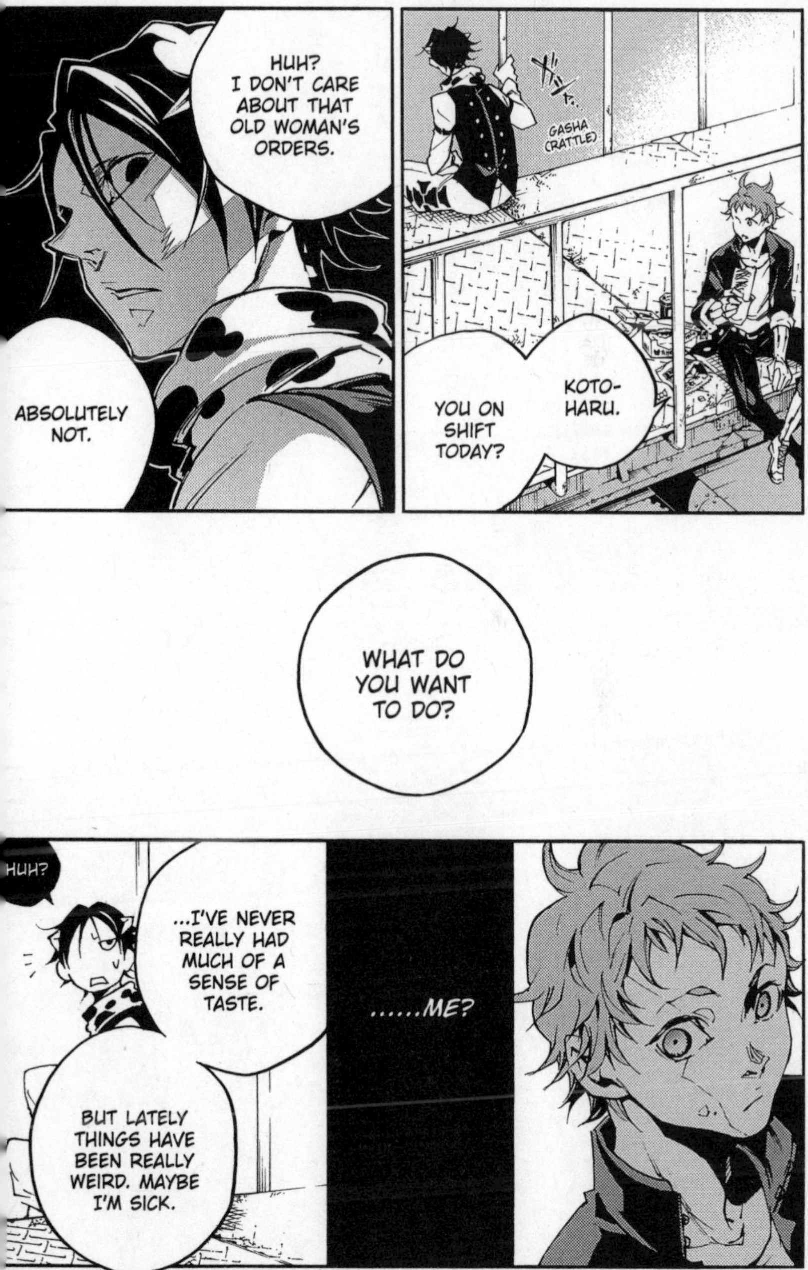
GASHA (RATTLE)
KOTO-HARU.
YOU ON SHIFT TODAY?
HUH? I DON'T CARE ABOUT THAT OLD WOMAN'S ORDERS.
ABSOLUTELY NOT.
WHAT DO YOU WANT TO DO?
......ME?
HUH?
...I'VE NEVER REALLY HAD MUCH OF A SENSE OF TASTE.
BUT LATELY THINGS HAVE BEEN REALLY WEIRD. MAYBE I'M SICK.

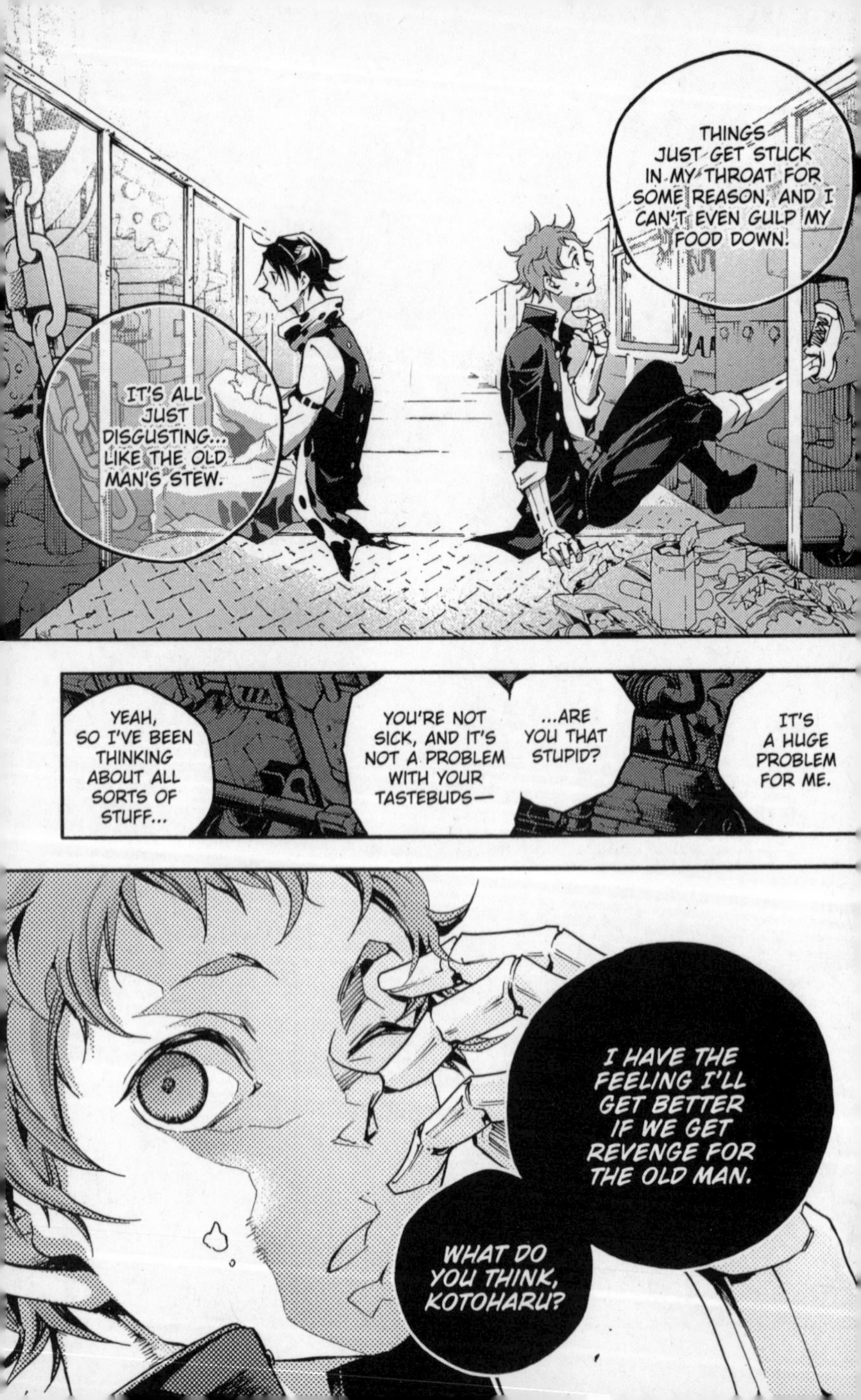
IT'S ALL JUST DISGUSTING... LIKE THE OLD MAN'S STEW.
THINGS JUST GET STUCK IN MY THROAT FOR SOME REASON, AND I CAN'T EVEN GULP MY FOOD DOWN.
YEAH, SO I'VE BEEN THINKING ABOUT ALL SORTS OF STUFF...
YOU'RE NOT SICK, AND IT'S NOT A PROBLEM WITH YOUR TASTEBUDS—
...ARE YOU THAT STUPID?
IT'S A HUGE PROBLEM FOR ME.
I HAVE THE FEELING I'LL GET BETTER IF WE GET REVENGE FOR THE OLD MAN.
WHAT DO YOU THINK, KOTOHARU?

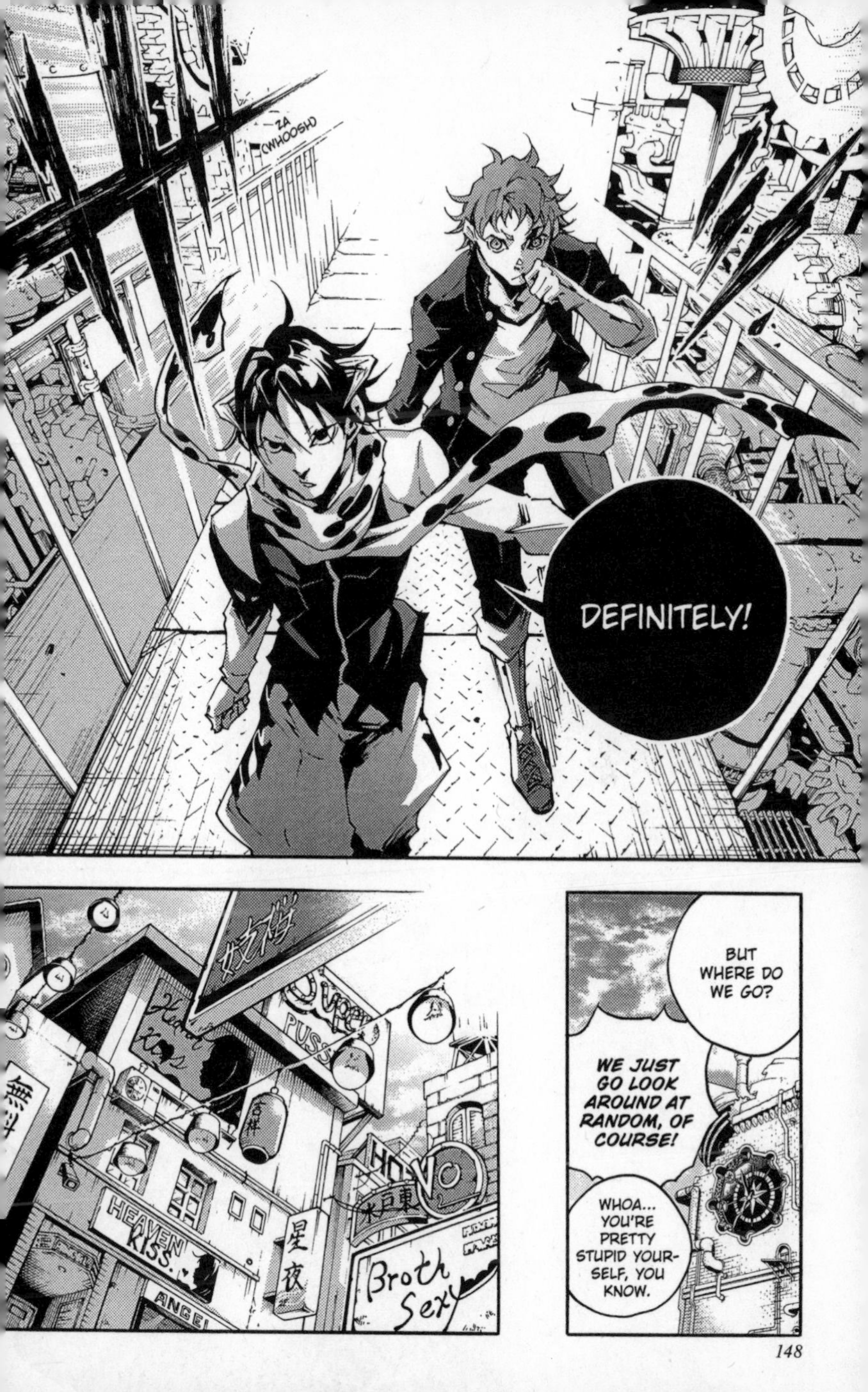
ZA (WHOOSH)
DEFINITELY!
BUT WHERE DO WE GO?
WE JUST GO LOOK AROUND AT RANDOM, OF COURSE!
WHOA... YOU'RE PRETTY STUPID YOUR-SELF, YOU KNOW.
HEAVEN KISS.
星夜
Broth Sexy

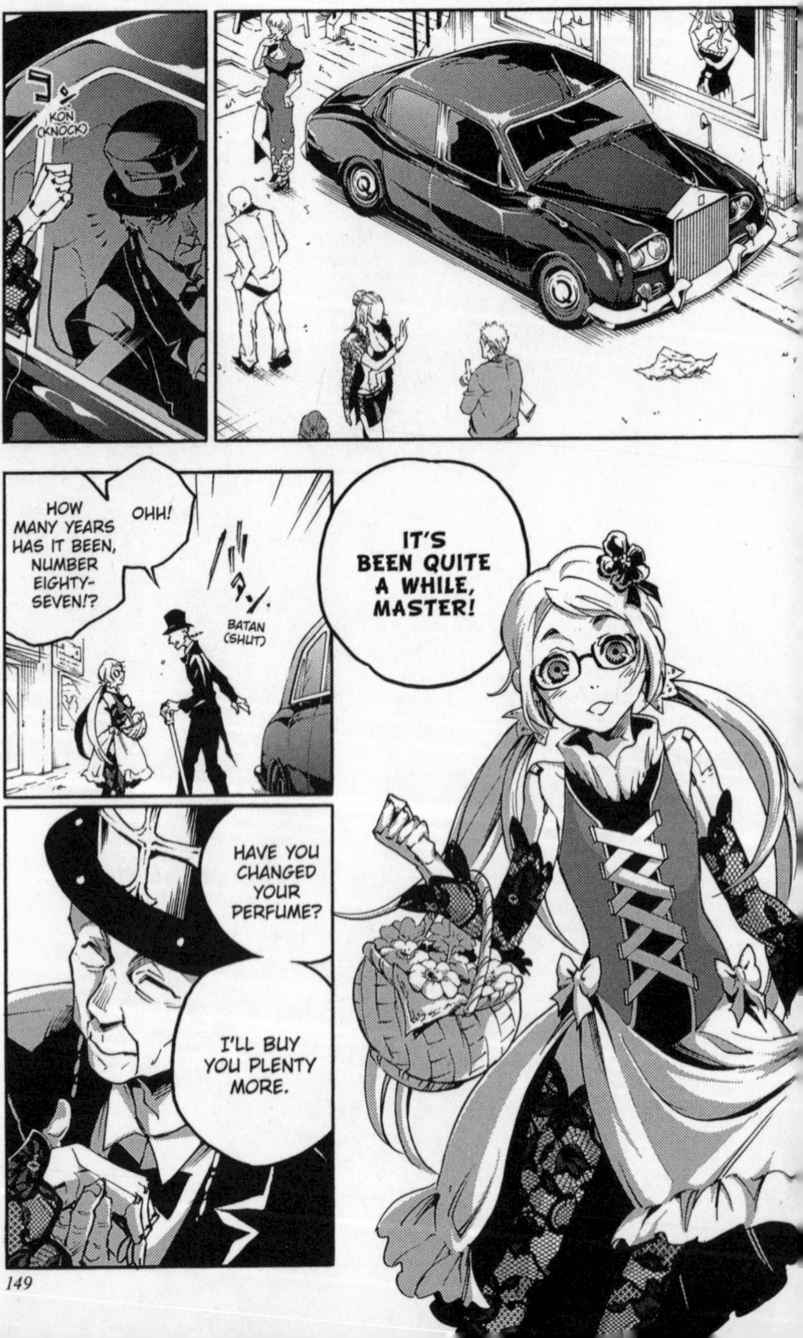
KON (KNOCK)
IT'S BEEN QUITE A WHILE, MASTER!
OHH!
HOW MANY YEARS HAS IT BEEN, NUMBER EIGHTY-SEVEN!?
BATAN (SHUT)
HAVE YOU CHANGED YOUR PERFUME?
I'LL BUY YOU PLENTY MORE.

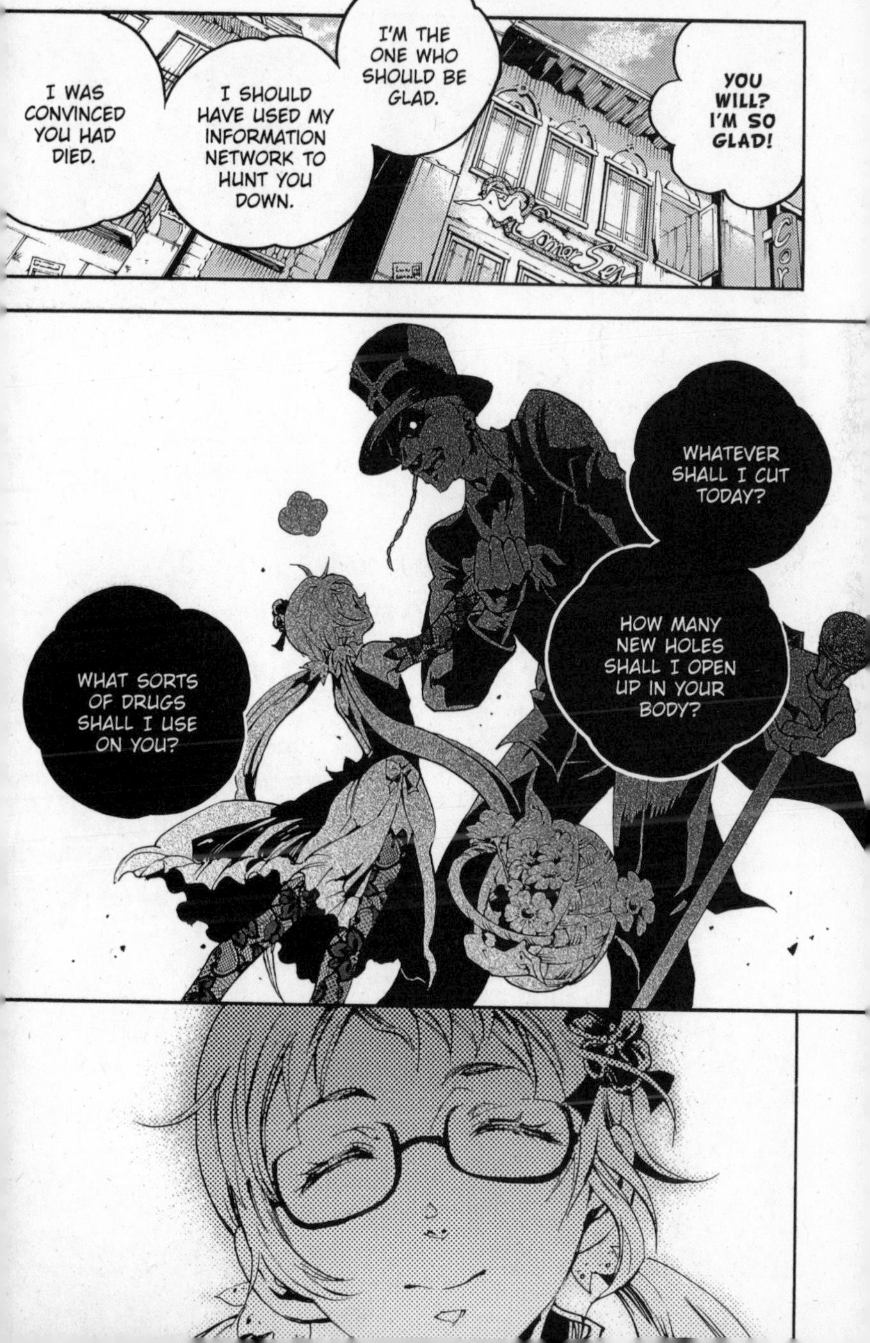
YOU WILL? I'M SO GLAD!
I'M THE ONE WHO SHOULD BE GLAD.
I SHOULD HAVE USED MY INFORMATION NETWORK TO HUNT YOU DOWN.
I WAS CONVINCED YOU HAD DIED.
WHATEVER SHALL I CUT TODAY?
HOW MANY NEW HOLES SHALL I OPEN UP IN YOUR BODY?
WHAT SORTS OF DRUGS SHALL I USE ON YOU?

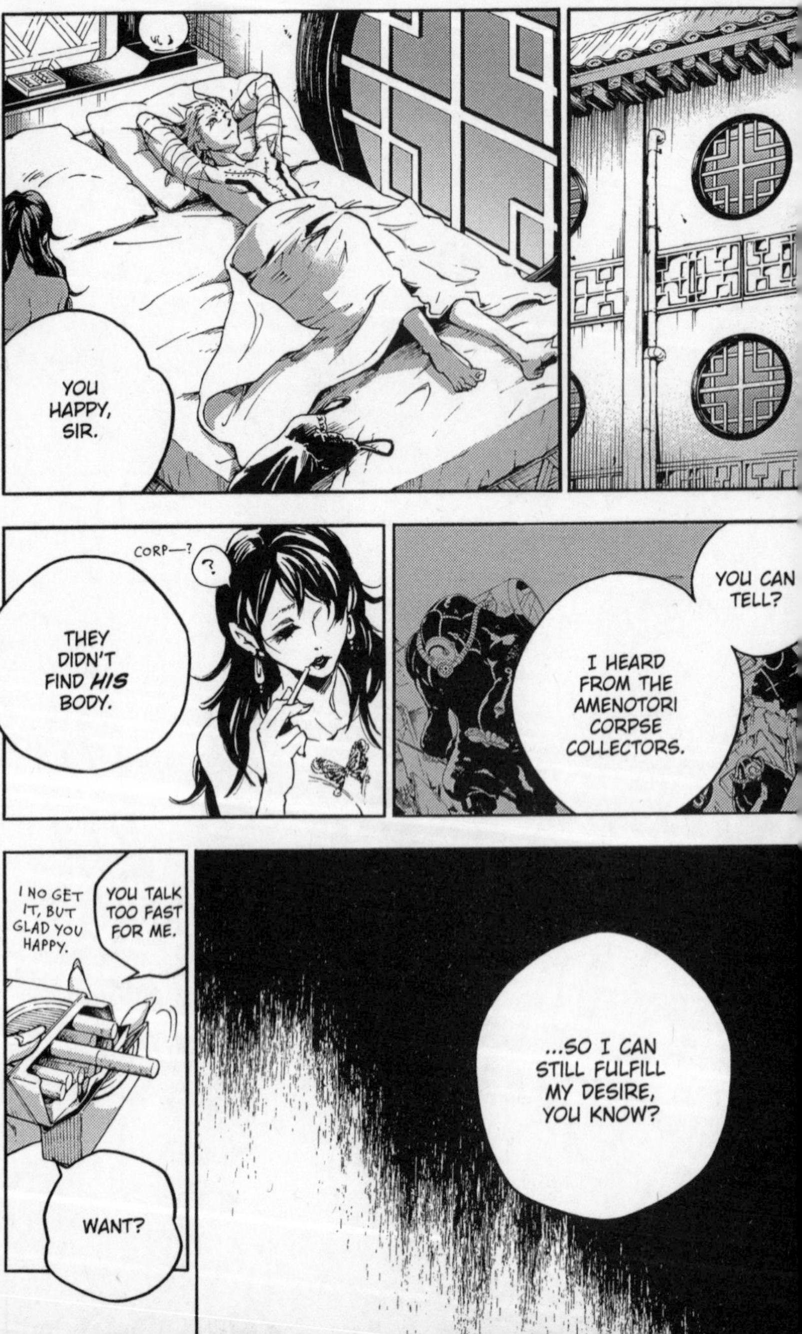
YOU HAPPY, SIR.
YOU CAN TELL?
I HEARD FROM THE AMENOTORI CORPSE COLLECTORS.
CORP—?
?
THEY DIDN'T FIND *HIS* BODY.
...SO I CAN STILL FULFILL MY DESIRE, YOU KNOW?
YOU TALK TOO FAST FOR ME.
I NO GET IT, BUT GLAD YOU HAPPY.
WANT?

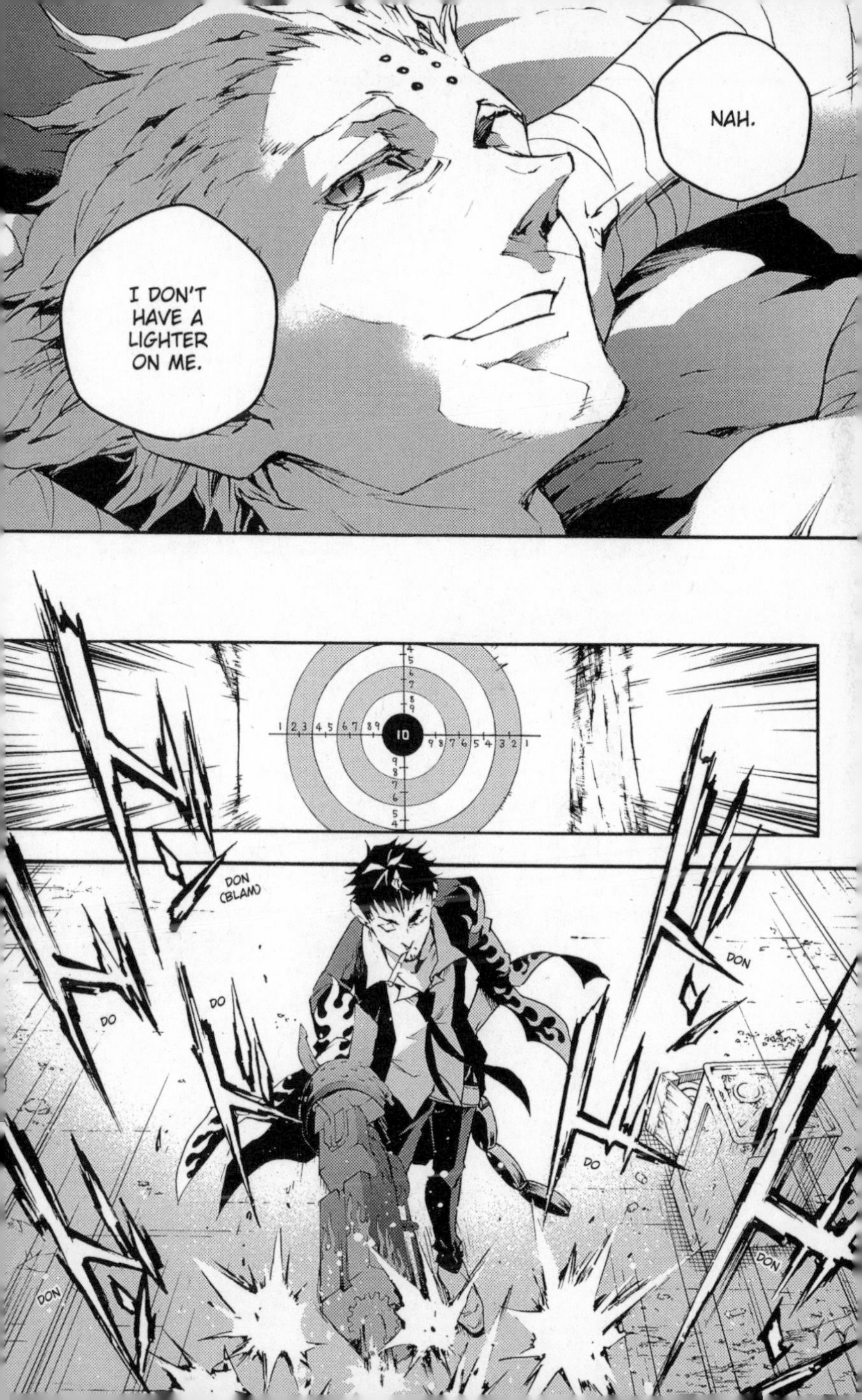
NAH.
I DON'T HAVE A LIGHTER ON ME.
DON
DON (BLAM)
DO
DO
DO
DON
DON

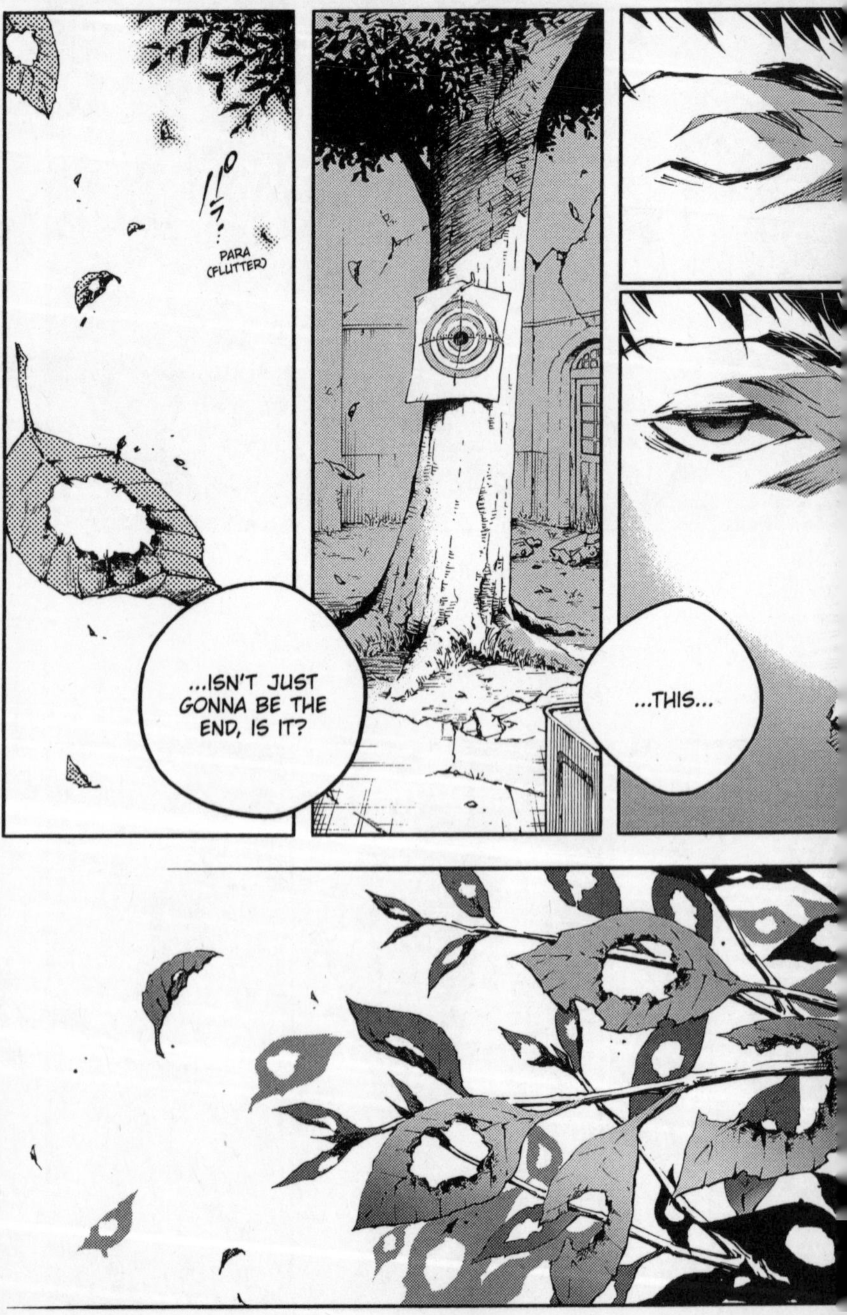
...THIS...
...ISN'T JUST GONNA BE THE END, IS IT?
PARA (FLUTTER)

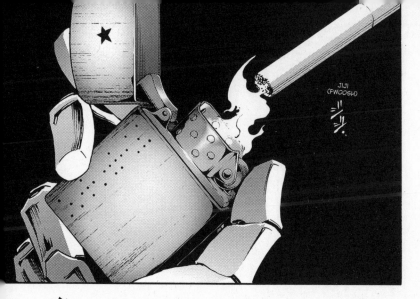

JIJI
(FWOOSH)

KACHIN
(CLICK)

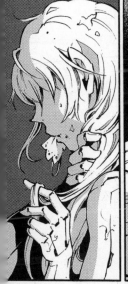

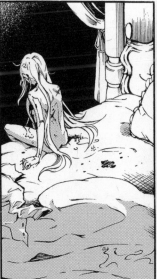

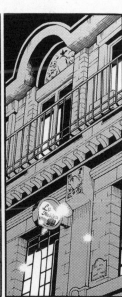

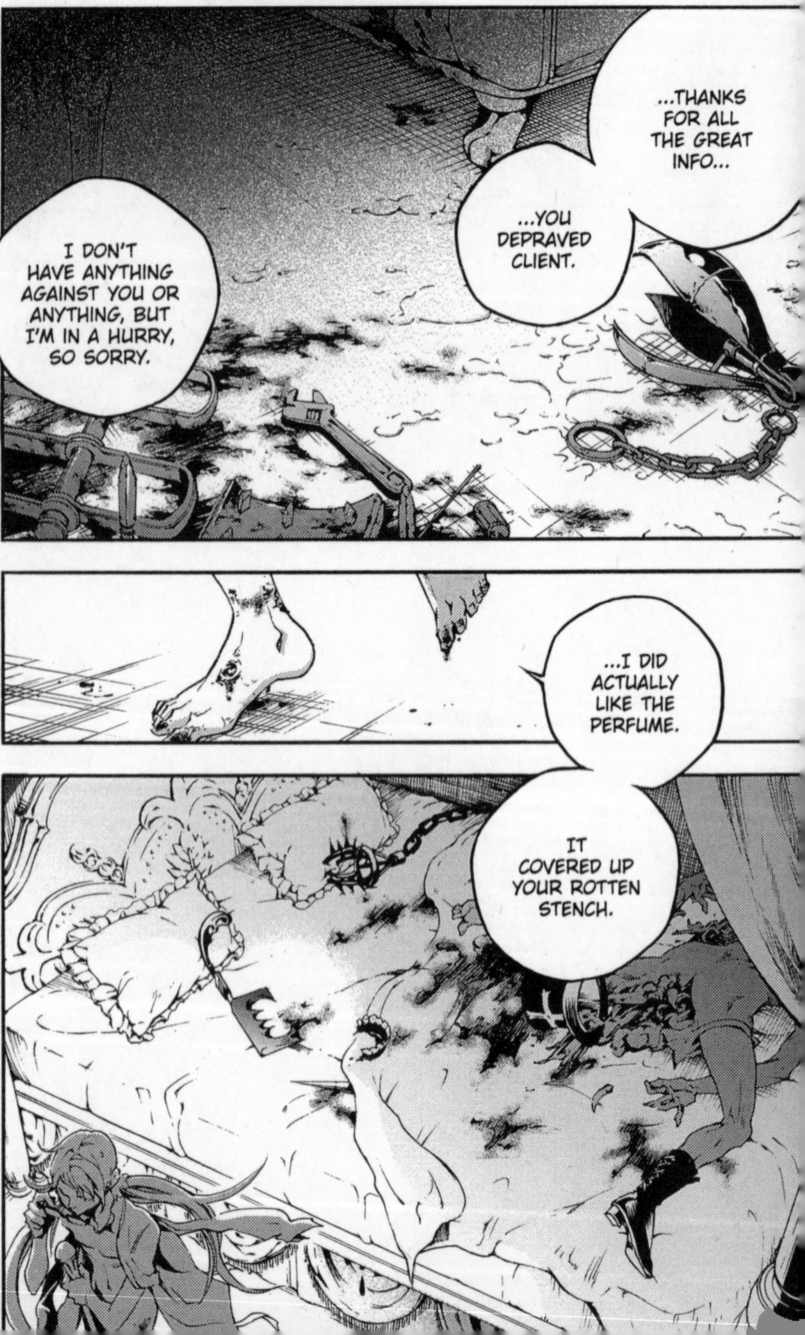
...THANKS FOR ALL THE GREAT INFO...
...YOU DEPRAVED CLIENT.
I DON'T HAVE ANYTHING AGAINST YOU OR ANYTHING, BUT I'M IN A HURRY, SO SORRY.
...I DID ACTUALLY LIKE THE PERFUME.
IT COVERED UP YOUR ROTTEN STENCH.

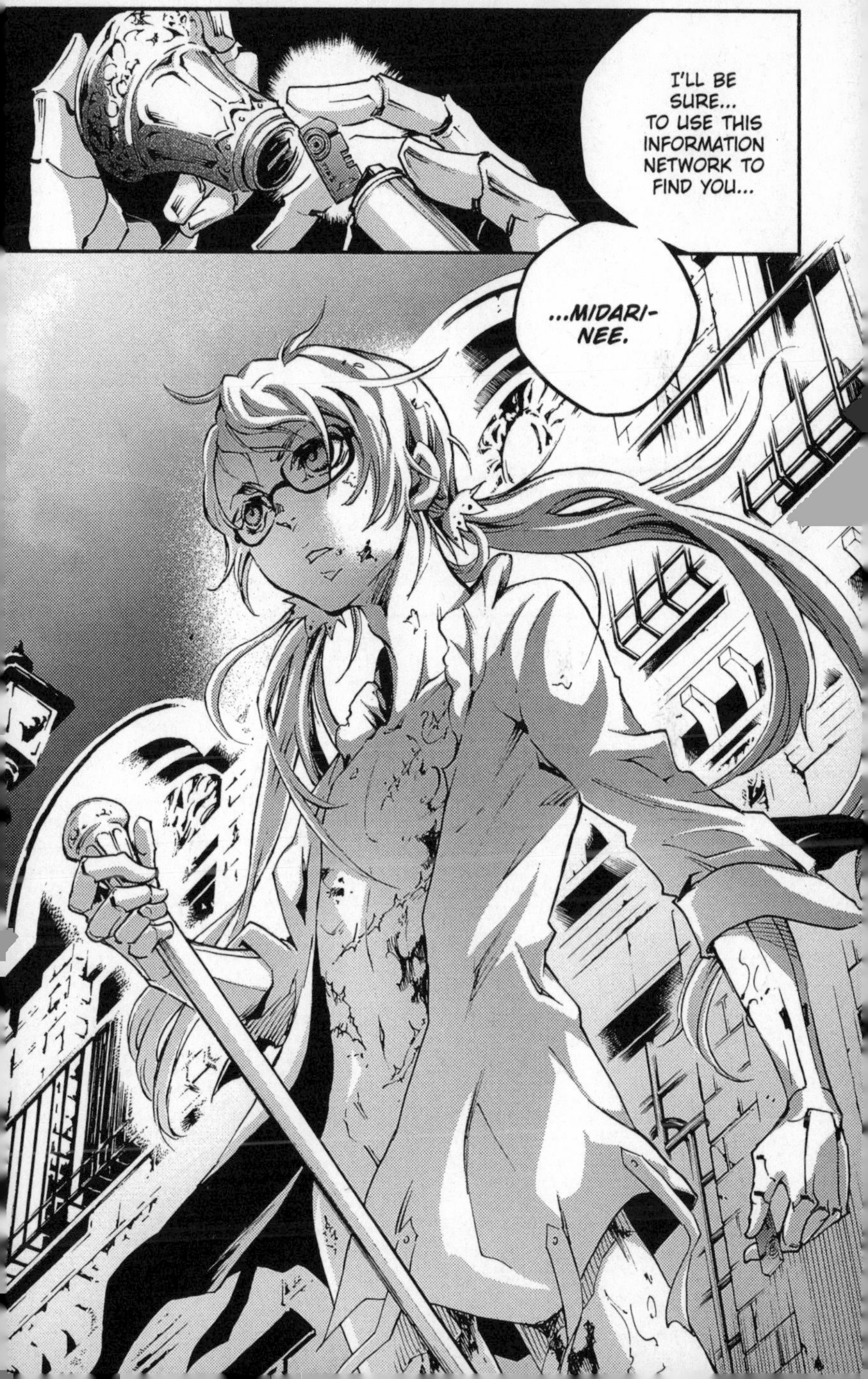
I'LL BE SURE... TO USE THIS INFORMATION NETWORK TO FIND YOU...
...MIDARI-NEE.

SMOKIN' PARADE

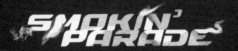

THE
WORLD IS
DEAD,
THE
PARADE
WILL
START.

SMOKIN'
PARADE

JINSEI KATAOKA
KAZUMA KONDOU

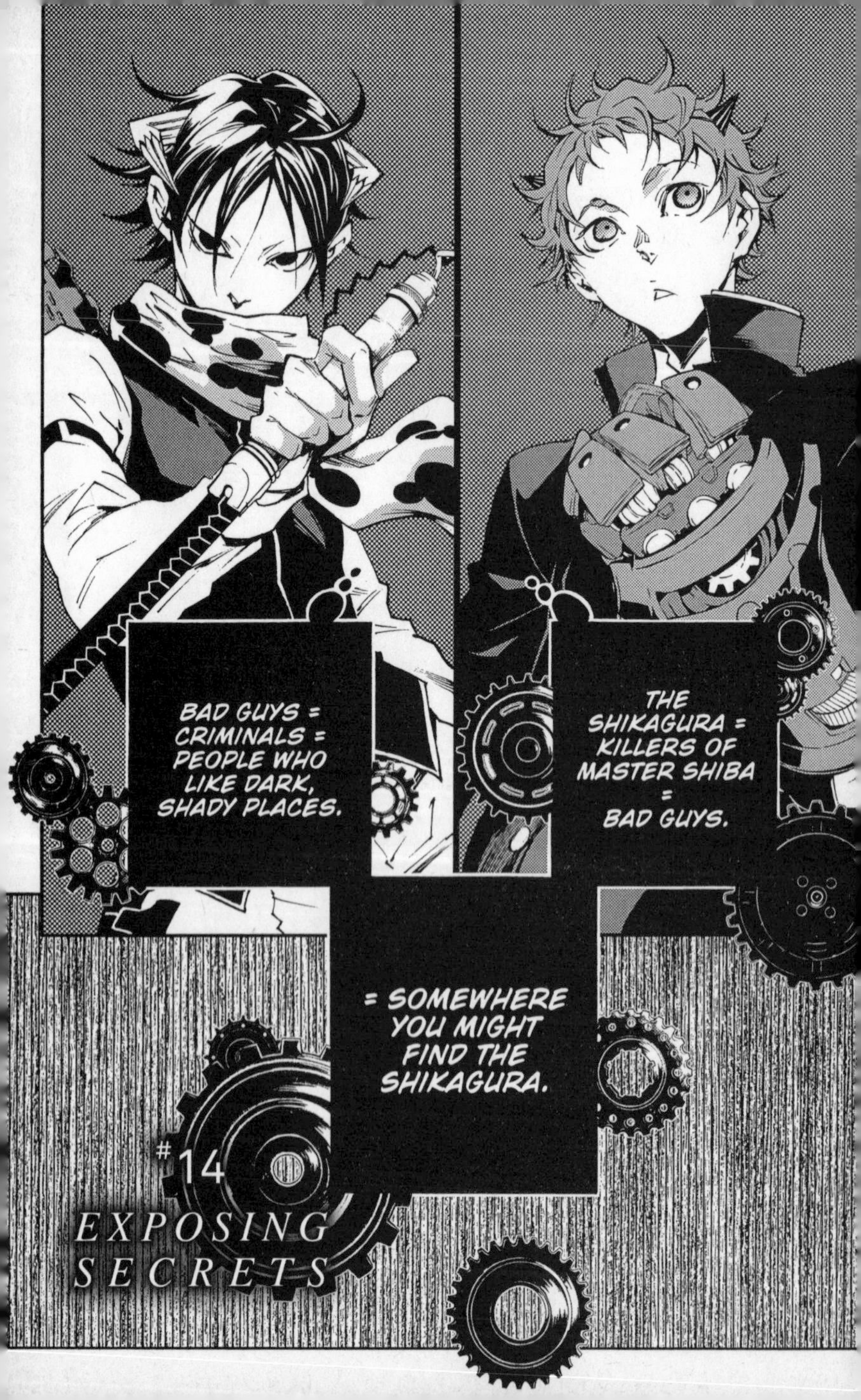
THE SHIKAGURA = KILLERS OF MASTER SHIBA = BAD GUYS.
BAD GUYS = CRIMINALS = PEOPLE WHO LIKE DARK, SHADY PLACES.
= SOMEWHERE YOU MIGHT FIND THE SHIKAGURA.
#14
EXPOSING SECRETS

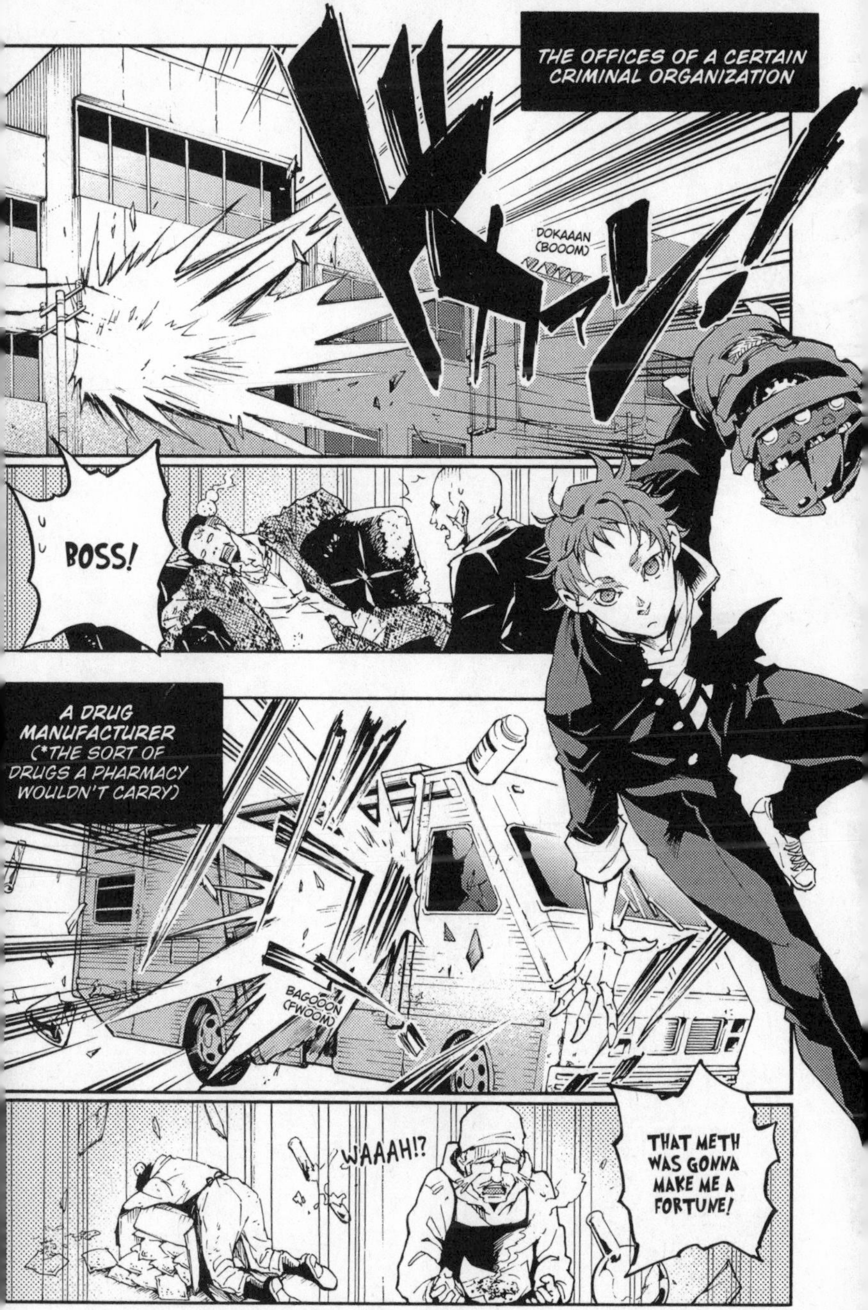
THE OFFICES OF A CERTAIN CRIMINAL ORGANIZATION
DOKAAAN (BOOOM)
BOSS!
A DRUG MANUFACTURER (*THE SORT OF DRUGS A PHARMACY WOULDN'T CARRY)
BAGOOON (FWOOM)
THAT METH WAS GONNA MAKE ME A FORTUNE!
WAAAH!?

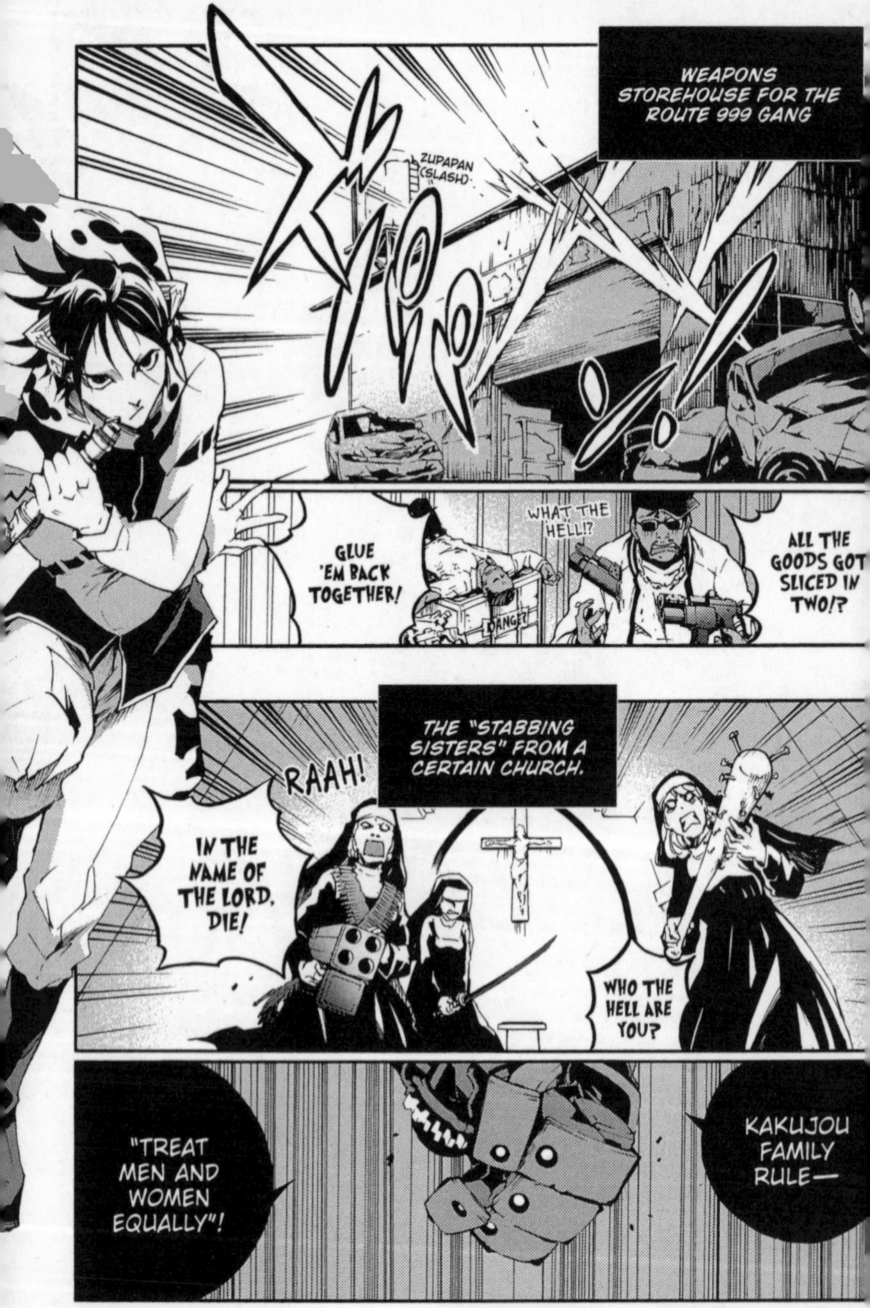
WEAPONS STOREHOUSE FOR THE ROUTE 999 GANG
ZUPAPAN (SLASH)
ALL THE GOODS GOT SLICED IN TWO!?
WHAT THE HELL!?
DANGER
GLUE 'EM BACK TOGETHER!
THE "STABBING SISTERS" FROM A CERTAIN CHURCH.
WHO THE HELL ARE YOU?
RAAH!
IN THE NAME OF THE LORD, DIE!
KAKUJOU FAMILY RULE—
"TREAT MEN AND WOMEN EQUALLY"!

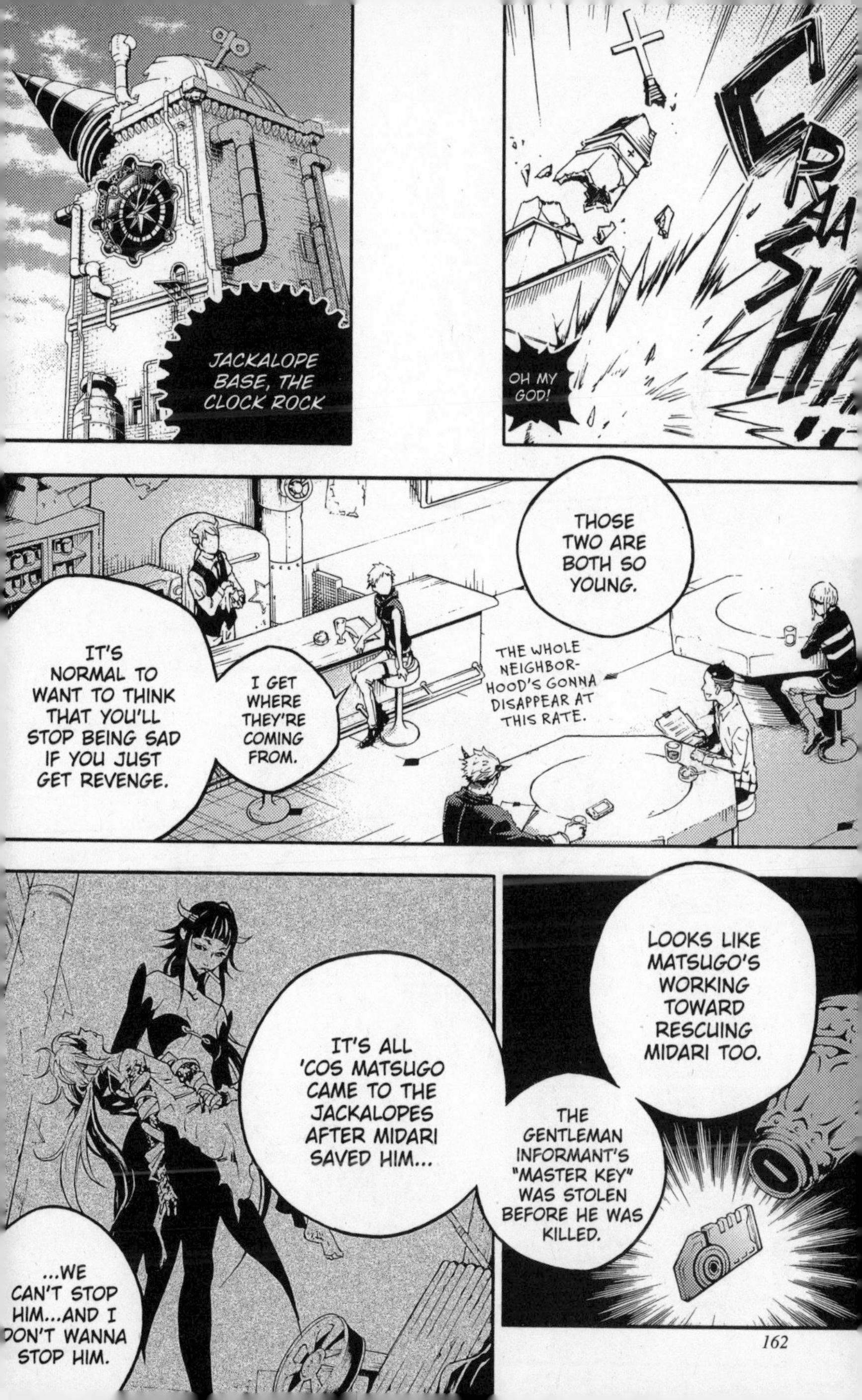
CRAASH!!
OH MY GOD!
JACKALOPE BASE, THE CLOCK ROCK
THOSE TWO ARE BOTH SO YOUNG.
THE WHOLE NEIGHBOR-HOOD'S GONNA DISAPPEAR AT THIS RATE.
I GET WHERE THEY'RE COMING FROM.
IT'S NORMAL TO WANT TO THINK THAT YOU'LL STOP BEING SAD IF YOU JUST GET REVENGE.
LOOKS LIKE MATSUGO'S WORKING TOWARD RESCUING MIDARI TOO.
THE GENTLEMAN INFORMANT'S "MASTER KEY" WAS STOLEN BEFORE HE WAS KILLED.
IT'S ALL 'COS MATSUGO CAME TO THE JACKALOPES AFTER MIDARI SAVED HIM...
...WE CAN'T STOP HIM...AND I DON'T WANNA STOP HIM.

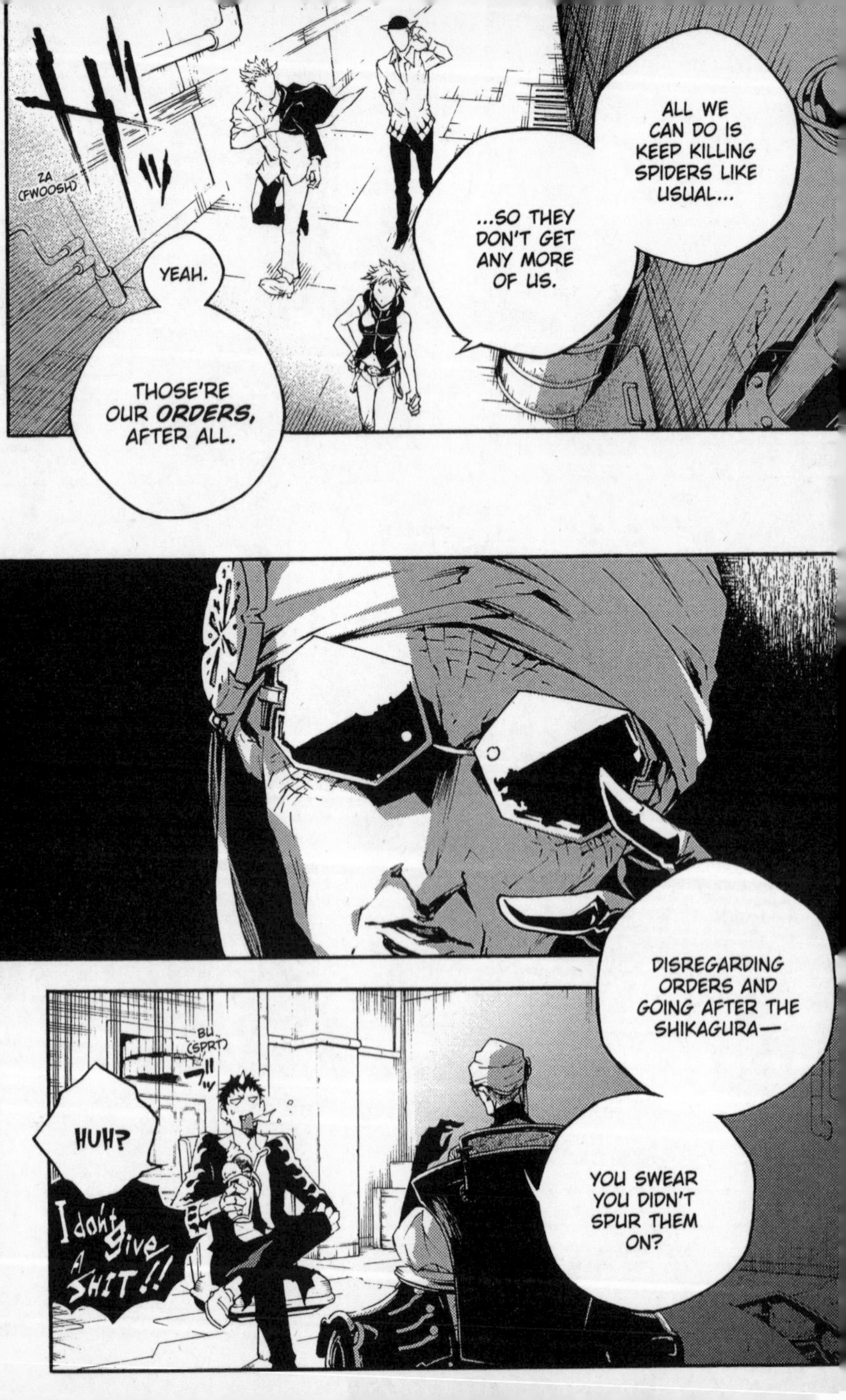
ALL WE CAN DO IS KEEP KILLING SPIDERS LIKE USUAL...
...SO THEY DON'T GET ANY MORE OF US.
ZA (FWOOSH)
YEAH.
THOSE'RE OUR ORDERS, AFTER ALL.
DISREGARDING ORDERS AND GOING AFTER THE SHIKAGURA—
YOU SWEAR YOU DIDN'T SPUR THEM ON?
BU (SPRT)
HUH?
I don't give a SHIT!!

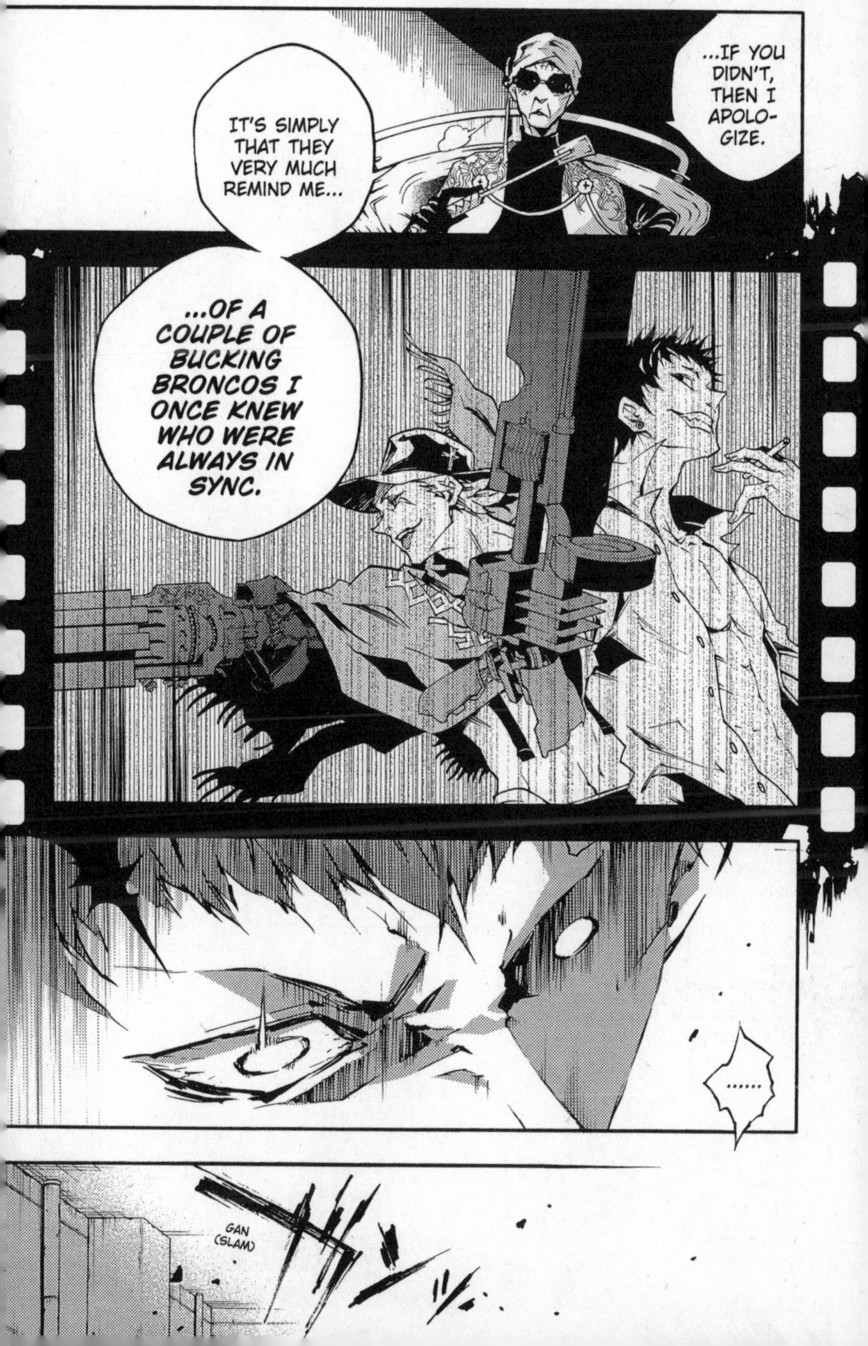
...IF YOU DIDN'T, THEN I APOLOGIZE.
IT'S SIMPLY THAT THEY VERY MUCH REMIND ME...
...OF A COUPLE OF BUCKING BRONCOS I ONCE KNEW WHO WERE ALWAYS IN SYNC.
......
GAN (SLAM)

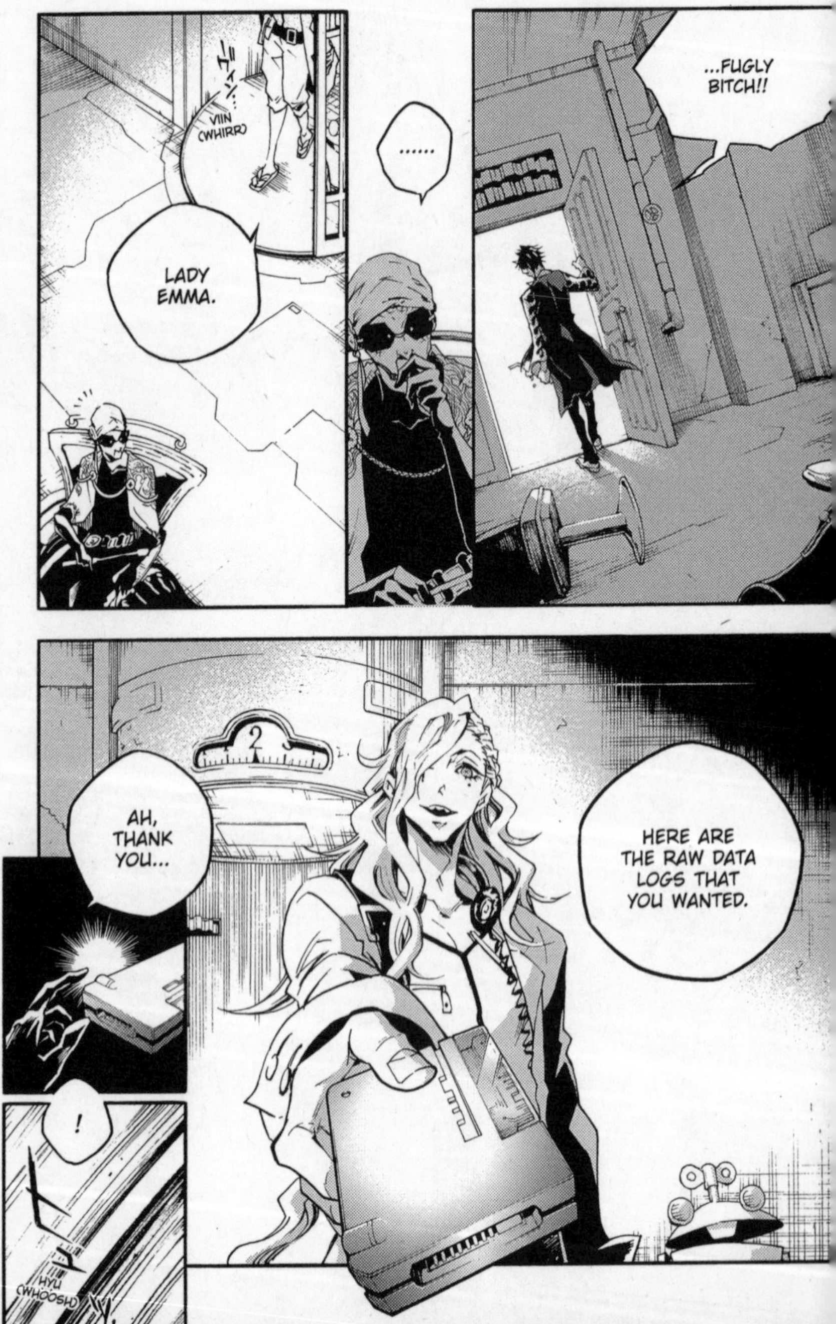
...FUGLY BITCH!!
......
VIIN (WHIRR)
LADY EMMA.
HERE ARE THE RAW DATA LOGS THAT YOU WANTED.
AH, THANK YOU...
!
HYU (WHOOSH)

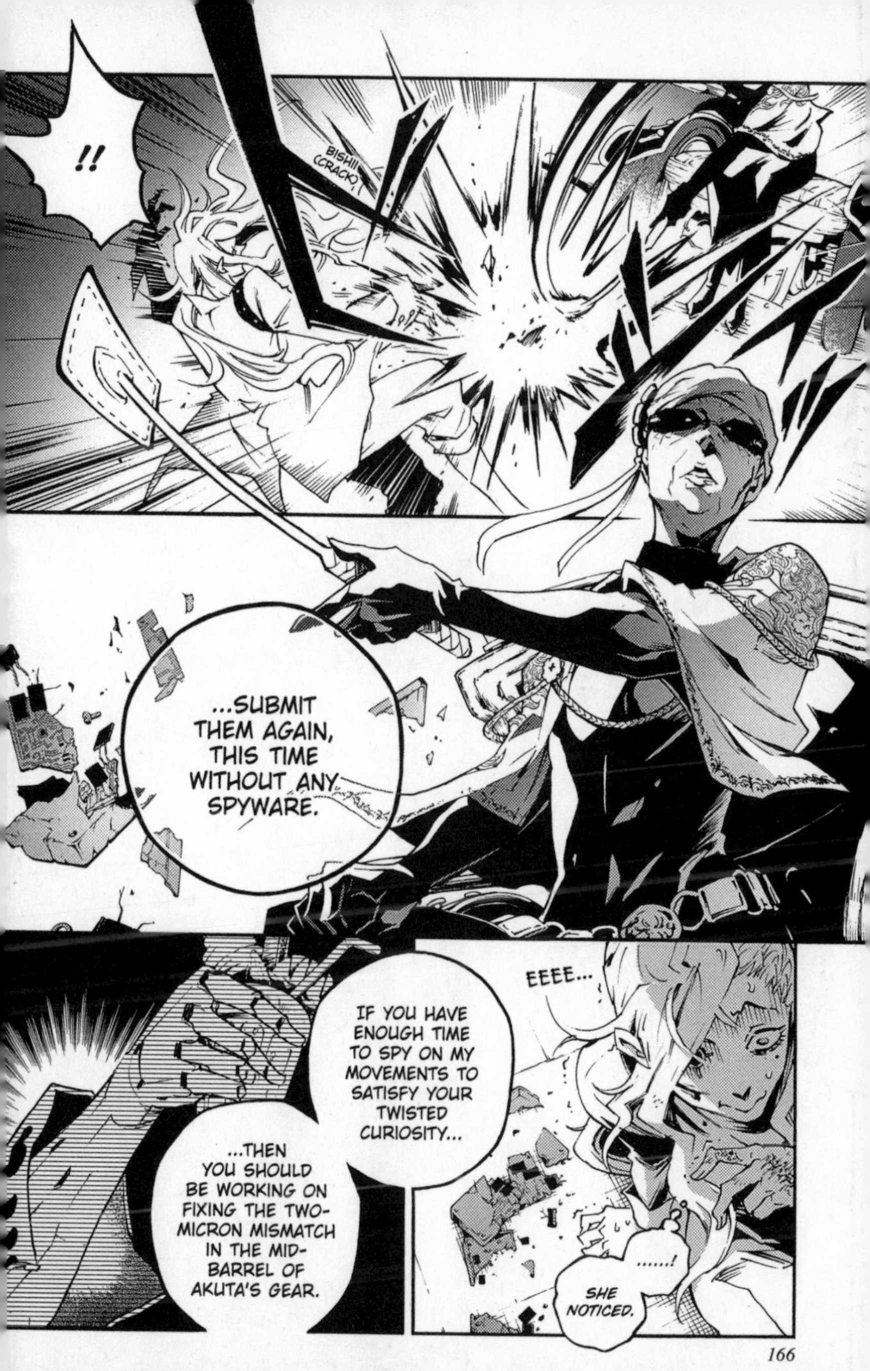
BISHI! (CRACK)
!!
...SUBMIT THEM AGAIN, THIS TIME WITHOUT ANY SPYWARE.
EEEE...
......!
SHE NOTICED.
IF YOU HAVE ENOUGH TIME TO SPY ON MY MOVEMENTS TO SATISFY YOUR TWISTED CURIOSITY...
...THEN YOU SHOULD BE WORKING ON FIXING THE TWO-MICRON MISMATCH IN THE MID-BARREL OF AKUTA'S GEAR.

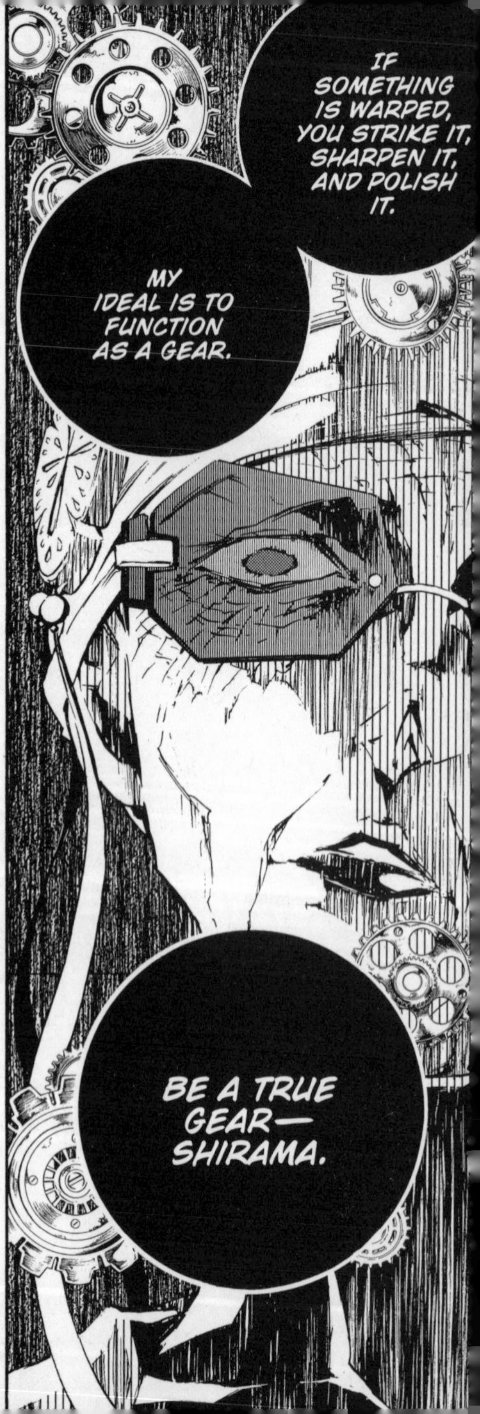
IF SOMETHING IS WARPED, YOU STRIKE IT, SHARPEN IT, AND POLISH IT.
MY IDEAL IS TO FUNCTION AS A GEAR.
BE A TRUE GEAR— SHIRAMA.

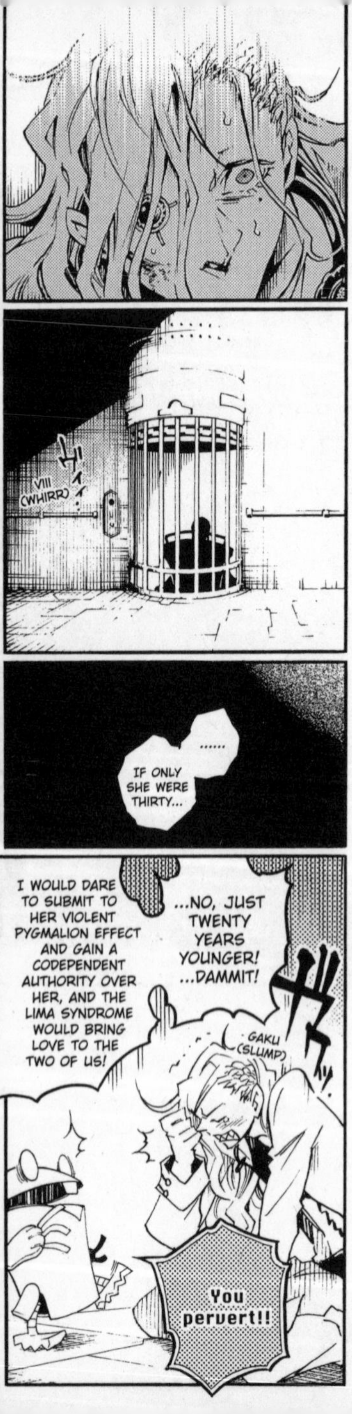
VIII (WHIRR)
......
IF ONLY SHE WERE THIRTY...
...NO, JUST TWENTY YEARS YOUNGER! ...DAMMIT!
I WOULD DARE TO SUBMIT TO HER VIOLENT PYGMALION EFFECT AND GAIN A CODEPENDENT AUTHORITY OVER HER, AND THE LIMA SYNDROME WOULD BRING LOVE TO THE TWO OF US!
GAKU (SLUMP)
You pervert!!

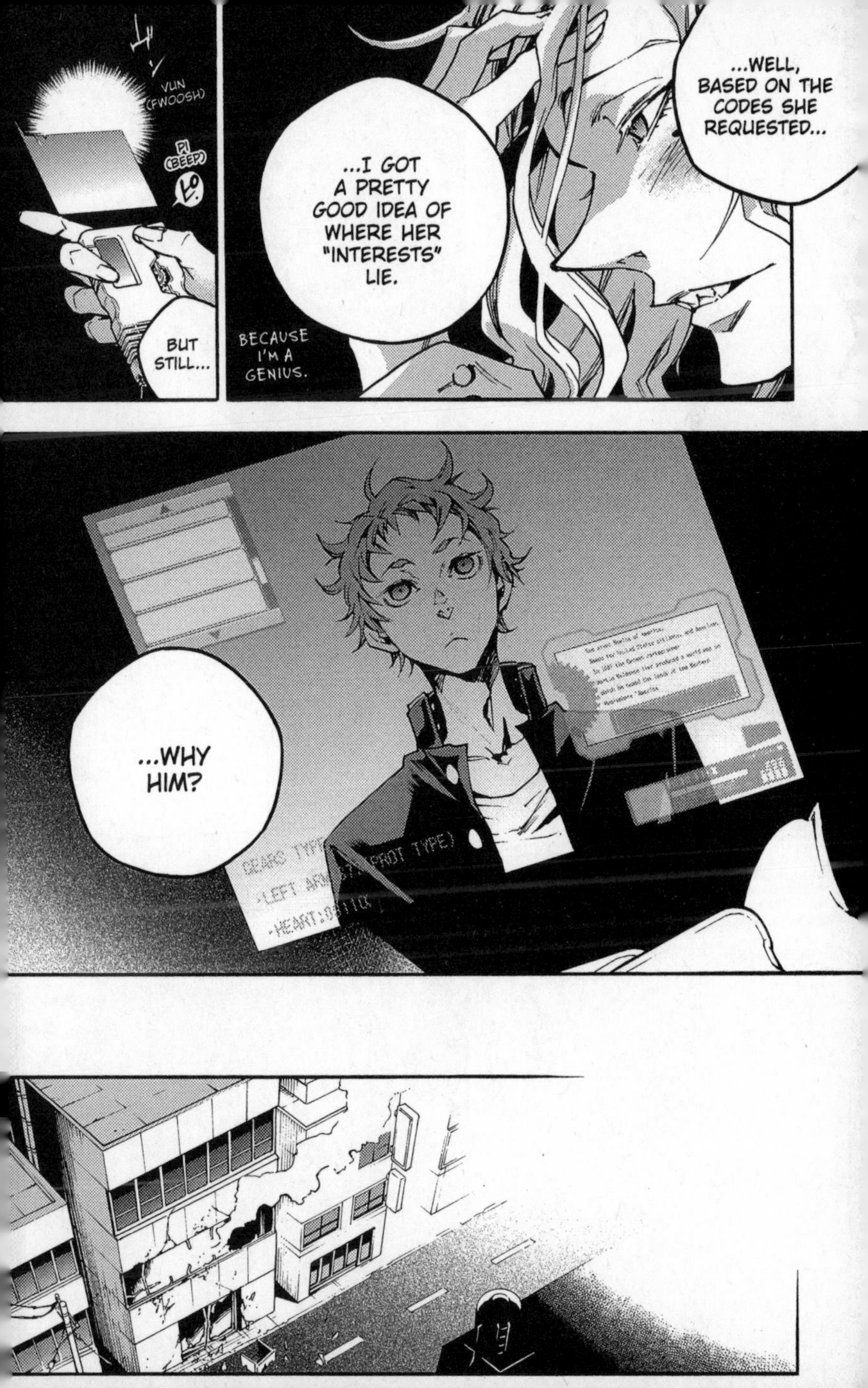
...WELL, BASED ON THE CODES SHE REQUESTED...
...I GOT A PRETTY GOOD IDEA OF WHERE HER "INTERESTS" LIE.
BECAUSE I'M A GENIUS.
VUN (FWOOSH)
PI (BEEP)
BUT STILL...
...WHY HIM?

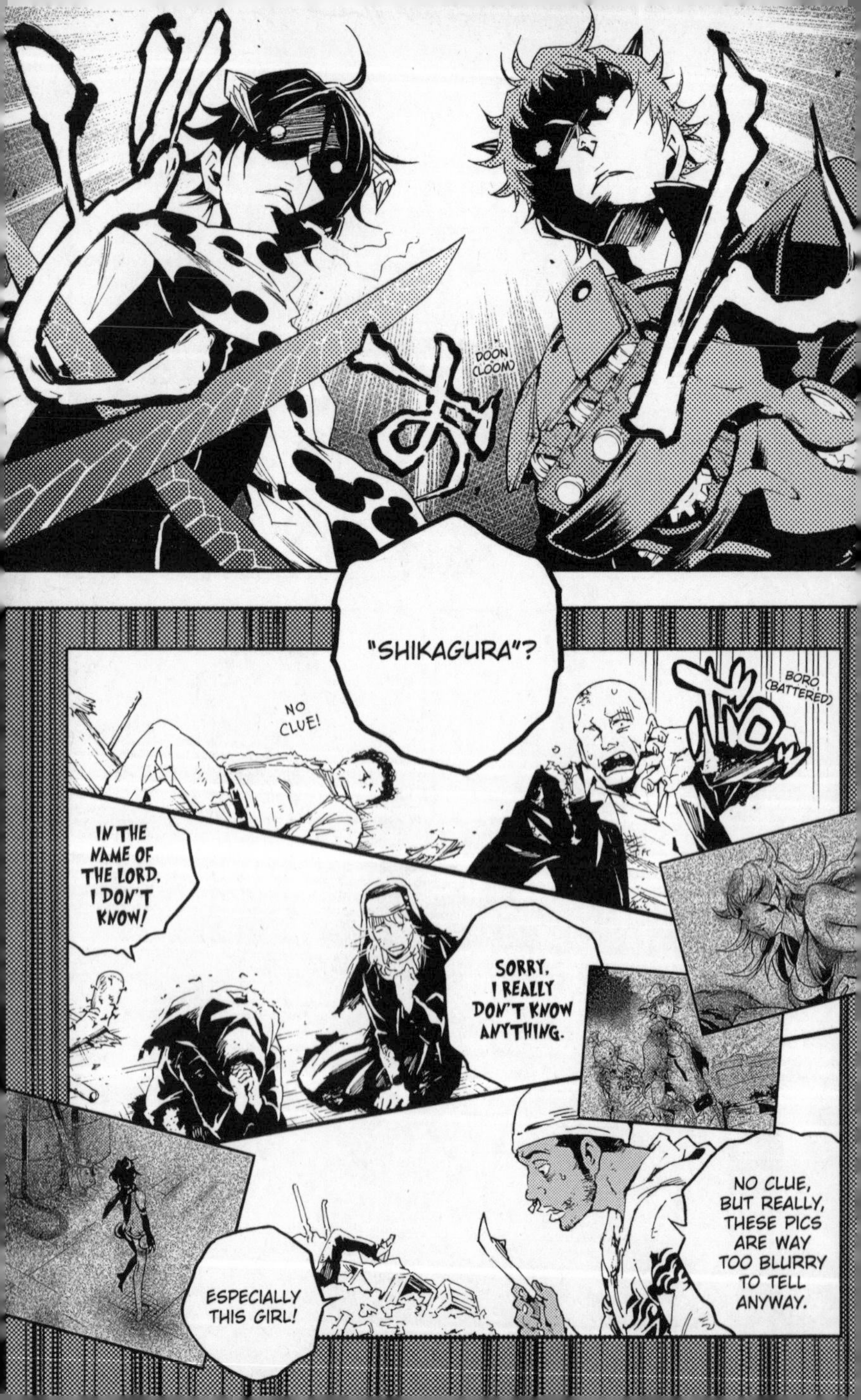
DOON (LOOM)
"SHIKAGURA"?
BORO (BATTERED)
NO CLUE!
SORRY, I REALLY DON'T KNOW ANYTHING.
IN THE NAME OF THE LORD, I DON'T KNOW!
NO CLUE, BUT REALLY, THESE PICS ARE WAY TOO BLURRY TO TELL ANYWAY.
ESPECIALLY THIS GIRL!

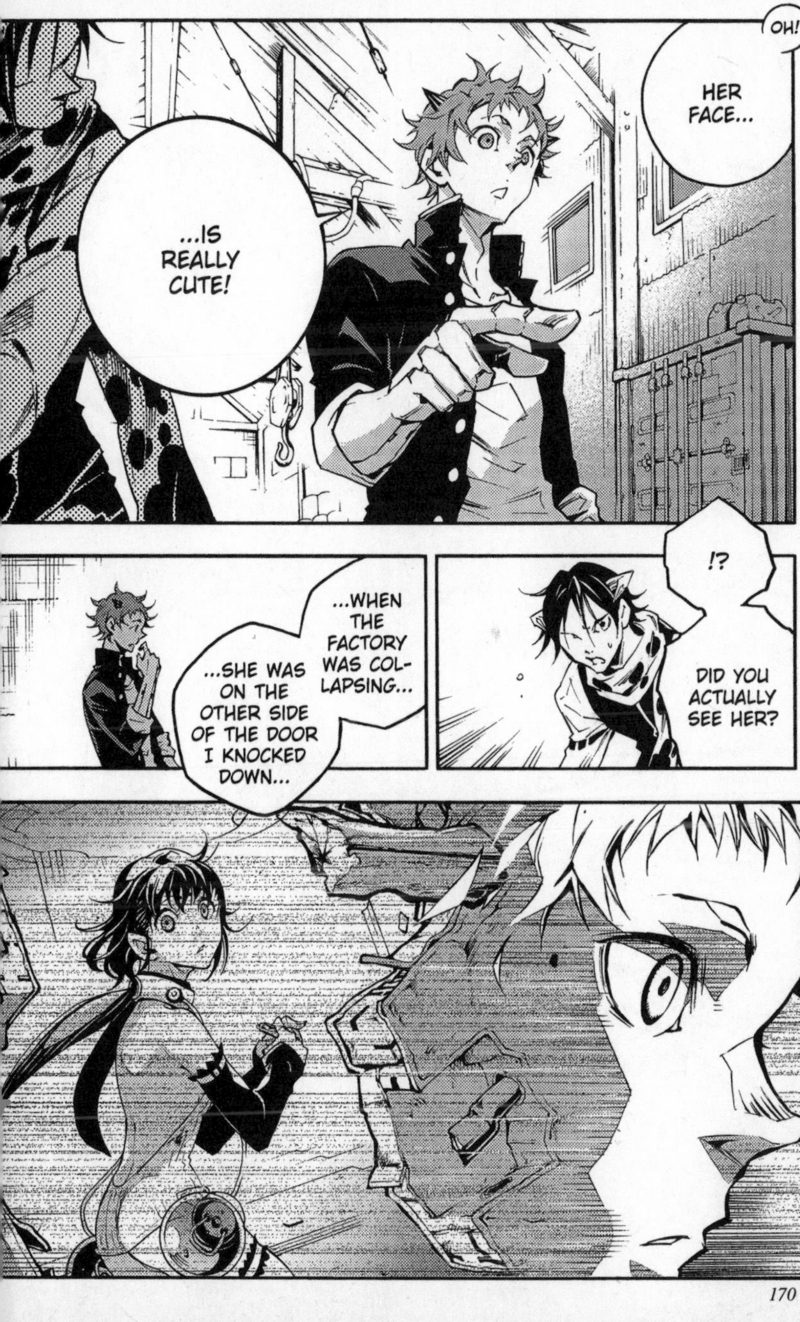
OH!
HER FACE...
...IS REALLY CUTE!
!?
DID YOU ACTUALLY SEE HER?
...WHEN THE FACTORY WAS COL-LAPSING...
...SHE WAS ON THE OTHER SIDE OF THE DOOR I KNOCKED DOWN...

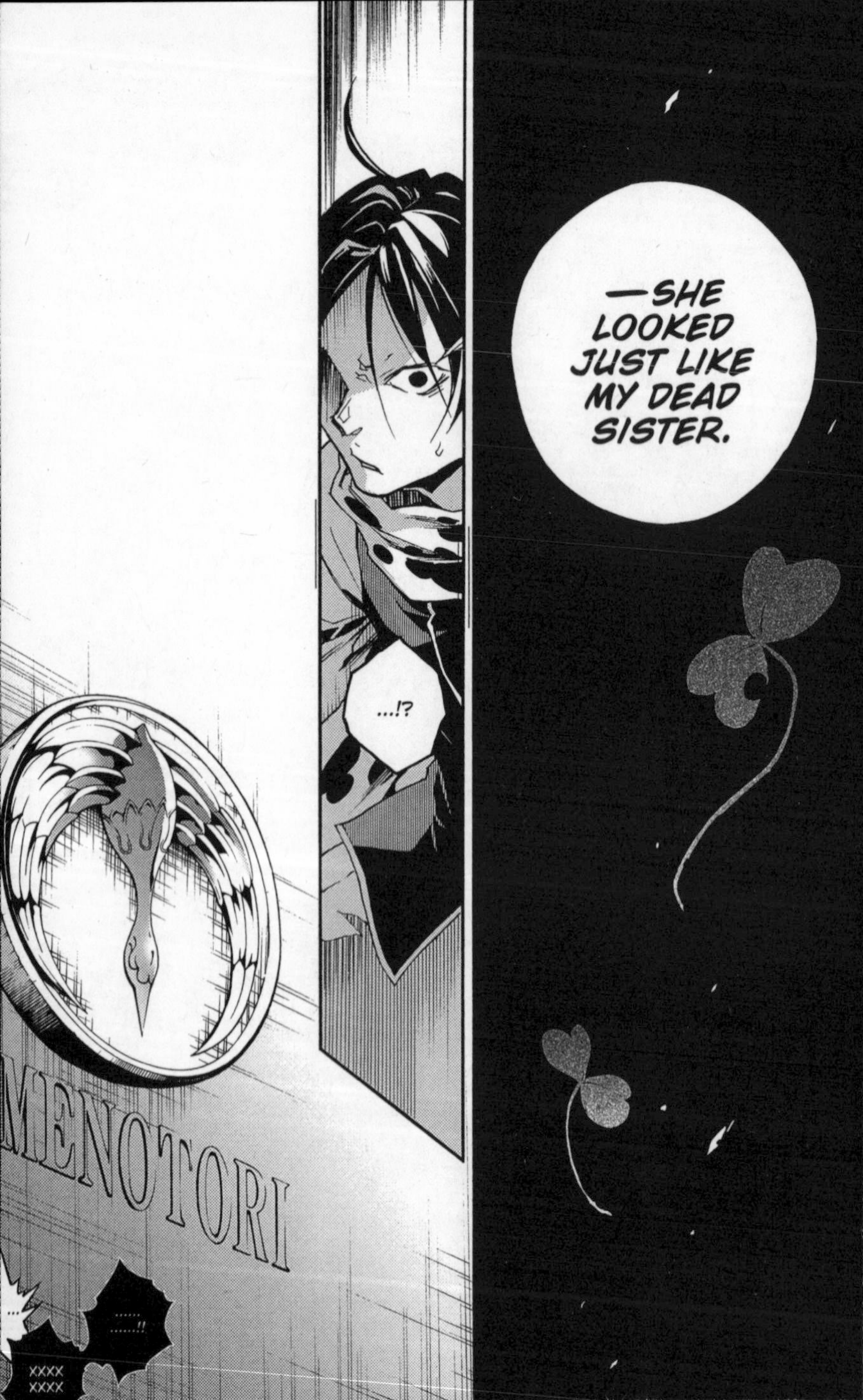
—SHE LOOKED JUST LIKE MY DEAD SISTER.
...!?
MENOTORI
......
......!!
...
XXXX
XXXX

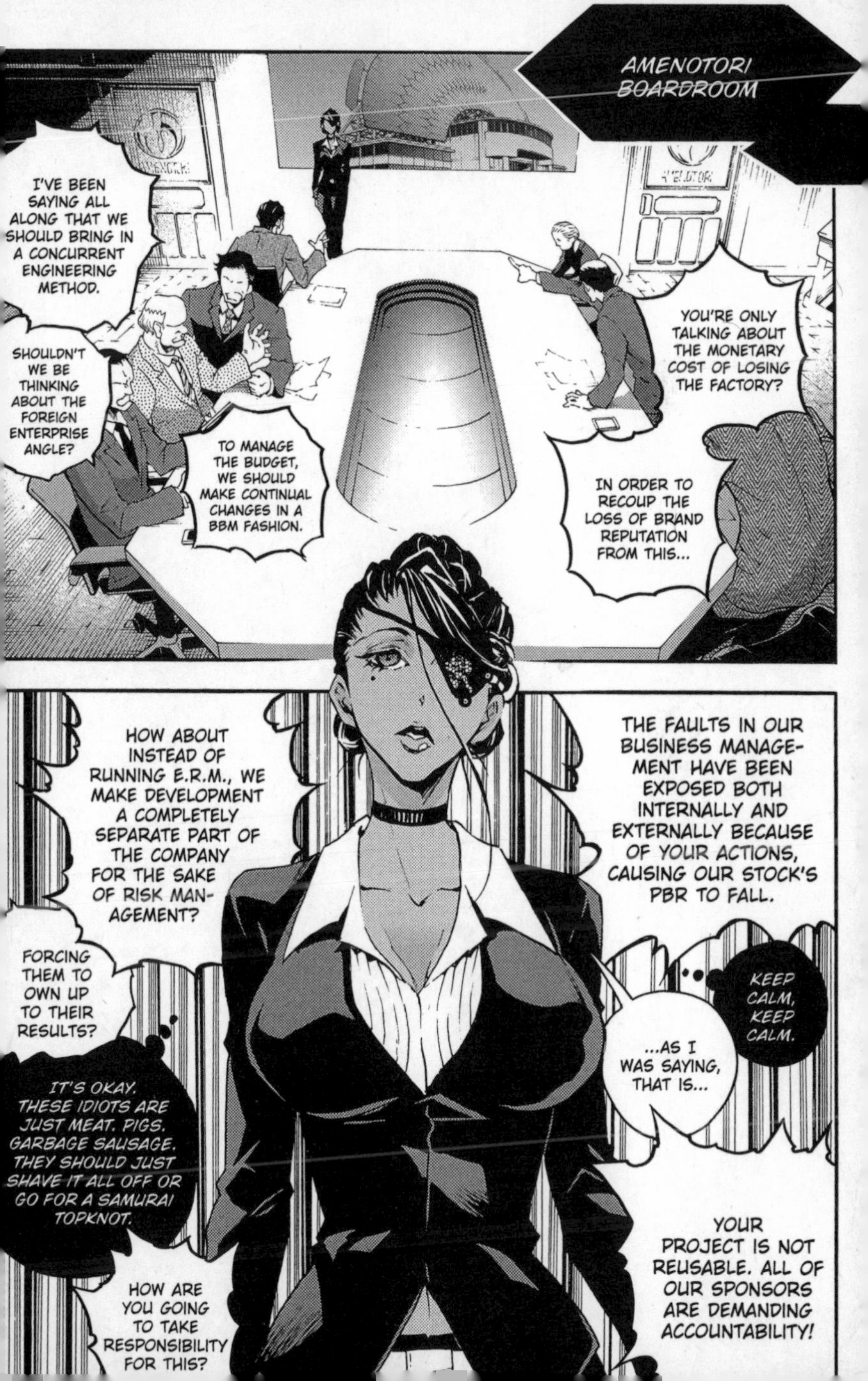
AMENOTORI BOARDROOM
YOU'RE ONLY TALKING ABOUT THE MONETARY COST OF LOSING THE FACTORY?
I'VE BEEN SAYING ALL ALONG THAT WE SHOULD BRING IN A CONCURRENT ENGINEERING METHOD.
SHOULDN'T WE BE THINKING ABOUT THE FOREIGN ENTERPRISE ANGLE?
IN ORDER TO RECOUP THE LOSS OF BRAND REPUTATION FROM THIS...
TO MANAGE THE BUDGET, WE SHOULD MAKE CONTINUAL CHANGES IN A BBM FASHION.
THE FAULTS IN OUR BUSINESS MANAGEMENT HAVE BEEN EXPOSED BOTH INTERNALLY AND EXTERNALLY BECAUSE OF YOUR ACTIONS, CAUSING OUR STOCK'S PBR TO FALL.
HOW ABOUT INSTEAD OF RUNNING E.R.M., WE MAKE DEVELOPMENT A COMPLETELY SEPARATE PART OF THE COMPANY FOR THE SAKE OF RISK MANAGEMENT?
KEEP CALM, KEEP CALM.
...AS I WAS SAYING, THAT IS...
FORCING THEM TO OWN UP TO THEIR RESULTS?
IT'S OKAY. THESE IDIOTS ARE JUST MEAT. PIGS. GARBAGE SAUSAGE. THEY SHOULD JUST SHAVE IT ALL OFF OR GO FOR A SAMURAI TOPKNOT.
YOUR PROJECT IS NOT REUSABLE. ALL OF OUR SPONSORS ARE DEMANDING ACCOUNTABILITY!
HOW ARE YOU GOING TO TAKE RESPONSIBILITY FOR THIS?

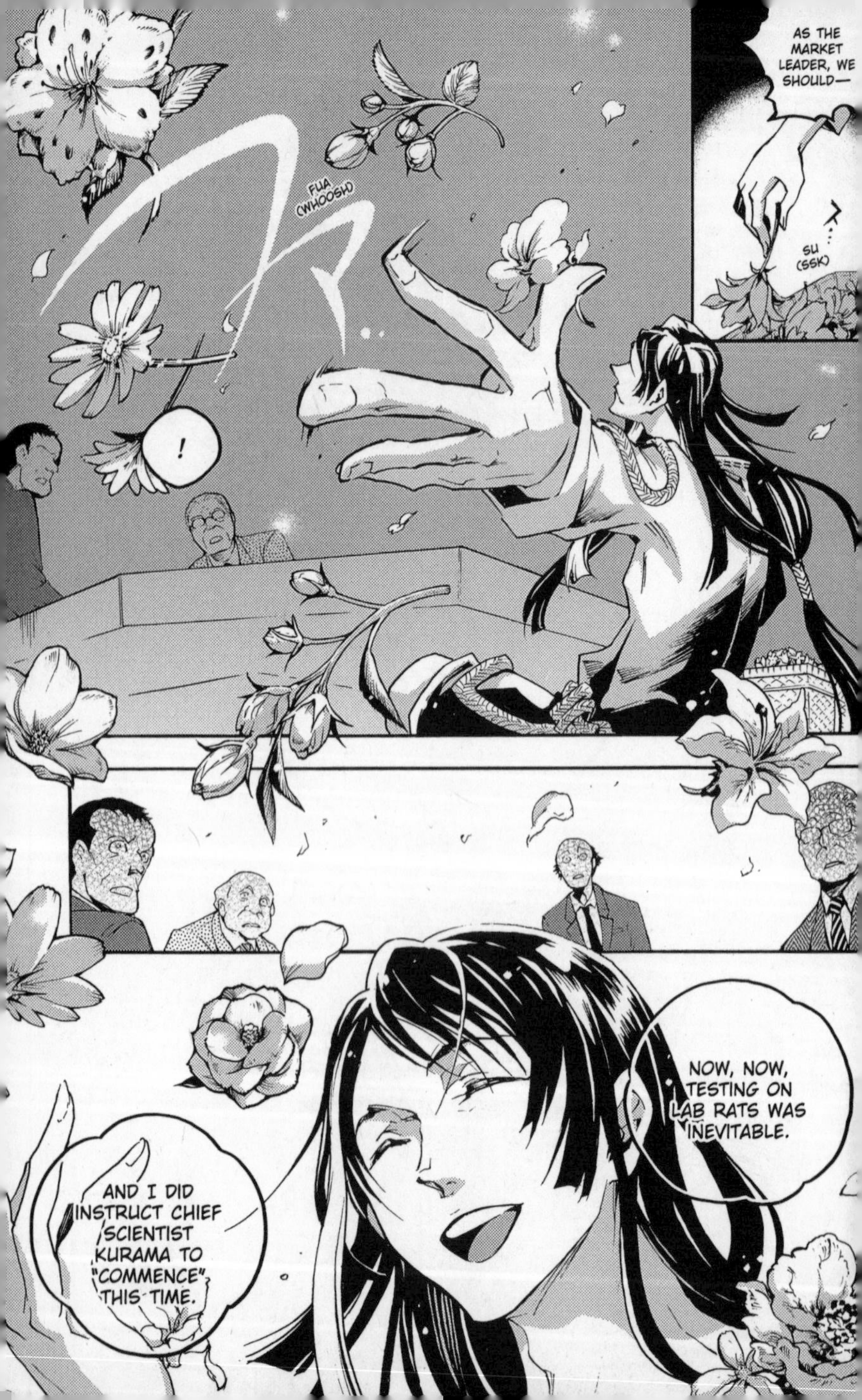
AS THE MARKET LEADER, WE SHOULD—
SU (SSK)
FUA (WHOOSH)
!
NOW, NOW, TESTING ON LAB RATS WAS INEVITABLE.
AND I DID INSTRUCT CHIEF SCIENTIST KURAMA TO "COMMENCE" THIS TIME.

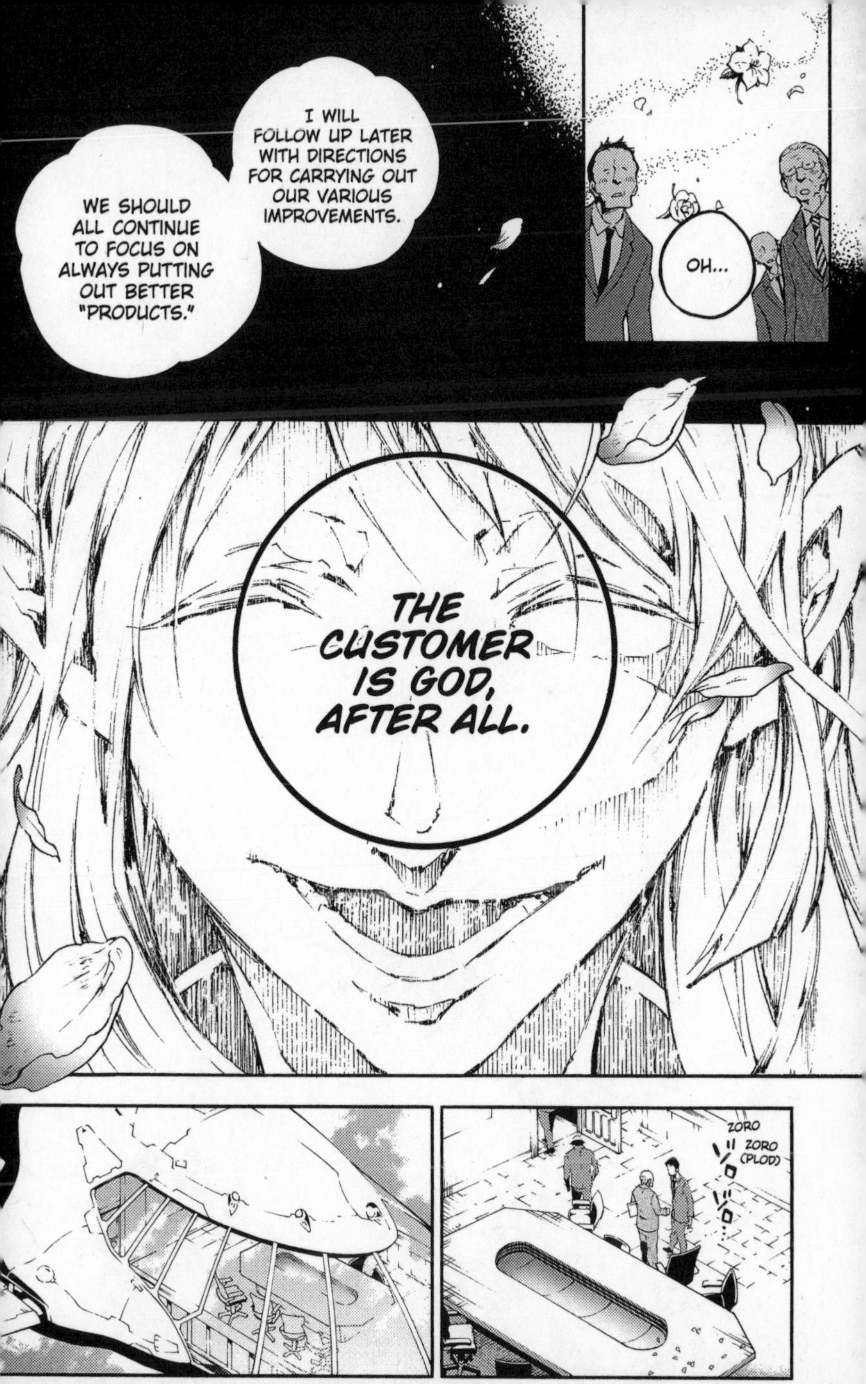
OH...
I WILL FOLLOW UP LATER WITH DIRECTIONS FOR CARRYING OUT OUR VARIOUS IMPROVEMENTS.
WE SHOULD ALL CONTINUE TO FOCUS ON ALWAYS PUTTING OUT BETTER "PRODUCTS."
THE CUSTOMER IS GOD, AFTER ALL.
ZORO ZORO (PLOD)

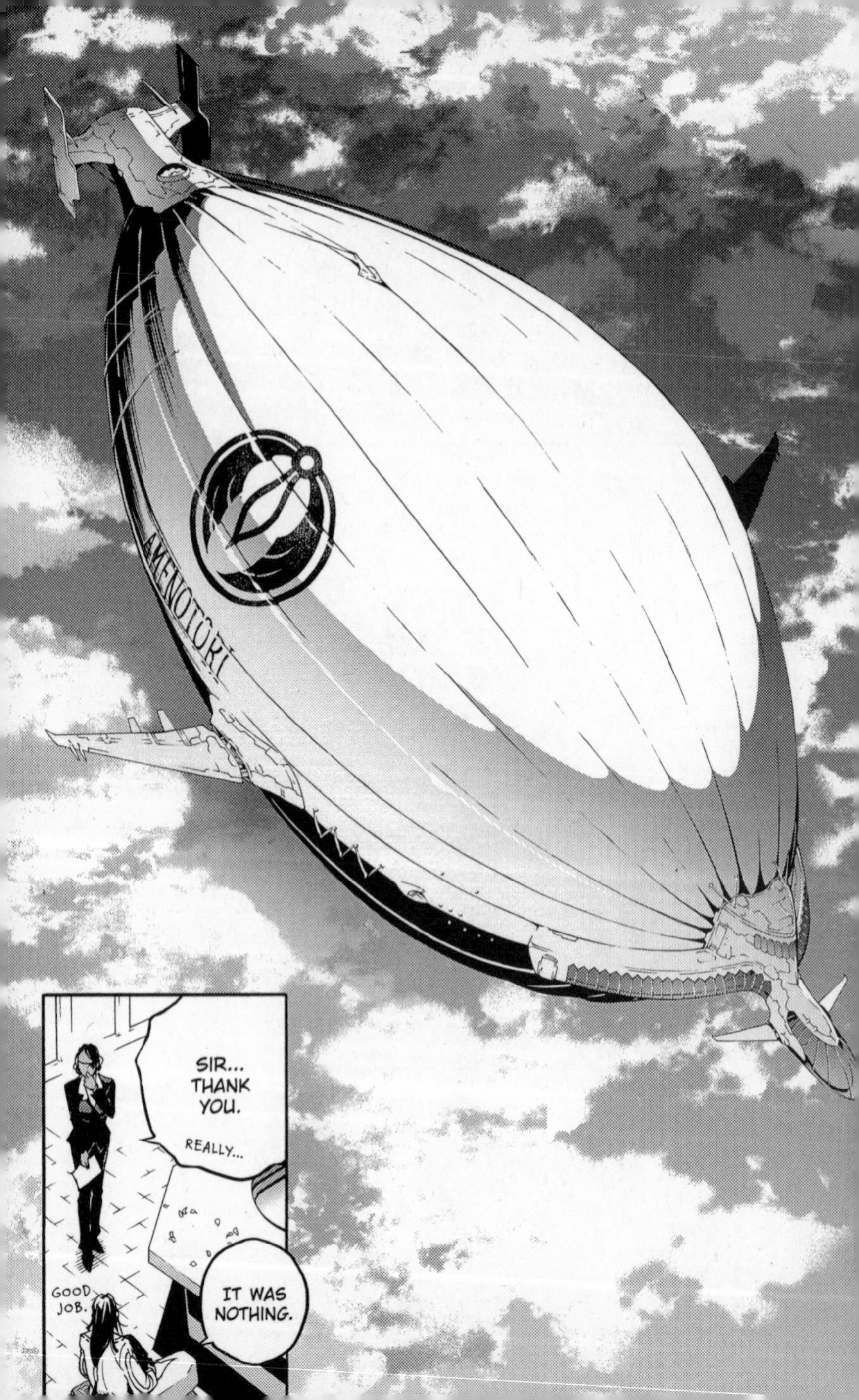
AMENOTORI
SIR... THANK YOU.
REALLY...
IT WAS NOTHING.
GOOD JOB.

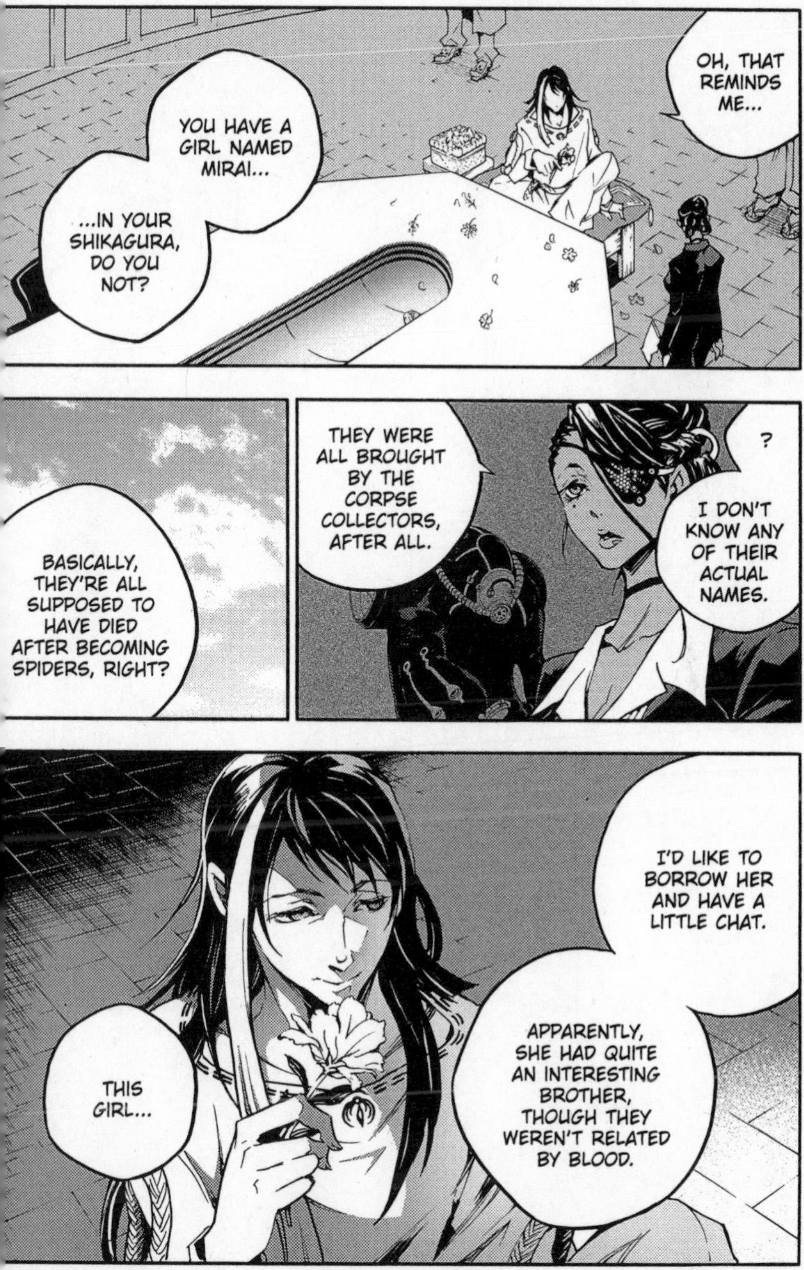
OH, THAT REMINDS ME...
YOU HAVE A GIRL NAMED MIRAI...
...IN YOUR SHIKAGURA, DO YOU NOT?
?
I DON'T KNOW ANY OF THEIR ACTUAL NAMES.
THEY WERE ALL BROUGHT BY THE CORPSE COLLECTORS, AFTER ALL.
BASICALLY, THEY'RE ALL SUPPOSED TO HAVE DIED AFTER BECOMING SPIDERS, RIGHT?
I'D LIKE TO BORROW HER AND HAVE A LITTLE CHAT.
APPARENTLY, SHE HAD QUITE AN INTERESTING BROTHER, THOUGH THEY WEREN'T RELATED BY BLOOD.
THIS GIRL...

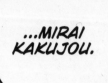

...MIRAI
KAKUJOU.

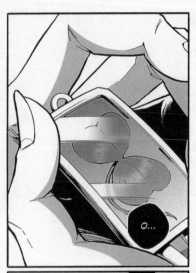

O...

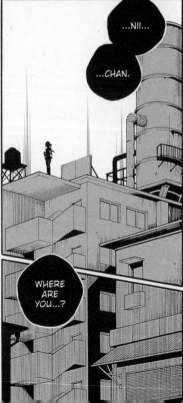

...NII...

...CHAN.

WHERE
ARE
YOU...?

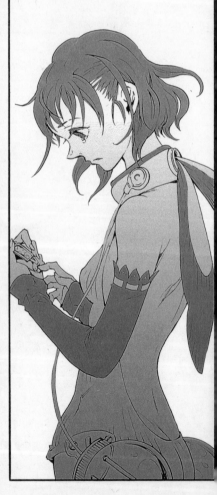

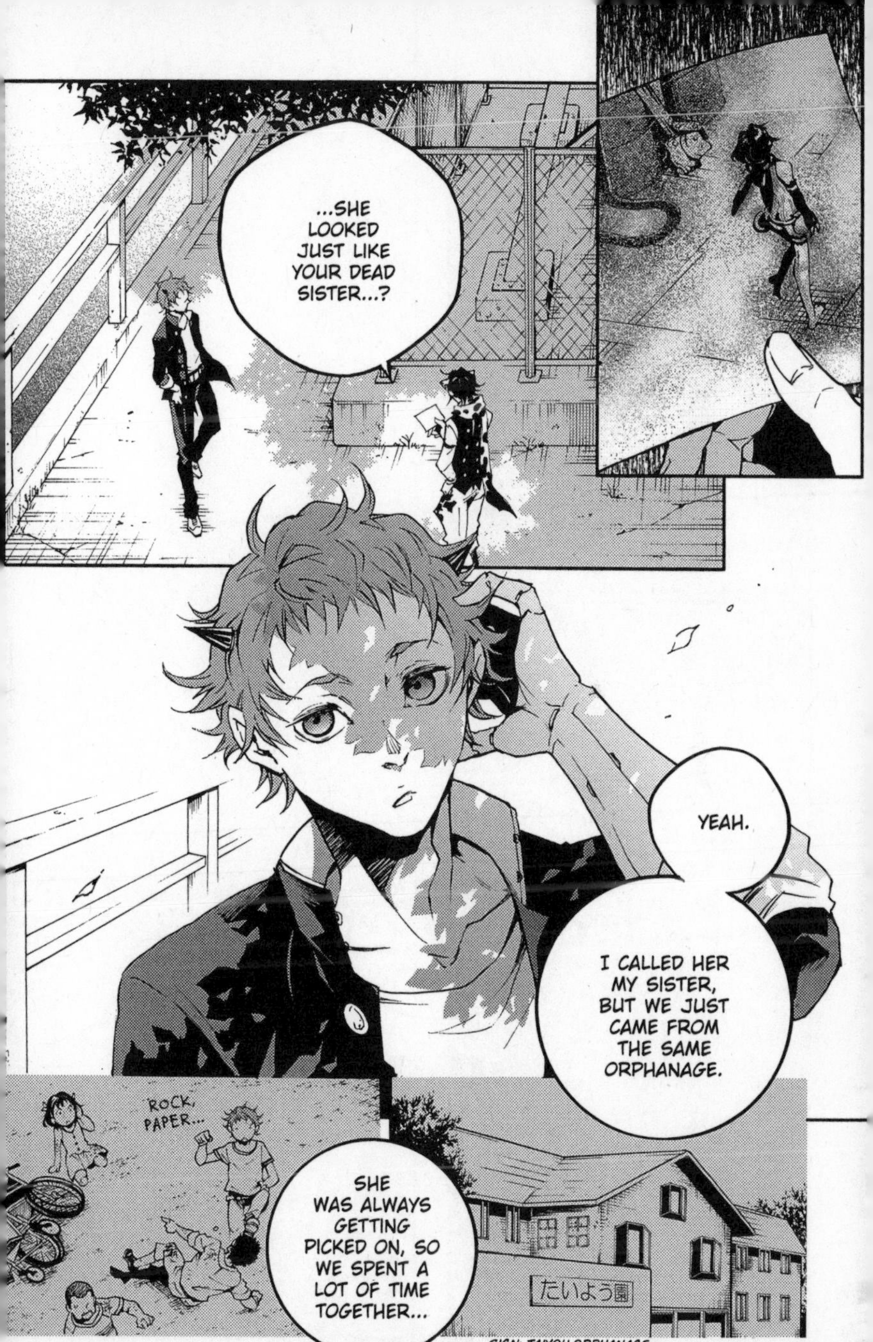
...SHE LOOKED JUST LIKE YOUR DEAD SISTER...?
YEAH.
I CALLED HER MY SISTER, BUT WE JUST CAME FROM THE SAME ORPHANAGE.
たいよう園
SHE WAS ALWAYS GETTING PICKED ON, SO WE SPENT A LOT OF TIME TOGETHER...
ROCK, PAPER...

SIGN: TAIYOU ORPHANAGE

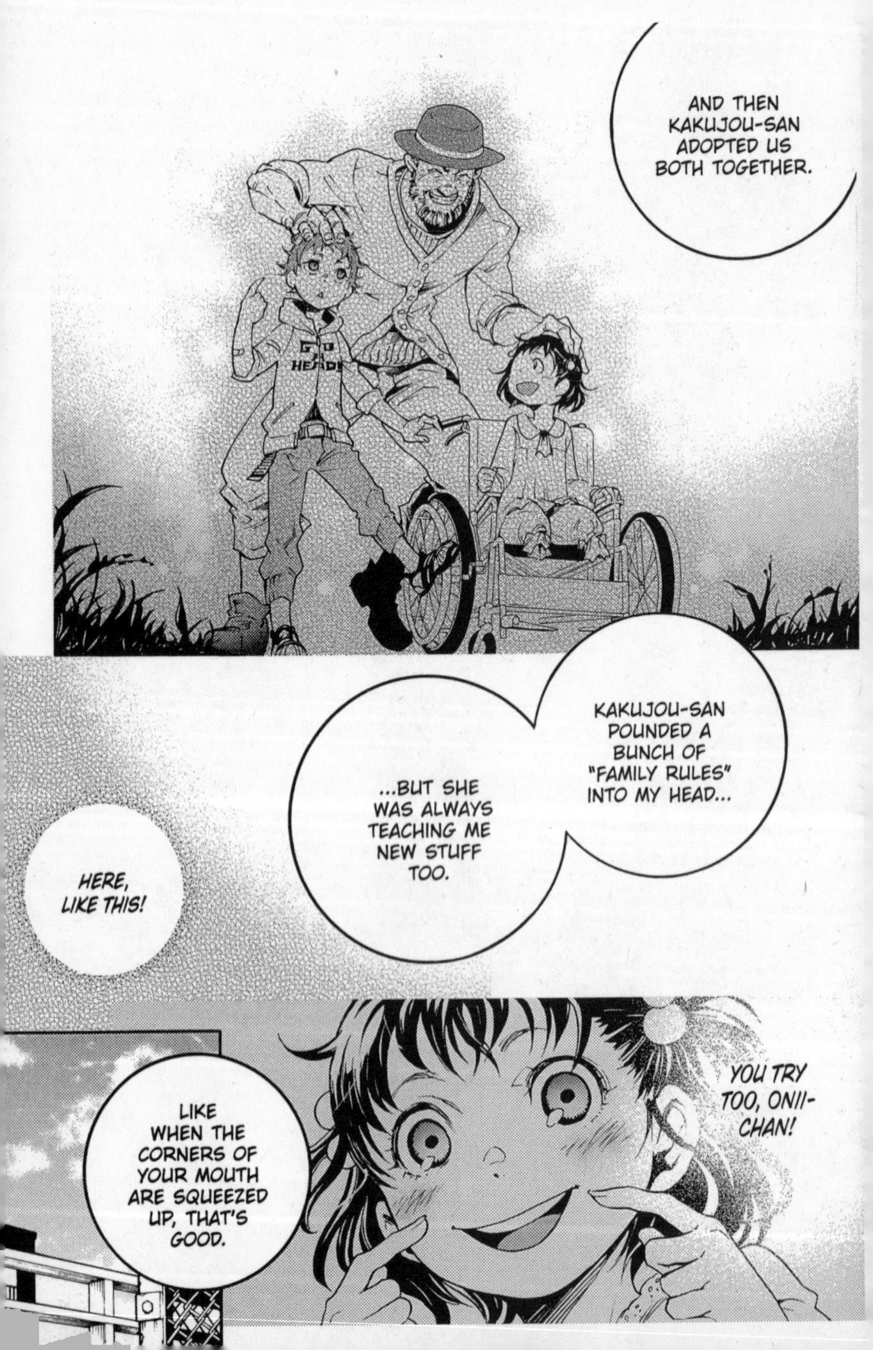
AND THEN KAKUJOU-SAN ADOPTED US BOTH TOGETHER.
KAKUJOU-SAN POUNDED A BUNCH OF "FAMILY RULES" INTO MY HEAD...
...BUT SHE WAS ALWAYS TEACHING ME NEW STUFF TOO.
HERE, LIKE THIS!
YOU TRY TOO, ONII-CHAN!
LIKE WHEN THE CORNERS OF YOUR MOUTH ARE SQUEEZED UP, THAT'S GOOD.

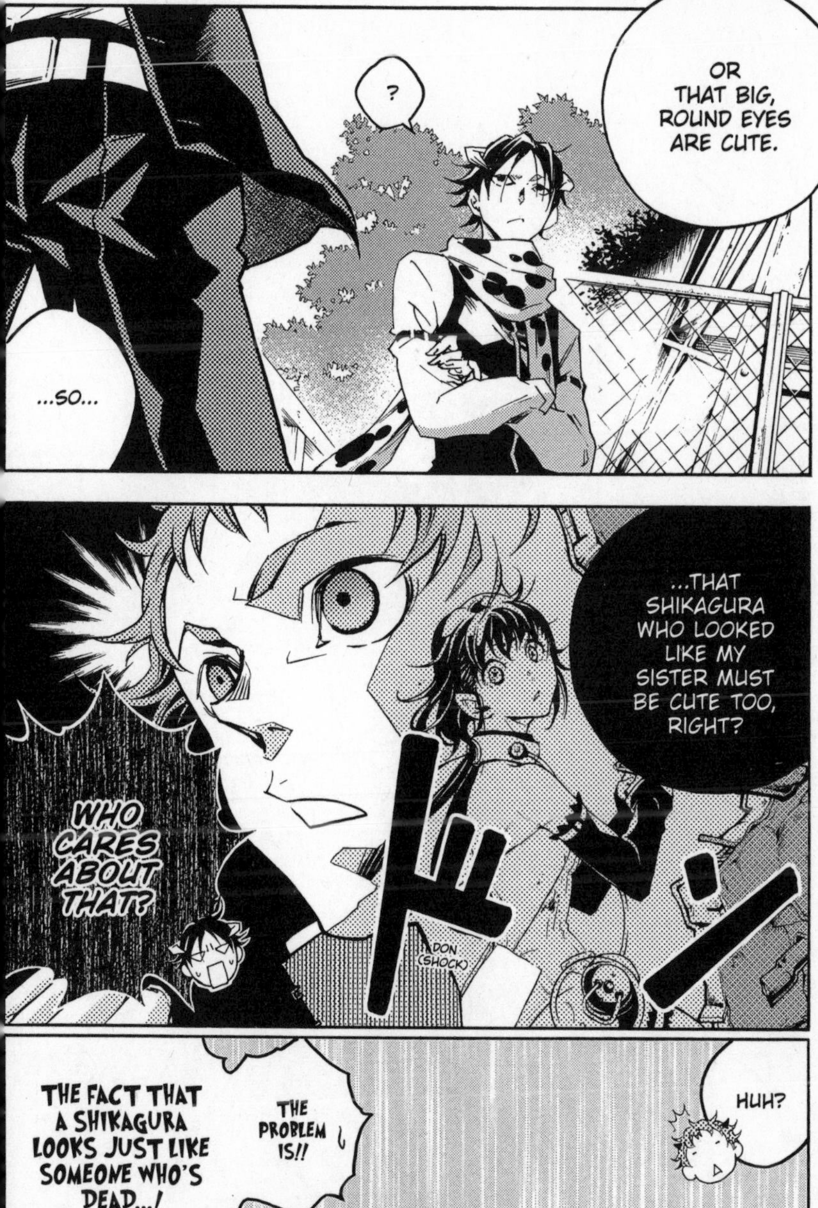
OR THAT BIG, ROUND EYES ARE CUTE.
?
...SO...
...THAT SHIKAGURA WHO LOOKED LIKE MY SISTER MUST BE CUTE TOO, RIGHT?
DON (SHOCK)
WHO CARES ABOUT THAT?
HUH?
THE PROBLEM IS!!
THE FACT THAT A SHIKAGURA LOOKS JUST LIKE SOMEONE WHO'S DEAD...!

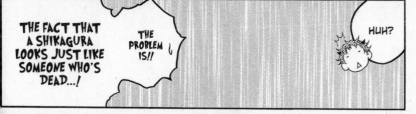

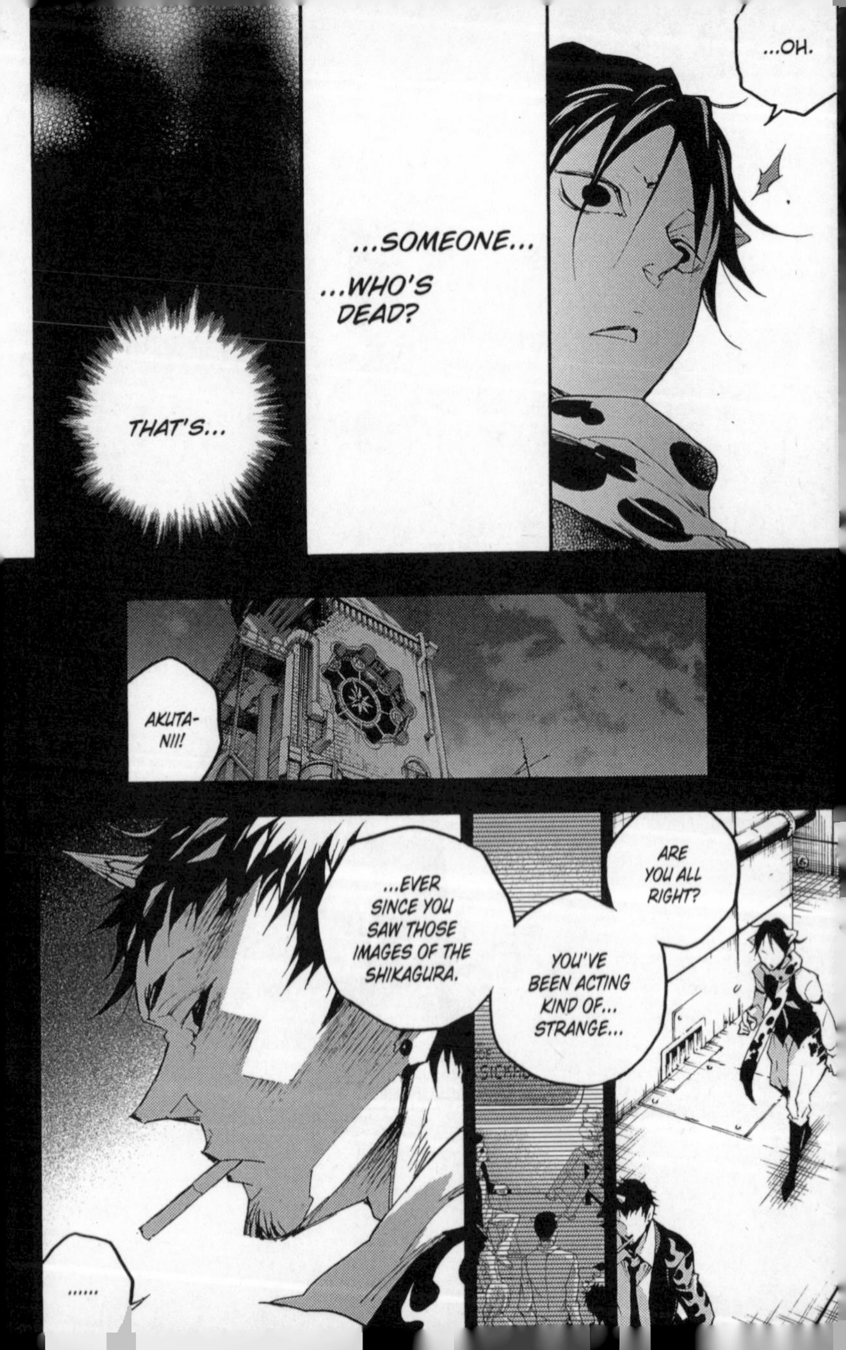
...OH.
...SOMEONE...
...WHO'S DEAD?
THAT'S...
AKUTA-NII!
ARE YOU ALL RIGHT?
YOU'VE BEEN ACTING KIND OF... STRANGE...
...EVER SINCE YOU SAW THOSE IMAGES OF THE SHIKAGURA.
......

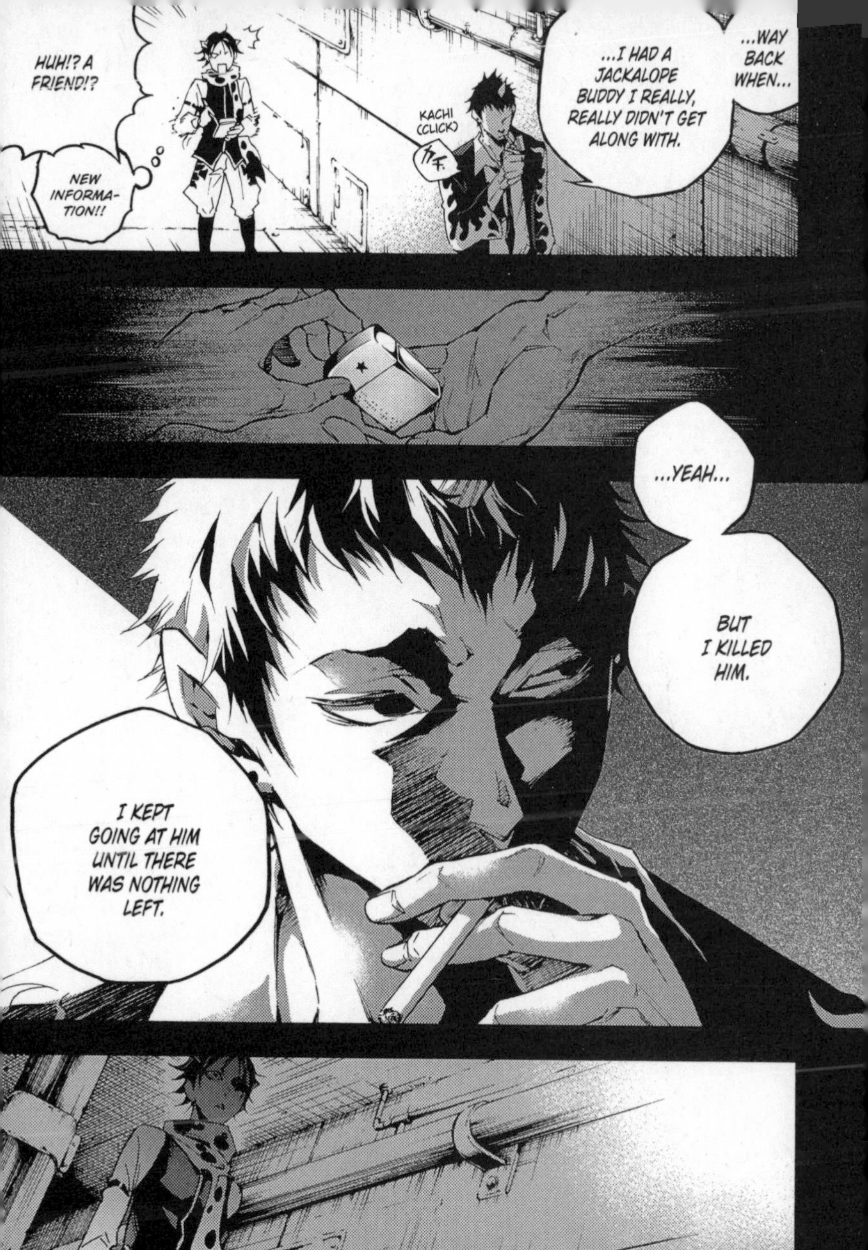
...WAY BACK WHEN...
...I HAD A JACKALOPE BUDDY I REALLY, REALLY DIDN'T GET ALONG WITH.
KACHI (CLICK)
HUH!? A FRIEND!?
NEW INFORMATION!!
...YEAH...
BUT I KILLED HIM.
I KEPT GOING AT HIM UNTIL THERE WAS NOTHING LEFT.

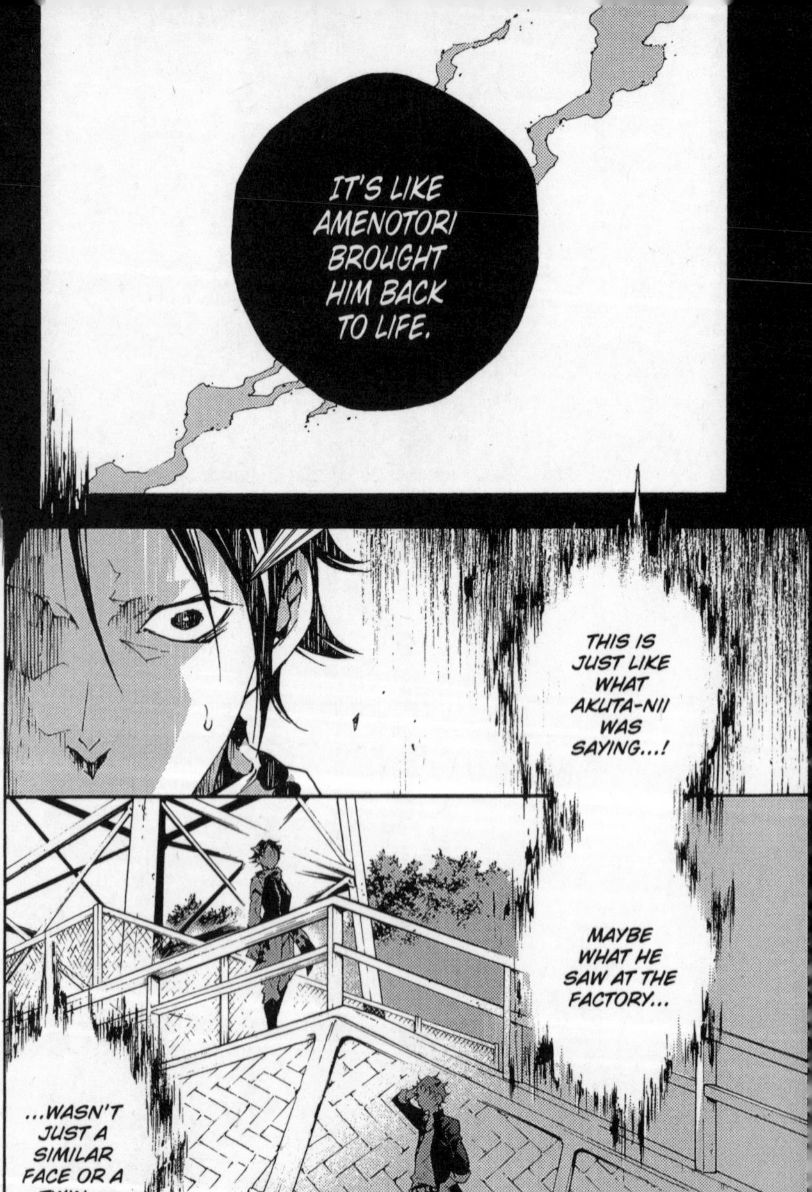
IT'S LIKE AMENOTORI BROUGHT HIM BACK TO LIFE.
THIS IS JUST LIKE WHAT AKUTA-NII WAS SAYING...!
MAYBE WHAT HE SAW AT THE FACTORY...
...WASN'T JUST A SIMILAR FACE OR A TWIN...

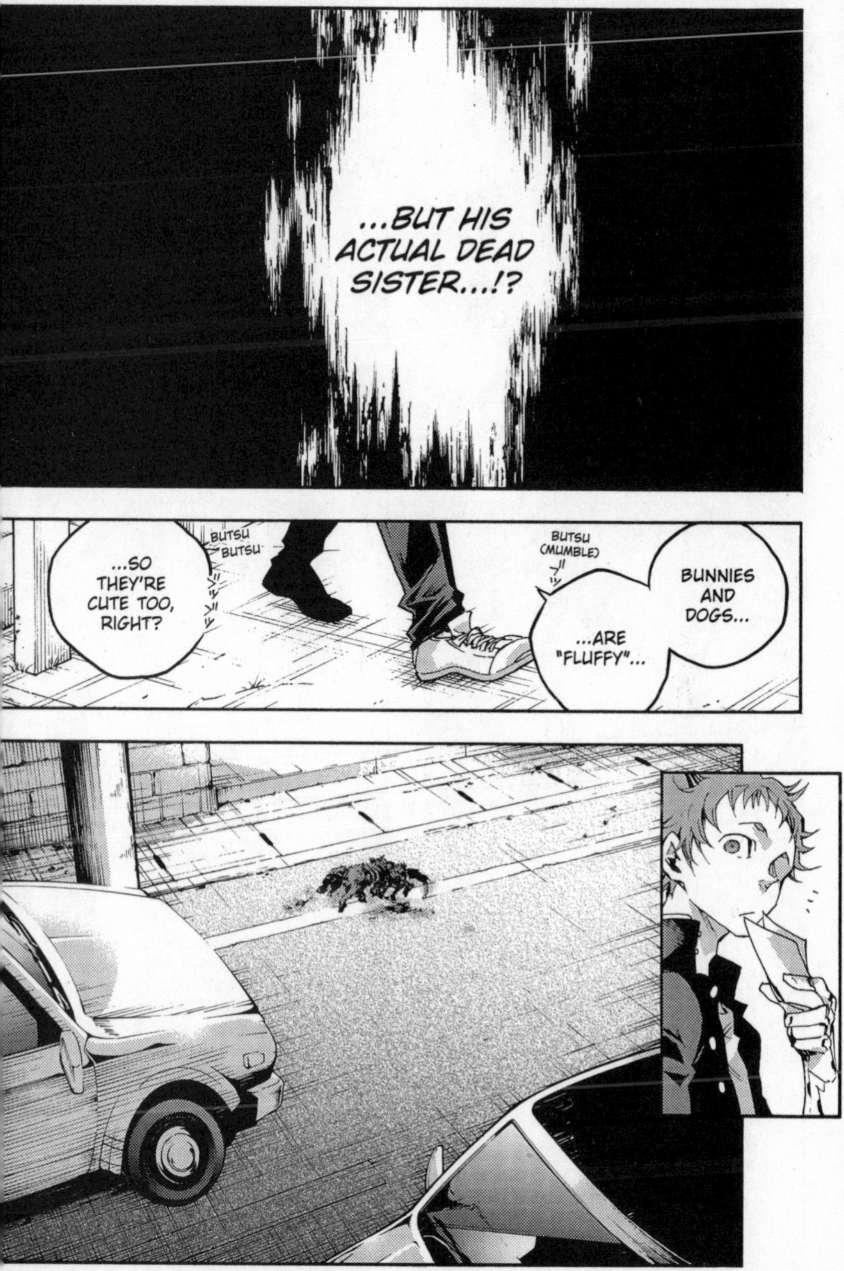
...BUT HIS ACTUAL DEAD SISTER...!?
BUTSU (MUMBLE)
BUNNIES AND DOGS...
...ARE "FLUFFY"...
BUTSU BUTSU
...SO THEY'RE CUTE TOO, RIGHT?

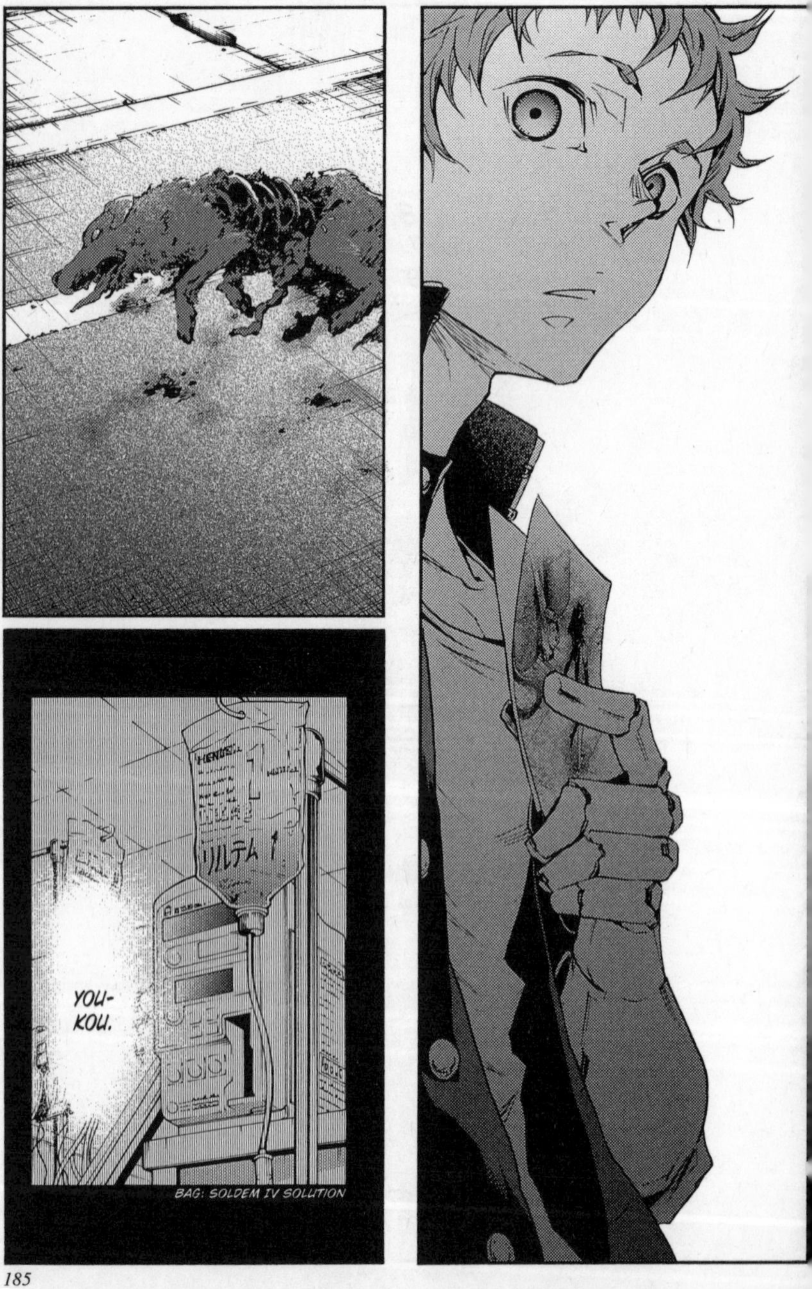
YOU-KOU.
BAG: SOLDEM IV SOLUTION

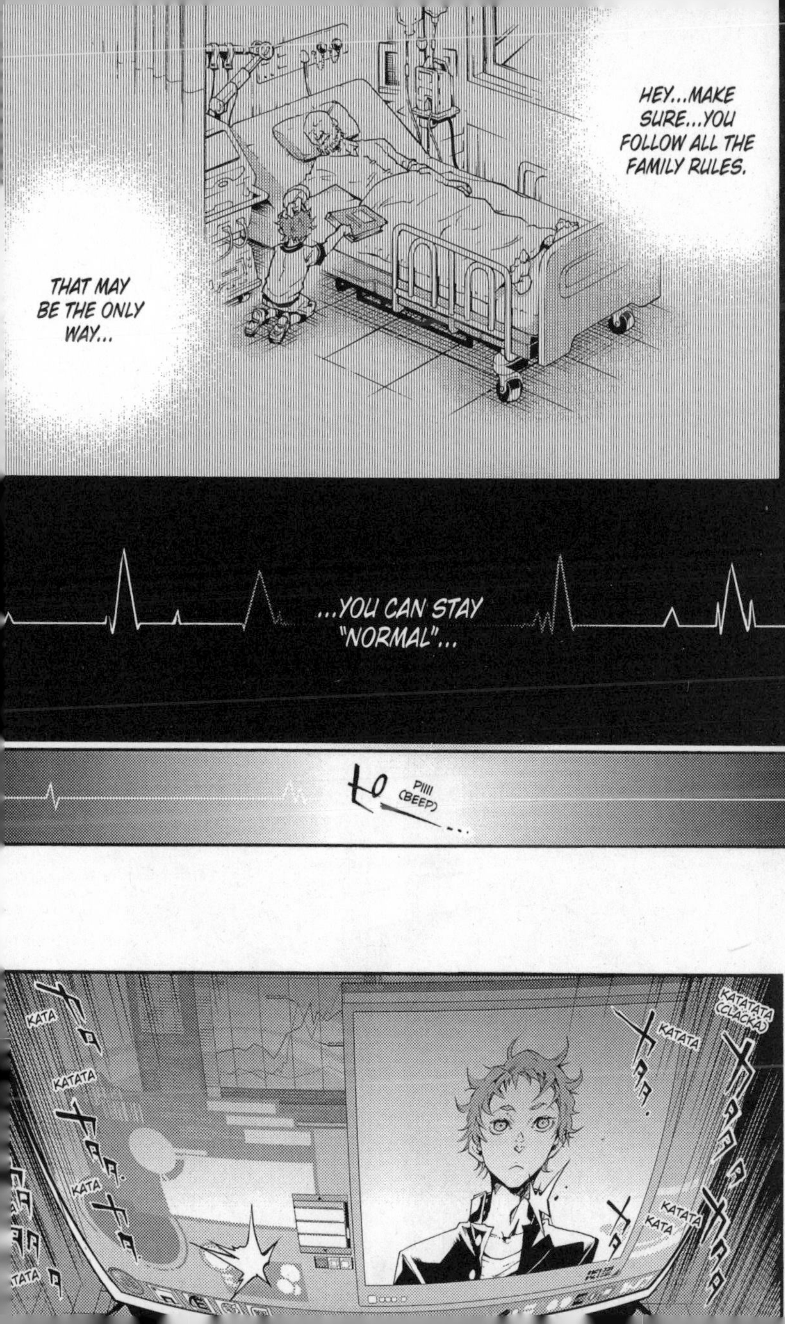
HEY...MAKE SURE...YOU FOLLOW ALL THE FAMILY RULES.
THAT MAY BE THE ONLY WAY...
...YOU CAN STAY "NORMAL"...
PIIII (BEEP)
KATATATA (CLACKA)
KATATA
KATATA
KATA
KATA
KATATA
KATA
KATA

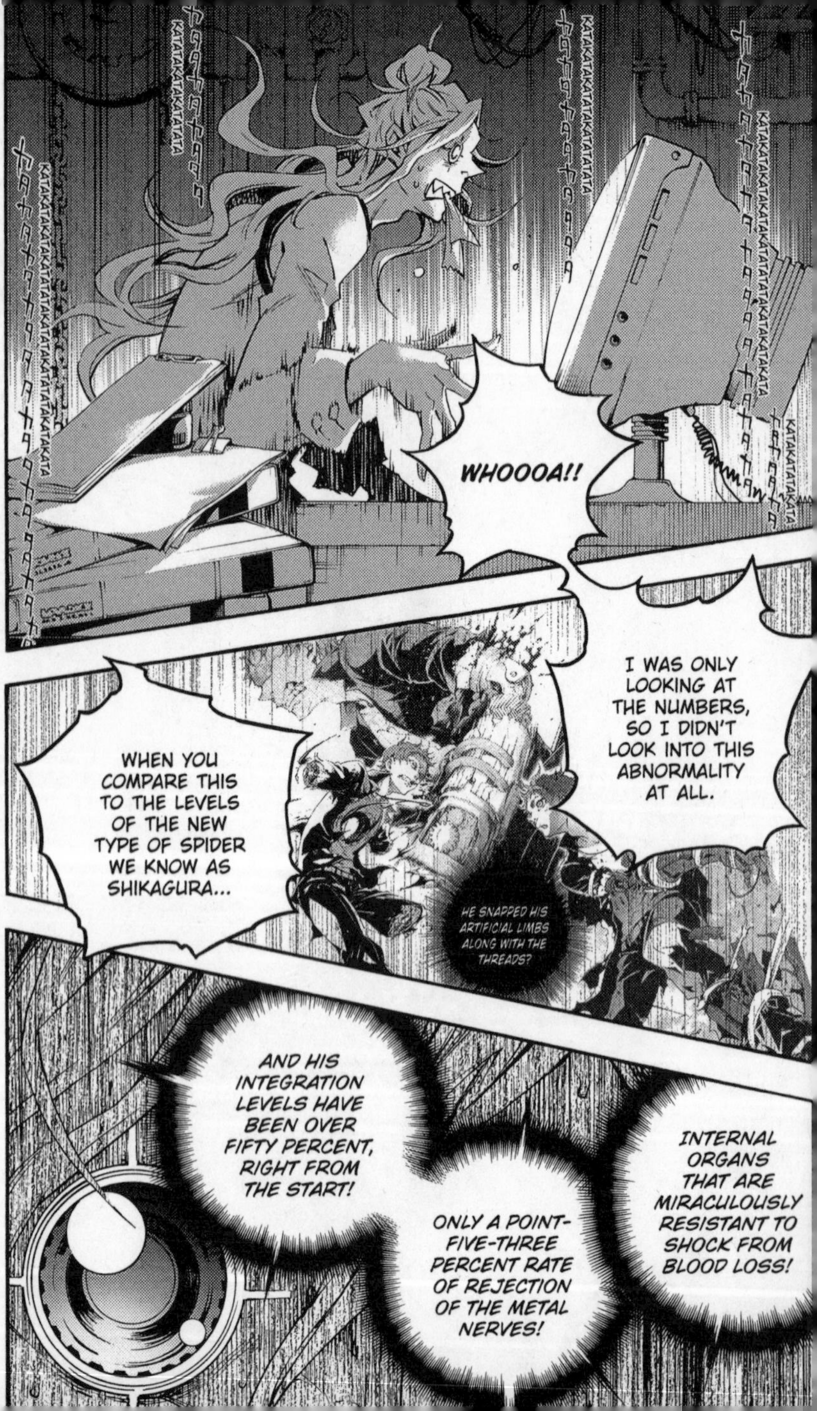
WHOOOA!!
I WAS ONLY LOOKING AT THE NUMBERS, SO I DIDN'T LOOK INTO THIS ABNORMALITY AT ALL.
HE SNAPPED HIS ARTIFICIAL LIMBS ALONG WITH THE THREADS?
WHEN YOU COMPARE THIS TO THE LEVELS OF THE NEW TYPE OF SPIDER WE KNOW AS SHIKAGURA...
AND HIS INTEGRATION LEVELS HAVE BEEN OVER FIFTY PERCENT, RIGHT FROM THE START!
INTERNAL ORGANS THAT ARE MIRACULOUSLY RESISTANT TO SHOCK FROM BLOOD LOSS!
ONLY A POINT-FIVE-THREE PERCENT RATE OF REJECTION OF THE METAL NERVES!

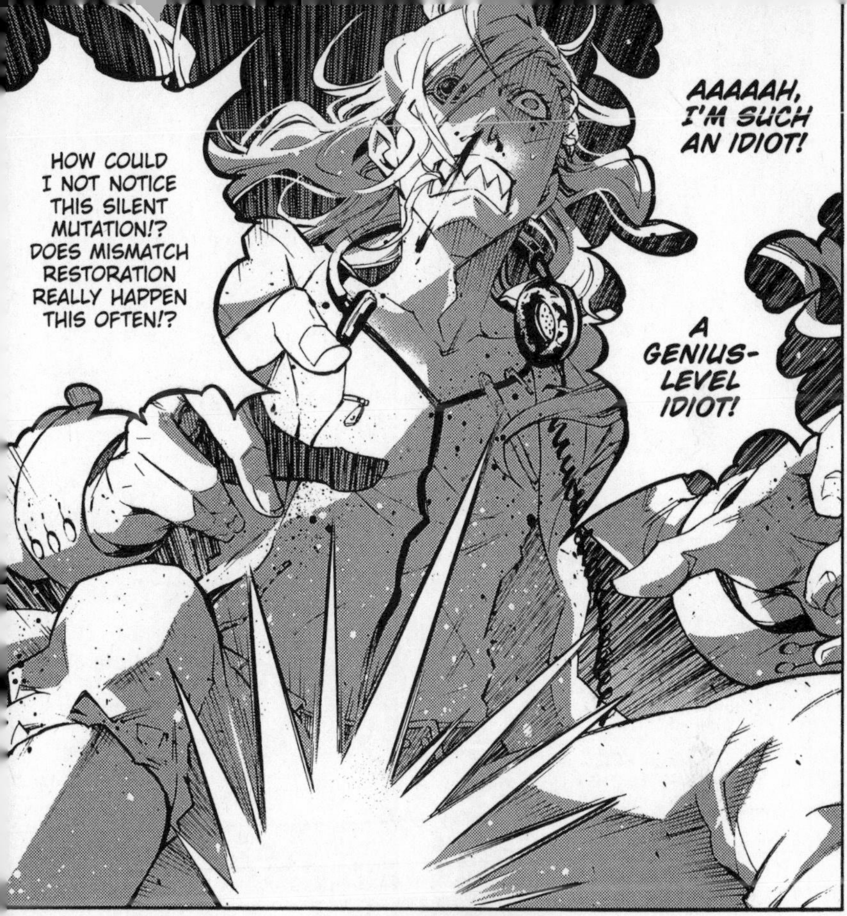
AAAAAH, I'M SUCH AN IDIOT!
HOW COULD I NOT NOTICE THIS SILENT MUTATION!? DOES MISMATCH RESTORATION REALLY HAPPEN THIS OFTEN!?
A GENIUS-LEVEL IDIOT!
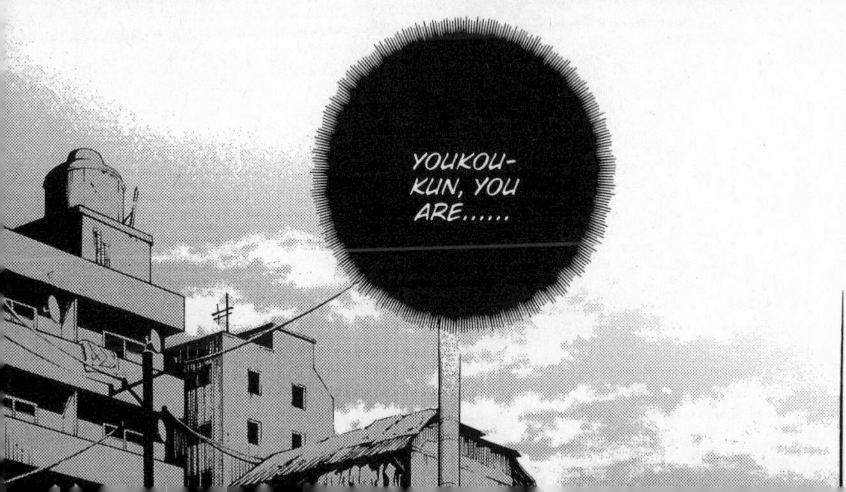
YOUKOU-KUN, YOU ARE......

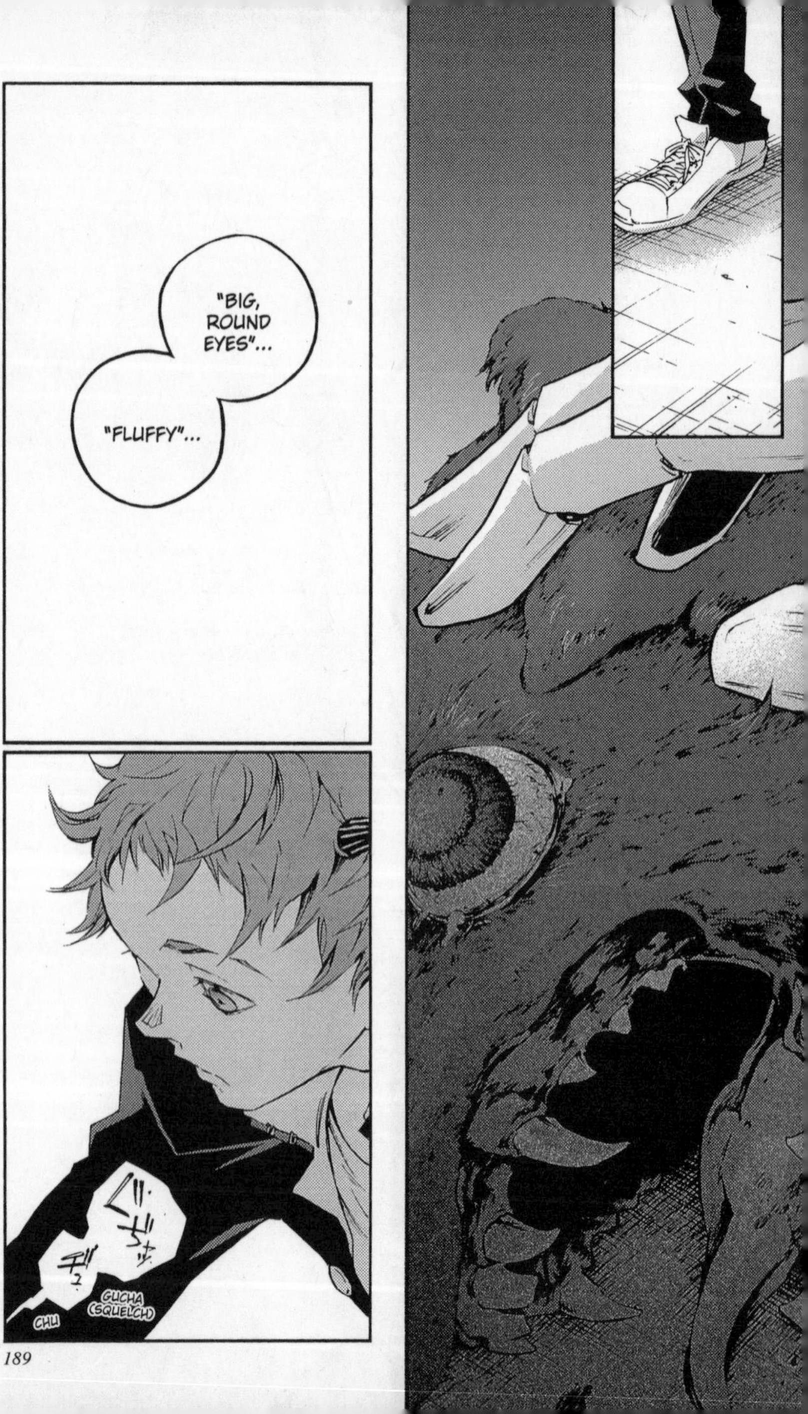
"BIG, ROUND EYES"...
"FLUFFY"...
GUCHA (SQUELCH)
CHU

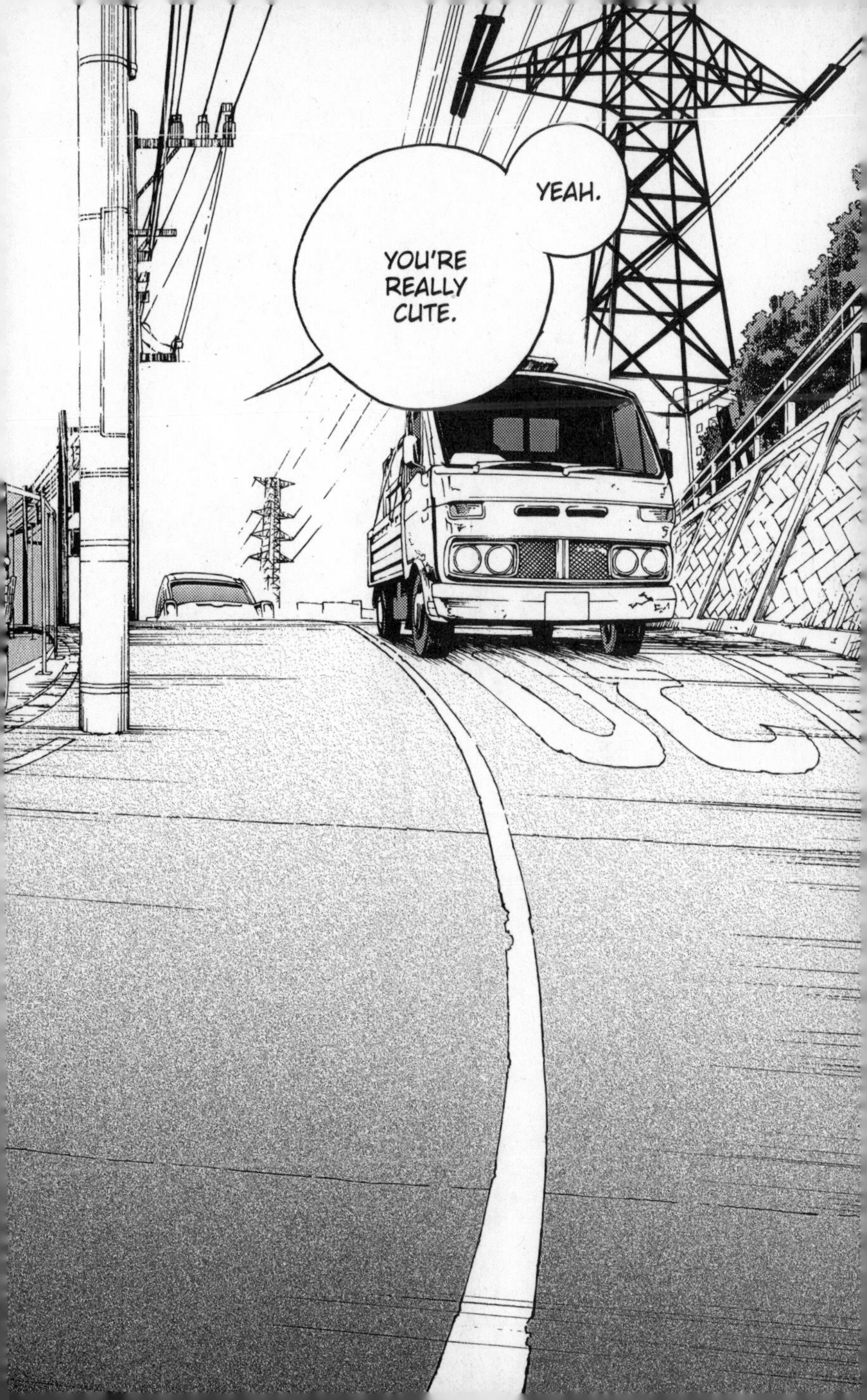
YEAH.
YOU'RE REALLY CUTE.

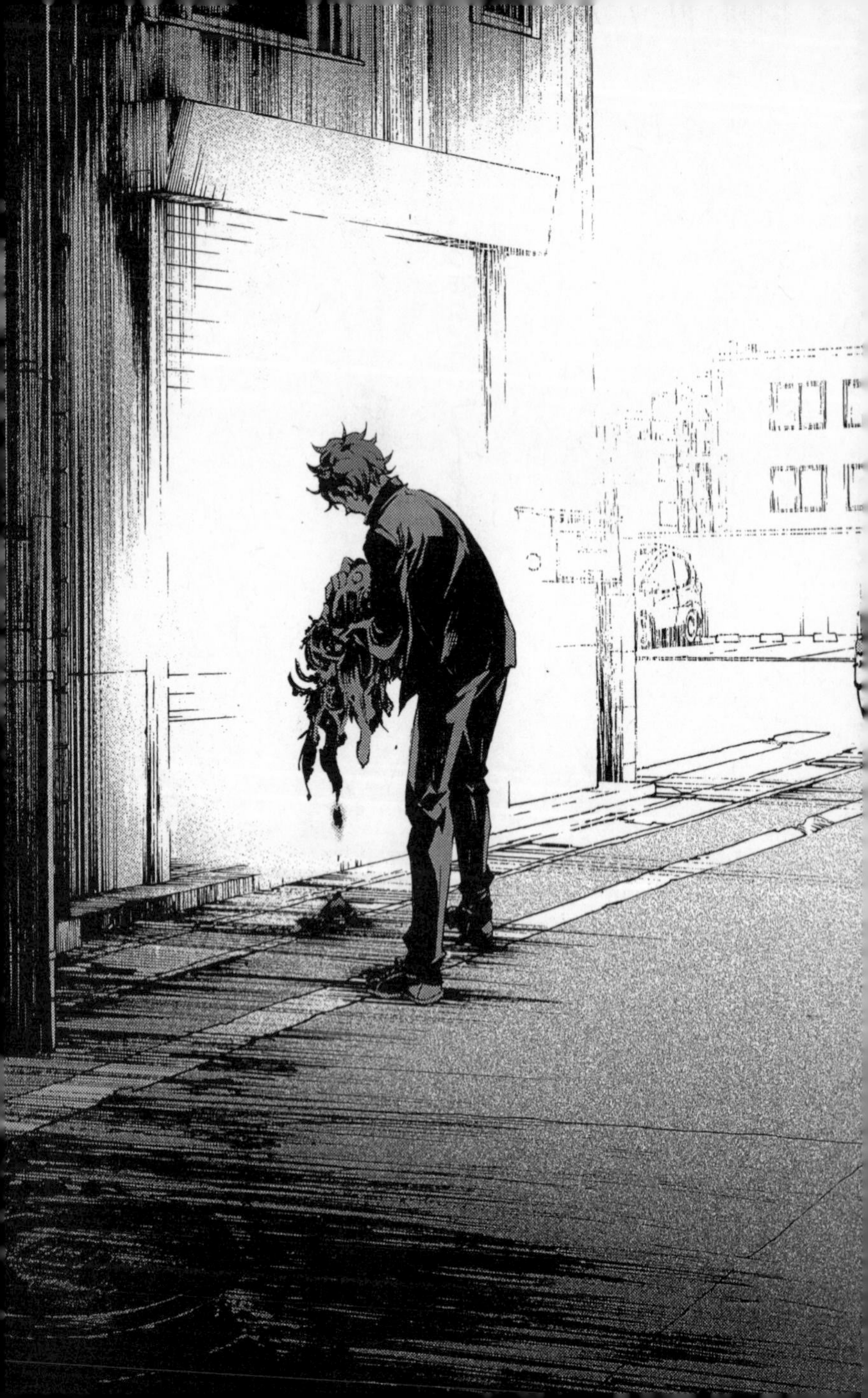

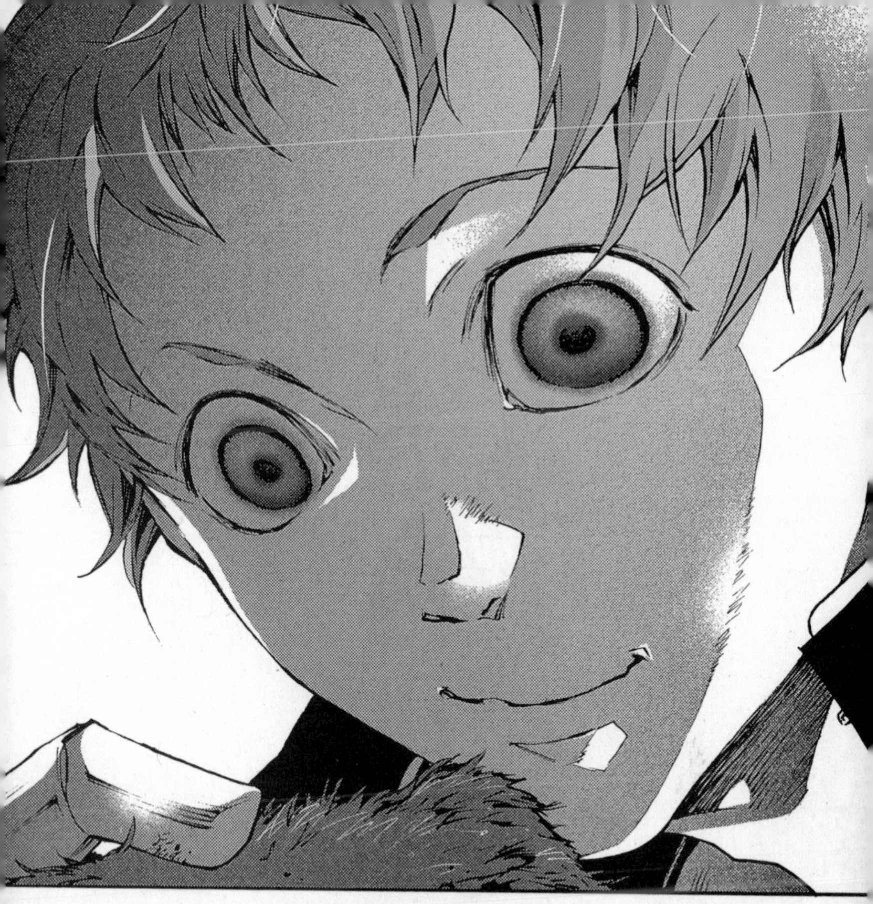

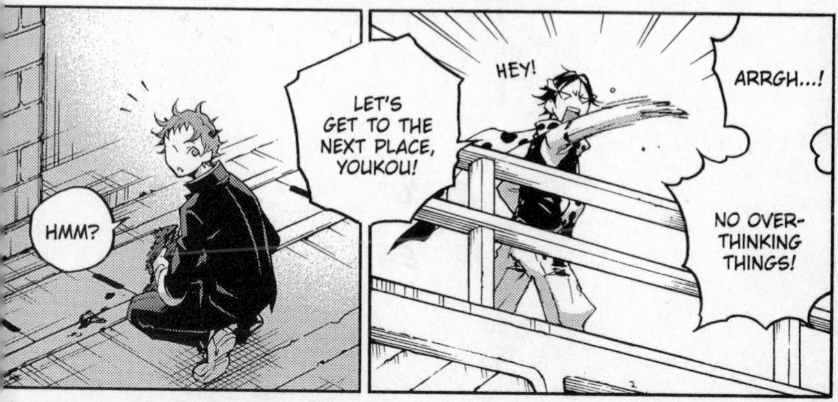
ARRGH...!
NO OVER-THINKING THINGS!
HEY!
LET'S GET TO THE NEXT PLACE, YOUKOU!
HMM?

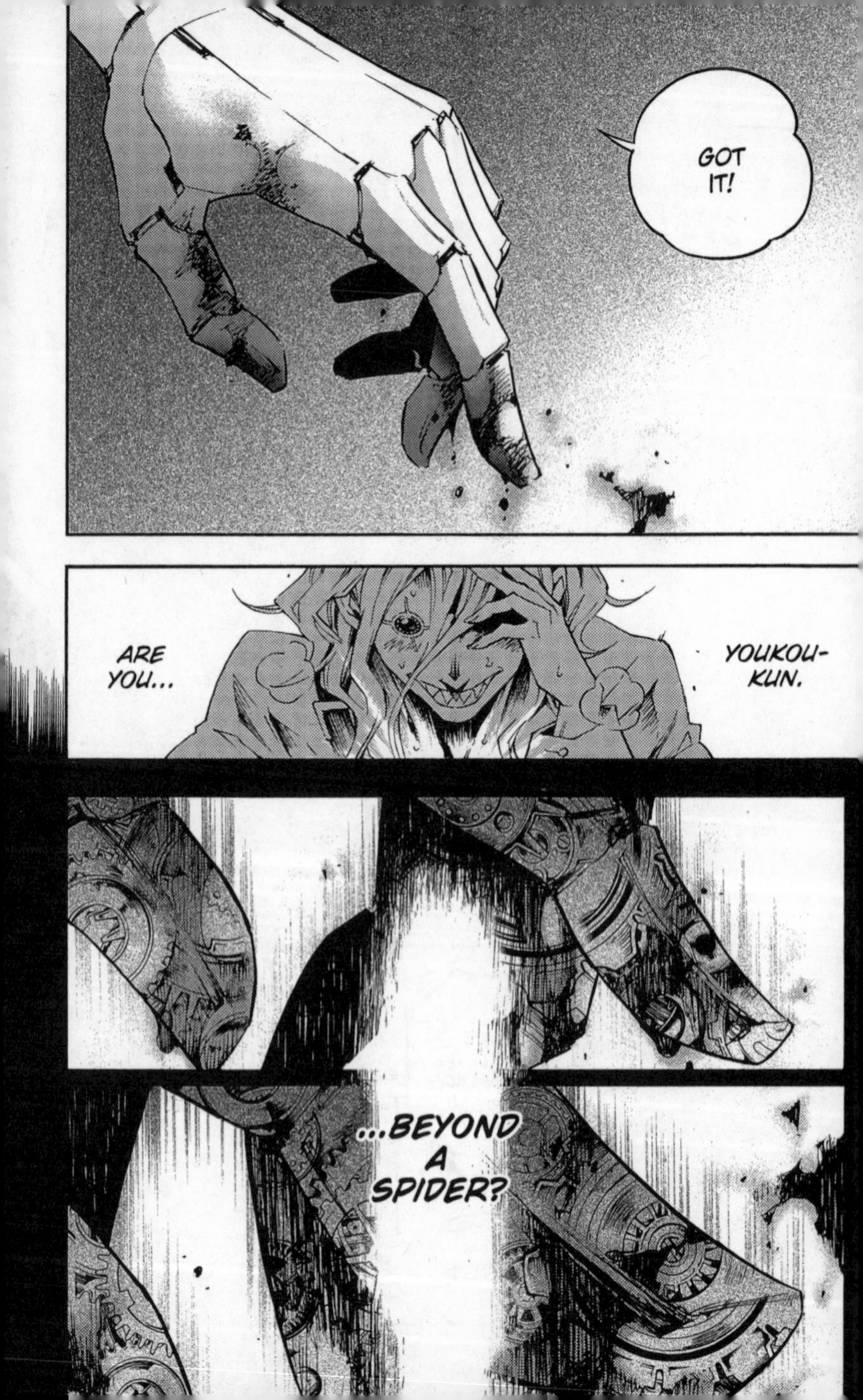
GOT IT!
YOUKOU-KUN.
ARE YOU...
...BEYOND A SPIDER?

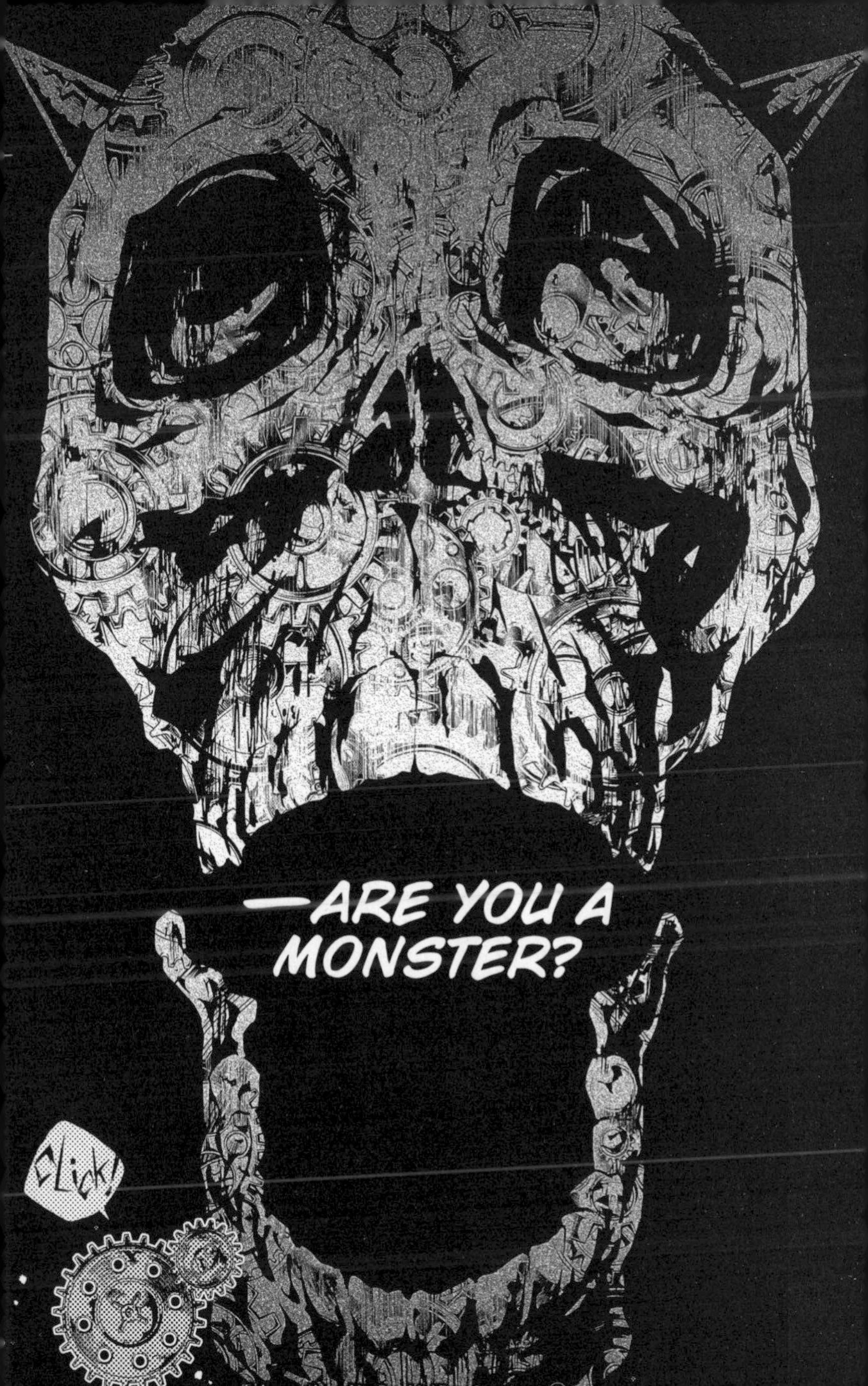
—ARE YOU A MONSTER?
CLICK!

To be continued in *Smokin' Parade*, Volume 4

THE MYSTERY OF THE JACKALOPES

Q: WHAT ARE THOSE HORNS THE MEMBERS WEAR?

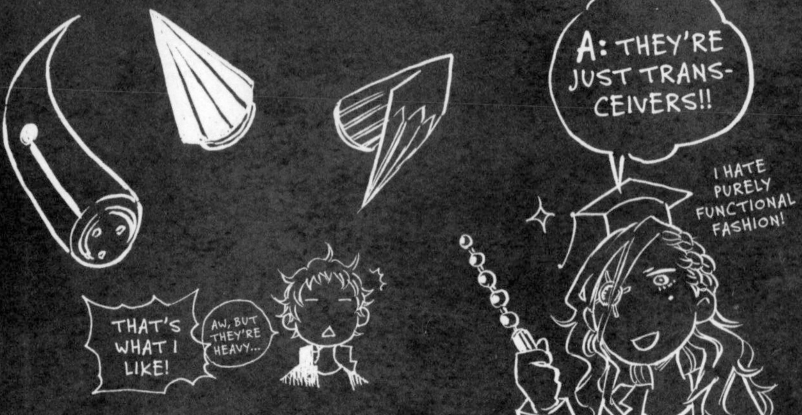
A: THEY'RE JUST TRANS-CEIVERS!!
I HATE PURELY FUNCTIONAL FASHION!
AW, BUT THEY'RE HEAVY...
THAT'S WHAT I LIKE!

*THEY'RE NOT MADE FROM A SPECIAL MATERIAL LIKE THE GEARS, SO THEY CAN BE MASS-PRODUCED! NOW ACCEPTING ORDERS FOR USE AS PARTY FAVORS AND THE LIKE!!

THE SECRET OF AMENOTORI

Q: WHY DO THE SPIDERS HAVE SUCH WEIRD FACES AFTER THEY TRANSFORM?

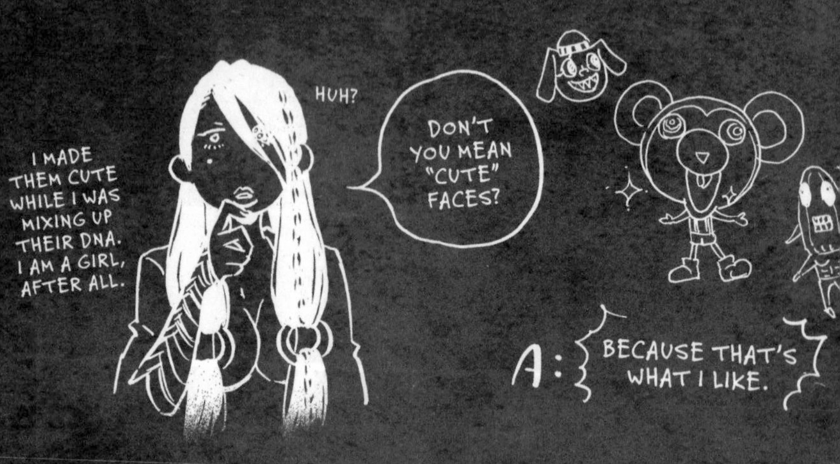
A: BECAUSE THAT'S WHAT I LIKE.
DON'T YOU MEAN "CUTE" FACES?
HUH?
I MADE THEM CUTE WHILE I WAS MIXING UP THEIR DNA. I AM A GIRL, AFTER ALL.

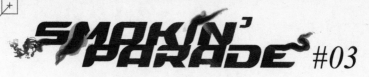

SMOKIN' PARADE #03

BY JINSEI KATAOKA, KAZUMA KONDOU

Translation: Leighann Harvey
Lettering: Abigail Blackman

SMOKIN' PARADE Volume 3
©Jinsei KATAOKA 2017
©Kazuma KONDOU 2017
First published in Japan in 2017 by KADOKAWA CORPORATION, Tokyo. English translation rights arranged with KADOKAWA CORPORATION, Tokyo through TUTTLE-MORI AGENCY, INC., Tokyo.

English translation © 2017 by Yen Press, LLC

Yen Press
1290 Avenue of the Americas
New York, NY 10104

Visit us at yenpress.com
facebook.com/yenpress
twitter.com/yenpress
yenpress.tumblr.com
instagram.com/yenpress

First Yen Press Edition: December 2017

Yen Press is an imprint of Yen Press, LLC.
The Yen Press name and logo are trademarks of Yen Press, LLC.

Library of Congress Control Number: 2016958477

ISBNs: 978-0-316-41409-8 (paperback)
        978-0-316-44650-1 (ebook)

10 9 8 7 6 5 4 3 2 1

BVG

Printed in the United States of America

S0-ACL-660